Corporate Networks in Europe and the United States

PAUL WINDOLF

OXFORD

UNIVERSITY PRESS

OXFORD
UNIVERSITY PRESS

Great Clarendon Street, Oxford OX2 6DP

Oxford University Press is a department of the University of Oxford.
It furthers the University's objective of excellence in research, scholarship,
and education by publishing worldwide in

Oxford New York

Auckland Bangkok Buenos Aires Cape Town Chennai
Dar es Salaam Delhi Hong Kong Istanbul Karachi Kolkata
Kuala Lumpur Madrid Melbourne Mexico City Mumbai Nairobi
São Paulo Shanghai Taipei Tokyo Toronto

Oxford is a registered trade mark of Oxford University Press
in the UK and in certain other countries

Published in the United States
by Oxford University Press Inc., New York

British Library Cataloguing in Publication Data
Data available

Library of Congress Cataloging in Publication Data
Data available

ISBN 0-19-925697-7

1 3 5 7 9 10 8 6 4 2

Typeset by Newgen Imaging Systems (P) Ltd., Chennai, India
Printed in Great Britain
on acid-free paper by
Biddles Ltd., Guildford & King's Lynn

Contents

Part IV. **Outlook**

9. From Corporatism to Shareholder Value   207

List of Figures

List of Tables

Acknowledgments

The origins of this book go back to 1996, the year I was a research fellow at the Haas School of Business at Berkeley. During this period, I had the opportunity to compile a data record on corporate networks in the United States. My discussions with Neil Fligstein, Michael Gerlach, and Michael Reich helped me considerably in this project. The data survey and analysis were financed by the German Research Foundation and the Volkswagen Foundation. I am deeply indebted to both of these organizations.

A leave of absence, financed by the German Research Foundation, enabled me to spend a research year at the Minda de Gunzburg Center for European Studies at Harvard in 1998. Several chapters of this book were written during this stay. I am very grateful for the stimulating discussions I had at the Center, particularly with Peter Hall and Charles Maier.

The data records for Switzerland and the Netherlands were made available to me by Michael Nollert, to whom I owe many thanks. I also extend my gratitude to Jürgen Beyer, who took part in the data compilation and analysis for several years. François Morin aided my work by giving me many suggestions and insights on the structure of corporate networks in France. Finally, several chapters of the book benefited greatly from the constructive criticism of John Scott and Mark Roe.

In the final chapter, I have included several suggestions that I received at a conference organized by Malcom Alexander and William Carroll and held in April 2001 at the Netherlands Institute for Advanced Study in Wassenaar. I thank the conference participants for their helpful criticism and ideas.

Last but not least, I wish to thank the many students of the University of Trier for the commitment and care with which they entered into the computer the data of more than 3000 companies and the names and titles of more than 12,000 managers from various countries. The comparative study presented here would not have been possible without their contribution.

I also extend my appreciation to Terry Barton, Dona Geyer, and Andrew Watt. They not only translated most chapters of this book but also helped me to overcome many idiosyncrasies of the German language.

P.W.

1

Introduction

1.1. PROPHETS OF REGULATION IN THE UNITED STATES

One of the very first studies to appear on corporate networks was published by the US Interstate Commerce Commission in 1908. The Commission wanted to know to whom the big railroad companies belonged and learned that, for the most part, they were owned by each other. 'The securities of one company are owned by another company; of the 8.9 billion US-$ in stock outstanding, the railway companies themselves owned 46%'.[1] Throughout the years, the managers of the railroad companies had created hierarchically structured combines, with the help of which they controlled regional and transcontinental railways. The Commission came to the conclusion that 'railway corporations once independent have been welded into highly centralized systems' (p. 7). Figure 1.1 shows a section of this 'centralized system'.

The study on the capital networks[2] in the railroad industry was not conducted by a university, but by a government agency that was primarily seeking to fulfill *political* aims rather than scientific ones. The purpose was to show that an enormous economic power was concentrated in the corporate networks and that this power represented a potential threat to the free market. Therefore, the Commission did not refrain from using governmental pressure to force the railroad managers to reveal detailed information on the capital networks: the Commission 'required from every [railway] corporation full and true answers under oath to the respective inquiries'. A university department would not have possessed the authority to force corporations to answer a questionnaire 'under oath'.

Not many years later, another study on corporate networks was conducted on instruction of the United States House of Representatives.[3] This study by the Pujo Commission focused on the interlocking directorates and capital networks between banks, insurances, railway companies, and large industrial firms. The principal

---

[1] The authors differentiate between securities 'held within the system' (the 46% of the shares that were held by the railroad companies themselves) and securities 'held outside the system' (the 'free float', meaning the 54% of the securities traded on the exchange). See pp. 44–5.

[2] When companies own other companies, networks develop that are called 'capital networks' here and in the following chapters. Examples for such networks are the '*Konzern*' in Germany, the '*keiretsu*' in Japan, and the '*groupes industriels*' in France.

[3] House Subcommittee of the Committee on Banking and Currency (Pujo Committee): Investigation of Financial and Monetary Conditions in the United States (Money Trust Investigation). Washington 1912–13: Government Printing Office.

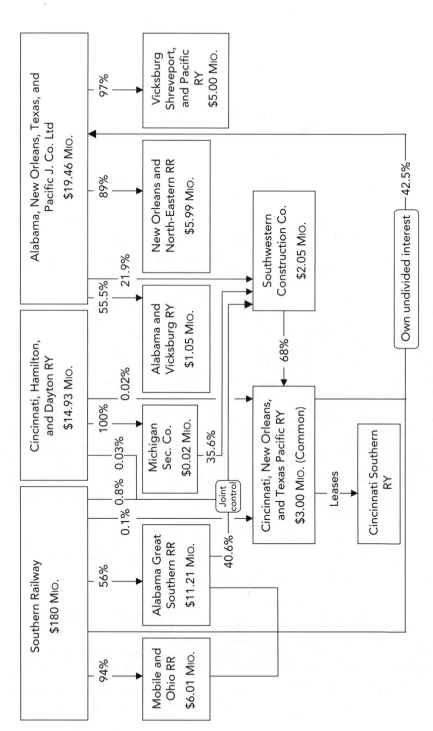

Fig. 1.1 *Railway corporations*

investigator conducting the inquiry was counsel Samuel Untermyer of New York. Mr Untermyer possessed the legal power to summon the leading American bankers before the Committee and have them testify 'under oath' about the 'banking and currency conditions of the United States for the purpose of determining what legislation is needed' (p. 3). On 9 January 1913, George F. Baker, Chairman of the Board of Directors of the First National Bank of New York, testified before the Committee. The following excerpt from the transcript of these hearings indicates the manner in which Mr Untermyer questioned the 'leading bankers':

Mr Baker:	Mr Untermyer, may I be allowed to make a little statement?
Mr Untermyer:	Yes.
Mr Baker:	You presented me before the public as such a great director man, more than I realized myself, that I would just like to interject here that I never have become a director or a voting trustee from solicitation of my own; it has all come to me, rather ...
Mr Untermyer:	[cutting him off] You recognize, Mr Baker, that we have just begun to examine you as to your directorships. Do you know how many you have?
Mr Baker:	I know I have too many.
Mr Untermyer:	Do you know how many?
Mr Baker:	No.
Mr Untermyer:	Have you got 25?
Mr Baker:	I guess so.
Mr Untermyer:	Have you got 50?
Mr Baker:	There must be 25 in the Jersey Central and those little companies ... (p. 1489).

Mr Baker was grilled like this for hours, and Mr Untermyer used the very same tenacity in questioning many other bankers and financiers, among them J. Pierpont Morgan, George W. Perkins (Vice-president of New York Life Insurance), and Jacob H. Schiff (partner of the Bank Kuhn, Loeb & Co.).[4]

The final report of the Pujo Commission is several thousand pages long and reports in minute detail on the 'Money Trust' created at the turn of the century by the leading American banks and insurances. The report also contains the first matrix of interlocking directorates that shows the ties between 269 directors of the largest financial institutions.[5]

---

[4] The transcript of the testimony of Mr Baker consists of more that 150 printed pages and is found on pages 1419–573. The testimony of J. P. Morgan is recorded on about 100 printed pages. Strouse (1999: 660) writes about Untermyer: 'Samuel Untermyer was an experienced trial lawyer and lifelong Democrat who specialized in corporate finance. In the late eighties and nineties, he had made a fortune organizing financial syndicates and industrial consolidations.... Untermyer has also worked in the nineties for the Boss of New York's Tammany Hall, Richard Corker'. Untermyer was indeed an 'expert' in many respects.

[5] *Source* Subcommittee of the Committee on Banking and Currency (Pujo Commission): Investigation of Financial and Monetary Conditions in the United States. Washington 1913: Government Printing Office, exhibit 134A,B.

Louis Brandeis, Justice of the Supreme Court since 1916, summarized and evaluated the findings of the Pujo Committee in a political commentary with the title 'Other People's Money'. In this work, he contended that the big banks and insurances were not only in control of the American financial markets, but that they also used interlocking directorates and capital networks to maintain a dominant position over major industrial corporations and railroad companies. The corporate networks were an important means to control competition and distribute lucrative contracts among the members of the trust, argued Brandeis. The Money Trust, around which these networks were centered, threatened not only the free market but also the democratic constitution and the liberal traditions of the United States.

The studies produced by the Pujo Committee had revealed that the market was not regulating itself, but was tending more and more toward trust and monopoly-building. In light of these findings, Brandeis concluded that it was the *responsibility of the state* to break up the Money Trust, to reinstate a free market with the help of government legislation, and to have government institutions monitor the behavior of corporations. By proposing these initiatives, Brandeis became the leading member of that group of reformers whom McCraw (1984) later called the 'prophets of regulation'.

Even today, the relationship between the market and the state is still plagued with the problem that Polanyi (1957: 139) has called the 'liberal paradox': the market does not regulate itself, but only functions when it is 'embedded' in institutions. The political program announced by Brandeis and implemented step-by-step in the decades that followed provided a *specific* solution for this problem. Starting with the Sherman Act of 1890 (antitrust law) and followed by the Clayton Act (1914) and the Security Exchange Act (1934), the United States created a system of controls that by the mid-1930s had produced the most regulated financial market existing—compared to Western European countries—and the only body of antitrust law that could be said to have been actually enforced (Bhide 1993; Roe 1994: 51–145).

The purpose of state regulation is to return repeatedly the market to a 'natural state' in which there is completely unfettered competition and no one individual is in a position to exert economic power. This is the paradise propagated by liberal economists in their models. However, the '*homo oeconomicus*' is forever being quickly banished from this paradise. In a study on the major entrepreneurs of American capitalism, Josephson (1962) shows that the 'robber barons' did not make their fortunes by working *against* the market, but by exploiting every opportunity it offered. This also holds true for the 'Money Trust': it was the brainchild of liberal competitive capitalism. Free markets are always in danger of being monopolized by 'robber barons'.

1.2. THE CULTURE OF CARTELS IN GERMANY

In Germany, the liberal paradox was resolved another way. At the close of the nineteenth century, cartels of leading corporations were established in nearly every economic sector. Quantity cartels stipulated by contract how much steel would be produced in a year or how much coal would be mined; in price cartels a minimum price was set for the respective commodity.

In 1897, the Reichsgericht, the Imperial Supreme Court in Germany, was asked to rule on the legality of cartel contracts. In the United States, cartels in which corporations work together specifically to control the quantity or prices of commodities are considered to be a 'conspiracy in restraint of trade' and are, therefore, prohibited by the Sherman Act of 1890 and by the subsequent antitrust laws. In Germany, the Reichsgericht drew a different conclusion. According to the Court, if producers joined together in order to ensure their economic survival and to guarantee a price level that enabled all companies to earn a 'reasonable' profit on the long run, then such an association would not constitute a 'conspiracy in restraint of trade'. Cartels were compatible with the legal system, and firms that broke cartel contracts could be sued for damages in German courts.[6]

In the United States, it is the responsibility of the Federal Trade Commission (FTC) to continually monitor various markets and to determine whether a joint venture, a fusion, or an interlocking directorate constitutes a 'conspiracy to fix prices'. Bok (1960: 228) criticizes this regulation by arguing 'that economists, as well as lawyers, lack the knowledge to make the predictions concerning the probable consequences of many of the mergers with which the [law] must deal'.

In Germany, the state left the job of regulating markets primarily to business. The Reichsgericht only guaranteed that the state would use its constitutional power to ensure the implementation of whatever *solution business itself decided upon* (cartel contract).

With cartels free to regulate the market themselves, one might think that this would hinder technological progress and create economic inefficiency.[7] However, this was not the case in Germany before the First World War. Cartels were never enduring nor steadfast forms of coordination between competitors. Often they were contractually set for a short period (2–5 years), and could break apart at any time. Before 1914, German corporations attempted to expand as quickly as possible during the duration of a cartel contract in order to receive a higher quota[8] in the next round of contractual negotiations. More specifically, they implemented aggressive rationalization measures in the attempt to prepare for the day when the cartel disbanded (Feldman 1998: 194–6).

1.3. DIFFERENT IDEOLOGIES

Both the antitrust laws in the United States and the ruling of the Reichsgericht must be seen in the context of the different political ideologies. For the 'prophets of regulation' there existed a direct correlation between a 'free' market and political democracy. In their view, the corporate networks were not only inefficient, but the

---

[6] Nearly every cartel had at its disposal an administration that was to monitor prices and production quantities of member firms. If a firm exceeded its production quota or sold commodities for less than the contractually stipulated price, it could be sued in court for damages.

[7] See more on this in Hicks (1935: 8): 'The best of all monopoly profits is a quiet life'.

[8] A 'quota' is the share of the entire production in an economic sector that is allotted to a company by the cartel.

economic power concentrated in them posed a threat to political liberty. Brandeis (1995: 76) argued that 'the compelling reason for prohibiting interlocking directorates is neither the protection of stockholders, nor the protection of the public from the incidents of inefficiency and graft...For even more important than efficiency are industrial and political liberty; and these are imperiled by the Money Trust. Interlocking directorates must be prohibited, because it is impossible to break the Money Trust without putting an end to the practice in the larger corporations'.

Like Adam Smith, Louis Brandeis also believed in the beneficial effects of the 'invisible hand'. The common good is best served when each citizen has free access to the market and can pursue his own economic interests. Only if the market and competition are free to develop unimpaired can social justice come about.

The Reichsgericht rejected this credo outright (Böhm 1948: 205–7). If producers joined together to correct the way the market was divided among competitors, then the results were not only more efficient but also more *equitable*. In a cartel, the market share of each corporation was not being determined by the anarchy of competition but by negotiations between the various companies. Competition would not be completely eradicated, but controlled and regulated. The court justified its opinion primarily by referring to the work of the economists from the Historical School of Economics (e.g. Schmoller 1906). In their view, cartels were an important developmental step in the evolution of society (Nörr 1995). Compared with the anarchy of the market, a cartel represented a higher form of organization and a central institution for 'organized capitalism' (Wehler 1974).

In Germany, organized capitalism was not regulated directly by the state, but by business itself. In a certain sense, the cartel was an example of a decentralized planned economy. For instance, the steel cartel would estimate the demand for steel for the year ahead and, on the basis of this estimation, allocated quotas for the entire steel production among the member firms. The cartel subjected the competition for a share of the market to *collective* regulation. The central aim was not to maximize profits of big business, but to achieve a 'reasonable' profit for all cartel members. At the close of the nineteenth century, there were many rich entrepreneurs in Germany, but very few 'robber barons'. This was because the cartel not only guaranteed a minimum price, it also prevented excessive monopoly prices from being demanded during periods of prosperity.

1.4. THE RECONSTRUCTION OF TRADITIONS

For fifty years, the ruling of the Reichsgericht on cartels in Germany remained legally valid. Not until February 1947 were cartels forbidden by the American and British occupational forces (Böhm 1948: 198), and it took nearly a decade until the first German antitrust law went into effect in 1956.

This cartel tradition has been described here rather extensively because we will argue in the following chapters that the structure of corporate networks in Germany (and in other European countries where a cartel tradition exists) can be viewed as a transformation of earlier cartel structures. Simplified: *The corporate networks replaced the cartels.* The networks are spread rather densely over the corporate landscape; they include nearly all big businesses, and there is a great deal of overlapping among interlocking directorates and capital networks. Compared with the anarchy of the market, corporate networks also represent a 'higher' form of organization, which enables the business world to impose collective self-regulation.

In Japan, the corporate networks were also transformed in a similar fashion. During Japan's period of industrialization prior to the First World War, complex corporate networks were created. Each of these was dominated by a family clan (*zaibatsu*). The control exerted within these networks can be described as being patrimonial: they combined the traditional form of authority within the family clan with an economic power attained through shareholdings and property rights. Although the *zaibatsu* were disbanded by the American occupational government following the Second World War, they were reconstructed in the 1950s by the leading Japanese businesses and expanded into large cooperative business groups (*keiretsu*).[9]

The structure of corporate networks, which emerged in the United States as a result of antitrust laws and which will be described in detail in the following chapters, can also be seen as a *reconstruction of traditions.* The Progressive movement abhorred the Money Trust, the railroad and steel trusts, the dominance of banks and the excessive wealth of the 'robber barons' as a distortion and betrayal of the original American tradition. Therefore, in their eyes, the Sherman Act, the Clayton Act, and a series of other laws were not so much measures to *reform* the economic system, but ones implemented to help *restore* the original American tradition.[10]

As mentioned earlier, the Interstate Commerce Commission concluded in its 1908 report that the railroad corporations had been welded into highly centralized systems, a section of which is shown in Fig. 1.1. Three railroad companies (Southern, Cincinnati, Alabama) were interlocked and controlled additional (smaller) railroads in a hierarchically structured system of shareholdings. These networks were disbanded in the interwar period, and one can say that the antitrust laws are at least *one* of the reasons that in America today there no longer exists any capital networks among its 500 largest industrial corporations.[11]

The Progressive movement and the laws it inspired revived traditions or at least made it appear as if the reforms had achieved the greatest possible proximity to a free market and to Jacksonian democracy.[12] The antitrust laws are not merely instruments

[9] A historical analysis of *zaibatsu* is found in Morikawa (1992), an analysis of *keiretsu* in Gerlach (1992).

[10] See also the speech by Senator Sherman: 'If we would not submit to an emperor we should not submit to an autocrat of trade, with power to prevent competition and to fix the price of any commodity.' 21 Congressional Record 2456 (1890), quote cited in Schmidt and Binder (1996: 131). This quotation makes it clear that the antitrust law was not only about ensuring free competition, but also about protecting democracy.

[11] This means that the matrix of capital networks among the 500 largest American non-financial corporations is empty. In other words, these 500 companies share no (mutual) shareholdings that are larger than 0.5%. See also Chapter 2.

[12] The Bank of the United States, which fulfilled the function of a central bank, was dismantled by President Andrew Jackson in 1832. He justified this step by criticizing the monopolistic power of this institution: 'The Bank of the United States enjoys a monopoly of favor and support ... [and] such a concentration

to regulate markets; they also need to be interpreted in the cultural context from which they emerged. With the passage of the antitrust laws at the dawn of the twentieth century, a part of American history and tradition was 'reconstructed'.[13]

1.5. NETWORK THEORIES

Theories explaining the meaning of corporate networks can be divided into two categories: the first group of theories, labeled here *functionalist theories*, explains networks by way of the economic and social functions they fulfill. For the second group of theories, labeled here *power or control theories*, networks are instruments used to monopolize markets or to exclude potential competitors from these markets. Adam Smith (1979: 232) already criticized networks as a 'contrivance to raise prices'. The analyses of the 'power elite' by C. Wright Mills (1956), of the 'higher circles' by Domhoff (1983) or the studies of 'social capital' by Bourdieu (1980) are classic examples of power and control theories. In the following, we will briefly explain the various theories and classify them according to these two groups. We will devote more attention to these theories later in the book.

(1) One of the most important functionalist explanations is the transaction cost theory. This theory assumes that the purpose of economic institutions is to reduce transaction costs (Williamson 1985). Networks are important instruments of coordination that increase the efficiency of the market and are used to help regulate competition. Furthermore, it is argued that networks can be used to enhance trust between firms and to reduce uncertainty (Uzzi 1996). In this manner, corporate networks help check transaction costs.

Information theories can also be classified as functionalist theories. Granovetter (1973) argues that through 'weak ties,' one receives information that is not obtainable through one's close circle of friends, including information about job vacancies, undervalued stock, or new market trends. Distant acquaintances can be useful in finding a new job, and many corporations use the social networks of their employees to recruit personnel (Windolf and Wood 1988). Many studies provided empirical evidence that innovations are disseminated particularly rapidly within networks (Burt 1987). They are also useful instruments to reduce information asymmetries between transaction partners. Many interlocks are 'weak ties' through which information is exchanged that is not available through the 'strong ties' within a company.

A final concept belonging to the group of functionalist theories is that of resource dependency (Pfeffer and Salancik 1978). Companies are not autarchic organizations; they rely instead on various different resources within their environment, including credit (banks), and raw materials and machinery (supplier firms). Companies attempt

---

of power in the hands of a few men irresponsible to the people' (Blum *et al.* 1968: 239). Jackson embodied the radical-democratic cause to which the antitrust legislation was also oriented at the time. With Andrew Jackson's veto, the American monetary and financial system was practically thrown back to a premodern level of development.

[13] Hobsbawm (1983) talks in this context of 'the invention of tradition'. Yet the case here is not so much about 'invention', as it is about adaptation of a tradition to the conditions of modernization.

to establish interlocks with those organizations on whose resources they are particularly dependent. Interlocks between banks and industrial firms are beneficial because they can be used, on the one hand, to guarantee the financing for new investment sought by industrial firms and, on the other, to reduce the risk taken by the banks in issuing the credit for such investment (see more in Section 2.3 in Chapter 2).

(2) The theory of resource dependency can also be grouped with those belonging to the second category, namely the *power and control theories*. Each and every dependency on a resource, regardless of what kind, implies vulnerability, and such a dependency can be strategically exploited by any player who controls the resource. As this example illustrates, it is not possible to clearly divide the various network theories into these two categories. Instead, such classification reflects the *theoretical perspectives* under which networks can be analyzed. Networks can be studied from a functionalist perspective, and then the focus of the analysis becomes their coordinating function. However, they can also be examined from a control perspective. What then becomes the focus of the study is the fact that they are instruments used to monopolize markets and to exclude potential competitors.

For Bourdieu, social networks are a specific form of social capital.[14] The alumni networks of elite universities are good examples of this. The members of such networks help each other get promoted to top executive positions in large corporations and establish thereby an 'old-boys' network'. These alumni networks are a closed market in which orders, contracts, positions, and insider information are exchanged.

Closely related to this is Max Weber's concept of 'social closure',[15] in which social networks have the function of distinguishing between 'insiders' and 'outsiders'. With the help of the concept, we can analyze Asian networks based on family relations. Examples of these are the '*chaebol*' in Korea or the '*guanxiqiye*' in Taiwan. A '*guanxiqiye*' is a business group consisting of several firms whose managers are recruited primarily from the same family clan (Numazaki 1996; Granovetter 1995). It is not always easy to tell whether such a business group is actually a corporate network or an example of 'crony capitalism'.

These various explanations for the existence of networks are not mutually exclusive. In an old-boys' network, transaction costs can be reduced (trust factor), while at the same time efforts to monopolize a market are being undertaken. Simultaneously, such a network can help diminish resource dependencies. Therefore, it is difficult to attribute the existence of networks to a *single* source or a *single* 'motive' of the members. This even holds true for cartels, which are networks established for the purpose of monopolizing markets, but could—under certain conditions—be more effective in reducing transaction costs than competitive markets. 'Mixed motive games' can be

---

[14] 'Le volume du capital social comme portefeuille de liaisons est d'autant plus important que les liaisons sont plus nombreuses, plus stables et plus rentables (c'est-à-dire d'autant plus que les institutions— par exemples, les conseils d'administration—ou les individus sur lesquels elles donnent prise possèdent plus de capital) et aussi, en beaucoup de cas, mieux cachées' (Bourdieu 1989: 516). See also Coleman (1990: 300–24); Bourdieu (1980).

[15] Weber (1956: 203) understood 'social closure' as being the monopolization of employment opportunities by erecting entry barriers, thus preventing competitors from entering a particular market.

played in any network: they serve to enhance social cooperation as well as to facilitate the self-seeking goal of maximizing profits. In Chapter 3, we will show that certain network configurations encourage cooperation (e.g. cliques) while others stimulate competition.

1.6. INSTITUTIONAL AND CULTURAL CONTINGENCY

Organizational sociology has a simple answer to the question concerning the structure or organization, namely that such structures are the product of an adaptation process to the environment. Firms that need to adapt to different environments will have a variety of different organizational structures. This type of explanation is known as 'contingency theory' in sociology.[16] Can the structure of *networks* also be conceived of as the product of an adaptation process to specific environments?

The 'environment' is an amorphous term, unsuitable in explaining causality. In order to make the concept more explicit, certain areas in the environment must be specified as causal factors. One such factor is the technology that a company uses in production and to which its organizational structures must adapt. Other factors include social and political institutions and the 'culture' of a country, which can influence the organizational structure through norms and values. So, we can speak of the technical, institutional, or cultural contingency involved, depending on whether the production technology, the institutions, or a country's culture is the *dominant* causal factor that has shaped the structure of the organization.

Examples of '*technical contingency*' are featured in the analyses by Burns and Stalker (1961), who assume in their study that the organizational structures of companies are influenced by the specific production technology involved. A mass production firm will often have a mechanistic–bureaucratic structure, whereas one specializing in problem-solving for individual customers will have a more organic decentralized structure.

In a similar fashion, the '*cultural contingency theory*' attempts to explain the structure of Japanese corporations with the help of the prevailing norms and values in Japan. The characteristics of Japanese companies, among which are flat hierarchies, lifelong employment, and the special work discipline of Japanese workers, are part of the heritage of Japan's Confucian 'culture'.[17]

Last but not least, an example of '*institutional contingency theory*' is the study done by Maurice *et al.* (1982) in which German and French companies are compared. These scholars conclude from their work that differences in the organizational structures between German and French companies are not caused by differences in culture but by differences in the educational and training institutions of the two countries. It is argued that the educational institutions of a country determine the qualification pattern of the labor force and that companies are forced to adapt their organizational structures to this pattern.

---

[16] See Lawrence and Lorsch (1967), compare also with the concept of 'isomorphism' (Hannan and Freeman 1989: 93).   [17] Dore (1987: 91–4), see also Lincoln and Kalleberg (1990: 27–9).

A major theme of this book is the description and analysis of corporate networks in various Western European countries and in the United States. Two questions are paramount in this study: first, what kind of structure do these networks have? Second, how can structural differences between countries be explained? The explanation presented in the following chapters in answer to the second question can be classified as an 'institutional contingency theory'. The hypothesis is that the network structure in each country is a product of an adaptation process to social and political institutions. Should these institutions change (e.g. the laws governing financial markets), then the structure of networks subsequently changes. However, an important factor to remember when working with this explanation is that the institutions themselves are influenced by culture, a point elaborated upon below.

This approach can be made more precise by specifying dependent and independent variables. The *dependent* variables are the structural characteristics of the corporate networks in each of the countries (e.g. density, centrality, largest component, multiple ties). The *independent* variables are the different social and political institutions of each country, such as the antitrust laws, laws regulating the financial market, employee codetermination, the structure of interest groups (unions, employers' associations).

1.7. INDEPENDENT VARIABLES

The theory states that it is possible to explain the structure of corporate networks by the political and economic institutions of a country. Yet this explanation is inadequate if it is not taken into consideration that the institutions themselves are influenced by culture and traditions. The Co-determination Act in Germany, for example, embodies corporatist traditions that date back far into the nineteenth century; the antitrust laws in the Unites States can only be properly understood if the political 'culture' of the Progressive movement is taken into account. Many institutions are the explicit manifestation of a cultural context.

Consequently, the institutional contingency theory (*institutions* are here the important independent variable) cannot always be distinguished from a cultural contingency theory (*culture* is here the important independent variable).[18] In many cases, the 'culture' is incorporated into the institutions. We illustrate this point with two examples:

(1) In Germany, *competition* and *anarchy* are equated time and again in social science literature: unregulated competition between independent individuals is not assumed to be guided by an 'invisible hand' that reconciles conflicting interests and leads to a harmonious order, as Adam Smith postulated. Instead, unregulated competition is assumed to lead to anarchy and chaos. Such a negative evaluation of competition can be found, for instance, in the publications of Otto von Gierke, who propagated the

---

[18] On the controversy between 'culturalists' and 'institutionalists', see Iribarne (1991) and Maurice *et al.* (1992). Whereas Iribarne defends the 'culture' standpoint, Maurice *et al.* emphasize the importance of institutions.

establishment of cooperatives as an alternative to the free market. Gierke (1954) maintained that the cooperation between producers and consumers was to replace capitalist competition or at least restrain it.[19] These ideas were adopted by the economists of the Historical School of Economics, in particular by Gustav Schmoller (1906), who developed the concept of 'regulated competition' and juxtaposed it to the supposed 'anarchistic' conditions in the United States.

In Germany, unrestricted competition on the market is rejected not only by the unions, but also by entrepreneurs. Fritz Berg, president of the *Bundesverband der Deutschen Industrie* (Federal Association of German Industry) expressed the opinion in 1953 that unregulated competition 'would inevitably degenerate into chaos'.[20] Therefore, he demanded that employers should have the right to enter into cartel agreements in order to regulate the market without being restricted by state control.

Cartels were the most important economic institutions to evolve from these traditions in Germany, and they regulated most facets of the economy until after the Second World War. Other such institutions born of German cultural influence include employee codetermination in large companies, the corporatist regulation (as opposed to state control) of the financial markets by banks and stock exchanges (Lütz 1997), and the close ties between banks and industrial firms (relational contracting). The structure of corporate networks in Germany, which will be analyzed later in this book, needs to be interpreted in the context of this cultural heritage.

(2) In the Anglo-Saxon literature, we find a different evaluation of competition. Here it is argued that in a free and open market powerful economic actors neutralize each other and that competition is the only institution that can effectively control power. Evolving from the work of Adam Smith, this liberal tradition has not only shaped economics, but also political science, as can be seen from the liberal axiom of the 'interdependence of orders': the institutional order of the market (free competition) and the institutional order of the political system (democracy) are mutually dependent on one another. Without a free market, democratic institutions cannot survive on the long run, and the reverse is true as well: without democracy, the free market is doomed.[21]

From this perspective, networks are doubly suspicious. They limit competition and, therefore, are suspected of facilitating monopolistic developments and the misuse of power. Networks nurture particularism (old-boys' networks, the power elite), and in the worst of cases, they degenerate into crony capitalism. Economists also find corporate networks a problem because they violate the criterion of economic efficiency. As a rule, they are inferior to the market as an instrument of coordination (Williamson 1991).

However, starting with the work of Polanyi (1957), a new research field has been established in the United States over the past few decades that provides empirical

---

[19] It goes without saying that Marx considered capitalism in principle to be an 'anarchic' production system. The point to be clarified here is that criticism of competition is not a genuine Marxist idea, but that Marx is part of a tradition that dates back to the early nineteenth century. See Hirschman (1982).

[20] Quotation cited in Mestmäcker (1984: 3).

[21] See Hayek (1973), Buchanan (1991), Friedman (1970).

evidence on networks which contradicts the 'liberal' paradigm. Here it is argued that economic transactions are always embedded in social relations. Networks are not just second-best solutions to problems in coordinating the market, they are also efficient in an economic sense because they nurture loyalty, commitment, and trust between economic actors and thereby reduce transaction costs.[22] We will devote more attention to these theories later in the book.

Still, it is undeniable that the greatest influence on American legislation, especially on the antitrust acts and the laws regulating financial markets, has been this 'liberal' tradition. Cartels were forbidden as early as 1890; corporate networks between competing firms in 1914. The deregulation of the markets and the deconglomeration of major American companies in the 1980s were further steps in the direction of establishing a free and open market (Davis *et al.* 1994).

1.8. DEPENDENT VARIABLES

The key dependent variable to be analyzed in the coming chapters is the structure of networks in various countries. Networks are instruments to regulate markets, to coordinate big business, and to communicate the economic interests of firms. Economic power can be concentrated more or less intensively in networks; likewise, the state can be linked more or less closely to them. This potential for power and influence is dependent on the specific structure of a network, which can be described through various variables, specifically through statistical coefficients.

The density of the network indicates how closely linked companies are with one another through shareholdings and/or interlocks. The denser the interlocking, the greater the chances to regulate the market and coordinate interests (*ceteris paribus*). Another important indicator is the percentage of isolated companies, meaning the percentage of large companies that are not linked to any other companies. In Germany, nearly 90 percent of all large firms are linked in *one* large network component. However in France, the structure is segmented since approximately half of the large firms are linked to one another and the other half are isolated. Among those in the first group are the big banks, insurances, and companies that were nationalized still in the early 1990s. Among those in the second group are companies that are chiefly family owned (family capitalism).

The final component important to a network is its configuration, which we interpret as being the specific, 'spatial' structure of the network. Networks can be configured as a star, a pyramid, an inverted star, or a circle.[23] The configuration is also characterized by the degree of centralization of the network, that is, the degree to which the entire network is concentrated on only a few large companies that are located at the center of the network. The configuration also determines how much opportunity member companies have to exert their influence and how much economic power is concentrated in the network.

---

[22] These studies originated chiefly in the context of economic sociology. See more in Granovetter (1985), Powell (1990), Uzzi (1996), and Baker (1984). [23] See the Fig. 3.1 in Chapter 3.

1.9. NETWORKS AS INSTITUTIONS

The structure of corporate networks is not only shaped by social and political institutions, they themselves constitute an important institution for regulating markets.
The relatively densely interlocked and heavily centralized networks in Germany,
which incorporate nearly every large corporation into a single component, facilitate
the coordination of economic interests and advance a specific form of corporatist
self-regulation.

Although this book does not analyze the institutions and the structure of economic
interest organizations in each country, it will be shown that there does exist an 'affinity' between the way in which the market is regulated and the way in which economic
interests are represented.

In Anglo-Saxon countries, the institutional structure of the market is shaped by
decentralized corporate networks featuring a relatively low level of density. Economic
interests are represented in pluralist associations that compete with one another, enjoy
no monopoly of representation, and demonstrate a relatively low degree of organizational density.

In Germany, the *structural* similarity between market regulation and the representation of economic interests can be described in the following manner: market regulation
is determined chiefly by cartel-like corporate networks, which are dominated by the big
corporations and include nearly all companies (making these networks both highly
centralized and very comprehensive). Likewise, the representation of economic interests is the task of corporatist organizations (unions, employers' association), which are
also highly centralized and monopolistically organized (see more in Chapter 2).

In every country, the economic institutions of capitalism create a 'system' in which
the elements adapt themselves to one another (Bratton and McCahery 1999).
Economic subsystems are regulated by the same laws, they are subject to similar cultural influences, and they are often headed by the same people. We will show in
Chapter 3 that the 'big linkers', those who assume important positions in corporate
networks, often also hold a top position in economic interest groups.

1.10. A TOPICAL OUTLINE OF THIS BOOK

1.10.1. *What is the Subject of this Study?*

Companies can be linked with one another through various types of relationships:
they can have some of the same directors sitting on each of their respective board of
directors; they can alternate between being customers or suppliers; companies can
own other companies (capital networks); and finally, they can take out loans from
banks (financial ties). The empirical analysis presented in the following chapters studies only the subjects of interlocking directorates and capital networks among companies. The reason for focusing the study on these two types of relationships is found in
the availability of data: Whereas relatively reliable data can be found on interlocking
directorates and capital networks in company reference books, no publicly accessible
data is available for supplier and financial ties in most of the countries studied here.

Despite this limitation, it is possible to say that interlocking directorates and capital networks are among the most important forms of interlocking. When we know that the chief executive officer (CEO) of one firm sits on the board of directors of another firm, then we know that this person has the opportunity to exercise considerable influence in filling of managerial positions and in determining the business strategies of the other company. This is also true for capital networks: when we know that one company is the (majority) shareholder of another, we also then know that the owner-company has the *potential* to control the other company extensively.

Finally, another structural characteristic can be derived from these two forms of linkage: we can also determine the degree to which interlocking directorates and capital networks overlap, that is, parallel one another. In this case, the owner-company delegates a CEO to the board of directors of the dependent company. The potential influence created by interlocking personnel and by capital networks can be accumulated and mutually enhanced.

A data matrix listing interlocking directorates and capital networks among companies offers structural data, meaning information on the *structure* of the linkages. However, the network matrix does not contain any data on behavior. It does not tell us what the CEOs who sit on the board of directors of other companies really do, with whom they communicate, and which decisions they actually attempt to influence.

What then can the reader expect to find in the following chapters? We offer a 'map' of the opportunities created by interlocking directorates and capital networks among large firms, opportunities that can be used by directors on company boards. However, this 'map' or analysis of corporate networks does not provide us with an evaluation of the actual use of such power, only its potential.

Even if directors do not exercise the power they possess, it remains a latent force that as such can be very effective. Corporate managers are quite aware that boards of directors have such sanctioning means at their disposal, although they may seldom resort to these means. Even Max Weber defined power not with respect to how one actually behaved oneself, but in the sense of one's potential to coerce others to change their behavior.

A manager who sits on the board of directors of another company meets other managers there, who in turn hold seats on other boards. The networks that thereby develop help mobilize a resource labeled by Bourdieu (1980) and Coleman (1990) as 'social capital'. In this context, 'social capital' is defined as a potential that exists in certain situations to mobilize the economic, political, and/or cultural resources of another person and to be able to use these in the pursuit of one's own interests.

A simple illustration demonstrates what is meant: the CEO of company A regularly meets the CEO of company C because they both hold seats on the board of directors of company B. Through this contact, the former manager can call the latter to ask for information about future developments at company C. The network matrices, which will be analyzed in the following chapters, show the probabilities with which companies/managers could indeed receive such information. However, we do not know whether or not these telephone conversations have ever taken place.

To determine that all the members of a network *can* be reached over a maximum of two path lengths is not to say that all of these members actually *do* mobilize 'friends of friends'. The structure describes the windows of opportunity open to the economic elite, from which those who do not have such network access are excluded. Therefore, 'social capital' describes—much like the definition of power—a chance, a potential, and not always actual behavior. Whether or not these opportunities are used is another question.

The structure of networks, which is analyzed in the following chapters, describes the structure of the potential influence that exists among large firms (distribution of power). Network structure further describes the distributional structure of social capital, in the sense of the potential to mobilize the resources of another person in order to pursue one's own interests.

The analysis of behavioral data is impossible because the minutes of board meetings are not available to us, meaning that we do not know what the people present at these meeting actually said or did. Even if we had such minutes, it would not be possible to fully analyze them in a large sample survey. The structural analysis presented in Chapter 2 encompasses nearly 2600 big companies in the six countries.

1.10.2. *Which Countries are Included in this Study?*

It has been argued that network structures are influenced by the institutions, culture, and political traditions of a country (see Section 1.6 on contingency theory). In selecting countries for this survey, we made sure that these characteristics (independent variables) varied greatly.

The first step was to select three large European countries, namely Germany, Great Britain, and France. In *Germany*, the 'culture' of cartels plays an important role, and traditions are shaped by corporatist and federalist structures. Unlike any other country, *Great Britain* represents the tradition of free trade. *France*, however, is characterized by mercantile, etatist, and centralist traditions. There is little distinction between the political and economic elite in France: The top managerial positions of the major corporations are often held by former governmental officials who once graduated from one of the 'Grande Ecoles'.

Switzerland and the Netherlands were included in the study to represent smaller European countries. The economic institutions of *Switzerland* are somewhat similar to those in the German model (e.g. cartel culture), whereas the *Netherlands* can be more closely associated with Anglo-Saxon traditions. The data record for the *United States* serves as a reference point for the various comparisons. The separation of ownership and control is the most advanced in major American companies. Investment and pension funds hold a large percentage of stock in American firms and have been propagating the ideology of shareholder value for more than a decade.

1.10.3. *Corporate Networks and Elite Networks*

Networks can be analyzed from two different perspectives. For one, they can be interpreted as a structure of relationships between *companies*. In this case, the relationship between companies is created by interlocking directors who sit on various corporate boards (= corporate network).

For another, networks can be understood as a structure of relationships between people (= elite network). In such a case, the boards of directors are the meeting places for people. Managers from the various companies meet several times a year, and often these same people meet repeatedly over a period of many years. From this perspective, the board of directors can be interpreted as a 'social circle'. In this book, we examine the corporate networks in Part I (Chapters 2–4) and the elite networks in Part II (Chapters 5 and 6).

Chapter 2 offers the reader a comprehensive analysis of corporate networks between major firms in six countries: Germany, Great Britain, France, Switzerland, the Netherlands, and the United States. It will be shown that the structure of networks can be compared with the dominant forms of intermediary interest representation[24] found in each country. The network between German companies is dense, comprehensive, centralized, and corresponds in this regard with the corporatist structures also existing in Germany. The network in Great Britain is sparse, non-comprehensive (a large percentage of isolated companies), and non-centralized. The potential influence in this network is diffuse and not geared toward the organization of markets.

Chapter 3 presents a detailed comparative analysis of German and British firms; Chapter 4 offers the same for France and the United States. In these chapters, three aspects will be closely examined, namely the degree of ownership concentration, the different types of owners, and the differences in the configuration of networks.

Our perspective changes in Part II of the book. We are no longer interested in the relationships between companies, but the relationships between individuals. Although this analysis is based on the same data as the analysis of corporate networks, new questions can be posed and answered from this perspective. We will investigate whether the network of multiple directors creates one large comprehensive network or whether it breaks down into various, separate social circles.

The way in which these two perspectives correspond can be illustrated by the following example. In Chapter 2, we will see that in Germany, corporate networks and capital networks overlap considerably, meaning that companies are not only linked together through interlocking directorates but also often through capital networks (ownership relationships).

With regard to individual directors, Chapter 5 outlines the way in which top German managers combine the power of their bureaucratic position with the power of ownership. Many members of the network are CEOs in the parent company (bureaucratic power), while they simultaneously represent the owners in the supervisory board of the dependent company (property rights).

---

[24] We interpret 'intermediary' interest representation as being organizations that represent the economic interests of their members relatively autonomously and with no direct governmental interference. Similarly, one can also understand the network of companies as an intermediary institution that defines, aggregates, and filters the economic interests of its members.

In Chapter 6, we take a look at the career paths of German and British multiple directors: their education, their fields of study, the course of the careers, and the speed with which they climbed the career ladder. It will be shown that the central position of individual managers in the elite network can be explained by the following variables: the manager's age, the company's prestige, and the membership in lobby and interest organizations.

Part III addresses post-socialist networks. First, the network among East German firms is analyzed. Does the East German corporate network have the same structural characteristics as its counterpart in West Germany? The analysis shows that this is not the case: the East German network is dominated by West German corporations (Chapter 7).

The analysis of post-socialist networks is expanded in Chapter 8 to include several other countries in Eastern Europe (Poland, Hungary). We seek to discover which type of capitalism is developing in Eastern Europe. In particular, we ask whether the emerging structures more closely resemble the model of (German) corporatism or that of Anglo-Saxon market liberalism.

PART I

CORPORATE NETWORKS

2

The Structure of Corporate Networks

2.1. MARKETS AND INSTITUTIONS[1]

One of the central hypotheses of institutional economics is that markets only function optimally within the framework of institutions (North 1990). Examples of economic institutions include corporate law, the Federal Trade Commission (FTC), or the networks in which firms are able to coordinate their strategies.[2] Fligstein (1996: 657) terms this institutional order 'the social structure of the market'.

In a way the relationship between markets and institutions is paradoxical: on the one hand markets are dependent on effective 'background institutions' (Rawls 1971: 274); on the other, this institutional order is perpetually being destroyed by competition. Schumpeter termed this relationship 'creative destruction'. Examples of this process are the dissolution of employers' federations in eastern Germany or union busting in the US. We are currently witnessing the dissolution of national market orders in the face of global competition, although so far scarcely any new, transnational market institutions have been created.

In recent decades, a systematic analysis of the relationship between markets and institutions has been developed by the proponents of transaction cost theory (North 1990; Williamson 1985), economic sociology (Granovetter 1985; Fligstein 1996; Swedberg 1994), and comparative institutional analysis; comparative analysis is concerned primarily with national and cultural differences between market orders (Orrú et al. 1997; Maurice et al. 1982; Stokman et al. 1985). We commence by summarizing these theories, before embarking, in Section 2.3, on the comparative analysis of corporate networks.

2.1.1. *Transaction Cost Theory*

Markets constitute a specific form of social order. The question as to how market orders are possible is merely a special case of the more general question as to how order and cooperation in society are possible. The lack of information, uncertainty, and 'bounded rationality', on the one hand, fraud and moral hazard, on the other, are some of the reasons why markets do not function, or do so only sub-optimally.

---

[1] A German version of this chapter was published in *Politische Vierteljahresschrift* 42 (2001), pp. 51–78; co-author: Michael Nollert. I gratefully acknowledge the research support of Christian Brandt and Martin Weber.

[2] Networks are here taken to mean interlocking directorates and capital networks. For a summary of research on interlocks, see Mizruchi (1996).

A market order consists of a system of institutions that are there to overcome these inadequacies of the market (Williamson 1985).

Davis and North (1971: 6) define the institutional framework in which markets are embedded as a 'set of fundamental political, social and legal ground rules that establishes the basis for production, exchange, and distribution. Rules governing elections, property rights, and the right of contract are examples of the type of ground rules that make up the economic environment.' In the absence of these 'fundamental' institutions, there can be no efficient markets. They are 'constraints on human action' (North 1990) and protect individuals against the consequences of uncertainty and inadequate information, and against fraud and the threat of violence.

If we then ask what type of institutions a society chooses in order to render markets more effective, transaction cost theory offers a simple answer: society chooses those institutions that reduce transaction costs. 'The economic institutions of capitalism have the main purpose and effect of economizing on transaction costs' (Williamson 1985: 17). In other words, the problem of the 'optimal' market order is resolved with reference to a meta-market in which institutions compete with one another. Those institutions will survive that, in the longer run, reduce transaction costs in a given country and thus raise its competitiveness. Competition on the meta-market for institutions, therefore, describes the mechanism through which institutions that have become an obstacle to innovation are replaced by new ones.

However, historical and empirical studies show that in many countries there are institutions that—seen from a purely economic perspective—are inefficient, if not completely obsolete. If the meta-market of institutional competition were working perfectly, then inefficient institutions would be expected to die out over time. North (1990) answers the question why inefficient institutions nevertheless survive by a repeated reference to transaction costs: institutional (or social) change itself causes transaction costs, and these can be very high (e.g. social reforms). The higher these costs, the less likely is social change. This explains the phenomena that North describes as 'lock-in' and 'path dependency'. A society is locked in to its institutional framework, and these institutions influence development paths in the future (path dependency). Inefficient institutions survive because the costs of social change are too high or appear too high to the members of the society. The modernization of economic institutions fails to occur, or is delayed in certain countries. Thus, differences in the modernization process offer one explanation of why different countries exhibit different market orders.

We, therefore, conclude that transaction cost theory cannot offer an unambiguous answer to the question as to which market order will emerge from institutional competition. This is because the theory is unable to specify the costs of social change. The competition of institutions is a political process the outcome of which depends on historical contingencies.

2.1.2. *Networks and Embeddedness*

Granovetter (1985) has criticized the arguments propounded by transaction cost theory and institutional economics by pointing out that the problems of the market order and of cooperation cannot be solved by institutions alone. The existence of an institutional order does not guarantee that this order will also be accepted and adhered to. Exchange processes on the market are already 'embedded' in a preexisting system of social relationships. Buyers and sellers do not meet on a market cleansed of all social relations, but rather economic transactions almost always occur within a framework of already existent social relations. These relationships constitute a normative framework in which the actors monitor each other's activities.

The 'ongoing social relations' to which Granovetter refers (1985: 482) are the concrete social networks in which the actors are embedded and which play an important role in coordinating market transactions. They may serve to reduce transaction costs, and they are also an important instrument with which to monitor competitors (Fligstein 1996). Within these networks, informational asymmetries between groups of managers can be reduced.[3] Stable social relationships enable 'trust' to be created between market actors, and market uncertainty to be reduced (Uzzi 1996). Moreover, within these networks, owners may be able to strengthen their control over managers, and thus defuse the principal–agent problem (cf. the analysis of parallel networks in Section 2.4). Networks integrate managers from different companies who, as a group, monitor their decisions (group control).[4] It can also be shown that it is possible to redistribute entrepreneurial risk between investors, banks, and companies (Section 2.3). Networks constitute an 'organizational field' (DiMaggio and Powell 1983) in which innovations diffuse rapidly and the resources necessary to push through an innovation can be pooled.

Every market order causes specific transaction costs, and this is also true of networks. Networks are not merely an efficient instrument with which to coordinate exchange processes and to limit the 'anarchy' of the market. In marginal cases, networks can entirely suspend competition (e.g. in a cartel). In many countries such networks achieve a relatively high degree of social closure. In Germany, for instance, in many companies, the members of the management board control the electoral lists for the supervisory board members, and it is members of the supervisory board that appoint managerial board members (mutual co-optation). Such networks are largely closed to external competitors (such as young companies), and they frequently degenerate into coalitions in defense of the status quo (Wood 1994). The 'crony capitalism' found in many Asian countries, and the financial crisis to which it gave rise offer an additional illustration of the fact that markets can be 'over-coordinated'.

2.1.3. *Comparative Institutional Analysis*

If markets can only function efficiently within an institutional framework, and given that institutions are influenced by the traditions and culture of a country, it is

---

[3] Granovetter (1973) argues that relationships to social groups with which one is not in continuous contact (= 'weak ties') are particularly useful to obtain valuable information. Many interlocks perform the function of such weak ties.

[4] Networks 'are forms of coordination by which actors collectively monitor one another' (Hollingsworth and Boyer 1997: 11).

inevitable that market orders vary between countries; there is not just one, there are many forms of capitalist market order. Variations in economic institutions thus arise from cultural differences and 'lock-in' effects, based on learning processes (Liebowitz and Margolis 1995).

Culture and tradition are resources that are at the disposal of each country in designing its market institutions. These resources may offer comparative advantages (e.g. the Protestant ethic) or comparative disadvantages (e.g. the economic ethic of Islam). The close relationship between economic institutions and culture also results from the fact that economic transactions are always embedded in social relations. Fukuyama (1995), for example, has argued that the structure of the Chinese economy, based on small-scale enterprises, can be explained in terms of the structure of its social networks. The family constitutes both the center and the boundary of social organizations, and Chinese families tend to exclude outsiders: 'In Chinese culture the strong distrust of outsiders usually prevents the institutionalization of the company. Rather than let professional managers take over management of the firm, family owners of Chinese businesses tend to acquiesce in its fragmentation into new concerns, or in its total disintegration' (p. 78).

Comparative institutional analysis has repeatedly been called upon to address the question of the 'one best way': which country has the best economic institutions? There has been a change in preferences over time in this regard. During the 1960s, the German model (in some cases, the Swedish model) was widely held to represent an optimal institutional configuration (Lehmbruch 1983). During the 1980s, the Japanese model was the favorite. The forms of external market organization predominant in Japan (e.g. *keiretsu*) and the prevailing internal organization of production (just in time, flat hierarchies) were accepted as superior even in the US (Womack *et al.* 1990). In the 1990s, the US model is held to be the most efficient on globalized markets.

To date there has been only limited success in importing and implementing a market order from abroad, however. In the 1970s, Great Britain attempted in vain to imitate German and Swedish corporatism (Crouch 1977). The US successfully imported the purely technical components of the Japanese production model (such as just-in-time production), whereas it failed to reproduce the social forms of organization characteristic of this model (such as group work). The greater the social and cultural distance between the domestic and the imported model, the higher are the (transaction) costs of social change.

To a degree, the various market orders constitute functional equivalents. They are alternative solutions to the problem of restraining the 'anarchy' of competition. The social costs they generate also differ. Corporatist market orders change relatively slowly in response to changes in technology and market preferences, but they reduce social inequality and the social conflict associated with it. Due to their informal nature (loose coupling), networks can react relatively fast to market signals, but they frequently tend to degenerate into closed social circles inaccessible to outsiders.

In a decade during which the market has become increasingly globalized and has developed outside and beyond national market orders, those countries that have only a 'weak' market order, and consequently can react relatively swiftly to changes in their environment enjoy a comparative advantage. In such cases, there is an affinity between the national and the global market order, in that both operate with a minimum of institutional regulation.

2.2. NETWORKS AS PART OF THE MARKET ORDER

As far as corporate networks are concerned, the arguments presented above can be summarized in the following hypotheses:

1. Networks form part of an institutional structure of the market whose aim is to reduce transaction costs. Networks enable firms to coordinate their behavior and regulate competition (Fligstein 1996).
2. Corporate networks perform a number of economic functions: reducing informational asymmetries (e.g. weak ties, Granovetter 1973); reducing uncertainty (e.g. trust, Uzzi 1996); the supervision of managers by owners (principal–agent problem); redistributing risk (risk-sharing); diffusion of innovations within an 'organizational field' (DiMaggio and Powell 1983); reducing (mutual) resource dependency (Burt 1982); selecting and recruiting successful managers (screening).
3. The structure of corporate networks is different in different countries. In Germany and Switzerland, for instance, large firms and banks come together in the networks (*Konzerne*); in France, the large companies, the state, and the financial companies (*groupes industriels*), and in Korea, the family-clans and the state (*chaebol*). The predominant network configuration is influenced in each country by its specific culture, traditions and experience (Stokman *et al.* 1985; Numazaki 1996).
4. Within the networks, actors with different economic interests form a coalition, whereby these coalitions may be 'modernization coalitions' or defensive 'rent-seeking coalitions'.

    Corporate networks can be compared with interest organizations (corporatism). They serve to improve the *collective* capacity of firms for self-regulation. The more comprehensive the networks and the more effective the mechanisms by which interests are filtered, the less their scope to organize narrow sectional interests.[5]
5. Conversely, networks that focus on a single branch approximate, in terms of their structure, to cartels and only organize narrow rent-seeking coalitions. Networks that are relatively confined and exhibit a high degree of social closure raise transaction costs and exacerbate social inequality.

Although networks are able to filter and aggregate heterogeneous interests, it is important to note that they are *not* formal interest organizations. They lack the legitimacy to represent business interests to the outside world, or to engage in bargaining.

---

[5] On this aspect, see Offe and Wiesenthal (1980) and Olson (1982); with specific reference to networks, see Useem (1984).

This reflects their lack of formal membership and bureaucratic organizational structure. The networks analyzed in the following sections are quasi-institutions[6] that transcend the boundaries of individual companies, and that filter and communicate the interests of large companies. Within these networks, interests negatively affected by innovations can receive compensation by way of multiple issue bargaining (cf. the notion of 'political exchange', Marin 1990).

The next section describes the networks of American and German banks toward the end of the nineteenth century. Sections 2.4–2.6 present a quantitative analysis of present-day network structures in six countries.

2.3. 'MORGANIZATION': REGULATED COMPETITION

Historical analysis shows that the differences in network structures that currently prevail between a number of west European countries and the US have not always existed. If one compares turn-of-the-century Germany with the US, more similarities than differences emerge. In both countries, the banks exerted a dominant influence on interlocking directorates: in the US, networks were monitored by the 'Money Trust', in Germany by the large Berlin banks.[7] In Germany, this structure has been largely preserved until the present day, whereas there was a radical change in the US in the wake of antitrust legislation.

2.3.1. *Networks in the US*

The major railway lines built in the second half of the nineteenth century in the US exemplify the hypothesis, formulated above, that markets do not function in the absence of institutions (market failure). If there was just one railway line between two American cities, the monopoly company frequently charged exorbitant prices for the transport of goods and passengers. These prices constituted a major incentive to construct a parallel railway line, inducing a murderous price war. Frequently this war led to both companies going bankrupt: 'Building two lines over the same route simply means enormous waste of capital which impoverishes society in general' (Josephson 1962: 297).

Pierpont Morgan, one of the most influential bankers in American history, recognized the problems of American competitive capitalism toward the end of the nineteenth century. He attempted to restructure not only the railway companies, but also the steel industry (US Steel Corporation) and engineering (Harvester), by introducing a market order. Strouse (1999: xiii) concludes that 'Morgan did not really believe in free markets'. The strategies which he deployed in his reorganizations and which have been termed 'Morganization', consisted of a number of elements.

---

[6] They acquire the character of 'institutions' by virtue of the fact that membership of a corporate network is indirectly tied to membership of the managerial or supervisory board of a large company, and the fact that in all countries the role of director is defined by corporate *law*. For Germany, it can be shown that the interlocks are relatively *stable* over time (see Chapter 5).

[7] For the US, see Brandeis (1995), McCraw (1984), Gourevitch (1996: 239); for Germany, see Riesser (1971), Jeidels (1905), Eulenberg (1906), Hardach (1995).

First, several competing firms were merged into a single company (trust). Second, the new company was financed via the equity market, and not by bank loans. Third, Morgan assumed a degree of responsibility for the creditworthiness of these financial transactions. This meant that Morgan's investment bank and/or associate financial institutions assumed a number of seats on the board of directors, in order to be able to exert control over the company (interlocks). The 'Money Trust'—a coalition of large banks and insurance companies in New York—formed the core of these networks.

One of the largest financial operations organized by Morgan was the founding of the US Steel Corporation in 1901. This merger marked the transition from atomistic competition between numerous small steel producers to mass production, and to the age of organized markets in the American steel industry. This merger proved possible because Andrew Carnegie—one of the pioneers of industrialization in the US—was willing, toward the end of his career, to sell his steel empire to Morgan for US$ 480 million.[8] Along with the steel firms owned by Carnegie, around two dozen independent steel firms were incorporated into the merger, enabling the largest company in the then world to be established, one that controlled around 50 percent of the American steel market. Morgan himself took a seat on the board of directors of the newly founded US Steel Corporation, and filled other positions with business friends (Mizruchi 1982: 46).

Frequently the restructuring schemes were prepared in the networks in which the owners and managers of the major railway lines, the steelworks, mines and financial institutes came together. They pushed through the modernization of American industry, that is, the transformation of small firms into large corporations which were able to organize mass production, to implement new technology and to enforce the Taylorization of the production process—often against the bitter opposition of trade unions.[9] The 'Morganization' of American industry has frequently been interpreted as a process of monopolization (trust) and financial control; but it was also a process of modernization and expansion.

In New York three banks formed the inner circle of the 'Money Trust': J. P. Morgan & Co., National City Bank, and First National Bank. Morgan held 16.5 percent of the share capital of the First National Bank and owned a holding of $6 million in the National City Bank. He and his partners sat on the board of directors of both these banks. Moreover, the three banks also held shares in numerous insurance companies (e.g. in the Equitable Life Assurance Society); in return, the insurance companies invested their income from insurance premiums in shares in the banks.

---

[8] The 'Morganization' of the steel industry was an important step toward managerial capitalism. Following this transaction, the US Steel Corporation was no longer controlled by its owners, but by its managers. In the year it was founded (1901), the firm had 15,997 shareholders; by 1931, it was 174,507 (cf. Berle and Means 1997: 52, table VI).

[9] In 1892, a steel workers' strike was held in Homestead which led to an armed conflict between Carnegie's private army and the striking workers, in the course of which several workers were shot dead. The strike ended with the dismantling of the craft unions (for skilled craft workers) and the introduction of partially automated mass production in the steel industry (manned by unskilled workers). In this case, a market order controlled by the craft union was replaced by an alternative order, namely an oligopolistic market order controlled by large corporations.

The Pujo Commission set up by Congress to investigate the interlocking directorates within the Money Trust revealed that the three large banks (together with
financial institutes under their control) held a total of 341 positions on the boards of
directors of 112 other companies: of these, 118 positions were in other financial institutes, 30 positions in 10 insurance companies, 105 positions in 32 railway lines,
63 positions in 24 industrial companies, 25 positions in water, electricity, and gas supply
companies. Just as in Germany, in many companies, the investment banks occupied
not just one, but several positions on the board of directors.[10]

The Interstate Commerce Commission, which published its report in 1908, came
to the conclusions that many railway companies consisted of a hierarchically structured combine in which small rail companies were controlled by large corporations
(cf. Fig. 1.1). The Harriman Group, for instance, included ten companies, with a total
of 33,000 miles of track; the Morgan Group encompassed eight firms with a total of
28,000 miles. This structure of capital networks closely resembles the corporate
structure still prevalent in modern-day Germany, France, and Switzerland.[11]

Summarizing this brief historical account, we come to the conclusion that Morgan
successfully replaced the anarchic competition characteristic of the pioneering phase
of industrial capitalism by regulated competition. It was not until a later stage that this
'private' regulation of the market was in turn replaced by government regulation. The
restructuring of firms and their control within corporate networks marked the transition from early industrialization to organized mass production, and more generally to
the 'corporate economy' (Hannah 1983). Morgan was a firm believer in the efficiency
of consolidated companies and saw the necessity of 'administered markets, but had no
faith in the government's ability to do the administering' (Strouse 1999: 303).

The networks in whose center Morgan operated performed an important economic function: they reduced the risk to potential investors by imposing a 'private'
supervision of the financial markets.[12] Morgan's power base lay not in owning a large
bank operating in many states, but in the charismatic influence he personally exerted.
The Robber Barons accepted his authority (and his brilliant financial techniques),
and the investors who bought shares put their faith not primarily in the US Steel
Corporation, but in Pierpont Morgan. Morgan justified the interlocks between his

---

[10] Cf. Subcommittee of the Committee on Banking and Currency (Pujo Commission), *Investigation of
Financial and Monetary Conditions in the United States.* Washington 1913: Government Printing Office,
Exhibit 134A,B. A summary of the results is given in Brandeis (1995), especially pp. 62–5. The multiple
interrelationships between banks and industrial concerns are analyzed in greater detail in Table 2.1 (see
Section 2.4).

[11] Interstate Commerce Commission (1908: 9); cf. also Liefmann (1923: 78–81).

[12] Brandeis (1995: 55) shows that the Directors of the Money Trust (Morgan, Baker, Stillman) sat on the
board of directors of the railway and industrial companies whose share emissions they bought as a syndi-
cate (i.e. they voted on the board on the emission price of the shares). At the same time the investment
banks also held shares in the insurance companies. George Perkins, Vice-president of the New York Life
Insurance Company, the largest of its kind, was actually simultaneously a partner at J. P. Morgan & Co. The
life insurance companies were important buyers of shares; they took over a significant volume of the share
emissions directly from the investment banks. As a result, the investment banks exerted substantial influence both on the firms emitting shares and on the buyers of those shares.

bank and the railway and industrial companies with the confidence placed in him by share-buying investors, a confidence he was forced to honor. When a rail company that Morgan had floated on the stock exchange encountered difficulties, Morgan justified his intervention (i.e. the dismissal of the management team) to a friend as follows: 'I certainly have no desire to be burdened with all this trouble, ... but there I am, representing interests which cannot be shirked' (Strouse 1999: 240).

2.3.2. *Networks in Germany*

We are now in a position to compare the financial operations performed by Morgan in the US with those of Deutsche Bank in Germany. Deutsche Bank was founded in 1870, and by the start of the First World War it was the largest of Germany's nine big banks (Hardach 1995: 916). Even in those early years, Deutsche Bank was a share company with several thousand shareholders; it had already purchased a number of German banks, and had close links to a number of other regional banks through cartel agreements; its network of branches extended throughout the industrialized areas of Germany.[13] An important element in Deutsche Bank operations was to collect savings from its depositors and to lend capital to industry (Riesser 1971: 723–32).

Entrepreneurial risk was distributed differently in Germany than in the US. Even though American banks were lending money to American firms and German banks floated stock on the Berlin stock exchange, it is correct to say that bank credit was the dominant external financial source for German firms while equity capital was the dominant external financial source for American firms. In Germany, the risk involved in lending money is divided between the firm and the bank, whereas the savers (investors) who deposit their money with the bank bear virtually no risk at all.[14]

In order to be able to assume such a risk, a bank must, first and foremost, be sufficiently large; it is only then that it can spread risk by lending to many different companies. Secondly, it must establish an information and control apparatus with which to monitor the firms to which it lends money;[15] this usually takes the form of nominating bank managers to the supervisory board of the firms. Hilferding (1968: 309) characterized this form of financial capital as follows: 'An ever greater part of the capital used in industry is finance capital, capital at the disposal of the banks and utilized by the industrialists.'

Around the turn of the century, the directors of Deutsche Bank held 115 positions on the supervisory board of German companies; in twenty-nine companies the chairman

---

[13] At that time Morgan was still running his company as a 'partnership', that is, as a group of four or five owners (under the leadership of Pierpont Morgan).

[14] American investment banks passed on risks to the investors (shareholders), without themselves bearing entrepreneurial risk.

[15] 'In Germany, the various incompetencies of the individual entrepreneurs were offset by the device of splitting the entrepreneurial function: ... From their central vantage points of control, the banks participated actively in shaping the major—and sometimes even not so major—decisions of the individual enterprise' (Gerschenkron 1968: 137).

of the supervisory board was nominated by Deutsche Bank. The Schaafhausen'sche Bankverein held 142 supervisory board positions, and in twenty-six companies it nominated the chairman of the supervisory board. At the end of December 1910, the Berliner Handelsgesellschaft was represented on the supervisory board of nine companies, which, in turn, sent a board member to sit on the supervisory board of Berliner Handelsgesellschaft (cross interlocks).[16]

In many companies the banks held several seats on the supervisory board: clearly, it was not merely a matter of gaining information—which could have been obtained just as well by a single board member—but also of control, that is, voting majorities. The strategies adopted by the industrial firms also affected the interests of the German banks. The economic function of these networks lay not only in reducing risks, but also in redistributing them, namely from the industrialists to the banks, which thus became co-entrepreneurs. Rigorous deconcentration of the Money Trust, called for and in part achieved by Brandeis in the US, would, in Germany, have put a question mark over the very financial base of large industrial firms.[17]

2.3.3. *State Regulation versus Self-regulation*

The market structures organized by Morgan proved short-lived. The antitrust laws—the Sherman Act of 1890 and the Clayton Act of 1914—destroyed the foundations on which the Morganization of American industry was based.[18] In the years after 1910, the American antitrust authorities became active, leading to the development of market structures subsequently termed 'competitive capitalism' by Chandler (1990). The networks that remained under the control of the Money Trust until the First World War were steadily dismantled during the following two decades. This form of 'private' control was replaced by state supervision of the financial markets.

The protagonists of the 'progressive movement' perceived a close link between market competition and political democracy: the Money Trust was not merely inefficient in economic terms, it also destroyed political democracy. For this reason, the various commissions that were set up to investigate corporate networks in the US were, at heart, political commissions that were guided by a specific image of American democracy (Hofstadter 1955). The antitrust legislation and the economic institutions to which it gave rise cannot be understood unless their political content is taken into account at the same time. The state authorities perceived themselves not

---

[16] The figures are taken from Riesser (1971: 304, 501, 651–72).

[17] In a series of publications, Edwards and his collaborators have challenged the conventional view that—in comparison to British banks—German banks lend more money to large German firms and that they played a crucial role in the process of German industrialization (Edwards and Nibler 2000; Edwards and Fischer 1996; Edwards and Ogilvie 1996). Edwards' analyses cannot be discussed here in detail, but it seems that there is still a lot of empirical evidence to support the 'conventional' view. See case studies in Gall *et al.* (1995); Feldman (1998).

[18] In anticipation of the Clayton Act (which came into force in October 1914), the partners/managers of J. P. Morgan relinquished thirty positions they had held on the board of directors of other companies (January 1914). Many of these interlocks became illegal under the new provisions introduced by the Clayton Act (Brandeis 1995: 155).

merely as market regulators, but also as the guardians of democracy (e.g. the FTC, the Securities Exchange Commission).

The 'spontaneous order' (Hayek 1963) of the market does not in fact occur spontaneously, but rather must be produced by state regulation. This was the paradoxical message of the 'progressive movement' and the 'prophets of regulation' (McCraw 1984). Polanyi (1957: 139) expressed this paradox succinctly as follows: 'Laissez-faire itself was enforced by the state'.

In Germany (and many other European countries), by contrast, it was the heyday of the organized cartels, leading to the development of an 'organized capitalism', whose institutions were characterized by the close links between the corporatist networks (cartels) and the welfare policy of the state. In contrast to anarchic competition, the market as regulated by the cartels was considered to be a 'higher order', and not as a threat to democracy.[19]

In 1905 George Perkins, Vice-president of the New York Life Insurance Company, and at the same time a partner of Morgan, was questioned by the Armstrong Commission on the Money Trust networks. He is on record as saying the following: 'The old idea that we were raised under, that competition is the life of trade, is exploded. Competition is no longer the life of trade, it is cooperation'. (Carosso 1970: 138; Strouse 1999: 545.) This statement is an accurate description of the networks that dominated the market around the turn of the nineteenth century in both the US and, especially, in Germany. However, Perkins underestimated the political impact of the Commission that recorded his statement. Two decades later he would have been forced to conclude: cooperation is no longer the life of trade, it is competition.

2.4. STRUCTURAL DIFFERENCES

Under the 'Corporate Networks in Western Europe' project, data were collected on capital networks and interlocking directorates between large companies in five countries: Germany, Great Britain, France, Switzerland, and the Netherlands. Data for the US were obtained from a supplementary investigation, permitting a comparison with the European data, and making a total of six countries.[20] A detailed list of the number of firms for each country and the data sources (handbooks) are given in Appendix A at the end of this book.

Two criteria were used in selecting the countries: the size of the country (three large and two small European countries) and differences in the social organization of markets. Three of the countries selected are examples of corporatist traditions (Switzerland, Netherlands, Germany), one has an 'étatiste' tradition (France), and two are 'market societies' (Great Britain and the US).[21]

---

[19] Cf. Wehler (1974), Nörr (1995), Feldenkirchen (1988).

[20] The source of the data was in each country the various handbooks on large corporations. Data were collected for the largest firms in each country: *c.* 700 German firms (1993), *c.* 520 British firms (1993), *c.* 500 French firms (1995), *c.* 300 Swiss firms (1995), *c.* 300 Dutch firms (1995), *c.* 500 US firms (1996).

[21] On this classification, see Albert (1991), Scott (1997), Hall and Soskice (2001).

TABLE 2.1   *Directed interlocks*

	G		UK		F	CH	NL	US	US[a]
1 Number of firms (N)	616	300	520	300	374	300	300	481	166
2 Number of interlocks (not dichotomized)	1456	757	389	235	586	1047	493	531	564[b]
3 Number of ties (dichotomized matrix)	1147	581	376	230	503	865	407	528	403
4 Proportion of multiple relationships (%)	21.2	23.2	3.3	2.1	14.2	17.4	17.4	0.6	28.5[b]
5 Financial/nonfinancial									
Outdegree (% of row 2)	—	37.9	—	9.1	34.3	22.5	43.2	15.1	20.6
Indegree (% of row 2)	—	13.4	—	13.4	14.8	26.5	42.6	19.8	21.8
6 Largest component (% of N)	75.8	75.7	47.1	53.0	51.1	74.7	65.3	69.4	c
7 Isolates (% of N)	20.5	19.7	41.3	38.7	46.4	17.3	31.0	28.9	22.9
8 All ties/firms with ties (dichotomized)	2.3	2.4	1.2	1.3	2.5	3.5	2.0	1.5	3.1
9 Highest									
Outdegree	69	53	8	7	25	39	17	7	c
Indegree	13	8	7	7	12	26	18	7	c
10 Density: all firms	0.30	0.65	0.14	0.26	0.36	0.96	0.45	0.23	1.47
11 Density: firms with ties	0.48	1.00	0.41	0.68	1.28	1.41	0.95	0.45	2.48
12 Centralization of network									
Outdegree	11.0	17.2	1.4	2.1	6.4	46.0	19.9	1.2	c
Indegree	1.8	2.0	1.2	2.1	2.9	29.4	21.2	1.2	c

Notes: [a] US data for 1904; *Source*: Mizruchi (1982: 105–6, 128); own calculations.

[b] Estimation based on Mizruchi (1982: 104) [c] Data not available.

G: (West) Germany (1993); UK: United Kingdom (1993); F: France (1997); CH: Switzerland (1995); NL: Netherlands (1995); US (1997).

Row 1: Number of firms in the sample; for Germany and the UK coefficients were computed for the total sample and for a reduced sample (N=300).

Row 5: Proportion of interlocks that financials delegate to nonfinancial firms (outdegree); proportion of interlocks that financials receive from nonfinancial firms (indegree).

Row 8: Coefficients were computed as follows: (total number of dichotomized ties)/(total number of firms− isolates). Example for Germany: Firms with ties have on average directed interlocks to 2.3 other firms.

Density was computed as follows: (Number of dichotomized ties)/(Number of firms) × (Number of firms − 1). This formula was applied to *all networks regardless of whether the matrix contains directed or undirected interlocks*.

The corporate networks in the various countries were initially analyzed on the basis of structural coefficients, enabling their macro structures to be compared. For Germany and Great Britain, the coefficients were calculated for two samples, both for the entire sample and a reduced sample (N=300); the reduced sample was chosen both to illustrate the impact of sample size on the coefficients and to facilitate inter-country comparison. The coefficients were calculated for directed (Table 2.1) and for undirected (Table 2.2) interlocking directorates.[22]

[22] If Company A delegates a member of its management to the (supervisory) board of Company B and also to the (supervisory) board of Company C, a 'directed' interlock arises between the firms (A → B) and (A→C). At the same time, an 'undirected' interlock is established between (B–C), because the same person is represented on the (supervisory) boards of the firms B and C. See Scott (1991).

TABLE 2.2   *Undirected interlocks*

	G		UK		F	CH	NL	US
1 Number of firms (N)	616	300	520	300	374	300	300	481
2 Number of interlocks (not dichotomized)	9280	4228	1106	696	2792	1267	1298	3428
3 Number of ties (dichotomized matrix)	6834	3198	1014	632	2224	982	1144	3196
4 Proportion of multiple relationships (in %)	26.4	24.4	8.3	9.2	20.3	22.5	11.7	6.8
5 Largest component (% of N)	87.7	89.7	57.3	63.0	52.9	80.1	72.0	83.0
6 Isolates (% of N)	9.4	8.0	36.5	32.0	43.1	13.7	26.7	14.3
7 All ties/firms with ties (dichotomized)	12.2	11.6	3.1	3.1	10.4	3.8	5.2	7.6
8 Highest degree (dichotomized)	73	47	12	11	55	45	78	29
9 Density: all firms	1.80	3.57	0.36	0.70	1.59	1.09	1.28	1.38
10 Density: firms with ties	2.20	4.21	0.93	1.53	4.92	1.46	2.37	1.89
11 Centralization of network	10.1	12.2	1.9	3.0	13.2	49.0	78.0	4.6

Note: G: (West)Germany (1993); UK: United Kingdom (1993); F: France (1997); CH: Switzerland (1995); NL: Netherlands (1995); US (1997).

The presentation commences with the analysis of the directed interlocks. Row 2 of Table 2.1 contains the total number of directed interlocks between the 616 German, 520 British, etc. firms (non-dichotomized matrix). If a company delegates more than one manager to the supervisory board of another company, these relationships are coded in terms of the number of co-opted members. In row 3, such multiple relationships are counted as just a single relationship.[23] The percentage figures in row 4 indicate the proportion of interlocks that consist of multiple relationships between two firms. The figure for Germany is 21.2 percent (N=616), for the US 0.6 percent, and for Switzerland 17.4 percent.

In cases where the company of origin delegates more than one manager to the recipient company, it can be assumed that the underlying strategies are not restricted merely to obtaining information or maintaining business relations, but rather that the aim is to exert influence over the company. In Germany, the supervisory board nominates the members of the management board and can dismiss them. It is

---

[23] This matrix is dichotomized. It contains only the figures one (there is a relationship between two companies) and zero (there is no such relationship).

possible for one company to control another by virtue of its representation on the supervisory board.[24]

A study of the 166 largest companies over the period 1904–74 provides some data on the structure of the network in the US around the turn of the nineteenth century (last column of Table 2.1). The comparison shows that the structure of interrelationships at that time was in some ways similar to that of German companies ($N=300$) in the present day. In 1904, the number of multiple relationships in the US had been relatively high (28.5 percent); the same is true of the density of the network (1.47) and the number of interlocks per company (3.1). Since 1919, however, the density of the network has declined continuously in the US. The frequency of multiple relationships has also fallen; by 1997, they amounted to just 0.6 percent of the total (cf. Mizruchi 1982: 105–7). These coefficients clearly confirm the historical analysis provided in the preceding section.

Table 2.1 also shows that in 1904, 20.6 percent of all directed interlocks in the US emanated from financial companies. At the same time, though, industrial companies delegated managers to the board of directors of financial companies; indeed, the figure here was almost as high, at 21.8 percent. This means that while banks and insurance companies sent large numbers of managers to the board of directors of industrial firms (outdegree), at the same time, they co-opted a roughly equal number of industrial managers to serve on their own boards (indegree). This structure of mutual co-optation suggests a balance of power, rather than a hegemony on the part of the financial sector. The results given in Table 2.1 confirm, on the one hand, the close interlocks that existed between the leading companies, but not the claim, frequently put forward, that banks exerted hegemonic control.[25]

In present-day Germany and France, the financial companies delegate many more managers to the supervisory boards of nonfinancial companies (outdegree in Germany: 37.9 percent) than they co-opt from nonfinancial companies in return onto their own supervisory boards (indegree in Germany: 13.4 percent). In other words, in Germany and France we encounter many bank managers on the supervisory boards of industrial companies, but rather few industrial managers on the supervisory boards of banks.[26] This appears to indicate that lending leads to a greater degree of dependency between banks and industrial firms than that which results from emitting shares. German banks, in particular, are reluctant to elect their debtors (i.e. industrial firms) onto their own supervisory boards.

---

[24] Similar arguments apply to the 'board of directors' in Great Britain and the US, the 'conseil d'administration' in France, the 'Verwaltungsrat' in Switzerland and the 'raad van commissarissen' in the Netherlands.

[25] Cf. Kotz (1979); Mintz and Schwarz (1985). The quotient of outdegree/indegree (financial firms/nonfinancial firms) evolved as follows: 0.94 (1904), 0.75 (1969), 0.77 (1974). This means that during this period, the financial firms co-opted more managers from nonfinancial firms onto their boards of directors than they themselves seconded to the boards of nonfinancial companies. Data source: Mizruchi (1982: 128); own calculations.

[26] Fohlin (1999: 317) found this network structure already in 1905 in Germany: many bank managers had a seat on the supervisory board of industrial firms, but only few industrial managers had access to bank boards. 'Between 15 and 20% of Berlin-listed companies maintained representation at banks by 1905.' But more than half of nonfinancial firms had bank directors sitting on their supervisory boards.

An additional structural characteristic that can be compared using these data is the degree of centralization of the network.[27] The coefficients in row 12 tell us the extent to which the network as a whole is geared around just a few large companies. Particularly striking is the high degree of centralization of the network in Switzerland (46.0).[28] This means that in Switzerland, there are a small number of large concerns that second their managers to the supervisory boards of many other large companies.

The national differences cannot be put down merely to the sample size—for $N=300$, we obtain a figure of 17.2 for Germany—but rather reflect, first, the size of the national economy. In a small country, a small number of companies can form the core of the entire national network. Secondly, the high degree of network centralization is explained by the pivotal role played by the large banks in Switzerland. In the Netherlands, the insurance companies play a comparable role, although the network as a whole is not so highly centralized. The network in the US is decentralized (coefficient: 1.2), and falls into a number of regional centers, the linkages between which are relatively weak (cf. Kono et al. 1998).

The coefficients in Table 2.2 refer to undirected interlocking directorates. Given that the implications of many of the coefficients have already been explained for the directed interlocks, the following comments focus on the most important structural differences between the countries.

Row 7 of Table 2.2 indicates the proportion of the companies that belong to the largest component. In Germany, 87.7 percent of the 616 largest companies belong to a component, that is, this group of firms is linked together in such a way that each company can reach any other company by way of a greater or lesser number of path-lengths. It is noteworthy that in France only 52.9 percent of all companies belong to a component. This is reflected in the proportion of companies that are isolated, that is that have no relationship to another firm that forms part of our sample. In France, 43.1 percent of firms are isolated, compared with just 9.4 percent in Germany. The structure of interlocks in France is thus segmented: rather more than half of the companies is relatively tightly integrated within a network—indeed, they have the highest density of all the countries, namely 4.92 percent (row 10)—whereas the other half is isolated.

The segmented structure of the French network is a reflection of the segmented structure of the French economy: large, closely linked companies frequently belong to the public sector (nationalized industries), and they are linked to one another by way of 'pantouflage'.[29] The isolated companies are frequently family firms: they are in

---

[27] 'A centralization measure quantifies the range of variability of the individual actor indices'. Cf. Wasserman and Faust (1994: 180). The degree of centralization in tables 1, 2, and 5 was calculated using the formula developed by Freeman (group degree centralization measure).

[28] This figure refers to the outdegree of Swiss firms. The outdegree is a measure of the number of firms in which a manager of the seconding firm is represented. The Schweizerische Bankgesellschaft (SBG), for instance, is represented on the 'Verwaltungsrat' (= Swiss Board of Directors) of thirty-nine other companies.

[29] 'Pantouflage' is the term used to describe the delegation/promotion of a high-ranking civil servant (Grands Corps d'Etat) to the 'conseil d'administration' of large French companies. Cf. Bourdieu (1989).

ideological opposition to the public sector, and defend the principles of private-sector capitalism (Morin 1974; Pastré 1992). An additional group belonging to the isolated firms are foreign-owned firms. The center of the interlocked firms is consti-tuted by the large French insurance companies and financial institutions, which until recently were nationalized enterprises (e.g. UAP, Suez, Paribas).

Rows 9 and 10 indicate the density of the network; in the first case with reference to all companies ($= N$), in the second with respect only to those firms that are linked at all. The greater the proportion of isolated firms, the greater the difference between these two coefficients. In Great Britain and France, the proportion of isolated firms is relatively high, and it is here that the density coefficients vary most. Although Great Britain and the US exhibit many structural similarities between their corporate net-works, it is interesting to note the major difference with regard to the proportion of firms that are isolated: in the US there are relatively few firms (14.3 percent) that have no link at all to other large firms, whereas the figure for Great Britain is 36.5 percent.[30]

2.4.1. *Discussion*

The structural coefficients brought together in Tables 2.1 and 2.2 describe the *macro* structure of the networks in each country and the structural differences between the countries. Is this macro structure the result of conscious strategies pursued by specific actors or actor-groups, or is it the unintended outcome of innumerable indi-vidual decisions?

It is assumed here that individual firms exert control over the *micro* structure of the network, that is, over the dyadic relationships with other firms into which they enter (local network structure). We do not believe, however, that there exist, in market societies, central actors that exert control over the macro structure of the net-work. Hayek (1963) terms the market, that is, the result of innumerable individual transactions, a 'spontaneous order'. In analogy to this terminology, the *macro* struc-ture of the network may provisionally be termed a 'spontaneous' configuration of relationships that have developed between the large companies in a given country.

Even so, it is clear that in each country the macro structure of the network exhibits certain similarities with other market institutions. The network in Germany, for instance, is relatively dense, encompassing virtually all the companies in the sample (largest component); it is characterized by a large number of multiple interlocks as a proportion of all relationships (control); and the network as a whole is relatively highly centralized. These characteristics are comparable with organizational struc-tures that Schmitter (1974) subsumed under the term 'corporatism'. Corporatist interest organizations are relatively highly centralized, they restrain competition, are comprehensive (i.e. all the potential members actually belong to an organization), and the structure of the system is legitimized by the state.

---

[30] However, it has to be noted that the low proportion of isolated firms for the US is misleading; it hides the regional fragmentation of the network. In the US there are regional networks with a relatively high density and a few 'bridges' that link the regional centers.

Networks, too, are legitimized by the state, albeit indirectly, namely by legislation on monopolies and cartels. In Germany, Switzerland, and the Netherlands, such laws are relatively mild; specifically, they permit many forms of interlocks that in the US are explicitly illegal (Schröter 1994; for the US cf. Roe 1991). These structural characteristics indicate a relatively high degree of autonomy and self-regulation in the corporate sector of all three countries. The structure of relationships permits long-term cooperation and control over the respective markets.

The network structure in Great Britain and the US, by contrast, exhibits a relatively low density and is decentralized; there are few if any multiple relationships and the number of isolated firms is, in Great Britain at least, relatively high. Such characteristics can be seen as analogous to what Schmitter has termed 'pluralist' forms of interest organization.

France's 'étatiste' tradition is reflected in the segmented structure of the network: the network falls into two components, one with very dense interrelationships, in which publicly owned companies play a central role, and one dominated by family firms between which interrelationships are weak or non-existent.

In the previous chapter it was argued that the structure of corporate networks is the result of an adaptation process with respect to the institutional environment in each country (cf. institutional contingency model). We can see here that there is an affinity between the structure of corporate networks on the one hand, and the structure of interest organizations on the other (corporatist, pluralist). Corporate networks are also influenced by the structure of the financial markets (e.g. bank credits versus equity capital). Finally, the strength and efficiency of the national antitrust law has a considerable influence on the structure of networks.

2.5. CAPITAL NETWORKS

If firms own firms, more or less complex ownership ties are created among the large corporations. In this section, the structure of these ties (capital networks) will be analyzed, and three questions will be addressed: (a) who owns the large corporations in each country? (b) are there structural similarities between the interlock networks and the capital networks? (c) how closely do the interlocks and the capital network coincide (degree of overlap between the two networks)?

2.5.1. *Ownership*

Ownership offers the opportunity of exerting control and influence. Thus the question 'Who owns the large firms?' implicitly raises the question 'Who controls these firms?' In a joint stock company, ownership may be divided up between thousands of small shareholders (separation of ownership and control). It is this decentralization of ownership and the associated loss of influence by shareholders that constitutes the basis for the bureaucratic power of managers (Berle and Means 1997). This means that the question 'Who controls the firms' can only be answered after the degree of ownership *concentration* has been analyzed for each country.

TABLE 2.3   *Degree of ownership concentration*

Proportion of stock owned %	Distribution (%)					
	G	F	US	UK	CH	NL
–4.9	9.5	37.3	95.0	48.6	17.8	23.7
5–9.9	7.8	14.2	3.5	31.0	17.6	30.0
10–24.9	17.8	15.1	1.4	10.5	17.9	9.6
25–49.9	13.9	9.4	0.1	2.6	15.6	10.1
50–74.9	12.9	8.1	—	2.4	8.0	6.8
75+	38.1	15.8	—	4.9	23.1	19.7
N=100%	821	1224	5925	1859	614	603

Note: Unit of analysis (N): shareholdings (= proportion of stock).
Germany (G): 650 largest firms (1993), N=821; France (F) : 500 largest firms (1997), N=1224; United States (US): 250 largest firms (1997), N=5925; United Kingdom (UK): 520 largest firms (1993), N=1859; Switzerland (CH): 300 largest firms (1995); N=614; Netherlands (NL): 300 largest firms (1995); N=603.
Example: In the US, 95% of the owners (investment funds) hold less than 5% of the stock of a company.

Table 2.3 indicates the degree of ownership concentration for six countries. In Germany, a total of 821 owners (shareholdings) are identified, in France 1224, in the US 5925, etc. In Germany, 38.1 percent of all owners hold 75 percent or more of the shares of the 650 largest companies; 51 percent of all shareholdings represent 50 percent or more of the shares of a company, and thus permit majority control. Given that for each individual company, there can only be one majority shareholder, this means that of the 650 largest companies more than half have a majority shareholder under whose control the company operates.

It proved impossible to identify a single majority shareholder among the large US companies.[31] Ninety-five percent of all shareholdings are smaller than 5 percent. Thus, whereas ownership in Germany is highly concentrated, in the US it is highly fragmented. In the US, there is practically no majority shareholder who can exert control over the company. In terms of the fragmentation of ownership, Great Britain tends toward the US model (48.6 percent of shareholdings are smaller than 5 percent of share capital), whereas France exhibits a higher degree of ownership concentration (23.9 percent of all shareholdings constitute at least 50 percent of the share capital).

Table 2.4 presents data on the distribution of ownership between various types of owners. These different types of owners do not all pursue the same goal. If the shares of a company are held by a large number of investment funds that are in competition with one another, it can be assumed that they will exert a different type of influence on the company than if ownership of the company is divided up between large

[31] Tables 2.3 and 2.4 show the owners of the 250 largest companies in the US. We also analyzed the ownership structure of the firms occupying positions 251–500 in the ranking list, but even here no majority shareholder (i.e. holding 50% or more of the share capital) was identified. The ownership structure of the 251–500 largest companies is very similar to that of the 250 largest companies.

TABLE 2.4   *Type of owner*

	G	F	US	UK	CH	NL
Individuals/ families	18.9	18.0	1.8	10.1	31.1	8.3
Nonfinancials						
Domestic	36.1	17.0	0.1	7.3	18.4	11.8
Foreign	11.7	16.0	0.5	7.0	12.9	20.8
Financial firms						
Banks	10.8	16.3	20.4	10.2	9.0	8.0
Insurance	10.6	10.4	5.7	18.8	2.8	28.9
Funds	2.8	8.4	71.5	44.6	18.3[a]	18.3[a]
Public bodies	9.1	7.5	—	2.0	7.5	4.1
Auto-contrôle	[b]	2.7	[b]	[b]	[b]	[b]
Workforce	[b]	3.7	[b]	[b]	[b]	[b]
N=100%	821	1224	5925	1859	614	603

Note: Unit of analysis (N): shareholdings (= proportion of stock); see Table 2.3.
[a] This category (funds) includes 'other financial institutions' for Switzerland (13.5%) and for the Netherlands (5%).
[b] Data not available/shares too small to be listed in handbooks.

numbers of private individuals (who are not competing with one another), or if it is owned by another company that is willing to foot the bill for losses, because it is interested in the know-how held by this company. Profit maximization is an abstract goal that may suffice to describe the objectives of investment funds, but is inadequate to explaining the complex strategies pursued within a German combine or a French 'groupe industriel', in which the owners are other companies.

In Germany, the largest group of owners is that of companies that own other companies (38.1 percent). The second largest group is that of individuals/families (18.9 percent), which in many cases still have majority ownership.[32] In France, too, a relatively large proportion of the share capital of large firms is held by families (18 percent).[33] Thus large firms in both Germany and France are even now dominated to a considerable extent by families or groups of families (clans), and have thus preserved elements of the family-based capitalism typical of the nineteenth century.

In the US and Great Britain, it is the investment and pension funds that are the dominant owners, owning 71.5 percent (US) and 44.6 percent (GB) of all the shareholdings we were able to identify in these countries. A cross-classification of Tables 2.3 and 2.4 would show that in all cases the shares held by investment funds account for less than 5 percent of the share capital of any one company. Thus ownership

[32] For more details see cross-classification of the variables 'type of owner' and 'concentration of ownership' in Chapter 3 (Germany and Britain) and Chapter 4 (France and the United States).

[33] In fact this figure is probably much higher than 18%. In a number of cases it was not possible to determine the owners of holding companies, although many of them are owned by families or groups of families.

structure in the US and Great Britain can be characterized in terms of two features: it is highly fragmented and the fragmented shareholdings are (in Great Britain: largely, in the US: almost exclusively) held by investment/pension funds and other financials. Thus the ownership structure accords with the model discussed in the US under the headings of 'investor capitalism' and 'shareholder value' (Useem 1996).

2.5.2. *The Structure of Capital Networks*

Whereas Tables 2.3 and 2.4 list all the owners of the large companies, Table 2.5 is restricted to presenting ownership relations *between* the large companies in each country. If companies hold shares in other companies, these relationships create capital networks between large firms. Table 2.5 shows the structural characteristics of these networks.

The first point to note is that in almost all countries the density of the capital network is lower than that of the interlocks (rows 7 and 8), and that the number of isolated companies is higher (in Germany, for instance, 30.7 percent; $N=300$). The degree of network centralization is also lower. This indicates that large companies exchange directors relatively frequently, but less frequently acquire a shareholding in another firm.

The above statements do not apply, however, to the US, and are only partially true of Great Britain. In the US, there is only a single isolated company, and the degree of centralization (outdegree) is very high (88.7). These deviations can be explained in terms of the ownership structure described in Tables 2.3 and 2.4. The 250 largest

TABLE 2.5   *Capital networks*

	G		UK		F	CH	NL	US
1 Number of firms (N)	741	300	520	300	374	300	300	235
2 Number of shareholdings (dichotomized)	722	263	766	353	327	157	244	1217
3 Largest component (% of N)	59.2	54.7	75.2	68.3	51.6	32.7	42.3	99.6
4 Isolates (% of N)	23.3	30.7	24.8	29.7	44.0	49.3	53.3	0.4
5 All ties/firms with ties (dichotomized)	1.3	1.3	2.0	1.7	1.6	1.0	1.7	5.2
6 Highest								
Outdegree	26	16	162	111	25	14	44	224
Indegree	17	11	6	5	11	13	23	15
7 Density: all firms	0.13	0.29	0.28	0.39	0.24	0.18	0.27	2.21
8 Density: firms with ties	0.22	0.61	0.50	0.80	0.75	0.68	1.25	2.21
9 Centralization of network								
Outdegree	2.4	5.1	31.0	37.0	6.5	17.2	54.9	88.7
Indegree	2.2	3.4	0.9	1.3	2.7	15.8	28.2	4.1

Note: See Table 2.1.

companies in the US include a number of investment banks, and they have acquired shares in virtually all the other companies (up to 5 percent of share capital in each case).

The structure in the US can be described with greater precision if the following fact is taken into account: there are no shareholdings at all *between* the 250 largest *nonfinancial* companies.[34] The density of the capital network and its high degree of centralization is due solely to the investment banks. Bankers Trust (= Deutsche Bank)[35] holds shares in 224 firms (of the 250 in the sample); College Retirement Equities holds shares in 218 firms, etc. In this light, the structure of ownership relations in the US becomes clearer: a small number of banks (funds) hold shares in virtually all the large American companies. If these investment banks were to coordinate their behavior, they could—as a collective actor—exert control over the large firms.[36] However, it is questionable whether a small group of investment banks can actually exert control over 250 large American firms, each of which itself constitutes a global empire.

The role played in the US by Bankers Trust is assumed in Great Britain by Prudential (outdegree: 162), that is, Prudential holds shares in 162 companies (among the 520 largest British companies). The degree of centralization of the British network (outdegree) is also relatively high (31.0). The same is true of the Netherlands, where insurance companies hold a substantial proportion of the shares in nonfinancial companies (centralization: 54.9).

There are a number of arguments in support of the view that the behavior of the investment funds is coordinated indirectly via the financial markets (invisible hand). The investment funds act in a very competitive market; their staff are highly trained and largely have the same educational background (business schools); they also receive the same information on the firms in which the fund holds shares (e.g. through Reuters, Bloomberg); finally, the money managers all subscribe to the ideology of shareholder value. In other words, the investment funds constitute an 'organizational field' whose members are constantly engaged in mutual observation. It can, therefore, be expected that they react to the same signals in similar ways, without the necessity of coordinating their behavior.

2.5.3. *Overlap of Networks*

We now turn to the third question, namely: to what extent do shareholdings and interlocks run in parallel, or, to put it another way, how frequently are the owners represented on the supervisory board (board of directors, *conseil d'administration*) of a firm in which they hold shares? It may be supposed that the extent of overlap is dependent upon the degree of ownership concentration in each country. Table 2.6 serves to confirm this assumption.

[34] A capital network matrix that contained only the 250 largest nonfinancial companies in the US would therefore be empty, and all the coefficients given in Table 2.5 would be zero.

[35] Bankers Trust was acquired by Deutsche Bank in 1999; the shareholdings of Bankers Trust have, therefore, been passed on to Deutsche Bank.

[36] Cf. the concept of the 'constellation of interests' in Scott (1990).

TABLE 2.6   *Overlap of shareholdings and interlocks*

	Proportion of share capital (%)					
	–9.9	**10–24.9**	**25–49.9**	**50–74.9**	**75–94.9**	**95–100**
G	22.5	50.6	61.5	68.8	51.3	64.8
F	33.0	37.1	37.2	41.9	27.3	25.5
UK	0.8	7.1	a	a	a	12.5
CH	32.8	40.0	76.9	90.0	83.3	85.7
NL	10.7	34.4	81.8	a	a	73.9

Note: Unit of analysis (*N*): shareholdings (= proportion of stock).
Germany (G): *N*=543 shareholdings; France (F): *N*=470 shareholdings;
United Kingdom (UK): *N*=808 shareholdings; Switzerland (CH): *N*=157
shareholdings; Netherlands (NL): *N*=244 shareholdings.
[a] Only ten or less shareholdings in the cell.

In Germany, Switzerland, and the Netherlands, the probability that owners send a representative onto the supervisory board of a company increases with the relative size of their shareholding. Where the shareholding represents less than 10 percent of share capital, a representative is delegated in 22.5 percent of cases; this figure rises to 64.8 percent where the shareholding is above 95 percent (Germany).

In France, the relationship between the size of the shareholding and the probability of being represented on the '*conseil d'administration*' is not linear. Among shareholdings below 10 percent, there is a parallel interlock in 33 percent of cases. A relatively small shareholding is frequently not merely seen as a financial investment, but is also linked to a strategic interest. Many of the large companies maintain cross-shareholdings, and the large financial institutions, in turn, hold shares in such companies. In most cases, such holdings are less than 10 percent of the total, and their aim is to integrate the large companies within a group. These (cross-)shareholdings can also be interpreted as a system of mutual hostages, the aim of which is to instill an '*esprit de corps*' in all participants. The proportion of parallel interlocks declines, however, among shareholdings above 75 percent, falling to 25.5 percent. It appears that in France, majority ownership is seen as an adequate means of control, and that in these cases no need is perceived for representation on the '*conseil d'administration*'.[37]

The US was not included in Table 2.6 because the number of parallel interlocks was too small. In the capital network matrix of the 235 largest firms there are a total of 1217 ownership ties (= shareholdings; cf. Table 2.5, row 2). In only eight cases was there a directed interlock running parallel to the ownership relation (= 0.7 percent of all cases). As we have already seen, Bankers Trust has small shareholdings in a total of 224 firms, but in only two cases did this investment bank delegate a representative onto the board of directors.[38]

---

[37] Why this is not the case in Germany is explained in more detail in Chapter 3 (see Section 3.6 on 'combine law').

[38] Specifically, in the case of Mobil Oil (shareholding 1.7%) and J. C. Penney (1.6%). J. P. Morgan holds shares in 88 firms (among the 250 largest) and seconds a manager to the board of directors of IBM (0.7% shareholding) and Anheuser-Busch (0.7%).

Clearly, the investment funds do not exert direct control over the firms in which they hold shares, at least not in such a way that they lay claim to a seat on the board of directors. Their shareholdings are too small for that purpose and, what is equally important, the ownership relations are unstable. A number of funds have high turnover rates, that is, they buy and sell their entire stock of shares two to three times a year. Such owners are clearly incapable of exerting direct control. Their control is exerted by way of the financial markets; they sell the shares of those firms with whose management they are dissatisfied.

In sum, we can conclude that interlocks that run parallel to capital relations perform the function of enabling the owner to exert direct control over the firm. Efficient control requires a relatively high degree of concentration of ownership (e.g. Germany, Switzerland). Where this concentration is less pronounced (as in France, for instance), owners can only exert control if they coordinate their behavior. If ownership structure is highly fragmented and the owners (investment funds) simultaneously hold shares in a large number of companies, control via parallel interlocks is virtually impossible. In such cases, control is exerted by way of the invisible hand of the financial markets.

2.6. CENTRALITY OF FIRMS IN THE NETWORK

Interlocking directorates create interorganizational networks within which the economic interests of large firms are communicated. The more comprehensive the networks and the denser the relationships, and thus the more intense the communication, the greater are the *chances* that what can be termed the economic interests of large companies (Useem 1984) can be effectively filtered, aggregated, and legitimized. Meetings of supervisory boards can be used to arbitrate between competing interests.[39]

The boundaries of the networks in our study were set arbitrarily by the sample size (300–600) of the largest companies in each country. In fact, though, the relationships reach out further from the edges of the network to other (smaller) companies that were not analyzed here. The network has neither a telephone number nor an office; its membership is not precisely defined, because the boundaries of the network are fluid. The network 'brings itself up to date' (ongoing social relations) periodically during management board and supervisory board meetings. An agreement reached in the network cannot be enforced in the courts. The 'strength' of the informal relationships lies in the trust that the members of the network build up by way of mutual observation of each other's behavior over an extended period.

A company that plays a relatively central role in a network, that is, maintains stable relations with a large number of firms, is able to reduce the risks it and others face. These ties provide it with valuable information, and, because the firm is permanently 'visible' in the network, other companies are better able to assess the reliability of the central firm. By this means firms reduce transaction costs.

---

[39] The conditions for hostile takeovers, for instance, can be discretely negotiated within the network. It can be assumed that the 'hostility' of some hostile takeovers is largely a show put on for the public.

We now turn to consider the characteristics of those firms that occupy a relatively 'central' position within the network, whereby centrality is operationalized in terms of its 'degree', that is, the number of firms with which the company has relations. For instance, in France it is Havas that has the highest degree in terms of undirected interlocks (55), in Germany it is Veba AG (73), and in the Netherlands ABN-Amro (78). The 'degree' is the dependent variable in the following regression analyses. The question is: which independent variables offer an explanation for the centrality of a company?[40]

The theory of bank hegemony—a theory rooted in the writings of Hilferding (1968)—starts from the premise that financial institutions are among the most central companies within a network (Mintz and Schwartz 1985). This view is justified with resort to the concept of resource dependency: capital is a scarce resource on which all firms are dependent and which is difficult to procure. For this reason, industrial companies are willing to co-opt bank managers onto their supervisory board. In Section 2.3, it was shown that prior to the First World War, German banks had built up a comprehensive system of information procurement and control, as a way of reducing the risks associated with money-lending.

An alternative hypothesis is that the financial institutions no longer belong to the most central firms in the network,[41] but rather that the age, size, and prestige of a firm are much more important variables in explaining its centrality. The accumulation of social capital (trust) takes time. Thus it can be assumed that older, more traditional firms that have grown over an extended period and have survived numerous crises will be among the central actors in the organizational field, with the highest prestige. Prestige is measured in terms of the company's size (employees) and whether the firm is listed in the leading share index of the country in question (e.g. Dow Jones, DAX, CAC). Firms selected by the financial markets for this index (blue chips) are highly 'visible' and are seen as trustworthy. Consequently, for firms that are less visible and are lacking in tradition, it is important that their managers are co-opted onto the supervisory board of these central firms or, conversely, that they elect managers from these firms onto their own board.

Another hypothesis relates to the type of ownership: firms owned by other firms (e.g. the French *groupe industriel*) are closely linked to one another, whereas firms owned by individuals/families or foreign owners occupy marginal positions within the network. Family businesses frequently stand in opposition to big business, and are concerned to defend their autonomy against pressure for corporate concentration. The hypothesis, therefore, is that firms owned by other companies (especially those owned by large banks and insurance companies) occupy a central position within the network, whereas those owned by individuals/families or foreign-owned firms are less central.

---

[40] The degree measures the centrality of a *single* company within a network. The index of centralization in Tables 2.1, 2.2, and 2.5, on the other hand, is an indicator of the structure of the network *as a whole*. Although the two indices are not independent of one another, they measure different characteristics.

[41] Davis and Mizruchi (1999), for instance, show in their study of commercial banks in the US that such institutes have lost influence since the mid-1980s.

Table 2.7 shows the regressions for six countries, in each case for the undirected and directed interlocks and for the capital network (only outdegree).[42]

For the directed and undirected interlocks, three variables are particularly significant in all six countries: age, size, and share index. Older firms, larger firms, and those listed in the leading share index of the country in question are particularly central. The 'finance sector' variable, by contrast, is not significant with respect to the directed/undirected interlocks in any of the countries. This means that—*if we control for size, age, and prestige*—financial institutions are not among the most central companies in the interlock network of the six countries.

The 'capital outdegree' variable is also significant for Germany, France, Switzerland, and the Netherlands, but not for Great Britain. This variable measures the degree of parallelism of the interlocks with shareholdings, and the significance of the coefficients confirms a result that emerged earlier (Table 2.6): in these countries there is a high degree of overlap between the shareholdings and the interlocks. Firms that are owners frequently delegate one of their managers to the supervisory board of the dependent company. In Great Britain and the US, this overlapping of the two networks occurs relatively seldom, because of the fragmentation of ownership in these countries. (This variable was not included in the regression for the US due to the small number of cases.)

Ownership-type, on the other hand, is a variable that is rarely significant. We expected the coefficients for the variable 'family/foreign owner' to be negative, and this is indeed always the case. But only few of the coefficients are significant (e.g. variable 'family' for Switzerland, interlocks). For the US, only the investment funds were considered as owners. Here the variable measures the proportion of the share capital of the firm held by the various investment funds. This variable is significant for the interlocks; this means that firms in which many investment firms hold shares are relatively central in the network. (The other owners were not considered due to the small number of cases.)

The control variable 'size of board' is almost always significant. A large (supervisory) board offers more opportunities for interlocks than a small one. But this variable is a control variable, rather than an explanatory variable.[43]

More generally it is to be noted that the explanatory power of the model is lower for the US than for the other countries studied. In the case of interlocks (outdegree) only 5 percent of the variation is explained ($R^2 = 0.05$), whereas for Germany 77 percent of the variation is explained ($R^2 = 0.77$). One reason for the lack of explanatory power is the only small variation of the dependent variable (degree).[44]

[42] The regressions for the indegree (directed interlocks, capital networks) are not included in Table 2.7; the results can be obtained from the author.

[43] This is true, at least, for Germany, where the size of the supervisory board is set by law (co-determination law). In Great Britain, the size of the board of directors is not really a control variable because British corporate law merely sets the minimum size of the board, but imposes no ceiling. A large board of directors (with a large number of non-executive directors) is thus implicitly a decision in favor of establishing close relationships with other firms.

[44] In Germany, the outdegree of interlocks varies between fifty-three and zero, in the US between seven and zero (cf. Table 2.1, row 9, highest outdegree). We also conducted regression analyses for the US for

TABLE 2.7 *Centrality of companies in six countries (OLS-regressions)*

Independent variables	Germany			United Kingdom			France		
	Interlocks out 1	Interlocks undir. 2	Capital out 3	Interlocks out 1	Interlocks undir. 2	Capital out 3	Interlocks out 1	Interlocks undir. 2	Capital out 3
Financial sector (D)	0.04	−0.07	0.50[a]	0.00	0.01	0.56[a]	0.04	0.03	0.38[a]
Size: ln(employees)	0.07[d]	0.26[a]	0.10[b]	0.14[c]	0.12[c]	0.05	0.11[b]	0.20[a]	0.24[a]
Age	0.06[d]	0.09[c]	−0.01	−0.06	0.09[c]	−0.02	0.04	0.17[a]	0.05
Index (DAX, FTS, CAC) D	0.19[a]	0.41[a]	0.32[a]	0.20[b]	0.25[a]	0.16[a]	0.12[a]	0.41[a]	0.33[a]
Capital (outdegree)	0.73[a]	*	*	0.08	*	*	0.70[a]	*	*
Type of owner									
Financials	−0.10[b]	0.11[c]	−0.14[c]	0.16[b]	0.08[d]	0.02	−0.06	0.08[d]	−0.01
Other firms	−0.01	0.02	−0.01	0.03	−0.01	−0.02	−0.01	−0.01	0.00
Families/individuals	−0.04	−0.07	−0.04	−0.04	−0.15[b]	−0.02	−0.07[d]	−0.17[b]	−0.08
State (nationalized)	−0.05	−0.12[c]	−0.08	−0.08[d]	0.09[c]	−0.03	−0.03	−0.01	0.04
Foreign	−0.04	−0.01	−0.04	−0.02	−0.23[a]	−0.03	−0.06	−0.11[d]	−0.05
Control variables									
Size of board	0.01	0.23[a]	*	0.19[a]	0.21[a]	*	0.11[b]	0.25[a]	*
Legal form of firm D	−0.03	0.09[c]	−0.04	0.05	−0.06	−0.01	−0.02	−0.05	−0.02
R^2	0.77	0.63	0.33	0.19	0.38	0.37	0.44	0.70	0.76
Number of firms (N)	250	250	250	335	335	335	255	255	255
Dependent variable	y	y	y	$\ln(y+1)$	$\ln(y+1)$	y	y	y	$\ln(y+1)$

	Switzerland			Netherlands			United States	
	Interlocks out	Interlocks undir.	Capital out	Interlocks out	Interlocks undir.	Capital out	Interlocks out	Interlocks undir.
	1	2	3	1	2	3	1	2
Financial sector (D)	0.00	0.07	0.20[a]	−0.02	−0.09	0.52[a]	−0.07	−0.09
Size: ln(employees)	0.27[a]	0.14[c]	0.31[a]	0.03	0.05	0.05	0.11	0.19[b]
Age	0.14[c]	0.15[b]	0.05	0.17[b]	0.11[d]	0.01	0.14[d]	0.32[a]
Index (SMI, AEX, DJ) D	0.10	0.18[b]	0.27[a]	0.21[a]	0.36[a]	0.33[a]	0.03	0.15[b]
Capital (outdegree)	0.22[b]	*	*	0.34[a]	*	*	—	*
Type of owner								
Financials	0.04	−0.03	0.04	−0.08	0.12[d]	−0.08	0.22[b]	0.14[d]
Other firms	0.08	−0.01	−0.04	−0.09	−0.10	−0.04	—	—
Families/individuals	−0.13[d]	−0.13[d]	−0.13[d]	−0.11[d]	−0.06	−0.02	—	—
State (nationalized)	−0.21[b]	−0.05	−0.03	−0.04	−0.03	−0.03	—	—
Foreign	0.02	0.01	−0.08	−0.26[a]	−0.11	−0.08	—	—
Control variables								
Size of Board	0.11[d]	0.47[a]	*	0.13[d]	0.28[a]	*	0.05	0.24[a]
Legal form of firm(D)	0.06	0.39[a]	−0.19[b]	0.05	0.15[c]	−0.07	0.03	−0.04
R^2	0.37	0.49	0.40	0.44	0.48	0.40	0.05	0.30
Number of firms (N)	198	198	198	183	165	184	234	234
Dependent variable	ln(y+1)	y	ln(y+1)	y	y	ln(y+1)	ln(y+1)	ln(y+1)

Note: [a] $\alpha \le 0.000$; [b] $\alpha \le 0.01$; [c] $\alpha \le 0.05$; [d] $\alpha \le 0.10$; D: Dummy variable.

For each country, three regressions were computed. The three *dependent variables* (y) are defined by the centrality (degree) of the firm: (1) number of firms in which a manager of the sender-firm is represented (directed interlocks, outdegree); (2) number of firms to which the firm is connected by undirected interlocks; (3) number of firms of which the firm is a shareholder (capital network, outdegree). (Regression 3 was not computed for the US.) If the dependent variable (y) was highly skewed, the transformation ln(y+1) was used.

Independent variables

Age: 1995-founding year of the firm. Financial *sector*: financials=1, all others=0 (dummy variable); *Share index*: Germany=DAX, France=CAC 40, Great Britain=FTSE, US=Dow Jones Industrial, Switzerland=SMI (Swiss Market Index), Netherlands=AEX (Amsterdam Stock Exchange) (dummy variables).

Capital (outdegree): Number of firms of which the firm is a shareholder (=outdegree of the capital network matrix). *Type of owner*: Sum of shareholdings (%) of the respective type of owner. Example: If a firm is jointly owned by a family (24%) and by several investment funds ($\sum$48%), the variable 'family' was coded '24' and the variable 'financials' was coded '48'. *Size of Board*: Number of members of the supervisory board/external directors (undirected interlocks); number of members of management board/executive directors (directed interlocks). *Legal form of firm*: joint stock company=1; all others=0; US: firms listed on the NYSE=1; all others=0.

In the regression for the capital network (outdegree) the 'finance sector' variable attained a high level of significance in all countries. This means that in all the countries banks and insurance companies own more shares in other companies than non-financial companies. (This regression was not computed for the US, because here the financial sector is almost the sole owner of nonfinancial companies.) The second most important variable explaining centrality in the capital network is the share index: those firms included in the leading share index of the country concerned hold more shares in other companies than those firms not listed.

2.7. CONCLUSIONS

The historical review with which we began revealed that the origins of the networks between large firms go back to the end of the nineteenth century, and that their structure at that time was largely determined by the dominant position occupied by financial institutes: in Germany by the large Berlin-based banks, in the US by the Money Trust. In Germany and a number of other West European countries, these structures have been maintained until the present day, whereas in the US they were transformed or entirely dismantled in the wake of antitrust legislation.

Germany and the US also differ with respect to the forms of financing: in Germany it was bank loans that were the most important source of external finance. This made the banks co-entrepreneurs in the large industrial concerns (risk-sharing). In order to underpin their lending risk, the banks were frequently represented on the supervisory board of the firms in question with several managers (control). In the US, by contrast, the stock market was the most important source of finance. The Money Trust—a network of banks and insurance companies—exerted a form of 'private control' over the financial markets. Here too, there was a close network of interlocks between banks and industrial firms, whereby, in contrast to Germany, not only were the banks represented on the board of directors of nonfinancial firms, but, conversely, the latter were also represented on the board of directors of the banks.

These corporate networks, and the market structures to which they gave rise (e.g. cartels), must be understood against the background of the political ideology and culture of the country in question. In the US, the model of liberal, competitive capitalism predominated, whereas in Germany and a number of other West European countries, the prevailing ideology was that of a corporatist-inspired, organized capitalism. In an essay published in 1915 that marked the start of a long debate on 'organized capitalism', Hilferding wrote: 'Finance capital—the domination of monopolistically organized industry by a small number of large banks—has the tendency to mitigate the anarchy of production, and contains the seeds of a conversion of an anarchistic capitalist into an organized capitalist economic order' (p. 322). In contrast to the anarchy of the market, cartels and the network dominated by the large banks were

several regions separately. The result for the mid-south for directed interlocks (outdegree), for instance, was an R^2 of 0.19 ($N=34$). The figure for the north-east, on the other hand was zero ($R^2=0.00$). The results are available from the author on request.

interpreted as a 'higher' form of the social organization of the market. This view was shared not only by social-democrats, but also by the (conservative) economists of the Historical School (cf. Schmoller 1906: 249).

The corporate networks that we have analyzed, in their present-day form, in six countries, have been heavily influenced by these traditions. Accordingly, we have drawn parallels between the structure of the networks and the prevailing market order in the countries under consideration. In Germany, Switzerland, and the Netherlands, the networks are relatively highly centralized, with dense interlocks incorporating virtually all the large companies of a country (largest component), and with a high proportion of relationships consisting of multiple representation (hierarchical control). We have drawn a link between this network structure and corporatist interest-representation structures, which also form part of the respective market order (trade unions, employers' federations).

In Great Britain and the US, on the other hand, we found relatively decentralized networks with a low density of relationships, a large number of isolated firms, and relatively few multiple relationships. This structure was linked to the pluralist model of interest representation.

The principal–agent problem—in this context, the uncontrolled power of managers in large companies—has not become as virulent in the continental European countries as in the US. The reasons for this are to be found in the different control relations between owners and managers. This analysis has shown that in Germany, Switzerland, the Netherlands and, to some extent, also in France, ownership is highly concentrated; firms (concerns), families, and the financial sector all hold a relatively significant proportion of share capital; and that the owners are represented on the supervisory boards of the dependent firms. There is a high degree of overlap between the interlocks and the shareholdings, that is, owners are also present, and exert a controlling function, on the supervisory board of the relevant firms (cf. Table 2.6).

The problem of 'agents without principals' (Davis 1991) is largely to be found in the US and Great Britain, where ownership is highly fragmented, distributed across the portfolios of hundreds of investment funds that are in competition with one another. Here, control is exerted by the 'invisible hand' of the financial markets. Hostile takeovers, which often incur high transaction costs, are the most important instruments at the disposal of the financial markets in exerting this controlling function. Given the highly fragmented ownership structure, a presence of the owners on the board of directors is seldom practical.

The concept of the 'centrality' of individual firms within the network—analyzed in the last section—aims to determine which firms occupy a relatively dominant and visible position in the network. The hypothesis of 'bank hegemony', which goes back to Hilferding, postulates that it is banks and insurance companies that constitute many of the central firms in the network. To the extent that it can be confirmed at all, this bank-hegemony hypothesis is true only of Germany and France: it is only here that the banks are frequently represented on the supervisory boards of nonfinancial firms.

In the US, Great Britain, Switzerland, and the Netherlands, the interlocks between the financial sector and industrial firms are mutual: representatives of the banks sit on the board of directors of the nonfinancial companies, but, conversely, non-financial firms also delegate representatives onto the board of directors of banks and insurance companies.[45] These structural differences can be partially explained with reference to the different financing forms used (bank loans versus equity capital).

It can be shown that the following relationship holds for the countries analyzed in this chapter: the higher the total capitalization of the stock exchange (as a percentage of gross domestic product), the higher the proportion of nonfinancial managers who have a seat on the board of banks and insurance companies (cf. Table 2.1, row 5).[46]

As far as present-day structures are concerned, we have shown that the financial companies no longer occupy the central position in the network of interlocks;[47] this is true of all the countries studied here. Firms founded around the turn of the century (age), that are listed in the relevant country's leading share index (dominant position on the financial market), and particularly large companies (size) tend to be the most central actors in the network, irrespective of the economic sector in which the firm is active. This means that *Daimler-Chrysler* is just as central an actor as *Deutsche Bank*, and in France *Vivendi* is just as pivotal as *Banque Nationale de Paris*.

---

[45] Cf. Table 2.1, row 5. As early as 1919, Wieser documented the mutual interlocks between British industry and the banks (p. 276). The results presented here show that some structural characteristics of the corporate network are very stable over time.

[46] *Source*: Deutsche Bundesbank, Monatsberichte, Januar 1997 (Die Aktie als Finanzierungs- und Anlageinstrument), p. 28. Capitalization in percent of GDP: GB: 152%; Switzerland: 135%; US: 122%; Netherlands: 93%; France 38%; Germany: 27%.

[47] However, the financial sector continues to occupy a central position in the capital network, i.e., banks and insurance companies have more shareholdings in other companies than nonfinancial companies (cf. Table 2.7, column 'capital out', variable 'financial sector ').

3

Network Structures in Germany and Britain

3.1. COOPERATIVE AND COMPETITIVE MODELS OF CAPITALISM

According to Chandler (1990), the development of capitalism at the end of the nineteenth century was based upon different forms of market regulation: the United States exemplify a pattern of competitive capitalism whereas Germany was a model of cooperative capitalism. Comparing the two countries Tilly (1982: 641) argues that there was 'no exact counterpart in German experience to the merger movement in the United States around the turn of the century, neither in terms of its sheer dimensions nor in terms of the important oligopolies it created. Not that concentration and control of competition among producers were absent in German business. Such controls were present and were growing between 1880 and 1913; but they largely took the form of cartels and communities of interest (Interessengemeinschaften) within which mainly autonomous and independent firms operated by agreement'.

In Germany, this restriction of economic competition was seen as being in the public interest.[1] In an address before the 'Verein für Socialpolitik'[2] Gustav Schmoller (1906: 249), a leading German economist, summed up the German attitude thus: 'I have always maintained that economic freedom is a blessing only in certain areas, and that ultimately only moderate, sometimes even substantially regulated, competition is healthy'. Abelshauser (1984) even describes Imperial Germany as the first 'postliberal' state, having succeeded in combining cooperation and competition as well as corporatist regulation and economic innovation.

Chandler traces the different priority associated with competition and cooperation in the two countries to the export orientation of German firms as opposed to the

Earlier versions of this chapter have been published in *Kölner Zeitschrift für Soziologie und Sozialpsychologie* 47 (1995): 1–36 and *British Journal of Sociology* 47 (1996): 67–92 (co-author Jürgen Beyer), reproduced with permission. I gratefully acknowledge the research support of Maike Becker, Thorsten Lange, and Viola Peter.

[1] Cartels imposed restrictions not only on minimum but also on maximum price levels. The goal of German cartel agreements was thus not profit maximization but rather the legitimation of commonly approved profit margins, and in this they, therefore, differed from trusts in the United States (Passow 1930).

[2] The 'Verein für Socialpolitik' had among its founding members Max Weber and was the most prestigious German professional association for the social sciences at the turn of the nineteenth century.

concentration upon domestic market in the United States. The domestic market that American firms faced was large enough that efficient mass production and marketing strategies would generally suffice to guarantee corporate success, and they, therefore, usually limited their concentration to this market. Such was not the case in Germany, however, where the relatively small size of markets *forced* firms to compete for survival on the world market; here they were under constant pressure to prove their competitive efficiency (Newman 1964). Thus, the cartel agreements that German firms entered into *nationally* represented only one aspect of their *international* survival strategy: cartels were 'internally' cooperative and 'externally' aggressive.

Chandler's view finds support through comparison with another country, Japan, whose rise to economic superpower status likewise rested upon an export orientation. Until the Second World War, relations among Japanese companies were dominated by the six large *zaibatsu*—groups of cooperating firms in various sectors that were under the common leadership of a single clan. Following the war, the American occupation authorities dissolved these corporate groups; however, in the 1950s many companies managed to recombine, albeit with more autonomy than previously, into groups referred to now as *keiretsu* (Morikawa 1992). As in Germany, regulated competition became an accepted form of market organization, as the pressure that firms faced to look outward increased their willingness to cooperate on the domestic market—what Gerlach (1992) refers to as 'alliance capitalism'. Only the institutions through which the competition is regulated differ between the two countries; in Japan, it is the *keiretsu* while in Germany it is the combine (*Konzern*). Nevertheless, both the *keiretsu* and the combine represent forms of corporate networks that facilitate intercompany cooperation and the regulation of competition.

Comparing Germany with Britain we also find a number of remarkable differences with respect to the governance structure of the large corporation, the type of economic specialization, and the structure of the market order. First, with respect to the *governance structure*, Chandler (1990) emphasizes the strong family traditions in British corporations while in Germany the model of the Prussian bureaucracy had a strong influence on the internal organization of large firms. Even during the interwar period, British families still had a strong impact on the management of the corporate sector, while German large firms had developed a more professionalized managerial bureaucracy.

Second, while Britain was a first mover in modernization and industrialization, Germany was a late comer. Gerschenkron (1962) refers to national differences in development to explain differences in the pattern of economic specialization: in the late nineteenth century, Britain had specialized in overseas trade; London accommodated the largest and most developed financial market; and Britain was regarded as a model of democracy and liberal trade. By contrast, Germany had been specializing in (heavy) industry and manufacturing; many technical schools and universities were founded to provide the steel plants and engineering firms with technically trained personnel; the stock market was underdeveloped and firms were financed and influenced by the universal banks of Berlin. When the Deutsche Bank was founded in 1870 as a joint stock company, the articles of association stipulated that the Deutsche

Bank should provide commercial credit for the German export industry. Until the 1880s, most German firms financed their exports through British commercial banks (Gall *et al.* 1995).

Third, cartels were not forbidden in Britain, but they were not sheltered against foreign competition. Britain had only low protective tariffs and in some industries no tariffs at all. A cartel that is exposed to the competition of foreign firms is unlikely to survive for any length of time. Compared to Germany where cartels were supported not only by the legal order (cartel contracts were legally enforceable), but also by high tariffs, in Britain these protective devices were rather weak. Therefore, cartels proved to be instable and short-lived (Hannah 1983: 313; Mathis 1988: 81).

The two countries also differ in another important aspect of the market order, that is, the organization of the labor market. While in Germany a corporatist tradition developed with strong unions, codetermination, and comprehensive employers' associations, British industrial relations were characterized in the 1970s as 'largely informal, largely fragmented and largely autonomous'.[3] The liberal market order which Flanders criticized as 'fragmented' and 'informal' also influenced the structure of the corporate networks and the type of interest coordination within these networks.

The following analysis concentrates on a comparison of corporate networks in Britain and Germany. We continue the analysis of the preceding chapter by providing more detailed information on the structure of networks in the two countries. The analysis focuses on a limited number of variables, such as network configuration, concentration of ownership, and type of owner. The following section begins by explaining the concept of network configuration, and the subsequent analysis compares national networks in terms of ownership concentration and the overlap of capital networks and interlocking directorates.

3.2. THE CONFIGURATION OF CORPORATE NETWORKS

The corporate network is an organizational form that has grown up 'between' markets and hierarchies and which possesses a 'structure' just as markets and bureaucracies do. Bureaucracies can have centralized or decentralized structures, and flat or steep hierarchies; markets can be characterized by perfect competition or by oligopoly. A number of the various organizational structures that have developed for corporate networks are illustrated below.

Figure 3.1(a) presents a *clique*, in which each company is tied to each other company through a series of reciprocal relationships. Cliques show a high degree of integration as a result of the multitude of relationships obtaining among the participants (density). If the capital shares each member holds of the other members are roughly equal, the network can be said to have an 'egalitarian' structure, that is, no single member is in the position to dominate the others. Collective decisions are reached in a reciprocal clique only by consensus. A noncooperative member, however, can be put under pressure by the other members, for each company is enfranchised to participate

---

[3] Royal Commission on Trade Unions and Employers' Associations (1980: 18).

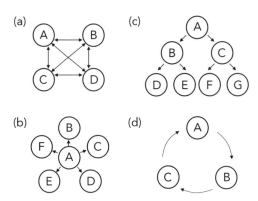

FIG. 3.1   *Network configurations. (a) Clique, (b) Star, (c) Pyramid, and (d) Circle*

in the decisions of every other company in the network, and this say in its affairs can be exploited so as to influence its decisions. Because of this, Williamson (1985, p. 169) refers to this structure of relationships as one of 'mutual hostage'.

The Japanese *keiretsu* provides an example of a reciprocal clique. Yamauchi (1994: 156) reports that the central member companies of the six *keiretsu* groups hold reciprocally about 2 percent of shares; all members together then hold some 32 percent of the stock of each individual member—enough to repel external affronts (e.g. hostile takeovers) but not enough for any one alone to dominate another. In his study on 'alliance capitalism', Gerlach (1992: 77) reports reciprocal relationships among the sixty largest Japanese firms of which 18 percent are connected by mutual capital participation. In Germany, on the other hand, only five reciprocal relationships can be identified among the 623 largest firms.[4] The 'clique' is not a dominant network configuration in Germany.

The *star* network is represented in Fig. 3.1(b), with one dominant firm surrounded by a number of 'satellite' companies in which it has a relatively high capital participation. In contrast to the reciprocal cliques, star networks have a hierarchical structure (Baker and Faulkner 1993: 849). In terms of both capital ownership and interlocking directorates, the parent company dominates the subsidiaries which do not interlock with one another, and hence the central enterprise of the network controls all formal communications and decision making. German combines frequently have such a star structure and, therefore, differ from the Japanese *keiretsu* by their hierarchical form and the lack of reciprocal relationships.

If the arrows in Fig. 3.1(b) were turned around, the structure would be that of an *inverted star*. The ideal typical structure of capital networks in Britain (and in the US) is the inverted star with relatively limited participations of several companies in a single large corporation. Firms in the financial sector (pension funds, insurance, investment

---

[4] These included, for instance, the reciprocal network of capital between 'Allianz Holding' and 'Dresdner Bank' and 'Allianz Holding' and 'Münchener Rückversicherung'.

funds) own 3–5 percent of the shares of a large enterprise, as for example, in British Aerospace, British Petroleum (BP), and Amec in Britain. The structure of capital networks in Britain and the US is *fragmented*[5] in a way which Scott (1990) terms as 'constellation of interest'. Up to twenty financial institutions own a small part of a company's stock which as such is not large enough to yield dominant power. Whereas the star structure has only 'one chief and many Indians', as it were, with the inverted star just the opposite is the case.

The *pyramid* structure in Fig. 3.1(c) is one in which a single dominant firm (A) owns a large share in other firms (B, C) which in turn dominate still further firms (D–G). Through its multitier organization the pyramid structure (which actually combines a series of star-patterned groups) enhances the hierarchical character of the corporate network. Firm A invests its own resources to control firms B and C, and can thereby utilize the resources of B and C to exert (indirect) control over firms D–G. The complete structure of a Japanese *keiretsu* consists of a reciprocal clique (of large enterprises) and numerous pyramids (primary and secondary supplier firms) and, therefore, combines hierarchical with egalitarian features (Gerlach 1992: 102). The pyramid structure is also common in Belgium (Daems 1978), France, and many German combines also belong to this form of network organization.

Figure 3.1(d) shows a circular network; here firm A is able through a series of intermediate steps (indirectly) to own part of itself. The *circle* is a functional equivalent of the reciprocal relationship, and has the effect of strengthening the hand of management *vis-à-vis* shareholders, who in effect stand 'outside' the circle. Through a series of 'vassal' firms a company can conceal its true ownership and indirectly control itself; this is sometimes employed as a protection against external influences (e.g. hostile takeovers). German banks, insurance companies, and large enterprises in the 'core' component of the capital network are linked to each other by circular capital holdings (Adams 1994: 150); 'circles' are also often exploited in France to ensure family control of large enterprises (Morin 1974: 43).

These four configurations do not exhaust all the possible structures that corporate networks can take,[6] but they illustrate some of the basic patterns that may be combined into more complex forms. While it is often remarked that new organizational forms have developed 'between' markets and hierarchies (Powell 1990), the question as to what *structures* these new organizational forms show is seldom asked, or whether countries differ as regards the typical structures that these take.[7] So far the

---

[5] *'Fragmented'* is not meant here as diffuse ownership. The five largest shareholders in the United States own an average of 28.8% of the stock in the 500 largest companies (Shleifer and Vishny 1986: 462; Brancato 1991). For Britain, Scott (1997: 91) shows that the 20 largest shareholders own 13.6% of ICI and 19.72% of Prudential Assurance. In public corporations which are in *'diffuse'* ownership, no single shareholder holds more than 1% of the total stock.

[6] See Burt (1982: 56), e.g. on the various forms in which three firms can be interlocking with one another (triad census); see also Wasserman and Faust (1994: 564–76).

[7] There are a few comparative studies on capital networks and interlocking directorates, as for instance, Gerlach (1992) who compares the structure of corporate networks in Japan and the United States, and Scott (1986, 1997) who presents a similar analysis for Britain, Japan, and the United States. The research project of Stokman *et al.* (1985) examined the structure of interlocking directorates in ten countries.

structure of different corporate networks has been presented. In the next section, we ask which network structures may facilitate cooperation between competing firms.

3.3. COMPETITION AND COOPERATION IN THE CORPORATE NETWORK

A corporate network bound together by ownership and/or interlocking directorates can be regarded as a collective actor whose freedom to maneuver is constrained by features of its own organizational structure. Among the possible forms that network structures can take, some are more favorable in promoting cooperation among members and the coordination of common strategies. Examination of the configuration of a network thus indicates the chances of cooperation among its members.

In the clique network, each member is dependent upon each other member, and no single member enjoys hegemonical power over the others. Cooperation is made possible by reciprocal dependence, but collective actions require a universal consensus. For instance, in the Japanese *keiretsu*, cohesion is strengthened not only by reciprocal shareholdings, but also by parallel interlocking directorates. The reciprocal dependence combines with the group's ethos, that is, ownership rights and the norms and values of the group become mutually supportive. 'In the case of what [is] called diffuse reciprocity, cooperation is contingent not on the behavior of particular individuals but on the continued successful functioning of the group' (Keohane 1986: 6).

Cooperation in the star network is guaranteed by hierarchical coordination. Here the dominant company buys a sufficient proportion of shares in the firm that it wishes to control in order to ensure that the latter is in a relationship of dependence.[8] German law ascribes to the dominant enterprise the responsibility of combine leadership (Hommelhoff 1982) which is reflected in the structure of interlocking directorates: members of the management board of the dominant firm also sit on the supervisory board of the dependent firm. The combine resembles the *keiretsu* in the high overlap of the capital network with the network of interlocking directorates, but it is different in its structure: whereas the *keiretsu* is integrated by the group's ethos and by consensus, the combine is governed by hierarchical coordination.

The inverse star network can be described in terms of the 'prisoner's dilemma': Among the owning enterprises there obtains a balance of power, as the relative capital participation of each is fairly equal to that of the others. Each of these actors, however, has its own specific set of interests, and there no formal organizational structure exists to coordinate their behavior. Cooperation must be *negotiated* on an ad hoc basis.[9] The ability to take collective action is relatively undeveloped in the

---

[8] This does not necessarily mean control of over 50% of stock in the subsidiary. An effectively *controlling* interest may be secured by less than 50% provided the rest is in diffuse ownership. German firms may buy high proportions of stock of public corporations without being forced by law to make a public offer to the remaining shareholders. Cf. discussion of the (non-statutory) Code on Takeovers and Mergers in Chapter 9.

[9] Scharpf (1985: 339) speaks of a 'bargaining' modus, and Williamson (1985: 21) of 'haggling'. Scott (1986: 114) has shown that institutional investors (insurance companies, pension funds, investment funds) own only a small proportion of shares of the large enterprises in Britain, and that there exists no (demonstrable) cooperation among share owners.

inverse star network, as no institutional framework exists to coordinate the autonomous shareholders. In a group of 'rational' egoists no one would be prepared to bear the organizational costs of coordination. Coordination generally results not from cooperation but from competition. Financial institutions which *jointly* own a substantial part of stock in large corporations may follow the option 'exit' or 'voice', but 'voice' requires the coordination of strategies among minority shareholders which is difficult to obtain in a competitive environment.

3.4. CONCENTRATION OF OWNERSHIP

Corporate networks can be based upon several types of exchange relationships: capital ownership, interlocking directorates, credit or supplier relationships, joint ventures. The following analysis considers only capital ownership and interlocking directorates, as no information is available on the other forms of networks. Data on corporate networks have been collected for the 650 largest firms in Germany and the 520 largest firms in Great Britain.

Table 3.1 describes the ownership structure of German and British enterprises in terms of two features: proportion of stock owned and the type of owner.[10] For the 500 largest German firms, 821 shareholders were identified, and for the 500 largest British firms, 1859. The concentration of ownership (last row) in Great Britain is relatively low: 48.6 percent of shareholders own less than 5 percent of company stock, and only 4.9 percent own more than 75 percent, while no more than 7.3 percent control a majority interest.[11] In Germany, the concentration is higher: only 9.5 percent of holdings are smaller than 5 percent, and 38.1 percent are larger than 75 percent, with 51 percent commanding a majority interest in the firm. This greater concentration of holdings means that in many large German companies only one shareholder exercises effective control over the company.

The second structural difference concerns the type of owner. In Great Britain, investment funds hold 47.3 percent of all shares smaller than 5 and 53.7 percent of shares between 5–9.9 percent, while they own none of the shares which permit majority control (50+ percent). The cross-classification of the two variables 'concentration of ownership' and 'type of owner' also shows that in Germany, 49.2 percent of shares between 50–74.9 percent are owned by domestic nonfinancial firms. These data indicate an initial difference in the structure of corporate networks: the combine structure is the dominant pattern in Germany whereas the 'inverse star' configuration

---

[10] In Table 3.1, *all* owners of the 500 largest German and British firms are considered, regardless of whether they themselves belong to the 500 largest firms. Therefore, families and (small) investment funds are shown as ownership categories in Table 3.1. In Table 3.2 only capital relationships among the *largest* firms are examined (matrix of capital networks). In addition, two units of analysis are used: shareholdings (proportion of stock) and the firm itself. Table 3.1 examines shareholdings (= proportion of stock owned by an individual or a firm); since a firm can be owned by many owners jointly, the number of such shares is substantially higher than the number of firms. Each table gives the unit of analysis and the number of shareholdings/firms (=N).

[11] 'Majority interest' refers to ownership of at least 50% of company stock; this includes the two last columns of Table 3.1 (50–74.9% and 75%+).

TABLE 3.1 *Distribution of stock ownership in Germany and the United Kingdom*

Type of owner	Proportion of stock owned (%)													Total (%)	
	-4.9		5–9.9		10–24.9		25–49.9		50–74.9		75+					
	G	UK	G	UK	G	UK	G	UK	G	UK	G	UK	G	UK
Individuals/families[a]	19.2	7.1	17.2	8.1	12.3	25.3	18.4	37.0	22.6	16.0	21.1	2.2	18.9	10.1
Nonfinancial firms														
Domestic	19.2	6.3	25.0	4.5	30.1	12.4	21.1	10.9	49.2	8.0	46.3	20.9	36.1	7.3
Foreign	6.4	1.8	6.3	2.9	2.7	7.2	5.3	26.1	9.4	12.0	21.4	72.5	11.7	7.0
Financial firms														
Banks	20.5	13.4	20.3	8.8	23.3	5.2	18.4	6.5	2.8	4.0	0.6	2.2	10.8	10.2
Insurance	16.7	23.8	26.5	21.3	12.3	4.1	19.3	6.5	3.8	—	4.2	2.2	10.6	18.8
Funds[b]	2.5	47.3	3.1	53.7	8.2	45.8	3.5	13.0	0.9	—	0.6	—	2.8	44.6
Public bodies	15.4	0.3	1.6	0.7	11.0	—	14.0	—	11.3	60.0	5.8	—	9.1	2.0
Total														
N=	78	901	64	577	146	194	114	46	106	50	313	91	821	1859
%=	9.5	48.6	7.8	31.0	17.8	10.5	13.9	2.6	12.9	2.4	38.1	4.9	100	100

Note: 500 largest firms in each country (1993).   Unit of analysis: shareholdings (= proportion of stock).
Germany (G): *N* = 821; United Kingdom (UK): *N* = 1859.
Each column adds to 100%, which means that each column category (= size of shareholding) can be compared between the two countries. For example: 78 holdings in Germany (= 9.5%) but 901 in the United Kingdom (= 48.6%) make up less than 5% of company stock. In the case of Germany, these 78 holdings are distributed as follows: 19.2% to individuals/families, 19.2% to domestic nonfinancial firms, 6.4% to foreign nonfinancial firms, 20.5% to banks, 16.7% to insurance companies, 2.5% to investment funds, and 15.4% to the government and other public bodies (e.g. labor unions). The bottom row adds separately for Germany and the UK to 100% and presents the percentage of holdings in each country falling within the respective share-size category. The two last columns give the proportion of shares in each country owned by the respective type of owner.
[a] Includes (family-) foundations. It was not possible in each case to determine whether family ownership was concealed behind the foundation.
[b] German sources designate only few investment funds because only shareholdings equal to or larger than 5% have to be published in Germany; in the UK, shareholdings equal to or larger than 3% have to be published.

characterizes the ownership structure in Great Britain, with a relatively high number of institutional investors owning only limited shares in large companies.

The percentage of stock in Germany possessed by individuals, families, and (family) foundations is noteworthy: 18.9 percent of all holdings (versus 10.1 percent in Great Britain). Even among large holdings, the proportion belonging to private persons is high: 21.1 percent of holdings accounting for at least 75 percent of the company stock (versus 2.2 percent in Great Britain) and 22.6 percent of those between 50 and 74.9 percent (versus 16.0 percent in Great Britain). The ownership distribution provides empirical evidence for the hypothesis that in Germany (and to some extent also in Britain) families still hold majority control over many large corporations.

Studies of the ownership distribution structure of the largest firms in the United States and Japan[12] show that the five largest owners hold an average of 24.4 percent of stock in the former and 33.1 percent in the latter. Assuming an equal distribution of these holdings among the five largest owners[13] would give an average of approximately 5 percent in Japan and 6.5 percent in the United States, thus resembling the actual case in Britain. From other sources, however, we know the corporate network patterns in Japan and the United States to differ, that in the former having typically the 'clique' form and that in the latter the 'inverse star' configuration. This demonstrates that similar distribution structures can be combined with differing network configurations. An analysis that only considers the concentration of ownership without looking at the network *configuration* may miss the point: the power relationship within a network of companies.[14]

Since the early seventies, the structure of ownership and control in large corporations has been changing in many countries. Individuals and families have become less important as shareholders whereas nonfinancial enterprises and financial institutions gained a dominant position as owners of large corporations. In *1950*, individuals/families owned 42 percent of all shares in (West)Germany, nonfinancial firms 22 percent and financial institutions 2.7 percent; by *1998*, these percentages had changed as follows: individuals/ families 15.0 percent, nonfinancial firms 30.5 percent, banks, insurance companies, and investment funds 36.9 percent.[15] A similar development is observed in Japan. In *1949*, about 70 percent of all shares were owned by individuals/families; 5 percent by nonfinancial enterprises; and 15 percent by financial institutions. In *1985*, the proportion of individual shareholdings had dropped to 25.5 percent, whereas nonfinancial firms held 25.6 percent and financial

---

[12] Data for the year 1984 on Japan cover 734 firms in the nonfinancial sector (Prowse 1992: 1124), and data for the year 1980 on the United States cover 511 firms, including those in the financial sector (Demsetz and Lehn 1985: 157).

[13] This assumption does in fact approach the actual distribution. See Demsetz and Lehn (1985: 1157, table 1) and Prowse (1992: 1125, fig. 1).

[14] For more details on the ownership structure in the United States, see Chapter 4.

[15] *Source: Die Aktiengesellschaft* 26 (1981), p. R79 and 39 (1994), p. R371–4. Deutsche Bundesbank: Ergebnisse der gesamtwirtschaftlichen Finanzierungsrechnung für Deutschland 1990–8, Statistische Sonderveröffentlichung 4. Frankfurt 1999.

TABLE 3.2   *The structure of capital networks*

Position of firm in network	G(%)	UK(%)
Parent/outdegree		
One participation	6.7	1.5
More than one participant	5.0	2.5
Subsidiary/indegree		
One owner	32.9	24.8
More than one owner	7.9	38.2
Intermediary	13.6	8.6
Isolated	33.9	24.4
Total	100	100

Note: Unit of analysis: firms.
Germany: $N = 623$ firms; United Kingdom: $N = 520$ firms.

institutions 45 percent of all shares (Gerlach 1992: 60). In the United States, the institutional shareholders have become more and more important during the last two decades: In 1950, they held 8 percent of all shares; in 1980 33 percent, and in 1988 45 percent (Coffee 1991: 1291).

So far we have identified three dimensions which characterize the control structure of large corporations in the different countries: the network configuration which may further cooperative or competitive relationships among firms; the concentration of ownership which may be high (Germany) or low (Britain); and the type of shareholder which may be a financial institution (Britain, US) or a nonfinancial firm (Germany). Cross-classifying these dimensions, we obtain different types of corporate governance in the countries compared here.

3.5. THE STRUCTURE OF CAPITAL NETWORKS

The data presented in Table 3.2 demonstrate that the 'star' pattern is a dominant form of corporate networks in Germany while the 'inverse star' is more frequent in Great Britain. Figure 3.1 gives an intuitive idea of national differences in network configurations, whereas Table 3.2 provides the empirical evidence for these differences.

Each of the companies examined was assigned to one of the categories in Table 3.2. 'Parent' here refers to a company owning part of one or more other companies, without itself being owned by another large company in our data matrix (only outdegree),[16] and 'subsidiary' to one belonging to one or more other companies, without itself owning another company. An 'intermediary' is one which both belongs to other companies and which owns still others in our data matrix; these are situated within a pyramid network (see Fig. 3.1(c)) dominant *vis-à-vis* those at the lower

---

[16] 'Outdegree' refers to the sum of relationships in which a firm acts as *sender*, e.g. it holds capital shares in another firm or sends a member of its own management board to the supervisory board of another firm; conversely, 'indegree' refers to the sum of relationships in which a firm acts as *receiver*, e.g. it is owned by a 'sender' or it 'receives' the manager of a 'sender' in its supervisory board.

hierarchical levels but subject *vis-à-vis* those at the higher levels. 'Isolated' companies are those which have no (capital) relationship with any of the other companies examined here.[17]

The data on Germany in Table 3.2 are drawn from 623 firms. The set of their relationships gives a network matrix of 623 × 623 cells, of which 628 are nonempty, that is, only 0.162 percent of all the possible relationships materialized.[18] The larger a network matrix, the smaller is the density coefficient because any single firm can realize only a fraction of all possible network opportunities. Similar considerations apply in the case of the British capital network (0.299 percent of all possible ownership relations exist).

The rows of the matrix show in which other firms a particular company participates (outdegree), and the columns show to which other firms it belongs (indegree). Every firm is 'embedded' in a network structure, that is, it is part of a particular configuration as shown by its indegree and outdegree; it was on the basis of this structure that it is categorized in Table 3.2.

A total of 11.7 percent firms are parent companies (outdegree)[19] in Germany and thus constitute centers of hierarchical control. These include not only banks and insurance companies but also many enterprises in the manufacturing and service sectors as, for instance, Daimler-Chrysler, Volkswagen, and Siemens. This compares to only 4.0 percent in Great Britain, where the respective firms are almost exclusively those of the financial sector.

An important structural difference between the two countries is found regarding the indegree: in Great Britain 38.2 percent of all firms show multiple ownership, with most shares being smaller than 5 percent (as seen in Table 3.1), but in Germany only 7.9 percent do so. Most subsidiary firms in Germany have only one parent (32.9 percent), which generally enjoys a controlling interest; in Great Britain, on the other hand, most subsidiary firms have multiple parents, not one of which commands a position of dominance. The data in Table 3.2 thus confirm to some extent the combine nature of German corporate networks (star pattern) and the 'inverse star' configuration in Great Britain.

3.6. A TYPOLOGY OF COMBINES

A comparison of the matrix of capital networks in Germany with that in Great Britain shows a major difference in the networks of the two countries: in Germany, many firms of the nonfinancial sector own other firms of the nonfinancial sector, while this is rarely the case in Britain. What is the reason for this difference?

Both countries have witnessed economic concentration, as certain large firms have absorbed others, but the structure of corporate networks in the respective countries

[17] 'Isolated' companies are frequently in foreign hands (e.g. Ford and Opel in Germany) or belong to a family.

[18] 623 × 622 = 387,506 cells (excluding the diagonal); of these 387,506 possible ownership relations 628 were observed (= 0.162%).

[19] Sum of 'one participation' (6.7%) and 'more than one participation' (5.0%).

nevertheless differ (Prais 1981). A firm that is absorbed by another generally retains its independence as a legal entity in Germany while in Britain (and the US) it typically ceases to exist outside of company-internal structures, thus losing not only its economic but legal independence as well and becoming merely a division or 'profit center' of the new parent (Baker 1992; Davis *et al.* 1994).

Does it make a difference whether a subsidiary that is 100 percent the property of a parent retains its legal independence from the parent or is completely absorbed within it? Is this independence nothing more than a mere facade for the pretense of economic autonomy? To answer these questions, one must first consider the distinctions in German corporate law among different types of combines.

In 1965, (West) Germany became the first Western industrial nation to pass a law on corporate combines which defines the rights and responsibilities of owners when these are not individuals but rather, themselves, other enterprises.[20] The law on corporate combines pertains to business groups and regulates relationships 'between' markets and hierarchies, which is the subject of the present analysis. German Combine Law recognizes that increasing numbers of firms belong to others, that is, that firms own firms and that it *makes* a difference of whether owners are individuals or corporations. It follows a brief description of two types of combines as defined by German Combine Law to show that the configuration of networks in Germany—as in other countries—is shaped by the institutional and legal environment.

3.6.1. *De facto Combine*

In a de facto combine there is a relationship of economic dependence between parent and subsidiary, but the organs of the subsidiary (management board, supervisory board) are required to continue representing the specific interests of the subsidiary. The dependent firm is an independently functioning unit, and its management must guarantee the maintenance of this organization. The de facto combine involves economic dependence, but 'at arm's length'; subordination to combine direction, but autonomous running of the firm's own business; cooperation on 'common' interests, but protection of the firm's own specific interests. It is this mixed nature of relationship that makes the de facto combine an exemplary organizational form 'between' markets and hierarchies.

In the de facto combine, the relationship between parent and subsidiary is no longer regulated through the market. The dominant of the two firms is able to influence the behavior of the dependent firm in a way that would not be permitted in the market. Complete subordination is nevertheless avoided, and therewith the inefficiency associated with large bureaucracies. A de facto combine comprises a system of semi-autonomous companies stabilized by legal regulation and hierarchical coordination.

The dependent firm enjoys a degree of autonomy and is responsible for its own debts. The principle of limited liability applies in de facto combines, with the parent liable only to the extent of its participation in the stock of the subsidiary.

---

[20] The corporate law of other countries has not as yet made this distinction. For the United States, see Blumberg (1987) on the difference between 'entity law' and 'enterprise law'.

3.6.2. *Contractual Combine*

In the contractual combine, an 'enterprise contract' binds parent and subsidiary, stipulating that the former may mandate certain actions on the part of the latter even if these are disadvantageous to it (Windolf 1993). Here it is, therefore, possible to do that which is precisely forbidden in the de facto combine, that is, act against the interests of the dependent firm. On the other hand, the parent firm in a contractual combine is liable for all the debts incurred by the subsidiary. The German legislation on combines intended this as the standard form of combine: the enterprise contract sets out clearly both the ultimate power of parent *vis-à-vis* the subsidiary and its ultimate liability as regards debts. The practice, however, has proven otherwise: the most frequent form of corporate network in Germany is not the contractual but the de facto combine.[21]

An enterprise contract can be concluded between two firms when the parent controls at least 75 percent of the stock in the subsidiary. Our sample included 313 cases of this level of participation; however, among these we counted only 54 cases (17 percent) of enterprise contracts. Since we can presume combines involving less than 75 percent capital participation to be of the de facto type, it is safe to say that the majority are of this type.

The difference between a British (or an American) firm and the de facto combine in Germany lies in the (limited) autonomy enjoyed by the subsidiary in the latter type and the resulting privilege of limited liability. A 'profit center' or a 'division' does not constitute a legally independent subsidiary. This explains why we have included legally independent subsidiary firms in our network matrix even when the firms in question belong entirely to another.[22] One must also consider that the legal independence of the subsidiary increases the opportunities for interlocking relationships in the overall system. If the subsidiary were to be completely absorbed, it would cease to have a supervisory board, which is the meeting place for interlocking directors.[23]

3.7. SECTORAL NETWORKS

A cartel is a group of firms in the same economic sector that form an association for the purpose of controlling prices and/or production. In the interwar period virtually

---

[21] The 'qualified de facto combine' is omitted from the consideration here as this is a degenerate (often fraudulent) form of de facto combine in which the parent firm does in fact completely dominate the subsidiary but attempts to evade the legal consequences (liability for debts).

[22] Ziegler (1984) and Pappi *et al.* (1987) omit partially the firms that are 'legally independent but economically dependent'.

[23] Germany has a two-board system with the *management board* equivalent to the *internal* directors of the British/American system and the *supervisory board* equivalent to the *external* directors. The supervisory board is the organ of interlocking: members of the management board sit on the supervisory board of other companies. German law does not allow executive managers to sit on the supervisory board of their own company. The more supervisory boards there are within a combine the higher the chances of interlocking with other firms. Within a de facto combine, many members of the group have their own supervisory board.

all economic sectors in Germany were subject to cartel agreements. If it is the case that this form of 'regulated competition' continues to influence the structure of corporate networks in Germany, one could expect to find more intrasectoral than intersectoral networks, that is, the interlocking structures would bind firms with one another that are in the *same* economic sector more frequently than they would firms in *different* economic sectors. The association of the combine structure (hierarchical coordination) with intrasectoral networks creates favorable circumstances for the coordination of competing firms. Tables 3.3 and 3.4 present the capital network (ownership) within and between economic sectors both in Germany and Great Britain.

The figures in the matrices are standardized density coefficients that represent the frequency of relationships between firms of different (same) economic sectors. The coefficients on the diagonal refer to the network density within the individual sectors. Virtually all of the highest coefficients in Table 3.3 are on this diagonal, which means that German firms form capital networks principally with other firms in the same economic sector. This confirms the thesis of 'regulated competition' in the German market. The combine is thus a group of firms in the same or closely related economic sector(s) and may be considered as a functional equivalent to the prewar cartel. The highest intrasectoral network density is found in the sectors of gas and petroleum (32.0), mining (23.8), and insurance (23.2).[24]

The marginals in Tables 3.3 and 3.4 (last column) show the outdegree: the higher the outdegree, the more frequently firms in a particular sector are *owners* of other firms. The marginals in the last row show the indegree: the higher the indegree, the more frequently firms in a particular sector *are owned* by other firms. Banks (5.9) and gas and petroleum companies (5.5) are frequently owners of other firms. In the sectors of mining (4.2) and nonferrous metals (3.7), there is a relatively high proportion of dependent firms (indegree, last row).

One might argue here that the only reason why the intrasectoral density is so high in Table 3.3 is that the purely subsidiary firms (100 percent dependence) are included in the dataset. To test this objection, we eliminated all firms with 95–100 percent dependence and calculated a new matrix.[25] The coefficient for intrasectoral density is highest in eighteen of the twenty-one sectors in the original Table 3.3; when the 95–100 percent dependent firms are excluded, the intrasectoral coefficients are still highest in twelve of the twenty-one sectors. Although the existence of pure subsidiary firms does increase the intrasectoral density, even without these, considerable interlocking is evident among the firms within most sectors.

The network matrix for Great Britain (Table 3.4) differs from that for Germany in two respects. First, in only seven of thirty sectors is density highest within the sector

---

[24] e.g. in the mining sector, there are 21 (legally) independent firms, among which there are $21 \times 20 = 420$ possible network connections. Of these 420, 10 ownership relations exist (=2.38%). The coefficients in Tables 3.3–3.6 are presented in per mill terms due to their small size (2.38% = 23.8 per mill).

[25] Due to the limited space available here, this matrix is not presented; it can be obtained upon request from the author.

TABLE 3.3 *Capital networks, Germany (intra-/intersectoral)*

	100	101	200	300	301	302	304	305	306	307	400	401	402	410	500	600	601	700	800	801	802	Average
Mining 100	**23.8**	**7.3**	6.1	0.0	4.0	2.3	0.0	0.0	0.0	3.0	6.0	0.0	0.0	0.0	**10.8**	3.1	0.0	3.2	0.0	0.0	0.7	3.3
Oil/gas 101	**14.7**	**32.1**	**19.6**	0.0	6.4	3.0	0.0	0.0	3.8	4.8	**13.7**	0.0	0.0	0.0	7.0	5.0	0.0	5.1	0.0	0.0	1.2	5.5
Electrical utilities 200	6.1	4.9	**13.4**	0.5	4.4	1.6	0.0	1.4	0.0	2.7	2.7	0.0	0.0	0.0	2.9	2.7	0.0	4.3	0.0	0.0	1.3	2.3
Iron and steel 300	2.1	0.0	0.5	**13.5**	0.0	4.2	2.1	0.8	1.1	4.1	0.0	0.0	0.0	0.0	2.0	2.1	0.0	0.0	0.0	0.0	0.7	1.6
Non-ferrous metals 301	6.0	3.2	**7.1**	0.0	**16.3**	4.4	3.0	2.1	2.1	**7.8**	4.5	0.0	0.0	0.0	3.8	**8.1**	0.0	0.0	0.0	0.0	1.3	3.2
Mechanical engineering 302	0.9	0.0	0.4	2.7	2.4	3.7	2.3	2.1	2.4	0.6	0.5	0.0	0.0	0.0	0.9	1.2	0.0	0.0	0.9	0.7	0.3	1.1
Motor cars 304	0.0	0.0	0.5	1.6	2.0	2.7	7.0	1.2	0.0	0.0	0.0	0.0	0.0	0.0	0.0	0.8	0.0	0.8	1.1	0.5	0.0	0.9
Electrical engineering 305	0.0	0.0	0.6	1.4	0.5	1.7	3.1	5.5	1.9	0.0	0.0	0.0	0.0	0.0	0.0	0.0	0.0	0.4	1.2	0.9	0.2	0.8
Instruments/optics 306	0.0	0.0	0.0	**7.6**	0.0	5.3	6.0	**7.1**	**7.9**	3.1	0.9	0.0	0.0	0.0	0.0	0.0	0.0	1.7	4.8	3.4	0.8	2.3
Metal products 307	6.0	4.8	1.3	1.4	**7.8**	4.8	1.5	5.5	3.1	4.2	2.2	0.0	0.0	0.7	0.8	2.0	0.0	0.0	1.1	0.0	0.0	1.7
Chemicals 400	6.0	2.7	1.5	1.2	6.0	2.4	0.0	0.2	1.8	2.2	**7.1**	4.5	**7.4**	0.0	0.0	1.6	0.0	0.0	1.1	0.0	0.0	1.9
Pharmaceuticals 401	0.0	0.0	0.0	0.0	2.6	2.4	0.0	0.0	3.1	0.0	5.6	**12.5**	0.0	0.0	0.0	2.6	0.0	0.0	0.0	0.0	0.0	1.2
Plastics/rubber 402	0.0	0.0	0.0	3.6	0.0	0.8	0.0	0.0	4.2	0.0	**7.4**	0.0	**7.6**	0.0	0.0	1.5	1.1	0.0	0.0	0.0	0.6	1.1
Food 410	0.0	0.0	0.0	0.0	0.0	0.4	0.0	0.0	0.0	0.0	0.0	0.0	0.0	**11.7**	0.0	2.6	0.0	0.0	0.0	0.0	0.0	0.8
Construction 500	**10.8**	3.5	1.9	1.0	3.8	2.6	3.1	1.3	1.6	2.8	1.6	2.0	0.0	1.3	**15.2**	0.9	1.7	2.2	0.0	0.0	0.6	2.1
Wholesale trade 600	4.6	2.5	1.4	**10.5**	**8.1**	**7.8**	3.1	1.3	1.6	6.0	2.3	1.7	0.0	3.2	2.9	6.5	1.7	1.8	0.0	0.0	0.0	3.2
Retail trade 601	0.0	0.0	0.0	0.0	0.0	0.0	1.6	1.3	0.0	0.0	0.5	0.0	0.0	1.3	0.0	1.1	**7.5**	0.9	0.0	0.0	0.0	0.8
Transportation 700	3.2	0.0	2.8	2.8	2.8	1.6	6.6	3.0	5.7	2.8	1.2	0.0	0.0	0.0	1.8	3.4	0.9	**9.2**	3.4	1.5	1.5	1.5
Banks 800	1.6	2.6	2.2	0.7	**7.2**	4.6	6.6	5.4	**12.1**	6.5	4.3	2.2	5.7	5.5	**9.4**	6.7	6.5	3.4	**13.8**	**9.4**	**9.0**	6.0
Insurance companies 801	0.0	2.7	1.5	0.5	2.8	3.1	4.3	3.0	5.7	2.8	2.4	4.3	1.9	0.0	3.1	3.7	0.0	1.5	**8.7**	**23.3**	3.1	3.6
Holding companies 802	2.9	2.4	5.6	4.3	2.6	4.1	4.4	2.8	3.8	3.8	2.5	2.9	1.3	3.7	4.2	4.5	1.2	2.6	2.9	6.6	2.6	3.4
Average	4.2	3.3	3.2	2.4	3.8	3.0	2.1	1.5	2.5	2.7	3.1	1.4	0.8	1.3	3.0	2.6	0.9	1.7	2.6	2.1	1.2	2.3
N	21	13	47	46	24	104	42	77	20	16	56	16	12	25	22	31	37	30	29	44	65	623

Note: N: Number of firms. Standardized coefficients have been computed as follows: coefficients in the diagonal cells $= (x/N_i \ast N_i - N_i) \ast 1000$. Coefficients off-diagonal $= (x/N_i \ast N_r - N_j) \ast 1000$. x = number of connections; N_i = Number of firms in industry i. Industries with less than 10 firms have been dropped. Firms have been assigned to industries on the basis of their most important divisions/products. On average each firm has been assigned to 1.42 industries. Coefficients larger than 7 are shown in bold printing. Highest coefficient in each row has been framed.

TABLE 3.4 Capital networks, United Kingdom (intra-/intersectoral)

Industry	9	14	18	19	21	27	31	35	38	41	42	47	48	49	51	53	54	66	68	70	71	72	75	76	77	80	81	86	87	89	Average
Water works (9)	7.6	0.0	0.0	0.0	0.0	0.0	0.0	0.0	0.0	0.0	0.0	0.0	0.0	0.0	0.0	0.0	0.0	0.0	0.0	0.0	0.0	0.0	0.0	0.0	0.0	0.0	0.0	0.0	0.0	0.0	0.3
Building materials (14)	0.0	1.1	1.3	0.5	0.8	0.0	0.0	0.8	2.4	0.0	0.9	0.0	0.0	0.0	0.0	0.0	0.0	0.0	0.0	0.0	0.0	0.0	0.0	0.0	0.0	0.0	0.0	1.0	0.0	0.0	0.3
Contracting & construction (18)	0.0	0.5	1.0	1.0	2.9	0.0	0.0	0.4	1.1	0.0	1.8	0.0	0.0	0.0	0.0	0.0	1.5	2.2	0.0	0.0	0.0	1.3	0.0	0.0	0.0	0.0	0.5	1.0	0.0	1.0	0.4
Electricals (19)	0.0	1.0	1.0	0.0	2.4	0.0	0.0	2.0	0.0	0.0	0.0	0.0	0.0	0.0	0.0	0.0	0.0	0.0	0.0	0.0	1.4	0.0	0.0	0.0	0.0	3.2	0.0	1.0	0.0	1.9	0.7
Aerospace (21)	0.0	0.0	0.0	0.0	4.0	0.0	0.0	0.0	4.3	0.0	0.0	0.0	0.0	0.0	0.0	0.0	0.0	0.0	0.0	0.0	0.0	0.0	0.0	0.0	0.0	0.0	0.0	0.0	0.0	0.0	0.4
Mechanical engineering (27)	0.0	0.0	0.0	0.0	0.0	0.0	0.0	0.0	0.0	0.0	0.0	0.0	0.0	0.0	0.0	0.0	0.0	0.0	0.0	0.0	0.0	0.0	0.0	0.0	0.0	0.0	0.0	0.0	0.0	0.0	0.2
Instruments (31)	0.0	0.0	0.0	0.0	0.0	0.0	0.0	0.0	0.0	0.0	0.0	0.0	0.0	0.0	0.0	0.0	0.0	0.0	0.0	0.0	0.0	0.0	0.0	0.0	0.0	0.0	0.0	0.0	0.0	0.0	0.0
Electronics (35)	0.0	0.0	0.0	0.0	0.0	0.0	0.0	0.0	0.0	0.0	0.0	0.0	0.0	0.0	0.0	0.0	0.0	0.0	0.0	0.0	0.0	0.0	0.0	0.0	0.0	0.0	0.0	0.0	0.0	0.0	0.0
Furniture and furnishings (38)	0.0	0.0	0.0	0.0	0.0	0.0	0.0	0.0	5.5	0.9	0.0	0.0	0.0	0.0	0.0	0.0	0.0	0.0	2.6	0.0	0.0	0.0	0.0	0.0	0.0	0.0	0.0	0.0	0.0	0.0	0.5
Motor components (41)	0.0	0.0	0.0	1.1	3.4	0.0	0.0	1.3	0.0	0.9	1.3	0.0	0.0	0.0	0.0	0.0	0.0	0.0	0.0	0.0	4.5	0.0	0.0	0.0	0.0	0.0	0.0	0.0	0.0	0.0	0.3
Motor distributors (42)	0.0	0.0	0.0	0.0	2.8	0.0	0.0	0.0	0.0	1.3	3.7	0.0	0.0	0.0	0.0	0.0	0.0	5.1	0.0	0.0	0.0	1.5	0.0	2.7	0.0	3.9	0.0	0.0	0.0	0.0	0.4
Hotel and caterers (47)	0.0	0.0	1.8	1.7	0.0	0.0	0.0	1.3	0.0	0.0	0.0	6.5	0.0	1.6	0.0	0.0	0.0	0.0	0.0	0.0	2.3	0.0	0.0	0.0	0.0	0.0	0.0	0.0	0.0	0.0	0.8
Leisure (48)	0.0	0.0	0.9	0.0	0.0	0.0	0.0	1.3	0.0	0.0	3.3	6.2	0.0	1.6	6.9	0.0	0.0	2.0	0.0	0.0	0.0	2.3	0.0	0.0	0.0	0.0	0.0	0.0	0.0	0.0	0.8
Food manufacturers (49)	0.0	0.0	0.0	0.0	0.0	0.0	0.0	0.0	0.0	0.0	0.0	4.6	0.0	1.2	6.9	0.0	1.1	0.0	0.0	0.9	0.0	1.2	0.0	1.3	0.0	0.0	0.0	0.0	0.0	0.0	0.1
Food retailers (51)	0.0	2.1	0.7	0.0	0.0	0.0	0.0	0.0	2.6	0.0	0.0	0.0	0.0	0.0	5.4	0.0	0.0	0.0	0.0	0.0	1.0	3.5	0.0	1.9	0.0	0.0	0.0	0.0	0.0	0.0	0.5
Printing (53)	0.0	1.7	0.0	0.0	0.0	0.0	0.0	0.0	0.0	0.0	2.9	0.0	0.0	0.0	0.0	4.2	0.0	0.0	0.0	1.5	0.0	2.6	0.0	0.0	0.0	0.0	0.0	0.0	0.0	0.0	0.3
Packaging and paper (54)	0.0	0.0	1.5	0.0	0.0	0.0	0.0	0.0	0.0	0.0	0.0	0.0	0.0	1.1	0.0	0.0	0.0	0.0	0.0	0.0	4.2	0.0	0.0	0.0	0.0	3.3	0.0	0.0	0.0	0.0	0.3
Plastic and rubber (66)	0.0	0.0	1.1	3.2	0.0	0.0	0.0	0.0	0.0	0.0	2.1	0.0	2.0	0.0	0.0	0.0	1.8	2.6	1.3	0.9	0.0	0.0	1.3	0.0	0.0	0.0	0.0	0.0	1.6	0.0	0.0
General chemicals (68)	0.0	0.0	0.0	0.1	3.0	3.0	3.0	0.0	0.0	0.0	0.0	0.0	0.0	0.0	0.0	0.0	0.0	0.0	0.0	1.2	0.6	1.3	0.0	1.3	0.0	2.4	0.0	0.0	0.0	0.0	1.0
Oil and gas (70)	0.0	0.0	0.0	0.0	0.0	0.0	0.0	0.6	0.0	0.0	0.0	0.0	0.0	0.0	0.0	0.0	0.0	0.0	1.2	1.1	0.0	0.0	0.0	0.0	0.0	0.0	0.0	0.0	1.6	0.0	0.1
Traders, wholesalers (71)	0.0	0.8	0.8	1.4	0.0	0.0	0.0	1.0	0.0	4.5	0.0	2.3	0.0	0.0	1.0	1.5	4.2	3.0	0.6	0.6	0.6	1.0	0.9	0.0	1.1	1.6	0.0	0.0	0.0	0.0	0.3
Transport and freight (72)	0.0	1.4	2.6	2.5	4.0	0.0	6.9	1.0	0.0	0.0	0.0	0.0	2.3	1.2	3.5	2.6	0.0	3.0	0.0	1.3	1.0	1.5	4.5	1.9	2.0	2.8	1.4	0.0	1.8	0.0	2.2
Support services (75)	0.0	2.6	0.0	0.0	0.0	0.0	0.0	1.1	0.0	0.0	0.0	0.0	0.0	0.0	0.0	0.0	0.0	0.0	0.0	0.0	0.0	0.0	0.0	0.0	0.0	0.0	0.0	0.0	0.0	0.0	0.1
Miscellaneous (76)	0.0	0.0	0.0	0.0	1.7	0.0	0.0	0.0	0.0	1.6	2.7	0.0	0.0	1.3	1.1	0.0	0.0	0.0	1.3	0.0	0.0	0.0	1.9	0.0	0.0	3.0	0.0	0.0	0.0	0.0	0.4
Banks (77)	11.9	28.6	32.5	30.3	24.9	23.8	7.9	22.7	17.0	11.9	28.0	26.5	39.7	15.4	19.8	20.8	28.6	20.4	23.8	20.0	27.2	27.8	34.0	28.1	42.9	19.0	14.8	32.7	16.6	17.9	23.9
Leasing and hire purchase (80)	0.0	0.0	0.0	0.0	0.0	0.0	0.0	0.0	0.0	0.0	0.0	0.0	0.0	0.0	0.0	0.0	0.0	0.0	30.8	25.6	0.0	0.0	0.0	0.0	0.0	0.0	0.0	0.0	0.0	0.0	0.0
Insurance (Life) (81)	34.5	31.0	36.1	31.3	29.6	48.9	43.1	29.6	22.2	23.4	32.5	32.6	34.5	24.3	24.4	17.2	36.2	32.0	0.0	30.4	30.4	27.3	17.2	26.6	21.3	27.6	11.1	21.6	28.5	23.7	28.5
Property (86)	0.0	0.0	1.0	1.9	0.0	0.0	0.0	0.0	0.0	3.1	0.0	0.0	0.0	0.0	0.0	3.9	0.0	0.0	0.0	0.0	0.0	2.6	0.0	0.0	0.0	8.7	0.0	0.0	0.0	0.0	0.3
Miscellaneous financial (87)	3.6	5.8	2.8	5.3	2.1	10.9	0.0	4.1	6.2	0.0	2.6	0.0	2.4	0.0	0.0	8.2	10.9	9.3	7.8	2.8	2.1	1.8	6.2	4.0	6.2	0.0	1.5	0.0	4.0	0.0	4.1
Electric utilities (89)	0.0	0.0	1.0	1.9	0.0	0.0	0.0	0.0	0.0	0.0	0.0	0.0	0.0	0.0	0.0	0.0	0.0	0.0	0.0	0.0	0.0	0.0	0.0	0.0	0.0	0.0	0.0	0.0	0.0	0.0	0.0
Average	1.9	2.4	2.8	2.6	2.7	2.8	2.2	2.2	2.0	1.8	2.8	2.6	2.7	1.7	2.3	1.9	2.9	2.6	2.4	1.7	2.1	2.3	2.2	2.1	2.5	2.6	1.0	1.8	1.8	1.5	2.2
N	12	30	63	33	21	12	12	42	14	28	17	18	18	34	24	16	20	14	28	31	42	24	28	22	21	15	29	16	23	16	520

Note: See Table 3.3. On average each firm has been assigned to 1.77 industries.

(highest coefficient on the diagonal).[26] In contrast to the German matrix, no pattern is evident here regarding the highest coefficients, and the distribution seems to be random. Secondly, Table 3.4 shows a clear participation by financial institutions in firms of the other sectors. The highest coefficients for network activity across all sectors (outdegree, last column) are those for banks (23.8) and insurance (28.5).

Table 3.4 (in comparison with Table 3.3) provides empirical evidence for the hypothesis that the *intra*sectoral network activity is lower in Great Britain than in Germany. British firms are often in association with firms in other sectors (conglomerates), and those in the financial sector with others in nonfinancial sectors. Networks among competing firms are rare and the structure of Table 3.4 is more compatible with a model of market regulation.

3.8. INTERLOCKING DIRECTORATES

The existence of an interlocking directorate can provide an enterprise the opportunity to exert power and influence over another.[27] A member of the management board of one firm who is elected to the supervisory board of another is enfranchised to take part in company decisions, can demand delicate information from the management, and can attempt to influence his colleagues on the board. Why does a company extend to another this power over it? Below, four potential answers are put forward to this question, which provide hypotheses on the importance of interlocking directorates (Koenig *et al.* 1979).

1. The concept of *resource dependence* begins by observing that firms are not self-sufficient but depend upon resources from their environment. These resources include goods, services, and information which are essential for the survival of the firm, and the acquisition of which may be difficult. Firms develop strategies to reduce their environmental dependence, one of which are interlocking directorates. The theory of resource dependence sees the structure of the interlocking directorates as reflecting the environmental dependence of the enterprise (Pfeffer 1992); thus, one would expect to find an interlocking of the enterprise with those organizations upon whose goods and services it is especially dependent.[28]

2. Almost all firms are dependent upon capital in the form of credit or securities. As a result, firms in the nonfinancial sector generally depend in some way upon institutions in the financial sector (banks, insurance companies). This dependence gives rise to the thesis of *bank hegemony*. The financial sector can exert influence upon the nonfinancial sector because the latter is dependent upon this difficult-to-acquire

---

[26] It must be noted here that the number of sectors in Table 3.4 is greater than that in Table 3.3. Since the sectors are consequently narrower, the probability is *lower* that network associations will be found within the same sector.

[27] If a member of the management board of firm A sits on the supervisory board of firm B, this relationship is called here a primary or directed interlocking directorate. When a person sits on the supervisory board of two firms simultaneously, this relationship is referred to as secondary, or undirected interlocking directorate.

[28] Burt *et al.* (1980: 823) maintain a similar hypothesis in terms of 'constraint on structural autonomy'.

resource which the former controls. A number of studies have shown the interlocking directorates between financial and nonfinancial sectors to be particularly
dense and that this network reflects the dependence upon capital. The centrality
of banks and insurance companies in those networks is often taken as an indicator
of the importance of financial institutions.[29]

3. German corporate law prescribes that the shareholders' meeting elect the supervisory board, and that this board appoint the management board (executive managers) and supervise its practices. This set of relationships is intended to
   guarantee the influence of shareholders over the running of the company.
   However, in addition to these formal procedures, there exist informal recruitment
   channels which have the effect of counteracting the legal stipulations. A list of
   candidates for the supervisory board are proposed by the management board to
   the shareholders, who then ratify the list. The managers recruit as their own
   'supervisors' persons whom they know and trust, thus giving rise to an 'old-boys'
   network'. This is the case not only for supervisory boards in Germany but also for
   'external' directors in the United States (Brudney 1981) and Great Britain. The
   third thesis is that interlocking directorates stabilize *managerial domination*. The
   supervisory board is not actually elected but merely coopted, and this in fact
   means that the influence of the owners is effectively negated. The supervisory
   board is supposed to be a puppet in the hands of executive managers.

4. Networks strengthen the *social cohesion* of a group (Friedkin 1984). The more
   dense a set of social contacts, the more integrated and capable of undertaking
   concerted action it is. In managerial capitalism, in which the control of the enterprise is entrusted to its managers, interlocking directorates are an important
   instrument for strengthening the social cohesion of the economic elite. Useem
   (1984) maintains that the 'big linkers', that is, managers with three or more positions in the network, are particularly prominent in sponsoring the interests of
   large enterprises. In his view, the structure of interlocking directorates is diffuse,
   and neither a resource dependence nor a bank hegemony can be discerned.
   Because of this, the 'big linkers' are not tied to the promotion of company-specific
   goals but can represent an overarching class interest. The network of interlocking
   directorates thus enhances the social integration of the economic elite.[30]

These are the principal hypotheses that have been put forward to explain the structure of the network of interlocking directorates. The data that we have collected on
interlocks do not allow to decide which of these competing hypotheses is correct. In
fact, they do not necessarily exclude each other. For instance, the argument that networks strengthen the social cohesion of managers does not contradict the hypothesis

---

[29] Mintz and Schwartz (1985), Ziegler *et al.* (1985). The bank-hegemony thesis is a diluted version of
the bank-control thesis (Kotz 1979). Pennings' (1980: 120) analysis of the structure of interlocking directorates among large firms in the United States led him to reject the bank-hegemony thesis. The thesis of
resource dependence, which has been tested in a number of studies on 'broken ties', has also not found
confirmation (Palmer 1983).

[30] A more detailed analysis of the elite network (big linkers) is given in Chapter 5.

of managerial domination. An organized group of managers connected to each other by interlocking directorates is all the more powerful *vis-à-vis* an unorganized group of owners.

The following analysis concentrates on a specific aspect of interlocking directorates, that is, its degree of overlap with the capital network. In Chapter 2, we have already shown the degree of overlap between the two types of networks for six countries (see Table 2.6). It was argued that interlocks that run parallel to capital relations perform the function of enabling the owner to exert direct control over the firm. Efficient control requires a relatively high degree of concentration of ownership. If ownership structure is highly fragmented and the owners (investment funds) simultaneously hold shares in a large number of companies, control via parallel interlocks is virtually impossible.

In Germany, concentration of ownership is high, that is, firms own high proportions of stock in other firms and the degree of overlap between the two networks is also high; in Britain, concentration of ownership is low and the degree of overlap between the two networks is also low. Thus, in Germany interlocking directorates are used to strengthen the hand of the parent in the affairs of the subsidiary. The parent's presence on the supervisory board of the subsidiary guarantees it at least an arm's length control of the strategic decision making of the dependent firm. In the case of a combine, erecting a comprehensive network of interlocks makes it possible to unite its various associated firms behind a common policy.[31]

The high overlap of capital networks and interlocking directorates within the combine structure produces a particular control structure in Germany. The managers of the central company in large German combines are managers *and* owners:[32] they are managers of the parent company *and* represent the owner towards the dependent companies on the supervisory board. In this control constellation owners have recaptured power from managers, but the puzzling fact is that the owners are managers. Managerial power and the power of ownership are not divorced in this control structure, but they join and reinforce each other.

The overlap of capital networks and interlocking directorates can also be observed to some extent in Japan. On average 11 percent of the members of boards of directors in Japanese firms come from the boards of other firms in the same *keiretsu* group (Yamauchi 1994). However, in contrast to the case in German firms, the overall coordination of the group derives not from the dominance of a single firm but through the agreements reached at the weekly meetings of the presidents of the various *keiretsu* members (*shachokai*).

In Great Britain, there are no combines as are common in Germany. As noted above, most of the network connections in the British data matrix are between firms

---

[31] This remark seems to contradict what has been said in Section 3.6 (combine). However, the supervisory board is not allowed to interfere with the business of executive managers. The question of where exactly 'supervision' ends and 'interference' begins, has given rise to much legal litigation in Germany. If the supervisory board 'interferes', the owners may lose the privilege of limited liability.

[32] This does not mean that the managers 'own' the company, but that they represent the owner (which is the firm over which they have managerial control).

in the financial and nonfinancial sectors, and although banks and insurance companies may invest simultaneously in several firms, the extent of capital participation rarely exceeds 5 percent in any of them. The costs would be prohibitively high for establishing a comprehensive network of interlocking directorates under these circumstances. Even if the financial institutions have a strategic interest in the firms that they invest in they would not be able to establish interlocking directorates with them, since they are part owners of too many of them.

We now turn to a comparison of the *sectoral* structure of interlocking directorates in the two countries (Tables 3.5 and 3.6). We have noted above, first, that capital networks in Germany are concentrated intrasectorally (Table 3.3), and, second, that German corporate networks tend to be based on the interlocking of both capital and personnel with the same firms. Therefore, it is not surprising to find that the interlocking directorates of German firms are also concentrated *within* rather than between economic sectors (i.e. on the diagonal, Table 3.5). This structure of interlocking directorates provides additional support to the thesis of regulated competition and cooperative capitalism in Germany (Schönwitz and Weber 1982: 18).

The structure of the marginals in Table 3.5 (last column, outdegree) shows that German banks still hold a central position in the corporate network. Banks are the firms that most frequently send representatives to the supervisory board of other firms (18.3). The next highest coefficient (gas and petroleum) is only 8.5. Similar results are reported in a study on German networks by Ziegler *et al.* (1985).

As in Table 3.4 (capital networks), the distribution in Table 3.6 shows no clear pattern in the data on interlocking directorates in Great Britain. In only two out of thirty sectors is the intrasectoral coefficient (diagonal) higher than the intersectoral ones.[33] The dominance of the financial sector, which was evident in the matrix for capital networks has disappeared. The fact that British banks and insurance companies lack significantly higher outdegree coefficients (Table 3.6, last column) contradicts the bank-hegemony thesis for that country. Banks do, however, have the highest indegree (4.1) of all sectors (bottom row). The figures in the appropriate column show British banks to be a meeting place for managers from other industrial sectors: German banks *send* managers to other sectors, British banks *receive* the managers from other sectors on their boards.

3.8.1. *Core of the Network*

Table 3.7 contains a part of the matrices on interlocking directorates in Germany and Great Britain, namely that part with the highest network density. Clique analysis was used to identify a core component of fifteen firms with the highest density. The figures in the table are the sums of directed and undirected interlocking directorates. The largest and most prestigious German corporations, such as Allianz (insurance), Daimler-Chrysler, Volkswagen, Deutsche Bank are connected to each other by interlocking directorates. For instance, the same five directors sit on the supervisory board

---

[33] In the US, *intra*sectoral interlockings are also rare (Pennings 1980: 84).

TABLE 3.5 Interlocking directorates, Germany (intra-/intersectoral)

	100	101	200	300	301	302	304	305	306	307	400	401	402	410	500	600	601	700	800	801	802	
Mining	40.5	18.3	9.1	8.3	6.0	3.7	1.1	0.0	0.0	3.0	6.8	0.0	4.0	1.9	23.8	3.1	0.0	4.8	2.3	5.4	0.0	6.8
Oil/gas	25.6	19.2	19.6	11.7	6.4	5.2	3.7	3.0	7.7	4.8	12.4	0.0	6.4	3.1	21.0	2.5	0.0	7.7	3.7	8.7	5.9	8.5
Electrical utilities	23.3	16.4	19.9	7.9	7.1	4.5	1.0	3.0	3.2	6.6	6.1	0.0	1.8	0.9	11.6	6.9	0.6	5.0	4.1	4.4	2.0	6.5
Iron and steel	7.2	1.7	1.9	14.5	3.6	7.1	3.1	1.4	3.3	6.8	1.6	2.7	1.8	0.0	3.0	2.8	0.0	0.0	7.2	3.5	3.0	3.6
Non-ferrous metals	6.0	6.4	5.3	13.6	14.5	7.6	4.0	1.6	6.3	13.0	4.5	2.6	6.9	0.0	9.5	5.4	0.5	1.4	2.0	0.9	3.2	5.5
Mechanical engineering	2.3	3.0	1.2	4.4	4.0	6.2	4.6	4.1	4.3	3.6	2.6	1.8	1.6	0.4	4.8	2.8	0.6	0.6	5.5	3.5	2.5	3.1
Motor cars	2.3	1.8	2.0	5.2	5.0	6.6	12.8	6.2	2.4	6.0	3.0	0.0	2.0	0.0	4.3	2.3	0.6	2.4	10.2	6.5	3.7	4.1
Electrical engineering	1.2	3.0	1.4	2.5	4.3	3.0	5.6	6.2	3.2	2.4	2.6	3.2	4.3	0.5	1.8	1.7	0.4	2.6	7.4	4.7	2.8	3.1
Instruments/optics	4.8	11.5	4.3	12.0	8.3	9.6	10.7	12.3	10.5	9.4	8.9	9.4	4.2	0.0	4.5	4.8	0.0	3.3	19.0	13.6	8.5	8.1
Metal products	6.0	4.8	0.0	8.2	7.8	5.4	3.0	0.0	0.0	8.3	0.0	0.0	5.2	0.0	2.8	2.0	0.0	2.1	0.0	0.0	0.0	2.6
Chemicals	7.7	0.0	2.7	4.3	3.7	2.9	0.9	1.2	3.1	3.3	7.5	3.3	6.0	3.6	7.3	1.2	0.0	1.2	6.0	2.8	2.2	3.8
Pharmaceuticals	0.0	0.0	0.0	0.0	0.0	3.0	0.0	0.8	4.2	0.0	6.7	16.7	5.2	0.0	8.5	0.0	0.0	2.1	6.0	4.3	1.0	2.9
Plastics/rubber	4.0	6.4	3.5	5.4	0.0	0.8	2.0	2.2	0.0	0.0	4.5	0.0	7.6	3.3	0.0	2.7	0.0	0.0	4.0	0.9	5.1	2.6
Food	0.0	0.0	0.0	0.0	1.7	1.2	0.0	0.0	0.0	0.0	0.7	2.5	0.0	10.0	0.0	3.9	0.0	0.0	0.0	0.0	0.6	1.0
Construction	8.7	3.5	1.0	5.9	1.9	3.5	1.1	0.0	0.0	2.8	0.0	0.0	3.8	0.0	17.3	0.0	1.2	1.5	0.0	1.0	0.0	2.5
Wholesale trade	6.1	9.9	2.1	16.8	9.4	9.6	4.6	3.8	9.7	12.1	1.7	6.0	2.7	0.0	10.3	4.3	3.5	3.2	10.8	2.8	5.5	6.7
Retail trade	0.0	0.0	0.0	0.6	2.3	0.3	0.6	0.0	1.4	3.4	0.0	1.7	0.0	1.1	0.0	0.9	6.0	0.0	2.6	1.8	0.8	1.1
Transportation	4.8	10.3	2.8	2.2	1.4	2.2	4.8	1.7	0.0	2.1	0.0	0.0	2.8	2.7	3.0	2.2	1.8	9.2	4.8	0.8	1.5	2.9
Banks	16.4	37.1	12.5	16.5	25.9	15.6	14.8	12.1	24.1	21.6	24.6	21.6	23.0	11.0	21.9	21.1	10.3	12.6	8.6	11.0	22.8	18.3
Insurance companies	2.2	5.2	1.9	1.0	3.8	3.5	2.7	3.2	3.4	3.4	3.2	7.1	0.0	0.0	1.0	3.7	0.0	2.3	11.9	14.8	1.0	3.4
Holding companies	7.3	7.1	6.5	10.4	10.3	6.4	4.4	4.0	2.3	8.7	5.5	2.9	1.3	4.3	8.4	7.4	2.9	3.1	7.3	10.1	3.6	5.9
Average	8.3	8.3	4.7	7.2	6.2	5.1	4.1	3.2	4.4	5.6	4.9	3.9	4.3	2.1	7.9	3.9	1.3	3.1	5.9	5.1	3.6	4.9
N= firms	21	13	47	46	24	104	42	77	20	16	56	16	12	25	22	31	37	30	29	44	65	623

Note: See Table 3.3; directed relationships only.

TABLE 3.6 Interlocking directorates, United Kingdom (intra-/intersectoral)

	9	14	18	19	21	27	31	35	38	41	42	47	48	49	51	53	54	66	68	70	71	72	75	76	77	80	81	86	87	89	Average
Water works (9)	0.0	0.0	0.0	0.0	0.0	0.0	0.0	0.0	0.0	0.0	0.0	0.0	4.6	0.0	0.0	0.0	1.7	0.0	3.0	0.0	0.0	0.0	0.0	0.0	0.0	0.0	0.0	0.0	0.0	2.1	0.3
Building materials (14)	2.8	1.1	2.1	1.0	7.9	8.3	8.3	3.2	0.0	2.4	0.0	0.0	0.0	0.0	1.4	2.0	0.0	0.0	2.4	1.1	1.6	1.4	1.2	0.0	7.9	0.0	0.0	0.0	0.0	3.0	2.1
Contracting & construction (18)	1.3	4.2	1.8	2.8	2.3	2.6	2.6	1.5	0.0	1.7	0.9	0.9	0.9	0.5	0.7	2.0	0.9	0.0	1.1	2.0	1.4	0.7	0.6	0.0	3.0	1.1	3.3	0.0	0.0	1.9	1.3
Electricals (19)	0.0	3.0	0.5	1.4	5.8	10.1	5.1	2.2	0.0	3.2	0.0	0.0	1.7	1.4	2.5	1.9	1.5	2.2	1.1	2.9	1.4	1.1	0.0	2.8	5.8	2.0	2.1	0.0	0.0	6.0	2.2
Aerospace (21)	4.0	4.8	2.3	2.5	2.4	4.0	4.0	1.1	0.0	0.0	0.0	2.6	2.6	1.8	2.0	3.0	0.0	1.8	3.4	0.0	1.1	4.0	0.0	2.2	9.1	0.0	0.0	0.0	0.0	0.0	2.8
Mechanical engineering (27)	13.9	8.3	4.0	2.5	7.9	22.7	6.9	2.0	0.0	3.0	0.0	4.6	4.6	2.5	3.5	0.0	0.0	0.0	0.0	2.7	2.0	0.0	0.0	7.6	11.9	5.6	5.7	0.0	0.0	0.0	3.8
Instruments (31)	0.0	2.8	2.6	2.2	4.0	6.9	2.0	2.0	0.0	0.0	4.9	4.6	4.6	2.5	3.5	0.0	0.0	0.0	0.0	0.0	1.1	0.0	0.0	5.4	7.9	5.6	0.8	4.5	3.6	3.0	2.1
Electronics (35)	6.0	3.2	2.6	0.0	0.0	0.0	6.0	1.7	0.0	1.7	1.4	0.0	0.0	0.7	2.0	0.0	4.2	0.0	0.0	1.5	1.7	1.0	0.0	0.0	1.1	1.6	2.5	0.0	0.0	0.0	1.5
Furniture and furnishings (38)	0.0	0.0	0.0	0.0	3.4	6.0	0.0	0.0	5.5	2.6	0.0	5.5	0.0	2.1	0.0	0.0	1.2	0.0	2.6	3.0	0.0	0.0	0.0	3.2	6.8	0.0	0.0	0.0	0.0	6.7	1.4
Motor components (41)	0.0	2.4	1.1	1.8	0.0	3.0	0.0	2.6	2.6	0.0	0.0	2.6	2.0	0.0	0.0	0.0	0.0	2.6	4.2	1.2	2.6	0.0	0.0	2.7	1.7	0.0	0.0	0.0	0.0	0.0	1.4
Motor distributors (42)	0.0	0.0	0.9	0.0	5.6	0.0	0.0	0.0	0.0	0.0	0.0	0.0	0.0	0.0	0.0	0.0	1.8	4.2	2.0	0.8	0.0	3.0	0.0	2.5	0.0	0.0	1.9	0.0	0.0	1.9	1.0
Hotel and caterers (47)	0.0	0.0	1.8	0.0	2.6	4.6	0.0	0.0	0.0	0.0	0.0	0.0	3.3	0.0	0.0	0.0	2.9	2.0	0.0	1.8	0.0	0.0	0.0	2.7	2.8	0.0	0.0	0.0	0.0	0.0	1.2
Leisure (48)	0.0	3.7	0.0	0.9	5.3	0.0	0.0	1.4	3.3	2.0	0.0	3.3	3.1	4.5	0.0	1.8	0.0	0.0	0.0	0.9	0.0	0.0	0.0	0.0	0.0	0.0	3.0	0.0	0.0	0.0	0.7
Food manufacturers (49)	2.5	1.9	0.7	0.0	0.0	0.0	0.0	0.0	0.0	0.0	0.0	2.3	3.3	0.0	0.0	4.2	0.0	3.0	2.2	2.7	0.0	4.6	0.0	6.0	6.0	2.8	1.4	0.0	1.3	5.2	1.1
Food retailers (51)	3.5	1.0	0.0	0.0	0.0	5.2	0.0	0.0	0.0	0.0	1.7	0.0	1.6	0.0	0.0	0.0	0.0	0.0	0.0	0.0	0.0	1.3	0.0	2.3	6.0	0.0	0.0	0.0	0.0	3.9	1.4
Printing (53)	0.0	0.0	0.0	0.0	3.0	4.2	0.0	0.0	0.0	0.0	2.3	0.0	2.3	0.0	0.0	4.5	2.1	4.2	0.0	1.1	0.8	1.7	0.0	0.0	0.0	3.3	0.0	4.5	2.7	3.1	1.3
Packaging and paper (54)	0.0	0.0	0.0	0.0	7.1	8.3	4.2	0.0	0.0	1.3	5.9	0.0	2.8	2.9	1.2	1.2	0.0	0.0	0.0	0.0	0.0	0.0	0.0	1.6	5.1	0.0	3.7	1.5	2.2	4.5	2.0
Plastic and rubber (66)	0.0	0.0	0.0	0.0	3.4	3.0	3.0	0.0	0.0	0.0	3.7	0.0	0.0	2.1	0.0	2.6	1.8	0.0	1.2	1.5	0.0	0.0	0.0	1.5	3.1	0.0	2.5	2.6	0.0	2.2	0.3
General chemicals (68)	3.0	0.0	0.8	1.5	1.5	3.0	0.0	0.0	2.6	0.0	0.0	0.0	3.6	0.0	0.0	0.0	1.6	2.2	0.0	2.7	1.2	0.0	0.0	1.1	5.7	0.0	4.3	2.2	0.0	4.0	1.6
Oil and gas (70)	0.0	1.1	0.0	0.0	1.1	0.0	0.0	0.8	3.0	0.0	0.8	0.0	0.0	3.2	2.1	1.5	1.2	0.0	1.5	0.0	0.0	1.3	0.0	1.9	6.0	0.0	0.0	2.8	0.0	1.5	1.0
Traders, wholesalers (71)	6.0	2.4	1.1	1.3	1.1	0.0	0.0	1.7	0.0	0.0	0.0	0.0	0.0	3.8	2.7	2.6	0.0	0.0	1.3	1.1	1.5	1.8	0.0	3.2	1.7	0.0	1.6	0.0	0.0	2.6	1.0
Transport and freight (72)	0.0	5.6	2.0	1.7	0.0	3.5	0.0	1.0	2.6	0.0	2.1	2.0	2.3	0.0	1.7	1.3	1.8	0.0	3.2	0.0	1.0	1.5	0.0	0.0	0.0	0.0	4.9	0.0	1.6	2.2	1.6
Support services (75)	0.0	2.4	1.7	2.2	3.4	0.0	0.0	1.7	1.7	1.6	2.7	0.0	2.0	0.0	1.5	0.0	1.5	0.0	1.7	2.8	0.0	0.0	0.0	6.5	4.8	4.9	0.0	0.0	0.0	2.8	1.4
Miscellaneous (76)	0.0	3.0	2.2	2.8	0.0	0.0	0.0	1.1	0.0	0.0	0.0	5.3	0.0	1.3	1.9	0.0	0.0	0.0	0.0	1.2	1.1	5.7	4.9	0.0	0.0	0.0	1.2	0.0	0.0	0.0	1.7
Banks (77)	4.0	1.6	2.3	1.4	0.0	0.0	0.0	1.1	6.5	1.2	0.0	3.8	7.9	0.0	4.0	6.5	0.0	0.0	0.0	2.8	0.0	4.0	1.7	1.6	11.5	3.2	8.6	0.0	0.0	0.0	2.1
Leasing and hire purchase (80)	0.0	0.0	0.0	0.0	4.5	0.0	0.0	0.8	0.0	0.0	0.0	3.8	0.0	2.0	0.0	0.0	0.0	0.0	1.1	0.0	0.0	0.0	2.5	0.0	6.0	0.0	0.0	0.0	6.2	4.3	0.0
Insurance (Life) (81)	2.9	1.1	1.6	0.0	1.6	5.2	0.0	0.0	0.0	3.1	0.0	0.0	3.8	0.0	5.7	0.0	0.0	0.0	0.0	0.0	0.0	4.3	3.1	0.0	4.1	4.6	0.0	0.0	4.5	3.9	2.2
Property (86)	0.0	2.1	1.0	0.0	0.0	0.0	0.0	3.1	0.0	0.0	0.0	0.0	0.0	0.0	0.0	0.0	0.0	0.0	0.0	0.0	0.0	0.0	0.0	0.0	0.0	0.0	0.0	0.0	0.0	5.4	1.0
Miscellaneous financial (87)	3.6	2.9	0.7	1.3	6.2	3.6	7.2	0.0	0.0	0.0	0.0	0.0	2.4	5.1	1.8	0.0	2.2	0.0	1.6	0.0	2.8	1.8	0.0	0.0	0.0	0.0	0.0	0.0	0.0	0.0	2.1
Electric utilities (89)	0.0	0.0	0.0	0.0	0.0	0.0	0.0	0.0	0.0	0.0	0.0	0.0	0.0	0.0	0.0	3.9	0.0	0.0	0.0	0.0	0.0	0.0	0.0	0.0	0.0	0.0	0.0	0.0	0.0	0.0	0.1
Average	1.8	2.0	1.1	1.0	2.8	3.2	1.8	1.1	0.9	0.8	0.8	1.2	1.8	1.4	1.3	1.1	0.8	0.5	1.1	1.2	0.6	1.2	0.6	1.8	4.1	1.0	1.7	0.6	0.7	2.5	1.4
N = (firms)	12	30	63	33	21	12	12	42	14	28	17	18	18	34	24	16	20	14	28	31	42	24	28	22	21	15	29	16	23	16	520

Note: See Table 3.3; directed relationships only.

TABLE 3.7 *Core component (interlocks)*

	Germany															United Kingdom														
	1	2	3	4	5	6	7	8	9	10	11	12	13	14	15	1	2	3	4	5	6	7	8	9	10	11	12	13	14	15
1	—	1	2	3	2	2	2	1	2	1	2	2	4		1	—	1			1	1	1	1	1	1	1	1		1	1
2	1	—	2	2	1	1	1	1	2	2	2	2	1	1	2	1	—	1			1						1			
3	1	2	—	1	2	2	4	1	2	2	2	1	2	1	5	1	1	—												1
4	3	2	1	—		1	2		2	2	1	2	1	1		1	1		—											
5	2	1	2		—	2	2	3	1	1	1		1		2	1				—	1						1			
6	1	1	2	2	2	—	2	2	1	3	1	1	2	1		1					—			1						
7	1	1	4	1	1	2	—	1	2		1	1	2	3		1	1	1				—								
8	1	1	1		2	2		—	3	2	1	1	2	1		1							—							
9	2	3	2	2	1	1	2	2	—	2	1	3	2	1	2	1		1						—	1				1	
10	1	2	2	2	1	1		2	2	—		1	1			1								1	—					
11	2	2	2	1	1	2	1	1	2		—	2	1			1		1								—				
12	2	2	1	2		2	1	1	2	1	1	—				1	1	1	1	1							—			1
13	4	1	2	1	1	1	1	2	1	1	1		—	2	2	1												—	1	
14		1	1	1		1	2	3	1	1	2		2	—	2	1			1									1	—	
15	1	2	5		2	2	1	1	2	1	1		2		—	1											1			—

Note: Germany
1 RWE; 2 VEBA; 3 Karstadt; 4 Allianz Holding; 5 Daimler-Chrysler; 6 Linde; 7 Thyssen; 8 MAN; 9 Münchener Rück; 10 Volkswagen; 11 Degussa; 12 Dresdner Bank; 13 Hochtief; 14 Commerzbank; 15 Deutsche Bank

density: 1.28 (all)
density: 0.79 (binary)

United Kingdom
1 Barclays Bank; 2 BP Company; 3 ICI; 4 Marks & Spencer; 5 BAA; 6 Smithkline Beecham; 7 Bass; 8 British Airways; 9 Whitbread; 10 Kingfisher; 11 Thorn Emy; 12 De La Rue; 13 Unilever; 14 The Telegraph; 15 Prudential

density: 0.20

In Table 3.7 (Germany, United Kingdom) figures give multiple interlocking directorates between companies (sum of directed and undirected interlocks). For example, Allianz Holding (4) and Deutsche Bank (15) have 5 common members on their supervisory board. Density (all) gives density computed on the basis of all directors two companies have in common. Density (binary): all multiple interlocks are counted as 1. For the United Kingdom there is no difference between the two density coefficients because there is no multiple interlock.

of both Allianz (4) and Deutsche Bank (15). In the case of Great Britain, one can hardly speak of a core component, as the density of the network is substantially lower than in Germany, and the network does not show every degree of closure (clique) that is attained in Germany. Data in Table 3.7 confirm an observation that was already made in the previous chapter: the core of the network which contains the most central firms includes not only banks and financial institutions, but also large and prestigious industrial firms.

In summary, we can observe that interlocking directorates in German enterprises parallel capital networks; that they are concentrated particularly within rather than between economic sectors; that they support and strengthen the power of ownership; and that there is a core component to which the largest corporations in the country belong. None of these features can be maintained in the case of British companies.

3.9. INTERLOCKING DIRECTORATES AND INTEREST REPRESENTATION

In Germany the principal organizations representing corporate interests in the political system and *vis-à-vis* labor unions and other social groups are the Federation of German Employers (Bundesvereinigung der Deutschen Arbeitgeberverbände, BDA) and the Federation of German Industry (Bundesverband der Deutschen Industrie, BDI). This section examines the hypothesis that the leadership of these organizations is recruited principally from the network of those sitting on many management and/or supervisory boards of the largest enterprises (so-called 'big linkers' or multiple-directors).[34]

In his study on firms in the United States and Great Britain, Useem (1984) demonstrated a personal union between the leaders of formal interest organizations and the network of 'big linkers'. The directors of large enterprises who occupy multiple positions in the network are also found more frequently in interest organizations for business, on government consulting bodies, and as sponsors for cultural institutions (e.g. theater, universities).

As a result of their activities in various large organizations, multiple-directors tend to transcend the narrow perspectives of company-specific interests and to represent instead the overall interest of big business. This role is further supported by the myriad social contacts that result from these activities, which also strengthen the cohesion and homogeneity of the group. Useem argues that the network of multiple-directors has the political functions of homogenizing the economic elite, aggregating business interests, and articulating them to the political system. Thus, the *formal* interest organizations and the *informal* network of multiple-directors can be seen as complementing one another.

To determine the degree of overlap between formal and informal systems of interest representation, we first listed those persons with some form of leadership position (e.g. president, honorary president, trustee, business manager) in either the BDI

---

[34] On the management/supervisory boards of the 623 largest German firms one can identify a total of 1423 multiple-directors with two or more positions in the network.

TABLE 3.8   *Officers of BDI/BDA*[a]

	Number of positions in the network				
	0	**1**	**2–3**	**4–6**	**7+**
N = 82	28	16	21	10	7
Σ100%	34.1	19.5	25.7	12.2	8.5

Note
[a] BDI and BDA are the leading German interest organizations representing business interests.

or BDA[35] and then sought these names among the 'big linkers' who connect the 623 largest German firms. The list included the names of eighty-two organization officers, almost half (46.4 percent) of whom had at least two positions in the informal network: 25.7 percent had two or three positions and 8.5 percent had seven positions or more (see Table 3.8).

These data thus verify the hypothesis that the two principal interest organizations representing German business recruit their leadership largely from the network of multiple-directors among the nation's largest enterprises. One can assume that the proportion of multiple-directors would decline in less centrally located interest groups.

3.10. CONCLUSIONS

In this chapter we have analyzed capital networks, interlocking directorates, and the *relationship* between them in more detail. For Germany it was shown that the structure of interlocking directorates must be understood in the context of the capital network. A high proportion of interlocking directorates reflect the capital network and serves to strengthen and ensure the power of the owner.

This should not be taken to mean, however, that the interlocking directorates are merely an epiphenomenon of the underlying property relations. In countries where the separation between ownership and control has progressed further than in Germany (e.g. in Britain and the US) and where many large enterprises are owned by investment funds (fragmented ownership), it is possible for interlocking directorates to divorce themselves from effective control by property. In fashioning the interlocks, such company managers can pursue their own interests to some extent undisturbed by owners. Such independence is not possible in Germany. As shown in Table 3.1, over half of all capital participations in Germany provide a single owner with a controlling interest in the company. Under these circumstances the dominant role that interlocking directorates can play lies in shoring up the strategic interests of the owner.

---

[35] As federations, both the BDI and the BDA have as members not companies but other, more specialized or regionally organized associations of companies, which in turn have companies as members. The list of officers included only those with formal functions in either of the two federations; the personnel at the level of the member associations of the federations were not examined.

In Britain there are two characteristic features of the capital network: the interlocking between financial and nonfinancial sectors is intense, and the shares held by the former in the latter are too limited to permit financial institutions to assume a dominant position (many chiefs, few Indians). Investment funds cannot delegate managers (monitors) to the board of directors of the many firms in which they have invested. As owners are weak, managers have more autonomy in designing the structure of interlocking directorates.

In Germany the 'regulated competition' (cartel) which had become a legitimate model of market organization by the end of the nineteenth century was superseded after the Second World War by the combine structure. There a number of factors that favored cooperation among competing companies: the high concentration of ownership; the related network of interlocking directorates; a core component uniting the largest enterprises into a single 'clique'; the integration of the banking sector in the interlocking directorates and its strong position in this network; and the personal union between the formal interest organizations for business (BDI, BDA) and the informal network of multiple-directors. The structure of overlapping capital networks and interlocking directorates is an example of 'cooperative' capitalism, because this type of market regulation permits structures of corporate networks which would not be accepted in a 'competitive' capitalism.

Interlocking directorates fulfill two—mutually contradictory—functions. The members of the supervisory board are supposed to supervise the company directors and prevent the misuse of their power. At the same time, however, they are part of a general network uniting the business elite, which serves its social integration and cohesion, and to which the individual economic leaders owe their positions. Conflicts of course arise between these two functions, and due to its personal importance for the individuals involved, the function of social cohesion may frequently prove the stronger.

We have shown that there are at least three dimensions which characterize different types of ownership and control: the network configuration (Fig. 3.1); the type of owner (financial/nonfinancial firm); and the concentration of ownership (high in Germany, low in Britain). In recent years the balance of power has shifted in favor of the owners, but in some countries (e.g. Germany, France) the owners are frequently nonfinancial firms which are represented by managers. Here, managerial power and ownership join and reinforce each other in a network of companies which own other companies and are owned by them. This overlap of interlocks and ownership and the mutual reinforcement of bureaucratic power (management) and power conveyed by ownership characterize the specific control structure of German capitalism.

4

The Evolution of French Capitalism

4.1. FROM FAMILY TO SHAREHOLDER VALUE CAPITALISM

The governance structure of large corporations has been transformed several times during the past one hundred years. At the turn of the nineteenth century, most firms were still owned and controlled by families or groups of families who exercised a patrimonial authority over their workforce. During the interwar period managerial capitalism developed, which is characterized by diffused ownership, a separation of ownership and control, and a managerial bureaucracy in command of the public corporation. Since the late 1970s, a new type of capitalism has evolved which is frequently termed 'shareholder value capitalism' and which many authors associate with a proliferation of financial institutions, new forms of financial control, and a recon-centration of ownership.[1]

These transformations affected not only the governance structure of large corpo-rations, but also the distribution of income and wealth and the structure of social classes and class conflicts (Zeitlin 1974). Investor capitalism and shareholder value is frequently associated with increasing income inequalities, new poverty, and what Bourdieu *et al.* (1993: 597) have called 'exclusion sociale'. This is particularly true for the United States where shareholder value is an institutionalized ideology, investment funds are the dominant owners in the large corporations, social inequality has increased considerably (Mishel *et al.* 2001), and hostile takeovers and financial control of large corporations are accepted practices for almost two decades.

First, two competing hypotheses will be discussed. The first hypothesis maintains that shareholder value capitalism and the attending social transformations are the product of a universal *modernization process*. Most advanced countries are likely to adopt this model of capitalism sooner or later under the pressure of global competi-tion. However, it can also be argued, and this is the second hypothesis, that several forms of corporate governance and capitalist institutions emerge as a consequence of recent adaptations to global markets. This suggests that shareholder value capitalism is a special outcome of an evolutionary adaptation, and it coexists and competes with

A first version of this paper was published in *Revue française de sociologie* 40(3) (1999): 501–29. Reproduced with permission of Éditions Ophrys.

[1] Consensus on terminology has not yet been reached. Rappaport (1990) uses the term 'shareholder value capitalism' which has become a catch word for recent changes in financial markets. Useem (1996) uses the term 'investor capitalism' to emphasize the growing power of investment/pension funds.

other forms of corporate governance. In this case, the process of *economic evolution* produces different path-dependent outcomes.

The evolution of French capitalism is a case in point. The analysis concentrates on the question whether the governance structure of large French corporations is an example of a lagged modernization process (Lévy-Leboyer 1980) or whether it represents a genuine type of corporate governance which may be as efficient as the shareholder value model.

4.2. MODERNIZATION THEORY

The transformations from family to managerial, and from managerial to shareholder value capitalism may be described as sequential stages in the evolution of the capitalist system (Clark 1980).

'Business historians describe the 19th century, before the age of giant companies and conglomerates, as an era of "entrepreneurial capitalism". Scholars from Adolph Berle to Alfred Chandler have described more recent times as an era of "managerial capitalism". We are now at the threshold of a new era in corporate purpose, one that may be remembered as an era of "shareholder value capitalism"... What we are witnessing today is an economic and political battle between management and shareholders over who will control the large public corporation and in whose interests it will be operated' (Rappaport 1990: 97–9).

Modernization is understood here as a unilinear process that produces a universal form of organization at each stage of development. The managerial bureaucracy which was implemented in many large corporations already before the First World War provided a more powerful form of organization than family capitalism (Chandler 1990). At a later stage, managerial capitalism itself is challenged by a more efficient governance structure which is more competitive in a global market. It strengthens financial control over the managerial bureaucracy, provides higher liquidity and a more efficient allocation of financial resources (shareholder value).

The governance structures of modern corporations are complex arrangements which are shaped by their legal, economic, and cultural environment. Table 4.1 decomposes the governance structures of the different stages of capitalism into their constituent parts, and each component is then analyzed separately. The main purpose of this analysis is to show in which way bureaucratic control (managerial capitalism) is different from financial control (shareholder value capitalism).

4.2.1. *Modes of Control*

The different types of capitalism shown in Table 4.1 incorporate different modes of control, among them control through ownership, bureaucratic control, and financial control. These modes of control differ in their institutionalized structures and their patterns of legitimation. Ownership confers discretionary power to an individual over his or her property. 'The exclusivity of ownership means that the owner has the right to choose what to do with his assets' (Pejovitch 1990: 28). The strategies of the

TABLE 4.1   *The process of modernization*

Type of capitalism	Modes of control	Concentration of ownership	Liquidity	Strategic option
Stage 1: Family	Patrimonial Ownership	High	Low	Voice
Stage 2: Managerial	Bureaucracy	Low (diffused)	High	Exit
Stage 3: Shareholder	Financial	Medium (fragmented)	High	Exit and voice

'robber barons' in the United States[2] or the regime of the large 'patrons' in France (e.g. Peugeot, Michelin) illustrate this discretionary power over the means of production. However, case studies on the history of entrepreneurial families in Germany also show that the discretionary power of the owner was restricted within relatively narrow limits by family traditions and quasi-feudal bonds to the workforce (Kocka 1969). Thus, the type of control exercised during the period of family capitalism was not a 'pure' type, but a combination of discretionary power of ownership and patrimonial traditions restricting this power.

The bureaucracy constitutes a different governance structure and provides a different type of legitimation. Max Weber describes this as the rational-legal form of authority. In contrast to discretionary property rights, authority based on bureaucracy is limited and governed by rules.[3] Bendix (1956) has argued that the process of modernization incorporates not only industrialization, the introduction of mass production, and modern technology but also legal-rational forms of authority. From this point of view, *managerial bureaucracy is a more modern form of authority than the regime of family owners.*

With the rise of shareholder value capitalism, an intense ideological battle has been fought about who controls the large corporation (owners versus managers), which type of regulation is most efficient (markets versus hierarchies), and for whom managers are responsible (shareholders versus employees). It will be argued below that the dominant mode of control which characterizes shareholder value capitalism is a combination of financial market power and property rights (ownership). The credible threat to sell their shareholdings ('exit') provides institutional investors with the power to influence the strategic decision making of firms ('voice').[4]

4.2.2. *Concentration of Ownership*

At the turn of the nineteenth century, the then large corporations were owned, managed, and controlled by the proverbial '200 families' of a country. In France, the

---

[2] Dobbin and Dowd (2000: 636) term these strategies the 'predatory business model'.

[3] Crozier (1963: 66) argues that bureaucratic rules have a protective function. They restrict the discretionary power of managers/owners over their workforce.

[4] See Hirschman (1970); the sale of shareholdings is identified here with the strategy of 'exit', while the attempt to influence the strategies of management is identified with 'voice'.

Rothschild's, Worms', and Lazard's; in Germany, the Siemens' and Krupp's; in the United States, the Rockefeller's and Vanderbilt's occupied the apex of economic power. Ownership in large corporations was highly concentrated and was the main power resource of the capitalist class. Typical of the regime of managerial capitalism is the diffusion and democratization of ownership. Dahrendorf (1959: 44), Bell (1960), and others praised the open and egalitarian regime of managerial capitalism. Workers could, at least theoretically, 'own' the factory in which they were exploited. Bell (1960: 42) argued that 'no longer are there America's Sixty Families. The chief consequence, politically, is the breakup of the ruling class'.

The regime of shareholder value capitalism is characterized by a reconcentration of shareholdings in the hands of institutional investors. This reconcentration has revalued property rights in the large corporation and has strengthened the power of owners. Some hostile takeovers illustrate in which way the 'new' owners exercise the discretionary power that ownership provides (Burrough and Hellyar 1989). In many large US corporations less than a dozen institutional investors are able to jointly nominate the majority of directors and to influence the strategic decision making of the firm.

4.2.3. *Liquidity and Strategic Options*

Liquidity is defined here as the chance to sell one's property at *any time* on the market. 'The liquidity of a securities market refers to the extent to which it is 'continuous', i.e. without large price changes between trades, and 'deep', i.e. with many buyers and sellers willing to trade just below or just above the prevailing price. Liquidity increases with the number of stockholders' (Bhide 1993). The family owners at the turn of the nineteenth century were unable to 'liquidate' their enterprise at any time: most of their capital was illiquid, because it was invested in real estate and machinery, and they would have had a hard time to sell the whole firm.

In his work on financial capital, Hilferding pointed to the duplication of assets which takes place on the stock market. A firm which incorporates real assets such as buildings, machinery, and tools, is illiquid as a whole. However, on the stock market, these assets are duplicated as 'fictitious capital' (Hilferding 1968: 111) and transformed into share capital. These shares are 'liquid', that is, they can be bought and sold at any time. The transformation of real assets into 'fictitious capital', their diffusion among many thousands of small shareholders, and the quasi-unlimited liquidity of shares were important conditions for the development of managerial capitalism. Small shareholders follow the 'golden Wall Street rule': they sell their shares if they are unsatisfied with management (exit), but they are unable to replace the incumbent management (voice). Rational choice theory has convincingly argued that thousands of shareholders are unable to coordinate their action.

The financial markets which are dominated by large institutional investors offer the chance to choose between 'exit' and 'voice'. The institutional owners may opt for 'exit' because their assets are liquid, that is, can be sold at any time.[5] However, they

---

[5] There is a controversy in the literature whether the shareholdings of institutional investors are really 'liquid' Useem (1996). In the United States 95% of all shareholdings in large corporations are below 5%

may also opt for 'voice' because of the reconcentration of ownership and the growing power of owners over the public corporation. Institutional owners may put management under pressure by threatening to sell their block of shares if management does not comply with their suggestions. *'Voice' becomes effective because 'exit' is a credible threat.*[6] The combination of liquidity with the power of a reconcentrated ownership characterizes the financial control of institutional investors.

The strategic options of institutional investors (exit or voice) may be *coordinated* in two ways: first, they may be coordinated through organizations of interest representation.[7] In the United States, a change in the rules of the Stock Exchange Commission allows institutional investors to meet (to 'collude') without publicly announcing these meetings (Useem 1996: 35). Second, institutional investors may also coordinate their actions because they belong to the same 'organizational field' (DiMaggio and Powell 1983). The managers of financial institutions are professionals who have obtained a similar university education; they are visible to each other in a small financial community; they receive their information from similar or even identical sources (e.g. Reuters, Bloomberg), and they are under similar market pressures (short-term profit expectations). It is therefore likely that they reach similar decisions in similar situations. Managers of large corporations *anticipate* in their strategic decisions the coordinated behavior of investors in the financial market.

Financial control which is one of the important characteristics of shareholder value capitalism can now be defined more precisely by the following characteristics: this type of financial control requires first a reconcentration of ownership in the hands of professional investors who are able to coordinate their strategies either by way of interest organizations or within an 'organizational field'. Second, financial control presupposes liquidity; without liquidity there is no financial control. The combination of liquidity and reconcentrated ownership (property rights) allows the investor to choose between 'exit' and 'voice'. While bureaucratic control is an internal mode of control, financial control is an external mode of control exerted in the financial markets through financial intermediaries.

4.2.4. *Critique of Modernization Theory*

It has been argued that managerial capitalism was so successful because it provided a solution to technological and economic challenges that could not have been solved within the organizational framework of family capitalism (mass production, high

---

(see Table 4.2). Institutional investors have the power to influence the strategic decisions of managers (voice) because they are able to coordinate their behavior.

[6] In the case of mass migration (exit) from East to West Germany in October 1989, Hirschman (1992) has argued that the strategic options of 'exit' and 'voice' do not exclude each other, but may be mutually reinforcing: the 'exit' of many citizens from East Germany strengthened the political influence (voice) of those who remained.

[7] In the United States, many investment funds are organized in the 'Council of Institutional Investors'; similar interest organizations exist in Britain and Germany (e.g. Bundesverband Deutscher Investment Gesellschaften, Frankfurt).

capital intensity, complex organization). The shortcomings of family capitalism have been, so to speak, the driving force which gave rise to the new institutions of managerial capitalism. A similar argument has been made for the transition from managerial to shareholder value capitalism. The conflict between managers (agents) and shareholders (principals) and the inefficiency of an uncontrolled management were the engine that generated the new control structure of shareholder value capitalism.[8]

However, mass production, capital-intensive technology, and complex organizational forms have been implemented by large French and German corporations still owned by families or groups of families.[9] In neither country has managerial capitalism ever been a *dominant* type of corporate governance. In the late 1920s, about 40 percent of all large firms in the United States were classified by Berle and Means (1997: 109) as being under 'managerial control'. In France, more than 50 percent of the 200 largest firms were still controlled by families or groups of families forty years later, even though these firms had introduced capital-intensive mass production as early as the interwar period.[10] Similarly, in Germany only a quarter of the 300 largest firms were directly under management control in the 1970s (Schreyögg and Steinmann 1981: 544).

Lévy-Leboyer (1980) argues that since the turn of the nineteenth century, French corporations have been lagging behind in modernizing their organizational structures. In 1980 he emphasized that 'today for the first time, the corporate sector in France seems to conform to the general pattern of economic structure and hierarchical organization that is evident in other major industrial countries' (p. 117). However, in the same article he admits that 'in 1950 far more of the largest firms were organized as loose-knit groups in which one firm had large shareholdings, or 'participations', to use the French term, in the others. For managerial purposes, they did not offer an efficiency comparable to that of the multidivisional organization; their predominance indicates a continuing preference, voluntary or not, for indirect rather than direct control over operations' (p. 119). As will be shown, even in 2000, French corporate managers still had a preference for this indirect mode of control.[11]

Thus, we come to the conclusion that even in the late 1990s, the majority of large French (and German) firms does not conform to the model of the Berle–Means type of corporation. Rather, these firms are integrated into and protected by complex capital networks in which coordination and control are organized on different hierarchical

---

[8] Dahrendorf (1967) has argued that social conflict may be a catalyst that generates processes of social change.

[9] Roe (1991) maintains that neither mass production nor high capital intensity can explain the spread of managerial capitalism (Berle–Means type of corporation). Rather, American antitrust law and the strict regulation of financial markets have prevented institutional investors from acquiring controlling blocks in the public corporations.

[10] See Morin (1974: 64). In a more recent survey, the 100 largest French firms are classified according to their dominant mode of control. Only 29 firms are submitted to direct 'management control' (Alternatives Economiques, no. 160, Juin 1998, p. 34–5; data source: Laboratoire d'étude et de recherche sur l'économie de la production, Toulouse).

[11] André Rousselet, former CEO of Canal+, criticizes the 'indirect' mode of control the French holding company Vivendi exercises over Canal+ (one of the largest European pay-TV channels. See Le Monde, 15 November 2000, pp. 1 and 19; 16 November 2000, p. 16.

levels (Morin 1994: 1459). Is it likely that these firms transform their control structure in the near future, in order to conform to the model of shareholder value capitalism?

Most modernization theories presume that the more advanced countries provide a 'model' for those countries which are lagging behind. The American 'public' corporation provided such a 'model' for the governance structure of large corporations in other countries, and Lévy-Leboyer asserts that it is only a question of time until the French firms will be catching up. However, even by the year 2000 this had not happened—despite an impressive modernization of the French economy. These anomalies and specifically the national developments which do not fit the modernization model require an alternative theory to explain the structure of corporate governance in France.

4.3. THEORIES OF SOCIAL EVOLUTION

Theories of social evolution are less holistic and less deterministic than modernization theories (Hannan and Freeman 1989). They do not argue that there is a sequence of stages that follow each other in a predetermined order. Also, they do not assume that social change is 'systemic', that is, that all relevant parts of a system change in the same direction. New organizational 'species' may evolve which combine components from different stages in a new governance structure which is neither 'managerial' nor 'financial' but is composed of parts of both organizational forms. Further, a random sample of organizations taken at any point in time would show that the *population* of organizations in a particular country is a mix of different organizational forms which compete against each other. Some proliferate, others perish, still others survive in small niches.

The key concepts of theories of social evolution are variation, selection, and retention (Campbell 1965). There is considerable *variation* in the legal and economic institutions of the different countries, and these variations constitute a pool of different governance structures from which each country is able to select. After the Second World War, the American diversified corporation, the German combine, the Japanese '*keiretsu*' and the French '*groupe industriel*' were innovative organizational structures (variations), some of which served as normative standards and were imitated in other countries (e.g. the '*keiretsu*' and the diversified structure). Few of these governance structures corresponded to the pure model of managerial capitalism, but rather combined components of different stages of development (see Table 4.1).

The various national governance structures compete in the global market, which exposes them to similar forces of competition (*selection*). Only those governance structures which survived this competition are finally institutionalized in the legal system and the economic order of a country (*retention*). Countries that are particularly successful export not only their goods and technology but also their institutions (United States, Japan), while less successful countries not only import goods but also try to implement foreign institutions—with more or less success (Ouchi 1981).

A model of evolutionary adaptation takes into account external pressures as well as *internal resources*. Internal resources may be the quality of the educational system, the organizational capacity of large firms to organize mass production, but also the ability of the state to pacify class conflicts, and to integrate capital and labor into a system of corporatist regulation. Last but not least, 'culture' is an important internal resource, as has been demonstrated in the long debates on the Japanese firm (Gerlach 1992). Depending on internal resources which are available to cope with external challenges, organizational forms differ between countries and within countries between different sectors of the economy.

Theories of social evolution do not claim that survival is proof of efficiency or superior adaptation. Today, the governance structure of most large corporations in the United States fits the model of shareholder value capitalism, even though many studies have shown that this model may cause high transaction costs (e.g. hostile takeovers). DiMaggio and Powell (1983) have argued that firms in an organizational field observe each other's behavior and imitate solutions that the 'leaders' in the field have already adopted. Meyer and Rowan (1977) emphasize that there may be no *causal* relationship between a particular organizational form (e.g. shareholder value capitalism) and the putative efficiency of this model. The relationship may be purely normative and symbolic. Given uncertainty and bounded rationality with respect to what is a 'good' governance structure, large corporations accept what most organizations in their environment have already adopted. 'Whether a given pattern of selection reflects planned adaptation, social imitation or organizational competition is difficult to find out' (Hannan and Freeman 1989: 14–15).

Chandler (1990) has argued that the implementation of managerial bureaucracy was one of the important factors in the success of large German and American corporations. This argument is correct insofar as many German firms had implemented formal bureaucratic structures already before the First World War. However, Chandler did not note that the governance structure which evolved in both Germany and France was *not* a Berle–Means corporation with a *separation* of ownership and control but a different type of governance which may be characterized as *interpenetration* of family ownership and managerial bureaucracy. In many firms the family owners controlled a majority of shares but kept themselves at arm's length from the firm and transferred most managerial functions to a professional technocracy. In a number of case studies, Bauer and Bertin-Mourot (1987) have shown that this interpenetration of patrimony and bureaucracy still characterizes many large French corporations today.

In France and in Germany, a managerial bureaucracy was implemented, but frequently in the name of a powerful (family) owner. Because of the high concentration of ownership—which has survived in both countries up to the present day—the separation of ownership and control was never able to develop to the same extent as in the United States, where strict stock market regulations implemented during the interwar period favored the small shareholder and the fragmentation of ownership.

A considerable number of French firms which belonged to the group of the 200 largest corporations in 1995 have been founded since the Second World War by unusually successful entrepreneurs (e.g. Bich, Bouygues); other large corporations have been transferred to the second or third generation and this patrimony served then as an endowment for further rapid growth (e.g. Arnauld/LVMH; Bel).[12] In any case, however, family capitalism has played a very important role for the growth, development, and modernization of France since the Second World War (Pastré 1992: 20). Far from being an obstacle to the modernization of France, family capitalism occupied a considerable segment of the French economy and was *at least* as successful as the large management-controlled corporations. Bauer and Bertin-Mourot (1995: 31) estimate that about 32 percent of the 200 largest French corporations are strongly influenced by their founders (entrepreneurs) or the heirs of founders.[13]

However, many of these entrepreneurs are not traditional family capitalists who stayed within the narrow limits of their patrimony, but they are outstanding financial virtuosi who constructed their empire on the French market for corporate control, and who were able to rival the most ingenious American raiders.[14] After the Second World War, French family capitalism integrated traditional forms of authority with most advanced financial techniques (e.g. hostile takeovers, external growth). French family capitalism has not been transformed into managerial capitalism but rather has merged with modern forms of financial control and has derived its dynamism from this marriage. The empire of Bernard Arnauld is an example of how family ownership, managerial bureaucracy, and financial control are merged on a transnational basis to form a new type of corporate control (see Fig. 4.1).

The new organizational forms combine elements of different evolutionary stages and are one of the remarkable characteristics of French capitalism. Many French corporations are *jointly* owned by different types of owners, and this 'recombinant property'[15] cannot be explained as the outcome of a unilinear modernization process. The new forms which combine different types of owners are adaptive responses to external challenges given internal constraints on such resources as financial capital, entrepreneurial qualification or 'culture'.

4.4. FRENCH NETWORK CONFIGURATIONS

The principal actors of French modernization—the entrepreneur, the financial institutions, and the state bureaucracy (Suleiman 1978)—are embedded in different networks with different network configurations. The first type of network in which the large private and state-owned corporations are interconnected is called here a

---

[12] Bauer and Bertin-Mourot (1995: 10) distinguish between founders, heirs of founders, and members of renowned French families.

[13] 'Contrairement aux thèses prônées par les théoriciens de la révolution manageriale, la logique du capitalisme familial pèse encore d'un poids non négligeable dans l'univers des grandes entreprises' (Bauer and Bertin-Mourot 1995: 32).

[14] Among them, for instance, Vincent Bolloré, (Groupe Bolloré), Bernard Arnault (LVMH), and François Pinault (Pinault-Printemps-Redoute).

[15] Stark (1996) uses this term to characterize the outcome of the privatization process in Hungary. The Hungarian state, financial institutions, private investors, and foreign corporations *jointly* own many privatized firms in Hungary after 1989.

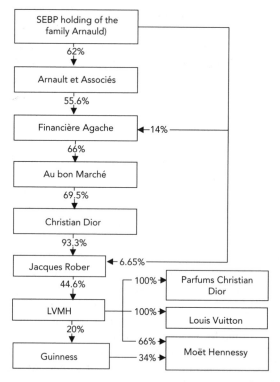

FIG. 4.1   *Holding company network (1996)*

'multilevel control network' (Fig 4.2). Within this network, smaller firms are linked to industrial groups (parent companies), and these groups are themselves connected with financial corporations. The second type of network is called the 'holding company network'. Within this network, entrepreneurs and family clans try to keep control over their patrimony which is threatened by economic concentration processes (mergers, hostile takeovers); this complex network structure also serves to conceal the underlying ownership relationships (see Fig. 4.3). Each network structure is now analyzed in more detail.

4.4.1. *Multilevel Control Network*

Morin (1994: 1459) has argued that within the capital networks of large French corporations *three levels of control* can be identified. At the lowest level, a parent company (e.g. Saint Gobain) holds a relatively high proportion of the share capital of its subsidiaries. Shareholdings are highly concentrated, and the mode of control is ownership. Morin terms this relationship 'relation de contrôle', and at this level, the French business group resembles the German combine (see Fig. 4.2, level III).

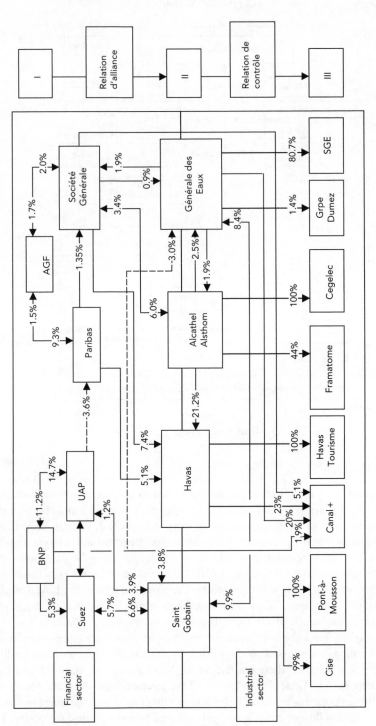

Financial Group II

Financial Group I

Financial sector

Industrial sector

Relation d'alliance

Relation de contrôle

I

II

III

FIG. 4.2 *Multilevel control network (1996)*

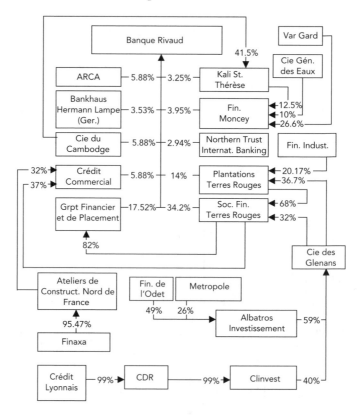

FIG. 4.3   *Who owns Banque Rivaud? (1995)*

At a second level, the different groups are linked to a financial network which is dominated by the large French financial corporations. These hold small to medium-sized shareholdings in the large (industrial) corporations (e.g. Paribas, BNP, UAP). One can see here that the groups are not isolated but integrated into a larger network at a higher level of integration. The core financial companies such as UAP and AGF (insurance companies) or Paribas and BNP (financial institutions) play the role of coordinators without being able to dominate the groups in which they hold a modest proportion of share capital. They coordinate their strategies and protect them from outside/foreign influence. Morin terms these links as '*relations d'alliance*'.

On the highest level, the large financial institutions (insurance companies, banks, financial holdings) are linked to each other by capital networks and interlocking directorates. For instance, there is a reciprocal shareholding between BNP and UAP and between Société Générale and AGF. These relationships structure the center (core) of the corporate network and Morin terms them as '*relations d'intermédiation*'. These connections do not exclude competition and ruthless contest for power. The cross-shareholdings may be interpreted as institutionalized forms of cooperation, but they are also a system of mutual hostages (Williamson 1985: 167).[16]

One may add even a fourth level to this hierarchical network structure: coordination at the top of this pyramid is exercised—more or less forcefully—by the French state bureaucracy. The links and coordination mechanisms between state and private industry may be described by such key concepts as *planification*, state ownership, and *pantouflage*.[17] The state is linked to some core groups, most of which are financial institutions which themselves coordinate the network on a lower level.

4.4.2. *Holding Company Network*

The expansion of large firms and their growing capital demands was one reason for the decease of family capitalism and the rise of managerial capitalism in the United States. In France, however, empirical evidence shows that a considerable proportion of the largest corporations are still controlled by individuals or family clans. How have these families been able to keep their firms under control and to defend them against merger operations and hostile takeovers? Most families use enigmatic holding structures to exercise a maximum of control with a limited amount of capital.

The owners construct complex networks, most of which have a pyramidal configuration: the parent company holds shares of its subsidiaries which in turn dominate smaller firms on a lower level. 'Holding companies issue shares to hold shares and other financial claims in industrial and financial companies' (Daems 1978: 18). These family networks consists of a cascade of intermediate holding companies[18] in which the family is frequently supported by an alliance with a financial institution.

Bernard Arnauld—son of Jean Arnault, former Président-Directeur Général (PDG) of the French group Ferret-Savinel (1947–76) and later PDG of the Société européenne de bâtiment—began his entrepreneurial career in 1978 as President of his father's group (Ferret-Savinel). In 1984, at the age of 35 years, he became PDG of the Financière Agache, and over a period of ten years he succeeded in capturing control over three of the most prestigious French companies producing luxury articles (Christian Dior, Louis Vitton, Moët Hennessy). The cascade of holding companies stretches over seven levels starting with SEBP (the family holding company) and Financière Agache and Au bon Marché at intermediate levels. This network configuration permits Bernard Arnauld to control 44.6 percent of LVMH—the direct holding company of

---

[16] For instance, in 1990, Paribas tried to gain control over the French group Compagnie de navigation mixte (hostile takeover). However, Navigation mixte itself held 12% of Paribas and could credibly threaten to take over Paribas. The 'coup' finally failed, and in the end, a German insurance company (Allianz) was in possession of Pariba's block shareholding in Navigation mixte. (*Source: Le Nouvel Economiste*, No. 732, Feb. 9, 1990, pp. 40–6, 'Paribas au milieu du gué'.)

[17] 'Pantouflage' denotes the transfer of a high state bureaucrat to a top management position in private industry (Bauer and Bertin-Mourot 1987: 175). It has also to be noted that the transfer of state bureaucrats to private industry is an important resource of social capital (Bourdieu 1989). In Japan similar career paths are called '*amakudari*' (Usui and Colignon 1995).

[18] 'The financial character of the holding company is sufficiently evident if the value of the portfolio is more than half the total assets' (Daems 1978: 13).

Dior, Vitton, and Hennessy. Integrated in the network as allies are Guinness (reciprocal shareholding) and the financial group Lazard (not shown in Fig. 4.1).[19]

The network shown in Fig. 4.1 presents a 'typical'[20] family holding which ensures control over a large corporation—without separating ownership and control. The cascade of holding companies permits the maximization of financial influence and to minimize capital expenditure. The control structures are complex and extremely difficult to disentangle for outsiders. The network integrates an individual entrepreneur (Arnauld), a large financial corporation (Lazard), and a foreign company (Guinness).

The network configurations shown in Figs 4.1–4.3 exhibit control patterns that resemble neither the diffused ownership structure of managerial capitalism nor the centralized family empire of the late nineteenth century. The network in Fig. 4.1 combines control through ownership (family) with financial control on the market for corporate control (the network has been restructured several times on the French market for corporate control between 1985 and 1995). The network in Fig. 4.2 shows overarching alliances in which state control, financial control, and managerial control are fused.

Despite some similarities in ownership structures and in network configurations between France and Germany, it has to be noted that the social mechanisms which have produced these structures are different in the two countries. In the case of Germany, capital networks and interlocking directorates are a complementary form of corporatist regulation, while in France, networks among competing firms have been stabilized by the state (nationalization, *pantouflage*). Whether these networks are likely to disintegrate as a consequence of privatization, the withdrawal of the French state, and the pressure of increased global competition is a controversial issue (Baudru and Kechidi 1998).

4.5. CAPITAL NETWORKS AND INTERLOCKING DIRECTORATES

Data analysis presented in this section concentrates on four variables which serve as indicators of the governance structure and the corporate networks in France: concentration of ownership, type of owner, core of network (interlocks), and intrasectoral networks. French data will be compared to those of the United States to illustrate structural differences between the two countries.[21]

4.5.1. *Concentration of Ownership*

Table 4.2 describes the ownership structure of French and US enterprises in terms of two features: proportion of stock owned and the type of owner. For the 500 largest French firms 1224 shareholders were identified, and for the 250 largest US firms

---

[19] Lazard had been an ally of Bernard Arnaud since 1985 when this financial group supported him in gaining control of the textile group Boussac Saint-Frères through the holding Financière Agache-Willot. In December 1996, Lazard withdrew from the Arnauld empire.

[20] Morin (1974) analyses similar network structures which were controlled in the 1970s by the Famille de Wendel (p. 41) and by the Famille Fould (p. 43).

[21] Data for the United States have been collected by Th. Brangs and F. Haver (University of Trier).

TABLE 4.2   *Distribution of stock ownership in France and the United States*

Type of owner	Proportion of stock owned (%)												Total (%)	
	−4.9		5–9.9		10–24.9		25–49.9		50–74.9		75⁺			
	F	US	F	US	F	US	F	US	F	US	F	US	F	US
Individuals/ families	15.5	0.8	14.4	8.4	23.2	21.7	21.7	56.5	30.3	—	13.4	—	18.0	1.8
Nonfinancial firms														
Domestic	14.2	0.1	16.1	—	17.3	—	25.2	14.0	21.2	—	17.0	—	17.0	0.1
Foreign	10.1	0.1	8.0	7.5	10.8	15.2	19.1	10.6	18.2	—	39.2	—	16.0	0.5
Financial firms														
Banks	20.8	19.2	17.2	10.8	15.1	9.1	13.0	—	10.1	—	11.3	—	16.3	20.4
Insurance	13.1	5.1	13.8	2.5	10.8	—	11.3	—	4.0	—	3.1	—	10.4	5.7
Funds	8.3	74.7	13.8	70.8	15.1	54.0	6.1	18.9	3.0	—	1.5	—	8.4	71.5
Public bodies	5.9	—	10.3	—	4.9	—	0.9	—	12.1	—	12.9	—	7.5	—
Auto-contrôle	5.0	—	2.9	—	1.1	—	0.9	—	1.0	—	0.5	—	2.7	—
Workforce	7.0	—	3.4	—	1.6	—	1.7	—	—	—	1.0	—	3.7	—
Total														
N=	457	5626	174	20	185	85	115	9	99	—	194	—	1224	5925
%=	37.3	95.0	14.2	3.5	15.1	1.4	9.4	0.1	8.1	—	15.8	—	100	100

Note: Unit of analysis: shareholdings (= proportion of stock).

France (F): N=1224; United States: N=5925 (only shareholdings larger than 0.5%). France: 500 largest firms (1995); US: 250 largest firms (1996).

Each column adds to 100%, which means that each column category (= size of shareholding) can be compared between the countries. For example, 457 holdings in France (= 37.3%) but 5626 in the United States (= 95%) make up less than 5% of company stock. In the case of France, these 457 holdings are distributed as follows: 15.5% to individuals/families, 14.2% to domestic nonfinancial firms, 10.1% to foreign nonfinancial firms, 20.8% to banks, 13.1% to insurance companies, 8.3% to investment funds, 5.9% to the government and other public bodies, 5.0% are classified as 'auto-contrôle', and 7.0% are owned by the workforce of the company. The bottom row adds separately for France and the United States to 100% and presents the percentage of holdings in each country falling within the respective share-size category. The two last columns give the proportion of shares in each country owned by the respective type of owner.

5925.[22] The concentration of ownership (last row) is much higher in France than in the United States. In France, 15.8 percent of all shareholdings are larger than 75 percent and only 37.3 percent of shareholders own less than 5 per cent of company stock. In the United States, 95 percent of shareholders own less than 5 percent of company stock, none owns more than 50 percent. The greater concentration of holdings in France means that in 293 French firms only one shareholder exercises effective control over the company, that is, about 59 percent of large French firms have a majority shareholder while none of the large US firms has a majority shareholder.

We assume that the higher the ownership concentration in the large corporation, the more likely is an *interpenetration* of managerial bureaucracy and ownership the dominant mode of control. And vice versa: the more diffused is the ownership, the

[22] We also controlled the ownership structure of the remaining 250 US firms on the Fortune 500 list, e. g. firms 251–500. Their ownership structure is similar to the structure shown in Table 4.2. We did not collect another 6000 owners to demonstrate it.

more likely is an independent management in power—unless the owners coordinate their behavior (e.g. coordinated action of pension fund managers).

4.5.2. *Type of owner*

The second structural difference concerns the type of owner. In France, 18 per cent of the 1224 shareholdings are owned by individuals, families, or a group of families. About 17 per cent of shareholdings are owned by nonfinancial (domestic) firms, 16 per cent by nonfinancial foreign firms. The financial sector (domestic and foreign combined) owns a total of 35.1 per cent of shareholdings. 'Auto-contrôle' denotes a circular structure of capital networks: large French corporations control about 2.7 per cent of their own stock via an intermediate financial holding (see Fig. 3.1(d)). In the United States, a total of 97.6 per cent are owned by the financial sector (last column); thus, ownership of large US corporations is concentrated—more or less completely—in the financial sector.[23]

We assume that the proportion of shareholdings owned by French families is underestimated. Many shareholdings are owned by obscure financial organizations the owners of which could not be identified.[24] Figure 4.3 gives an example of a complex capital network which can be found in many French companies. It is almost impossible to answer the question 'Who owns Banque Rivaud?' without having access to insider information.[25]

A comparison of the type of owners shows that in the United States and in Great Britain small shareholdings (fragmented ownership) are owned by the financial sector, particularly by investment/pension funds (see Chapter 3). In France, individuals and groups of families are a dominant type of owner (their proportion is higher than indicated in Table 4.2), while in Germany, most firms are owned by other nonfinancial firms (combine structure).

Data which have been presented for ownership structure illustrate that ownership structures have been transformed in different ways during the past hundred years. France, the United States, and Germany do not have a dominant ownership pattern in common; only Britain and the United States show similar structures of ownership. We assume that the higher the proportion of shares held by financial institutions, the more likely is the financial mode of control the dominant form of corporate governance.

4.5.3. *Core of Network (Interlocking Directorates)*

Table 4.3 contains a part of the matrix on interlocking directorates in France, namely that part with the highest network density. Clique analysis was used to identify a core

---

[23] For the United States, only shareholdings larger than 0.5% are given in Table 4.2. Therefore, all small shareholdings below this threshold are excluded from our data set. This bias does not affect our conclusions, because we are not interested here in the distribution of wealth, but in the control structure of large corporations.

[24] For instance, 'administration d'entreprises' or 'organismes de placement en valeurs mobilières'. We assume that the owners of many of these 'firms' are individuals or groups of families.

[25] We used the list of the 500 richest people in France to identify some of the family owners. 'Behind' the network of the Banque Rivaud we were able to identify two families (owners): Jean Bonin de la Bonninière (Comte de Beaumont) and Edouard de Ribes. *Source*: Challenges, Novembre 1996, pp. 89–160 (Les 500 français les plus riches).

TABLE 4.3   *Interlocking directorates—core component France*

	1	2	3	4	5	6	7	8	9	10	11	12	13	14	15
1	—	1	1	2	1	2		1	2	2	1	2	1		1
2	1	—	3	1	2	2	3	1	1		1	1	4	3	2
3	1	4	—	1	6	1	1	1	2	1	2	1	2	2	1
4	2	1	1	—	2	1		1	1	1	1	1	1	3	1
5	1	2	6	2	—	1	2	1	1	1	1	1	1	2	1
6	1	2	1	1	1	—		2	1	1	1	2	1	1	2
7	1	3	2	1	2	1	—	2	2	1	1	2	1		2
8	1	1	1	1	1	2	1	—	2		3	2		1	1
9	2	1	1	1	1	1	2	3	—	1	1	1	1		
10	2	1	1	1	1	1	1	1	1	—	1	1	1		
11	1	1	2	1	1	1		3	1	1	—	1	1		
12	1	1	1	1	1	3	1	2	2	1	1	—	2		
13		3	1	1	1	1	1		2	1			—	1	1
14	1	3	2	3	2	1		1			1	2	2	—	2
15		2	1	1	1	2	1						1	1	—

1 Groupe Paribas; 2 Générale des Eaux; 3 UAP; 4 Rhône Poulenc; 5 Saint Gobain; 6 CEP Communication; 7 BNP; 8 Crédit Commercial de France; 9 Elf Aquitaine; 10 Renault; 11 Galeries Lafayette; 12 Lafarge Coppée; 13 Alcatel Alsthom; 14 Société Générale; 15 Pinault-Print.-Redout.

Density: 1.28 *(all)*

Density: 0.87 *(binary)*.

Note: Table 4.3 shows directed and undirected relationships. The figures give multiple interlocking directorates between companies. For example: Saint Gobain (5) and UAP (3) have 6 common members on their 'conseil d'administration'.   Density (all) gives density computed on the basis of all directors which two companies have in common. In Density (binary) all multiple interlocks are counted as 1.

component of fifteen French firms with the highest density. The figures in the table are the sums of directed and undirected interlocking directorates. In France, the largest and most prestigious corporations are connected to each other by interlocking directorates (Swartz 1985). Paribas, Générale des Eaux, and UAP belong to this core group of firms. For instance, the same six directors sit on the 'conseil d'administration' both of Saint Gobain (5) and UAP (3). The fifteen firms constitute almost a clique in which all firms are connected to each other. Thus, France and Germany (see Chapter 3) are very similar with respect to the core component that includes financial as well as nonfinancial corporations.

In the case of the United States (and Great Britain) one can hardly speak of a core component, as the density of the network is substantially lower than in France, and the network does not show every degree of closure (clique) that is attained in the French network.

In Tables 2.1 and 2.2 it was shown that centrality coefficients are higher for the German and French networks than for the British and US network. Table 4.3 illustrates the hierarchical structure and status differentiation within the French network. The 'core' has a high visibility and involvement in network activities, while density is substantially lower in the periphery of the network. In Britain and in the United States, we could not identify a group of central firms being able to dominate the

TABLE 4.4 *Differences in network structure and corporate governance*

	Internal control[a]		External control[a]	
	France	**Germany**	**UK**	**US**
Concentration of ownership	High	Very high	Low	Very low
Type of owner	Families/ firms	Firms/ families	Financial sector	Financial sector
Overlap of networks	High	Very high	Low	Very low
% foreign[b]	18	13	8	1.3
Network configuration	Multilevel hierarchy	Star[c] (pyramid)	Inverse star[c]	Inverse star[c]

Note:

[a] The notion of internal/external control is explained in Franks and Mayer (1995).

[b] Percentage of shareholdings held by foreign individuals/firms.

[c] In the 'star' configuration there is a single central parent firm with numerous dependent subsidiaries (satellites). In the 'inverse star' configuration there are numerous (financial) institutions that own a single large corporation (fragmented ownership).

network. It is also to be noted that the French and German networks are not dominated by a *single* firm nor by a group of financial institutions (bank hegemony), but by a group of large interconnected financial and nonfinancial corporations.

4.6. CONCLUSIONS

Table 4.4 summarizes the major differences between France and Germany, on the one hand, and the United States and the United Kingdom, on the other. The model of shareholder value capitalism characterized the United States and the United Kingdom, where ownership is fragmented and dispersed. France and Germany, by contrast, lack such characteristic features; here one finds ownership to be relatively concentrated in the hands of nonfinancial enterprises and families rather than of investment funds.

The overlap of capital networks and interlocking directorates is relatively extensive in France and Germany, relatively uncommon in Britain, and virtually nonexistent in the United States (see Table 2.6). In the case of France and Germany, this overlap indicates the high degree to which corporate control is characterized by a combination of property rights and managerial bureaucracy. Large corporations which are often the owners of smaller firms are headed by executives who themselves sit on the supervisory boards of these dependent firms. Their power is based not only on bureaucratic control within the parent company, but also on property rights *vis-à-vis* the dependent firm. The overall network is controlled by a group of top managers who typically fulfill an executive function in one of the companies and a supervisory/proprietary function in others.[26]

---

[26] A detailed analysis of the combination of executive and supervisory functions is given in the following chapter.

While France and Germany appear largely similar in regard to this aspect of corporate control, there are a number of other aspects in which they differ substantially.
In Germany, the structure of networks is shaped by a corporatist tradition, whereas
in France, it rests on a bureaucratic elite the members of which hold positions in the
state administration as well as in large corporations.

As regards France, two types of networks have been differentiated in this chapter.
Figure 4.2 depicts a network that is integrated through several levels of hierarchical
coordination. At the highest level we find the state bureaucracy, which ensures the
control and internal integration of the network by means of two mechanisms: equity
participation by the state and *pantouflage*. As Bauer and Bertin-Mourot (1999) have
shown, the French elite is a relatively homogeneous body and comprised of persons
who have been socialized at a number of different institutions. They generally attend
an elite university, and many assume leadership positions in the state bureaucracy
before being named as chief executive officer of a large enterprise. The board of directors of the 'core' enterprises (Fig. 4.3) are largely controlled by members of this elite.

Figure 4.1 demonstrates a type of network in which the internal integration stems
from ownership and family relations. The network depicted here, however, hardly corresponds any longer to the traditional form of family capitalism. This network would
not be viable were it not for the support and active participation of the financial sector. The executive control exercised by the family in such networks is unstable and
fragile. The owners themselves can be replaced by a merger or a hostile takeover. When
this occurs, the company becomes subsumed under the aegis of a corporate network
(Fig. 4.2), and control over it passes to the network's central actors.

The mechanisms of social closure differ in the two types of networks. In the
corporate network, social closure results from selection processes based upon
bureaucratization, centralization, and meritocracy. The criteria for selection here are
basically those that are important for gaining access to elite universities. In the
second type of network, on the other hand, social closure follows lines of social background and economic capital. Here ascriptive characteristics play a major role in
obtaining the support of the financial sector, such as aristocratic titles and the
'symbolic value' attached to certain families. The presence of such considerations to
some extent shows the remnants of the social structure of the *ancien régime*.

The corporate type of network is of greater importance for the overall French
economy. Many expect the current privatization program of the French government
to produce changes in the network structures and its mode of control. The precise
nature of these changes, however, cannot necessarily be foreseen. Some social scientists predict that the network will soon be largely dismantled, and that its various
components will fragment.[27] While this scenario is certainly a possibility, we consider
it to be more probable that the network will reconstruct itself, and that this will take
two different forms.

---

[27] See 'La fin du capitalism à la française', in *Alternatives Economiques*, no. 160, June 1998, p. 28. The
data analyzed there are from LEREP, Toulouse.

A specific goal of the privatization program as drafted by the French government is to prevent complete disintegration of the network. Only a portion of the stock is floated on the market, with a relatively large proportion being sold to other French enterprises. In this way, the government has sought to promote stability in the ownership of the newly privatized companies and simultaneously to shield them against the threat of foreign influences (e.g. hostile takeovers). State control is to be replaced by self-regulation. Since the privatization program is not yet complete, it is too early to determine whether the government strategy has been successful.

Another way in which the corporate network could be protected from disintegration might be through the development of transnational networks. Of the four countries examined here, it is France which shows the greatest foreign participation in large enterprises (18 percent), with almost 70 percent of this coming from other countries in the European Union.[28] The 'globalization' of financial markets is clearly finding its first expression in the transnational capital networks and interlocking directorates *within* the European Union.

[28] A total of 252 participations have a non-French owner (18.2%). The distribution of these is: United States/Canada 19.8%; Western Europe (European Union, Switzerland, and Norway) 69.1 percent; Japan 9.1%. The highest proportions from European countries are Germany (13.5%), Switzerland (11.5%), and the Netherlands (10.7%). Some of the apparently foreign participations, however, are not genuinely so. E. g. several participations in French companies by *organismes de placement en valeurs mobilières* from Luxembourg very probably conceal French (family) owners.

PART II

ELITE NETWORKS

5

Elite Networks in Germany and Britain

5.1. CORPORATE NETWORKS VERSUS ELITE NETWORKS

Networks may be analyzed from two different points of view. First, they may be considered as a configuration of firms which are connected to one another by managers. The 'nodes' of the graph represent firms, and the 'lines' represent managers who connect pairs of firms.[1] This type of network was termed in previous chapters the *corporate network* (interlocks). Second, networks may also be considered as a configuration of managers who meet each other on the board of directors of large firms. In this case, the nodes of the graph are managers, and the lines represent boards of directors where managers meet. This type of network is termed here the *network of the economic elite*, the structure of which will be analyzed in this chapter.

5.1.1. *Who Belongs to the Elite?*

Before the elite network and the relationship between ownership and managerial control within this network can be examined in more detail, the question needs to be addressed as to who belong to the 'elite'. In elite studies, two selection criteria are usually referred to: positions and decisions.[2]

Modern societies are 'societies of organizations' in which important regulatory functions are performed by organizations (Presthus 1979). In the political system, these organizations include the political parties and the government bureaucracy, and in the economic system, the large corporations. Those who have successfully gained access to the formal positions of leadership in these central organizations belong to the elite; they dominate the dominant organizations (Giddens 1974). Because this study is limited to the economic system, according to this definition the

A first version of this chapter was published in *Leviathan* 25 (1997): pp. 76–106 and *Sociology* 32 (1998): 321–51. Reprinted by permission of Sage Publications Ltd from Windolf, P., 'Elite Networks in Germany and Britain', Copyright © BSA Publications Ltd, 1998. I gratefully acknowledge the advice of John Scott (University of Essex) and the research support of Maike Becker, Philip Herrey, Hanne Konz, and Thorsten Lange.

[1] In technical terms, there is an *incidence* matrix which contains in its rows agents (managers) and in its columns firms (meeting places). This incidence matrix can be transformed into two *adjacency* matrices. The first adjacency matrix contains firms which are listed in its rows and columns (corporate network); the second matrix contains agents (managers) who are listed in its rows and columns (network of the economic elite). Each of these three matrices contains the same set of information. See Scott (1991: 40–3), Wasserman and Faust (1994: 95, 150–3).

[2] Reputation is an additional selection criterion, but one which is not discussed here (cf. Giddens 1974).

members of the management and supervisory boards of the large corporations clearly belong to the 'elite'.

This selection criterion can be criticized for a lack of clarity in two dimensions: on the one hand it is too inclusive, as it assigns people to the elite who, while they hold positions of leadership, are mere figureheads who neither exert power nor participate in important decisions; on the other it excludes people on the lower hierarchical levels, although they have considerable power resources (e.g. information) at their disposal and are in a position to exert an indirect influence on decision making. Thus 'position' as a selection criterion is simultaneously too wide and too narrow: it includes people who should be left out and excludes people who actually belong to the elite (Pahl and Winkler 1974).

In the case of the second criterion, it is not positions but decisions that constitute the point of departure. The researcher selects suitable decisions taken within the political system or in large corporations and attempts to identify those who have had a decisive influence on the decision-making process. This circle of persons is then defined as the 'elite'. This selection criterion is subject to the criticism that power frequently manifests itself in the fact that certain alternatives are not admitted to the decision-making process. Economic or political elites interested in maintaining the status quo will ensure that alternatives are not placed on the agenda (Bachrach and Baratz 1970).

In this study it is the formal position within the large corporation that is adopted as the selection criterion. Selection on the basis of participation in important decisions is all but impossible to implement for a large sample in the economic sector due to the non-public nature of most of the decision-making processes. Although the objections to the 'position approach' are in principle valid, the critics have failed to provide an answer to the question why 'figureheads' are called upon to perform functions on managerial boards and—as will be shown later—remain in office for an extended period. If they were completely 'powerless' it would be expected that they would be forced out of their positions after a short space of time by a younger counter-elite.

The members of the elite network are those managers who occupy several posts on management and/or supervisory boards in large corporations and who, by virtue of these multiple boardships, are involved in a more or less intensive social contact with one another. Such managers are also termed 'multiple-directors' in the course of the study. This selection criterium shows that the positional approach was somewhat modified here: having one top-management position in a large corporation was not enough to be included in this investigation. Only managers who hold at least two leading positions and are thus a member of the elite *network* were selected for the analysis.

It is assumed here that the members of the elite network determine the dominant strategies of the large firms, they control the external relations of the firm to the political system and to other economic agents, for instance, to unions and business associations. On many occasions, these big linkers also influence the program of political parties and distinguish themselves as donors of universities and cultural institutions (Mizruchi 1992).

Approximately, 300 big linkers were identified in Britain and in Germany holding several positions in the largest corporations in each country. These managers meet each other several times a year on the board of directors/supervisory board of the large firms. They are able to build up a comprehensive and cohesive social network and to influence the strategic decisions of those firms which are a member of the corporate network (Stokman *et al.* 1985; Bearden and Mintz 1987).

It will be argued in this chapter that the resources on which the dominance of this economic elite is based are bureaucratic power, property rights, and social capital. The top managers do not only have a leading position within large corporations (bureaucratic power), but they also represent the owner *vis-à-vis* the dependent firm on whose supervisory board they sit (German combine structure). Thus, the economic elite is defined here not only by its relationship to the means of production,[3] or with respect to its technocratic competence or social capital (networks), but rather by the specific combination of *all* the relevant resources (Bourdieu 1984: 106).

Economic, cultural, and social capital are resources that are available in specific institutional forms and that can be accumulated and, under certain conditions, converted.[4] For instance, economic capital can be converted into cultural capital, as is illustrated by the cultural patronage practiced by large companies. What is important in this context is to show how *bureaucratic control* over a company is linked with *property rights* in the context of specific *network configurations*. These network configurations vary between countries and lead to differing forms of managerial control in Germany and Britain.

Thus managers base their dominance on a number of different resources and on various forms of legitimation, including bureaucratic power, property rights, and social capital. It is the combination of these various resources that enables managers to underpin their position of power. The following hypotheses show more precisely how different resources are combined: (1) executive and controlling functions on the Board of Directors; (2) managerial and ownership functions within a network of firms which are linked to one another by shareholdings (ownership) *and* by interlocks; (3) bureaucratic power and (4) social capital within the elite network.

Hypothesis 1   The institutional structure of German and British firms differ (board of directors in Britain; management board and supervisory board in Germany). Thus, it is to be expected that the structures of control will also vary between the two countries. Specifically, a clearer separation between nonexecutive (supervisory) and executive functions is to be expected in German firms, whereas in Britain, both functions are likely to be performed by one and the same person. The combination of executive and controlling functions gives more power to managers compared to a system where both functions are separated and embodied in different institutions.

Hypothesis 2   Germany is characterized by a relatively high concentration of ownership (combine structure), whereas the ownership structure in Britain is fragmented (institutional owners).[5] It is to be expected that in Germany, managers

---

[3] There are three types of relationship to the means of production: property (without control), control (without property), and property *and* control. The recombination of ownership and control is one of the important characteristics of shareholder-value capitalism.

[4] Cf. the discussion on the 'conversion' of political capital into economic capital in the transition countries of Eastern Europe (Szelényi and Szelényi 1995).

[5] See analysis of ownership structures in Germany and Britain in Chapter 3.

frequently combine executive functions with ownership functions, whereas this combination is encountered less frequently in Britain. In Chapter 2, it was shown that there is a high degree of overlap between the capital network and the interlocks in Germany (and France), but not in Britain. The top manager of one company—which is the shareholder of another company—usually sits on the supervisory board of the dependent company and represents the 'owner'.

Hypothesis 3   Elite networks serve to promote social integration and to consolidate positions of power (Useem 1984). Given its corporatist tradition (*Gemeinschaft*), it is to be expected that in Germany the network of multiple-directors will be both relatively diffuse and comprehensive and that all members of the economic elite are integrated into a single network. In the light of its liberal tradition (market), it is expected that in Britain the members of the elite are in competition with one another, and that there is evidence of separate social circles (pluralism).

Hypothesis 4   Networks are social institutions that offer their members both protection and opportunities on the market. The denser the network, the more stable it is over time and the longer its members can maintain their position in the network. Because of the higher density of the German network, we expect it to be more stable over time than the network of the British elite. It will be shown that a high proportion of German managers was able to keep their position within the elite/corporate network over a period of 10 years or longer (longitudinal analysis).

The following section describes the database for the subsequent analysis. In the ensuing sections, the four hypotheses are discussed.

5.2. THE SAMPLE

The point of departure for the empirical survey was a list of the 694 largest firms in (West) Germany and the 520 largest firms in Britain. For the German firms, each member of the management and supervisory boards was identified ($N=8952$). For the British firms, all the members of the boards of directors were listed ($N=4599$), whereby a distinction was drawn between executive and nonexecutive directors. The executive directors are roughly equivalent to the German management board (*Vorstand*) and the nonexecutive managers can, with certain reservations, be compared with the members of the supervisory boards (*Aufsichtsrat*). The German managers hold a total of 11,866 positions in the network of large firms, British managers 5258. The distribution of the managers across the positions indicates that in Germany, 83.1 percent of managers held just one position and 3.4 percent ($N=308$) more than four positions.[6] A comparison of the distributions of persons across positions reveals that on average German managers hold more positions than their British counterparts, so that the German elite network is more tightly woven than the British (Table 5.1).

---

[6] A study of multiple-directors carried out in Germany in 1981 presents an almost identical distribution as given in Table 5.1 (Biehler and Ortmann 1985: 5): 83.5% of German managers held only one position, 10.0% held two positions, and 6.5% held three or more positions ($N=5325$ managers; 330 largest German companies).

Table 5.1 *Managers and their positions in the elite network 1993*

Number of positions	G %	UK %
1	83.1	89.7
2	10.4	7.5
3	3.1	2.0
4+	3.4	0.8
Σ managers	8952	4599
Σ positions	11,866	5258
Σ companies	694	520

Note: G=Germany; UK=United Kingdom.

It is assumed here that the managers with the greatest number of high-ranking positions in the large firms form the core of the economic elite. Such persons are not merely a member of a board of a leading corporation, but by virtue of their seat on a number of supervisory boards can also exert an influence on decisions in other large firms. Because they have not just one, but several positions in institutions of corporate leadership, they collectively constitute a network that can be used to exchange information, as a means of control or co-optation, or to manage resource dependencies (Koenig *et al.* 1979).

For the purposes of this study, the elite network is defined as follows. In Britain, all managers holding three or more positions and half of those occupying two positions in the network were included in the analysis (N=302 multiple-directors). In Germany, managers holding four or more positions were selected for the network analysis (N=308). For the German and for the British managers, an adjacency matrix was drawn up into which all the formal relations held by these managers with each other were entered.[7] These include the different boards in which the managers from the various companies regularly meet.

The data were drawn from various handbooks and refer to 1993. Because managers clearly change their positions, a number of the positions are no longer held by the managers indicated here at the time of publication. This is true, for example, of the relationships portrayed in Fig. 5.1. No attempt has been made to bring the data up to date, as it is structures and not individuals that are the object of this analysis. Structures remain relatively stable while individuals come and go.

5.3. INTERDEPENDENT RELATIONSHIPS (HYPOTHESIS 1)

Even prior to the First World War, German legislation stipulated that executive and supervisory organs were to be separated in all joint stock companies. This institutional

---

[7] Each Board of Directors (supervisory board) is a meeting place for top managers coming from different firms.

structure provides for a clear functional division between the management board (*Vorstand*) and the supervisory board (*Aufsichtsrat*). The management board is the executive organ, the supervisory board the controlling organ; those managing the firm may not exercise a supervisory function, and those responsible for supervision may not manage the firm.[8]

In Britain, as in the US, there is no institutional division on these lines within large companies, merely a differentiation between roles: executive and supervisory managers sit together on one board of directors. The supervisory directors may originate from the firm itself (internal directors) or be recruited externally (external directors).[9] Internal directors face conflicts of loyalty in situations in which they are to supervise the activities of executive managers who are their superiors in the corporate hierarchy. Such cases lead to a dual—executive and supervisory—responsibility in the hands of one person: 'Several non-executives and chief executives commented on the awkwardness of having both chief executives and other executives on the board. In terms of the managerial hierarchy, the other executives were the chief's subordinate, but as directors they sat in judgement on his actions and two chief executives disliked this confusion of the line of command' (Hill 1995: 253).

In Germany, the institutional structure of corporate governance to some extent mirrors the division of powers within the political system. Firms are large-scale bureaucracies that are run by managers (agents), who pursue interests that differ from those of the owners (principals), and whose activities are to be monitored by shareholders and/or experts. It is, therefore, to be expected that a division of labor would develop within the German network between executive and nonexecutive (supervisory) managers: one group would thus be largely active on management boards, the other group performs the supervisory function as professional members of supervisory boards.

Characteristic of the group of multiple-directors studied here, however, is not the division of labor, but functional fusion (personal union): most managers occupy positions on both management and supervisory boards (are executive and nonexecutive directors), a phenomenon that applies to both Germany and Britain irrespective of the different institutional structures. Table 5.2 shows how even in the German system with its separation of supervisory and executive organs, there is little sign of specialization. Almost half (48.3 percent) of the managers holding two or more positions in the elite network are members of both a management and a supervisory board (in different firms). Thus hypothesis 1 cannot be confirmed.

Against this finding, it can be objected that a clear division of functions does prevail among those managers that are *not* examined in Table 5.2, namely those managers—around 7440 in Germany—holding only one position within the network and who are thus self-evidently either executive or nonexecutive managers, but not both. Although at first sight this argument appears convincing, it is not conclusive

---

[8] The various amendments of the German company law illustrate the historical evolution and the ensuing division of labor between executive and supervisory functions (Hommelhoff 1985).

[9] The 4599 British directors hold 5258 positions (see Table 5.1); 32.2% of these are held by external directors (nonexecutive). In a survey on large British corporations, a proportion of 44% is given (Hill 1995: 262).

TABLE 5.2   *Combination of executive and supervisory functions*

Position in company	G (%)	UK (%)
Executive and nonexecutive	48.3	53.4
Only executive	13.8	16.1
Only nonexecutive	24.6	∑ 30.5
Only nonexecutive, but former executive[a]	13.3	
Total	100%	100%

Note: Table 5.2 has been computed on the basis of *all* multiple-directors. G=Germany: N=1.118; UK=United Kingdom: N=474.

[a] 148 German managers (= 13.3%) are only members of supervisory boards (nonexecutive), but they had been executive managers earlier in their professional career; on reaching retirement age, they were elected into the supervisory board of their company. For Britain, comparable data are not available.

counter-evidence. The boundaries of a network are defined arbitrarily by delimiting a sample (such as the 694 largest firms). The survey method means that the network comes to an end at some point (Doreian and Woodard 1994). Consequently we cannot know whether these 7440 managers also hold additional executive and non-executive positions in smaller firms not examined here. And even if this is not the case, it is evident that the most influential directors holding positions in the largest and most reputable firms perform both functions simultaneously (albeit in different firms). Generally those holding more than one position within the elite network perform both executive and supervisory functions.

Thus, the fusion of functions that is forbidden in Germany at the level of the individual firm occurs in spite of this ban at the level of the network as a whole. The top managers of large firms are executive directors of their firm and members of the supervisory board of another. The supervisory board elects the members of the management board, but the supervisory board is composed to a greater or lesser extent of management board members of other large companies. As a collective the multiple-directors hold executive powers and at the same time are responsible for supervising this power.[10] At the level of the network as a whole it is no longer possible to distinguish between executive and nonexecutive managers. Most multiple-directors are electors and are elected, are supervisors and are supervised, and, as we will see in the next section, in Germany they are owners and at the same time are subject to owner control.

Discussions are under way in a number of countries on whether changes in institutional structures would enable executive managers to be subject to closer supervision. In the United States, for instance, it has been proposed that the supervisory function should primarily be performed by independent *external* directors.[11] In Germany, all

[10] This holds also true for the United States. It is estimated that in the Fortune 1000 US corporations about 63% of the external (nonexecutive) directors hold executive functions in the same 1000 corporations many of which are CEO positions. 'For the most part, directors form a relatively uniform pool' (Lorsch and MacIver 1989: 18–19).

[11] For an early critique of this institutional reform, see Brudney (1981). It is estimated that 70% of all directors in the Fortune 1000 US corporations are external directors; however, in about 80% of these

the supervisory directors are de facto external directors, but Table 5.2 illustrates that at the collective (network) level it is, nevertheless, not the division of labor but functional fusion that predominates. This recombination of functions at the network level can be explained in at least two ways, and these explanations are not mutually exclusive, but rather complement one another.

First, like the division of powers within the political system, the distinction between supervisory and executive functions in the economic system faces two problems: informational asymmetry and the lack of professional specialization. Independent supervisors recruited from other social systems (e.g. politics, academe or the cultural establishment) lack the information on a company required in order to supervise it adequately; in this respect they are at a disadvantage *vis-à-vis* internal management. Thus the fact that in both Germany and Britain (and the US) supervisors are recruited largely from within the network of executive managers can be explained with reference to the need to guarantee a minimum of information and professional competence.

A second explanatory approach emphasizes the hegemonic aspect: networks are instruments by means of which the position of the dominant elites are to be maintained. The network of multiple-directors serves to integrate and homogenize the managerial class and to stabilize their economic power. The link between the executive and the supervisory function closes the network to external competition and prevents the economic elite being subjected to external control.[12]

5.4. MANAGERS AS OWNERS (HYPOTHESIS 2)

Most of the large firms in Germany and Britain are owned not by families or individuals, but by other firms. For Germany, it was shown in Chapter 3 that nonfinancial firms are the dominant type of owner (combine structure). Within the combine, the dependent firms are frequently controlled by managers who represent the owner on the supervisory board. In the following, 'managers as owners' is used as an abbreviation for the fact that the leading managers of the dominant firm represent the owners and perform their supervisory function. Once a manager has attained a dominant position in a company that owns another firm, this position offers the opportunity to exert power not merely within the first company, but this manager can act as if he or she 'owned' the second company, supplementing bureaucratic power with the power of ownership.

Of the 308 managers in Germany belonging to the 'inner circle' of the economic elite, 139 of them occupy a position on the supervisory board of another company in which the corporation in which they are executive directors holds an equity stake. In other words, around 45 percent of the multiple-directors are executive managers of

corporations, the CEO still holds the powerful position of the Chairman of the Board (Lorsch and MacIver 1989: 2,17,19).

[12] This argument can be illustrated by the resistance put up against the German system of codetermination under which employee representatives hold positions on the supervisory board. The supervisory board is an important institution within the elite network. If employee representatives gain access to this organ they are in a position to interfere in the network 'from outside'. In view of this, informal meetings of the supervisory board are often held in which employee representatives do not participate.

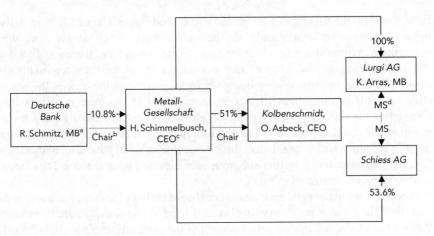

FIG. 5.1   *Managers as owners (1995)*

Notes: [a] MB: Member of the Management Board; [b] CEO: Chief Executive Officer;
[c] Chair: Chairman of the Supervisory Board; [d] MS: Member of the Supervisory Board.

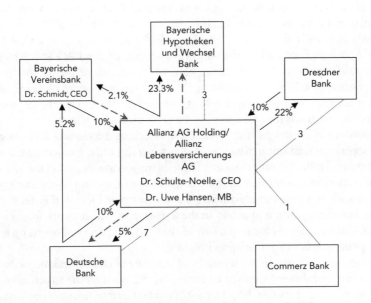

FIG. 5.2   *The core of the German finance sector (1996)*

Notes:
—2.1% ⟶ Capital ownership
- - - -▶ Interlocking directorate (directed)
········ 3 ······· Interlocking directorate (undirected).

Firm A and on the supervisory board of Firm B (and Firm C) in which Firm A also holds an equity stake. Firms B and C are themselves among the 694 largest companies in Germany. Within the network of leading German companies there are a total of 396 relationships in which an executive manager simultaneously represents the owner (i.e. is on the supervisory board).[13] In 96 percent of these cases the equity stake amounts to more than 10 percent. A total of 942 executive managers were counted in the dependent companies, of which 110 (= 12 percent) belong to the group of 308 multiple-directors. The 308 multiple-directors are not merely simultaneously executive and nonexecutive directors, some of them have also assumed the function of owner, and a further subgroup is subject to owner control. These interrelationships are illustrated in Fig. 5.1.

R. Schmitz is a member of the management board (MB) of Deutsche Bank and at the same time chairman of the supervisory board (Chair) of Metallgesellschaft. By virtue of the fact that Deutsche Bank owns 10.8 percent of the share capital of Metallgesellschaft, R. Schmitz represents on the supervisory board the interests of the largest shareholder and the interests of the creditor.[14] H. Schimmelbusch is CEO of Metallgesellschaft and the chairman of the supervisory board of Kolbenschmidt AG and represents in this firm the owner interest at a subordinate level in the chain of control depicted in Fig. 5.1. Schimmelbusch supervises the management board of Kolbenschmidt AG and, as the representative of the owner, he decides whether the shareholding (51 percent) in Kolbenschmidt AG is to be sold, retained or additional shares acquired. O. Asbeck is CEO of Kolbenschmidt and on the supervisory board of Lurgi AG and Schiess AG, where he, too, represents owner interests, namely the interests of the parent company (Metallgesellschaft). K. Arras, member of the management board of Lurgi AG and 'last man' in the chain of control belongs himself to the group of 308 multiple-directors: he, too, holds four positions in the network analyzed here.

The network of capital participation and interlocking directorates forms a system of interdependent relations in which managers supervise and are supervised, are owners and are controlled by other owners. Some managers are located at the end of the chain of control in one segment, but are at the head of the chain in another segment of the network. It is only those managers that are integrated within this network that can maintain their position of power in the longer term. The network forms a social institution that underpins the hegemony of the economic elite and opens up specific power opportunities to the managers involved.

Whereas Fig. 5.1 illustrates the hierarchical structure of control and ownership relationships in a multilayered German combine, Fig. 5.2 portrays the structure of interlocking relationships between the six largest (private) German financial institutes. This network can be described as follows: most of the leading banks are not directly linked, but all five banks are linked to the Allianz insurance company through both personal and capital linkages; the Commerzbank is the one exception here in which the link is

---

[13] The 139 managers are 'owners' in 396 cases, that is, there are approximately 2.9 ownership relationships per manager.

[14] In 1993, Metallgesellschaft received from Deutsche Bank a loan of appr. 540 mill. DM.

purely personal. The Allianz forms the center of a 'star' on which the banks are dependent, but on which they can also exert an influence (reciprocal shareholdings).

Although it is not possible to draw direct conclusions from network structures, it is extremely unlikely that the structural pattern shown in Fig. 5.2 emerged coincidentally: it is to be assumed that mutual coordination of capital stakes and the distribution of board positions has occurred, a coordination based on three principles: first, the Allianz largely protects four leading German banks from external influence (e.g. hostile takeovers); second, the banks themselves gain influence on the center in the form of positions on the supervisory board and reciprocal shareholdings; third, no one firm in this star configuration can dominate another. A further striking feature is that the interlocking directorates are redundant (Burt 1992: 21): there are a total of seven managers with positions on the supervisory boards of both Deutsche Bank and Allianz Insurance (two of which are employee representatives).[15] Germany's financial center has a network configuration similar to the Japanese '*keiretsu*' group. From a strategic point of view, the pattern of mutual control can also be interpreted as 'exchange of hostages' (Williamson 1985: 167).

As has already been shown, due to the often parallel capital and personal interlocks, there are a total of 396 relationships within the German network in which an executive manager represents the owner on the supervisory board of the dependent firm. There are only twenty such relationships in the British network. Reciprocal relationships such as those illustrated in Fig. 5.2 are entirely absent in the British system. On this point the researcher can merely conclude that network configurations that in Germany can be interpreted as hierarchical power relationships (Fig. 5.1) or as mutual control (Fig. 5.2) cannot be observed in the British system.[16] The British network is rather diffuse and, as will be shown in the next section, is focused on the financial sector. The parallel system of capital stakes and interlocking directorates only occurs in situations where ownership is highly concentrated. Such a strategy is difficult to realize in countries in which the structure of ownership is fragmented. This serves to confirm hypothesis 2.

5.5. SOCIAL CIRCLES (HYPOTHESIS 3)

The multiple-directors constitute a social network in which supervisors and the supervised are mutually linked at the collective level and in which the bureaucratic power of managers is linked with the power of ownership (in Germany). In this section, we will consider the question of whether the managers form a network in which each individual is connected with every other individual, or whether there are a number of separate cliques which, to take up a term coined by Simmel (1908), can be termed 'social circles'.

A social circle is defined as an informal social group which does not keep a list of members, which lacks formal (written) rules, and hierarchical structures or leaders. A social circle and its delineations are defined by the mutual relationships between its

---

[15] They received their supervisory board position on the basis of the German system of codetermination.
[16] In Chapter 4 (Fig. 4.1), it was shown that the French corporate network is to some extent hierarchically structured.

members. Individuals bound by close social relationships constitute a social circle, while those without contacts to these persons do not belong to the circle (Alba and Moore 1978; Kadushin 1995).

Useem (1984) has postulated that multiple-directors holding leading positions in several firms transcend the narrow horizons of firm-specific interests and represent the collective interests of large corporations as a whole. Due to the competing obligations placed upon them by their multiple boardships, they are forced to pursue 'global' interests shared by many large firms. If this hypothesis is correct, we would expect the network of multiple-directors to form a single large circle, the structure of which is relatively diffuse. The connections would not be restricted to separate groups of managers or corporate groups, but would be relatively open and unstructured and would encompass more or less all managers. In Germany, the trend to comprehensive social circles is reinforced by the traditions of corporatism and cartel organization.

An alternative hypothesis, one postulating a number of separate social circles can point to the following line of argument. The managers of the large corporations are subject to tough competition on the market for corporate control, irrespective of whether or not they produce competing products (Fligstein 1990). In the recent decades, the expansion of large corporate groups has been achieved largely through external growth, that is, by acquiring firms on the market for corporate control. Only those companies that are in a position to acquire other firms and thus to accelerate their own expansion have the chance of becoming and remaining one of the one or two hundred largest corporations in a country. These objective competitive relations between firms influence the structure of the elite network, splitting it up into social circles, the relationships between which are competitive in nature. In view of its liberal market tradition, it is expected that this network configuration predominates in Britain. In the following, these hypotheses will be examined in the light of the empirical data.

A matrix was drawn up for the 308 multiple-directors into which all the relationships were entered which these persons had with one another on the basis of their joint membership on the organs (Vorstand and Aufsichtsrat) of the 694 largest German firms. A similar matrix was drawn up for the 302 British multiple-directors. A number of statistical procedures were used in order to identify separate social circles (cliques) within these matrices:[17] block model analysis, clique analysis, cluster analysis, and factor analysis. Two criteria are decisive in evaluating the results: the density of the relationships *within* a group should be as high as possible, the density of the relationships *between* the groups should be as low as possible. The various procedures generated similar results. Tables 5.3 and 5.4 present the results of the factor analysis, as it was this procedure that met the two criteria most closely.

From the matrix of German managers, twenty factors were extracted which are interpreted here as 'social circles' (see Table 5.3). The density of relationship *within* these circles varies between 0.97 (DBV Holding) and 0.37 (Daimler-Benz/RWE; see column 3).

---

[17] The matrix for the German directors has $308 \times 308 = 94,864$ cells (adjacency matrix, directors-by-directors). It is symmetrical as it contains only undirected relationships: if A meets B on a supervisory board, then B meets A there. Thus, there are a total of $(308 \times 307)/2 = 47.278$ possible relationships. Of these 7.8% are actually realized in Germany (3690 dyads). In the matrix of British managers, the density is 2.0% (897 dyads); see Table 5.7.

TABLE 5.3   *Social circles of managers in Germany*

Social circle	Director	Positions	Density	Combine %	Executive %	Super-visory %	Variance %	1978–82
	1	2	3	4	5	6	7	8
1 DBV-Holding[a]	12	70	0.97	95.7	74.3	25.7	5.1	6
2 Daimler-Benz	21	120	0.94	71.6	17.5	82.5	5.7	5
3 Metallges./ Allianz[a]	11	61	0.91	65.5	21.3	78.7	3.3	4
4 Thyssen	15	95	0.69	61.0	16.8	83.2	3.6	6
5 VEBA	15	91	0.76	57.1	25.3	74.7	3.9	3
6 RWE	11	81	0.80	56.7	17.3	82.7	2.6	2
7 Hoesch-Krupp/ ABB	11	62	0.75	54.8	17.8	82.2	1.7	2
8 Dillinger Hütte/ Volksf.[a]	8	36	0.82	50.0	25.0	75.0	1.4	0
9 Mannesmann	12	83	0.64	49.4	9.7	90.3	2.1	4
10 Stora/ Metallgesellsch.	11	58	0.80	46.5	18.9	81.1	1.8	2
11 Ruhrkohle/ Allianz[a]	13	78	0.53	37.1	14.1	85.9	2.1	4
12 Kaufhof (Metro)/Asko	12	53	0.56	35.8	15.1	84.9	1.5	3
13 Victoria-Vers.[a]/ Hoechst	12	62	0.42	29.0	19.4	80.6	1.4	4
14 MAN	15	91	0.60	26.3	15.4	84.6	2.3	4
15 VIAG/ Bayernwerk	14	79	0.51	25.3	13.9	86.1	1.5	6
16 Preussag/VW	10	56	0.84	25.0	14.3	85.7	1.6	4
17 Daimler- Benz/RWE	18	100	0.37	20.0	11.0	89.0	1.9	0
18 BHF Bank[a]/ Babcock	13	64	0.89	18.7	9.4	90.6	2.8	6
19 Dresdner B.[a]/ Fam. Quandt	21	122	0.54	11.4	13.2	86.8	2.2	6
20 Deutsche Bank[a]/ Siemens	24	148	0.57	10.8	13.5	86.5	3.1	8
Total/average	279	1610			18.3	81.7	51.5	79

Note: [a] Financial institution (bank, insurance company). *Social circle*: The group of managers (= social circle) was named after the firm/combine in which many of them hold positions on the management/supervisory board. *Director*: Number of directors in social circle (total number of directors: 279). *Position*: Number of positions which are held by directors in this social circle (total number of positions: 1610). *Density*: Density within the social circles. *Combine*: Proportion of positions held in combine. *Executive*: Proportion of executive positions (positions on the management board). *Supervisory*: Proportion of nonexecutive positions (positions on the supervisory board). *Variance*: Proportion of variance explained by this factor (=social circle); total variance explained 51.5%. *1978–82*: Number of directors who belonged to the same social circle back in 1978–82.

The relationships *between* the circles is described in Table 5.5. The highest densities between two circles are 0.22 (circle 2 with circle 17) and 0.20 (circle 3 with circle 10).

The core of a circle is often formed by a group of managers connected with a single corporate group (e.g. Daimler-Benz, Thyssen, RWE, etc.), which is then used as the name of the circle. The twenty-one managers (column 1) assigned to social circle no.

TABLE 5.4   *Social circles of managers in the United Kingdom*

Social circle	Director	Positions	Density	Firm/group %	Executive %	Nonexec. %	Variance %
	1	2	3	4	5	6	7
1 Trafalgar House	9	26	0.50	34.6	50.0	50 0	1.7
2 BBA/Securicor Group	9	24	0.44	33.3	45.8	54 2	1.5
3 Charter Consolidated	10	25	0.42	32.0	20.0	80 0	1.4
4 Bank of Scotland[a]/Stand. Life[a]	9	23	0.56	26.0	26.1	73 9	2.0
5 Legal & General[a]/Bowater	12	31	0.52	25.8	19.4	80 6	2.2
6 Lloyds Bank[a]/Boots	10	24	0.33	25.0	45.8	54 2	1.2
7 Barclays Bank[a]	12	34	0.48	23.5	20.5	79 5	2.0
8 General Accident[a]/Roy.Bk.Scot.[a]	11	26	0.47	23.0	15.4	84 6	1.8
9 HSBC Holdings[a]/Sears	14	40	0.34	22.5	47.5	52.5	1.7
10 Kleinwort Benson[a]/Abbey Nat.[a]	8	23	0.50	21.7	39.2	60.8	1.3
11 Guard. Royal Exch.[a]/Hambros[a]	15	37	0.39	21.6	43.3	56.7	2.3
12 Nat. Westminster Bk.[a]/Hanson	16	43	0.46	20.9	30.3	69.7	2.6
13 Enterprise Oil	10	26	0.40	19.2	34.7	65.3	1.6
14 Warburg[a]/United Biscuits	12	33	0.42	18.1	36.4	63.6	1.6
15 Prudential[a]	11	28	0.33	17.8	17.9	82.1	1.4
16 Inchcape/Shell Transp.	14	40	0.35	15.0	35.0	65.0	1.7
17 Rank Org./Westland Group	12	36	0.33	13.8	33.4	66.6	1.2
18 T&N	8	22	0.32	13.6	18.2	81.8	1.2
19 British Aerospace	14	38	0.30	13.1	36.8	63.2	1.2
20 Grand Metropolitan/BOC	13	34	0.31	11.7	38.2	61.8	1.5
Total/average	229	613			33.1	66.9	33.2

Note: [a] Financial institution. *Social circle*: the group of managers (=social circle) was named after the firm/group in which many of them hold positions on the board of directors. *Director*: number of directors in social circle (total number of directors 229). *Density*: density within the social circles. *Position*: number of positions which are held by directors in this social circle (total number of positions 613). *Firm/group*: proportion of positions held in core firm/group. *Executive*: proportion of executive positions. *Nonexecutive*: proportion of nonexecutive positions. *Variance*: proportion of variance explained by this factor (=social circle); total variance explained 33.2%.

2 (Daimler-Benz) hold a total of 120 positions, (column 2); each member occupies 5.7 positions on average. Of these 120 positions, 71.6 percent are held within the Daimler-Benz combine itself (column 4), whereby the combine includes any firm in which the Daimler-Benz Holding has a stake of at least 50.1 percent. The periphery of the circle consists of managers from a large number of other firms who occupy positions on

TABLE 5.5   *Relationship between social circles (density)*

Germany

	1	2	3	4	5	6	7	8	9	10	11	12	13	14	15	16	17	18	19	20
1	—	0.00	0.02	0.01	0.00	0.09	0.01	0.00	0.01	0.00	0.02	0.01	0.01	0.03	0.01	0.00	0.06	0.00	0.00	0.00
2	0.00	—	0.05	0.02	0.02	0.02	0.04	0.02	0.04	0.01	0.02	0.01	0.01	0.03	0.11	0.07	0.22	0.06	0.04	0.07
3	0.00	0.00	—	0.01	0.00	0.16	0.02	0.06	0.06	0.20	0.05	0.02	0.04	0.07	0.03	0.03	0.09	0.03	0.10	0.12
4	0.00	0.00	0.00	—	0.06	0.16	0.04	0.05	0.12	0.08	0.11	0.01	0.02	0.09	0.01	0.15	0.06	0.11	0.03	0.12
5	0.01	0.00	0.02	0.03	—	0.05	0.06	0.04	0.11	0.02	0.18	0.01	0.06	0.08	0.10	0.18	0.07	0.13	0.10	0.14
6	0.00	0.01	0.00	0.00	0.02	—	0.03	0.05	0.17	0.02	0.19	0.01	0.03	0.15	0.03	0.15	0.14	0.07	0.13	0.11
7	0.00	0.00	0.00	0.06	0.03	0.02	—	0.01	0.03	0.05	0.13	0.01	0.05	0.02	0.01	0.12	0.03	0.13	0.07	0.02
8	0.00	0.00	0.00	0.01	0.00	0.00	0.05	—	0.06	0.02	0.13	0.00	0.01	0.03	0.04	0.00	0.02	0.12	0.03	0.10
9	0.00	0.00	0.01	0.00	0.00	0.00	0.02	0.00	—	0.04	0.04	0.01	0.10	0.04	0.04	0.08	0.07	0.16	0.12	0.09
10	0.00	0.00	0.00	0.03	0.00	0.03	0.00	0.03	0.00	—	0.00	0.04	0.04	0.10	0.00	0.00	0.00	0.04	0.05	0.08
11	0.00	0.00	0.03	0.04	0.00	0.01	0.04	0.00	0.00	0.00	—	0.02	0.03	0.06	0.03	0.09	0.03	0.04	0.04	0.05
12	0.01	0.00	0.01	0.00	0.01	0.00	0.00	0.03	0.05	0.01	0.02	—	0.01	0.03	0.01	0.00	0.02	0.00	0.04	0.05
13	0.00	0.00	0.00	0.00	0.03	0.00	0.01	0.01	0.01	0.03	0.02	0.03	—	0.03	0.04	0.03	0.07	0.04	0.04	0.03
14	0.00	0.00	0.00	0.01	0.01	0.00	0.04	0.00	0.00	0.02	0.00	0.03	0.04	—	0.09	0.06	0.07	0.09	0.10	0.14
15	0.01	0.00	0.00	0.00	0.01	0.01	0.02	0.03	0.03	0.01	0.00	0.01	0.04	0.04	—	0.09	0.04	0.03	0.06	0.09
16	0.01	0.00	0.00	0.01	0.00	0.03	0.03	0.00	0.01	0.00	0.00	0.02	0.00	0.02	0.01	—	0.03	0.08	0.10	0.12
17	0.00	0.01	0.01	0.00	0.02	0.00	0.03	0.00	0.00	0.02	0.01	0.01	0.02	0.01	0.02	0.00	—	0.02	0.06	0.11
18	0.00	0.01	0.00	0.00	0.01	0.00	0.01	0.00	0.00	0.02	0.00	0.00	0.00	0.00	0.00	0.00	0.00	—	0.04	0.05
19	0.00	0.00	0.01	0.02	0.02	0.00	0.07	0.00	0.01	0.01	0.01	0.04	0.02	0.02	0.03	0.01	0.04	0.03	—	0.09
20	0.00	0.00	0.00	0.00	0.00	0.02	0.03	0.04	0.02	0.03	0.01	0.01	0.02	0.02	0.01	0.02	0.01	0.01	0.01	—

United Kingdom

Note: Tables 5.3 and 5.4, column 2 show density *within* social circles; this table shows density *between* social circles. The right-hand part of the matrix (above diagonal) shows the relationship (density) between social circles in Germany; the left-hand part of the matrix (below diagonal) shows the relationship (density) between social circles in the United Kingdom. Example: The density between the social circles 3 (Metallgesellschaft/Allianz) and 6 (RWE) amounts to 0.16; the density between the social circles 19 (British Aerospace) and 7 (Barclays Bank) amounts to 0.07. In the right-hand part of the matrix (Germany), 17 fields are empty (=0), that is, there is no link between the social circles; in the left-hand part of the matrix (United Kingdom), 89 fields are empty (=0).

supervisory boards alongside managers from Daimler-Benz. Of the 120 positions, 17.5 percent are on management boards, 82.5 percent on supervisory boards (columns 5 and 6).

The social circle 'Deutsche Bank/Siemens' consists of twenty-four managers in all, who together occupy 148 positions in the elite network (an average of 6.2 positions). Of these 148 positions, however, just 11 percent are in firms belonging to the Deutsche Bank combine (column 4); the remainder are held in other firms.

These two examples illustrate the fact that the social circles within the elite network are structured in different ways. Two types of social circle can be distinguished.

5.5.1. *Integration Networks*

In the 'Daimler-Benz' social circle (and in other circles exhibiting a high percentage value in column 4), a large proportion of the positions are held within the combine itself. Moreover, the interrelationships within these circles tend to be very dense (e.g. density in the Daimler-Benz circle 0.94; Metallgesellschaft 0.91; column 3). The high density means that within these combine-centered circles almost every manager is in direct contact with virtually all other members.[18] These circles are inwardly oriented, their aim is integration within the group. Their structure is less suited to maintaining contacts to the external environment or to obtaining information on other firms. This does not mean that such circles consist solely of managers from the combine itself, although in such circles the number of managers from other firms is relatively small. The fact that even here the 'world outside' is not neglected is shown, among other things, by the presence within the 'Daimler-Benz' circle of two politicians from the State of Bavaria.

5.5.2. *Cosmopolitan Networks*

These networks are characterized by the fact that only a small proportion of the positions are held within the combine and by a lower internal density. In such networks, managers occupying positions in a large number of firms/combines meet. They are frequently dominated by managers from the banking sector (Deutsche Bank, Dresdner Bank, etc.). The aim of these networks is to procure information, particularly those relevant to the careers of banking and finance managers. Their positions on supervisory boards provide them with insider information on firms in receipt of large-scale loans or in which the banks hold a significant equity stake.

In Table 5.3, the social circles (factors) have been ranked according to the number of positions held within the dominant combine (column 4). The top position on this criterion is held by DBV Holding (95.7 percent); Deutsche Bank/Siemens brings up the rear with (10.8 percent). The classification into integration and cosmopolitan networks is based on the two terminal points of a continuum, and Table 5.3 (column 4) shows clearly that the borderline between them is fluid.

---

[18] The correlation coefficient (r) between the proportion of positions held within the combine (column 4) and the density within the social circle (column 3) is 0.67 ($N=20$).

The network of the British economic elite was also examined for evidence of separate social circles. The results of the factor analysis are summarized in Table 5.4. Comparing these results with those for the German economic elite, three central structural differences emerge. First, the density *within* each circle is substantially lower than in Germany. This finding reflects the generally lower density of relationships within the British economic elite. Second, the proportion of positions held within the corporate group is lower. This implies that the social circles in Britain are less centered around a single corporation, encompassing managers from different corporate groupings.[19] Third, in the majority of British social circles it is a financial corporation that forms the central core; this is true of eleven of the twenty circles.

While the financial networks (cosmopolitan) in Germany and Britain are structured in similar fashion, integration network patterns do not exist in Britain. The highest percentage figure in column 4 (proportion of positions held within the dominant group) amounts to 34.6 percent in Britain (Trafalgar House). In Chapter 3, it was shown that the combine is a predominant mode of intercorporate relationship in Germany, but not in Britain. These differences are reflected in the structure of the elite network.

This section concludes with a discussion of whether the structural data analyzed so far offer evidence that the German or British economic elite is decomposing into competing groups. The findings presented in Tables 5.3 and 5.4 reveal at first sight an unambiguous structural pattern: the economic elite, defined here as the set of multiple-directors, can be decomposed into relatively clearly delimitated social circles within which the density of interrelationships is relatively high, between which this density is rather low. This finding points to separate elite groups belonging to different corporate groupings and in competition with each other regarding the position and prestige of their respective firms. On the other hand, the structure also shows that the various social circles are not completely isolated from one another, but that reciprocal links between them exist, although the density of such links is lower. Of the total of 190 possible linkages between the twenty social circles in Germany,[20] only seventeen are not utilized (see Table 5.5; 17 cells=0). On average, virtually every circle is linked to all the others through two, not infrequently three or more people. Information exchange, control, and dependency exist between the circles. It seems appropriate to term this sort of competition 'controlled competition'. The competing groups are embedded in a cooperative system that permits competition (separate circles), but which at the same time provides the institutional framework required to put forward common interests *vis-à-vis* the outside world (linkages between the circles).

---

[19] For Britain, the correlation coefficient (r) between the proportion of positions held within the dominant group and the within-density of social circles (correlation of column 3 with column 4) is 0.64 ($N=20$) and is thus almost as high as in Germany.

[20] Between the 20 social circles there are a total of $(20 \times 19)/2 = 190$ possible relationships (see Table 5.5). The factors (social circles) were regrouped with the help of cluster analysis in order to determine whether or not larger social circles, composed of subgroups of the 20 social circles, exist. The findings were unstable, however, and are not discussed further here.

Elite Networks

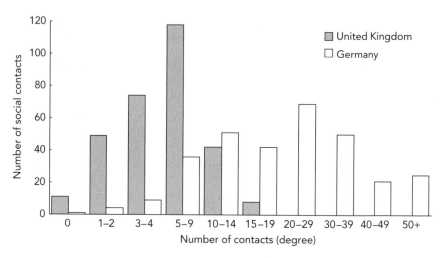

FIG. 5.3 *Frequency distribution of social contacts (1993)*

In Britain, the majority of social circles are not linked to one another; of the 190 possible linkages 91 are not in use (cells=0). Whereas in Germany virtually every competing circle is linked to all the others, most of these groupings in Britain are isolated. Networks are institutionalized forms of communication, control, and co-optation. The structure of the networks in Britain exemplifies the fact that the market order there is regulated to a greater extent by competition than in Germany.

The difference between the two networks is also evident in the frequency distribution of degrees (see Fig. 5.3). In Germany, twenty-five managers have a degree of fifty or higher,[21] in the British network, the highest degree is 18. The degree denotes the number of multiple-directors any manager meets on the different Boards of which he or she is a member (marginal distribution of the adjacency matrix). German managers meet more multiple-directors in the network than their British counterparts.

5.6. THE STABILITY OF SOCIAL CIRCLES (HYPOTHESIS 4)

The analysis of interlocking directorates presented in the previous section has frequently been criticized by claiming that the 'meaning' of such relationships is unclear (Stinchcombe 1990). What does it really mean when two people over a period of 1 year attend between two and four supervisory board meetings together? Indeed, have they ever communicated directly with one another? Do they coordinate their voting behavior on the supervisory board? Do they represent similar political interests? These and similar questions cannot be answered on the basis of the data analyzed here. What we

---

[21] Dr. Röller, former CEO of Dresdner Bank, has the highest degree in the German network: he meets 78 multiple-directors on the different Boards of which he is a member. For Germany, the mean of the degree frequency distribution is 24.0, for Britain 5.2 (see Frank 1981: 113). The degrees range from 0 to 78 in Germany and from 0 to 18 in Britain.

can do, however, is to determine whether two people who met regularly on a supervisory or management board in 1993 were linked 10 years earlier through an interlocking directorate. This addresses the issue of the stability of the networks.

If the members of an elite network change rapidly (elite circulation; Pareto 1968) or if with every change of board position the manager joins another social circle, there is little chance that such interlocking directorates will develop into stable social relationships. They would be more comparable to accidental encounters, the importance of which should not be overstated. If, on the other hand, it can be shown that many managers holding several positions within the elite network in 1993 were part of the network 10 years earlier, and perhaps were even in contact with the same individuals, such interpersonal relationships could no longer be seen as merely chance meetings.

During a period of 10 years, numerous elections to the supervisory board (Board of Directors) are held in each firm, and the term of contract of all management board members has repeatedly expired. If, in spite of this, the network consists of the same individuals, this stability indicates a high degree of social integration. Even if these relationships originally derived from resource dependencies between firms, it seems plausible to assume that over such a long period they would be transformed into social relations which have reinforced the integration and normative homogeneity of the social group.

Once again the starting point for the analysis is the set of members of the economic elite holding several positions in the 1993 network (308 German managers; 302 British managers, see Table 5.1). For these individuals, a list was made of all the positions (management and/or supervisory board) occupied between 1978 and 1982 using the handbooks available for these years. Subsequently, a matrix was drawn up into which all the relationships between these persons (by virtue of their position as management or Board members) during the period 1978–82 were listed. This matrix was again analyzed with the help of factor analysis in order to determine which social circles existed a decade ago, and the extent to which they overlap with the social circles identified in 1993.

In the following analysis, a distinction is drawn between two types of 'stability': the stability of positions and the stability of relationships (dyads). We can first ask whether a manager held a position on the boards of one of the 694 largest firms in Germany 10 years ago (or earlier). If this is the case, it is an example of 'stability of position'; if, in addition, this position is within the same combine, it is termed 'combine stability' (Table 5.6). The stability of relationships cannot be calculated at the individual level as an individual may have many relationships of which some are stable and others not. Consequently, such stability is calculated on the basis of dyads: the question addressed here is what proportion of the dyads making up the elite network in 1993 were in existence 10 years ago (or earlier) (Table 5.7).

We begin with the analysis of positional stability as this is a precondition for stable dyads. Managers who did not occupy a position on a management/supervisory board (Germany) or Board of Directors (Britain) 10 years ago do not belong to the elite network and were not included in the matrix for 1978–82. Relationships, as

TABLE 5.6   *Stability of positions: Germany and United Kingdom*

	Germany	**UK**
Combine stability	59.1	
Stability of position	14.7	$\sum$ 43.1
Employee representatives	4.3	—
Lower level position[a]	5.9	
No information	16.0	$\sum$ 56.9
	100%	100%

Note: Germany $N=308$; United Kingdom (UK) $N=302$. $\sum$: for British managers no distinction was made between 'combine stability' and 'stability of position'. Among the 308 German multiple-directors, there are 13 ($=4.3\%$) who hold four or more positions as employee representatives on supervisory boards (German system of codetermination). These representatives are not analyzed here.

[a] These German managers had been working between 1978 and 1982 in the same combine or in a company which belongs to the 694 largest ones in Germany, but on a lower hierarchical level, that is, they did not yet have a position on the management/supervisory board. For Britain, this distinction was not made because appropriate data are not available.

TABLE 5.7   *Stability of dyads*

	1993		**1978–82**	
	G	**UK**	**G**	**UK**
Dyads	3690	897	1481	203
Density(%)	7.8	2.0	3.1	0.4
Average/manager	12.0	3.0	4.8	0.7
Stable dyads 1978–93				
Stable dyads	667	32	—	—
Average/manager	2.2	0.1	—	—

Note: Germany (G): $N=308$; United Kingdom (UK): $N=302$.

defined here, exist only by virtue of Board membership of the 694 (520) largest firms in Germany (Britain).

As can be seen from Table 5.6, almost 60 percent of all German managers held a board position 10 years ago in the combine in which they held these positions in 1993 (combine stability). Almost 15 percent of the managers were on a management or supervisory board 10 years ago, although in a large corporation different from that in which they held the position in 1993 (positional stability). Thus, a total of 73.8 percent of the German managers held a management or supervisory board position 10 years ago, either in the same combine or in another large firm. For British managers, no distinction between the two types of stability was made because the combine is not a dominant network structure in Britain. Of the 302 British managers,

43.1 percent were members of the Board of directors in one of the 520 largest firms between 1978 and 1982. Thus the stability of managers within the network of the largest British firms is considerably lower compared to Germany.

An age-shift effect must be taken into account in evaluating this figure. In 1993, around 7 percent of the managers were aged less than 50; 10 years earlier, they were therefore under 40. Yet it is only seldom that managers join management or supervisory boards of large corporations before the age of 40. The youngest cohort of the managers could not belong to the elite network in 1978–82 simply because they were too young at the time. If this cohort is subtracted from the group of multiple-directors (308−22), a total of 286 managers could potentially have belonged to the elite network 10 years earlier. Of these, 227 or *c.*79 percent were stable. Similar considerations apply to the younger cohorts of British managers.

Thus, as a preliminary result, one is forced to the conclusion that in Germany the members of the economic elite attain their leading positions (on management or supervisory boards) at an average age of around 45, where they then remain for a relatively long period, as a rule until retiring from an active managerial function (management board). This does not mean that the same position is held throughout, but merely that a manager obtaining a position on the management or supervisory board of one of the 694 largest German firms is very likely to be occupying a leading position of this type in one of these firms 10 years later. This stability is considerably lower in Britain. Table 5.6 shows that combine stability explains most of the overall stability of the German management and this specific network structure is less important in Britain.

Though the financial press frequently reports that managers or chairmen of supervisory boards were fired this is only the first part of the story. The way in which such a career then continues is not usually reported on. On many occasions board members lose their position in a large corporation—for whatever reasons—and within just a few months they join the board of another large corporation, a move mediated by networks which we have described elsewhere as the 'extended internal labor market' (Windolf and Wood 1988). Table 5.6 shows that this is far from an exceptional case, but rather the rule.

Let us now consider the stability of the dyads. The German elite network of 1993 consisted of a total of 3690 dyads (897 in Britain); in other words, between the 308 managers constituting the network there are a total of 3690 relationships (*c.*12 relationships per manager). The density of this network is 7.8 percent (2.0 percent in Britain). The German elite network of 1978–82 consists of a total of 1481 dyads (203 dyads in Britain); this means that between the same 308 managers, a total of 1481 relationships existed back in 1978–82 (*c.*4.8 relationships per manager). The density of the 1978–82 network was 3.1 percent (0.4 percent in Britain). The lower panel of Table 5.7 shows the stable dyads, that is, those dyads that existed in 1993 *and* in 1978–82. The difference between Germany and Britain can be seen in the following relationship: in Germany, 3690 dyads existed in 1993 of which 667 could be identified in 1978–82 (=18 percent); there existed 897 dyads in Britain in 1993 of which only 32 could be identified in 1978–82 (=3.6 percent). Of the twelve relationships held on average by each German manager in 1993, 2.2 dated back 10 years (or longer). The respective figures for Britain are 3.0 and 0.1.

A summary interpretation of these results, one that clearly holds only at the average level, runs as follows: each of the 308 German managers making up the 1993 network was linked with 12 other managers from this group.[22] On average he/she has known somewhat more than two of these twelve managers for more than 10 years. This interpretation can be taken a stage further: in the period 1978–82, a total of 1481 dyads were registered; 667 of them remained stable. The remaining dyads (=814) constitute a *virtual* network, consisting of 'distant acquaintances' (Wegener 1987) that a manager met sometime back on a management or supervisory board (2.6 per manager). Contact can be reestablished with some of these if the need arises. The virtual network raises the density of the interrelationships of the current (1993) network. There is only a small virtual network among the British managers.[23]

In the same way as the 1993 matrix, the 1978–82 matrix of interrelationships was examined with the help of factor analysis in order to identify social circles. Once again twenty factors were extracted. As can be seen from Table 5.3, a total of seventy-nine managers belonged to the corresponding circles back in 1978–82 (column 8). For instance, of the twenty-one managers assigned to the 'Daimler-Benz' social circle in 1993, five managers belonged to it back in 1978–82. On average, 28 percent of the managers had been in the same social circle 10 years earlier.

For Britain, we were not able to identify stable social circles because of the small proportion of dyads that remained stable over a 10-year period. Of the 302 British managers in the sample, only 86 could be identified to meet at least one of their colleagues on the Board of Directors during the period 1978–82.[24] Table 5.8 at the end of this chapter shows that British managers belonged to different social circles in 1993 compared to 1978–82. For instance, of the seven managers who were assigned to social circle 1 in 1978–82, two managers belonged to social circle 4 in 1993, one manager to circle 5, two managers to circle 6, etc. In other words, membership in a particular social circle in 1978–82 has no significant influence on the assignment to a particular social circle in 1993.

We started out with the hypothesis that dense networks are stable over time and that they offer their members both protection and job opportunities on the labor market. This hypothesis could be confirmed by a comparison of networks among managers in Germany and Britain. There seems to be a relationship between the density and the stability of networks. The higher the density of networks, the more stable they are over time (*ceteris paribus*).

---

[22] This figure indicates the average degree. In actual fact, this degree varies between 0 and 78. Dr Röller (former CEO of Dresdner Bank) has a degree of 78; see frequency distribution of degrees in Fig. 5.3 for Britain and Germany.

[23] The reader is reminded that we report and analyze here only relationships which are created by Board membership. Whether these managers are linked to each other by family bonds or joint Club membership we do not know.

[24] Hundred and twenty-five managers were included in the matrix 1978–82, but only 86 had a degree >0; the remaining 39 managers were 'isolated' (degree=0).

TABLE 5.8 *Social circle membership 1978–82 and 1993 United Kingdom*

Social circle 1978–82	Social circle 1993	N
1	4,5,6,7,12	7
2	1,6,8,9,10,18,20	7
3	5,8,10,12,14,17	9
4	1,4,5,6,7,16,17	9
5	3,4,12,19	7
6	11,14,16,18,19	5
7	9,14,16,19	6
8	8	2
9	2,10	3
10	17	3
11	3	1
12	8,10,13	4
13	4,9,10,13	5
14	11,14,18	4
15	13,15,17,18	6
16	16,18	3
17	5	1
18	11	1
19	13,16	2
20	14	1

Note: N=86 British managers.

Example: The 7 British managers who were members of social circle 1 in 1978–82 were assigned to the following social circles in 1993: 4,5,6,7,12. The 4 British managers who were members of social circle 12 in 1978–82 were assigned to the following social circles in 1993: 8,10,13.

5.7. CONCLUSIONS

The 'classical' model of managerial control, formulated by Berle and Means back in the 1930s and since refined (Herman 1981), is based on the assumption that managers have been able largely to free themselves from external control. Neither owners, nor their peers nor the market can exert effective control over managers, who in advanced industrialized societies have taken over the function of the economic elite from owners. The owners (shareholders) are unable to exert effective control due to their large number (separation of ownership and control), and the peers are frequently dependent on precisely those managers they are supposed to be supervising. Under such conditions managers can become 'agents without principals' (Davis 1991), able to create huge business empires largely without hindrance.

What then are the differences between the new forms of control and ownership (shareholder value-capitalism) and the classical model of managerial control? In comparing the two it should be borne in mind that the differences are due to two causes: on the one hand, social changes that have transformed the structures of economic power during the past 20 years, and on the other, national variations rooted in cultural differences and different historical experiences.

5.7.1. *Control through Ownership*

In shareholder-value capitalism, it is no longer individuals or families that own companies, but rather other companies. This transfer of ownership has served to reconcentrate ownership and has thus increased and expanded the influence of owners. But in Germany, the owners are the large firms that are controlled by managers. Many, although not all, German managers have supplemented their bureaucratic power with the power of ownership. Managers are supervised by owners, but these 'owners' are other managers. The control function of ownership has been internalized in the network of multiple-directors and is collectively performed by those managers who control the dominant firms (internal control).

In Germany, where ownership has become highly concentrated, the managers of the dominant company frequently have a seat on the supervisory boards of the dependent companies, where they play the role of owner (cf. Fig. 5.1). The structure of ownership that has developed in Britain, by contrast, is fragmented. Here, control through ownership depends on whether institutional investors coordinate their behavior (Scott 1997: 49). In both countries, the ownership function has been bureaucratized and professionalized. It is no longer exercised by amateurish shareholders but by financial experts.

5.7.2. *Control by Peers*

More than half of the managers examined here perform executive and nonexecutive (supervisory) functions simultaneously in spite of the different statutory regulations in Germany and Britain. The supervisors are recruited from among the executive managers. At the collective level, the multiple-directors have executive power and the same collective also has the power of supervision and control. Most multiple-directors are electors and are elected, supervisors and the supervised. This does not preclude the fact that within this collective separate social circles are formed, with competitive relations prevailing between them. The social circles serve either to promote integration within the corporate group (primarily in Germany) or are 'cosmopolitan' financial networks open to a large number of managers. Control by peers is also internalized in the network of multiple-directors in order to protect the managers of large companies from external interference. Within the network itself competition is permitted, but at the same time restricted through ties that exist between the different circles and which may be used to mitigate conflicts (cf. Table 5.5, Germany).

5.7.3. *Control by the Market*

The question as to the extent to which managers are subject to market control was not considered directly in this study. However, a number of conclusions can be drawn from the structure of ownership relations which show the way in which market competition is effective within the elite network under the changed conditions of a globalized economy. Leading companies are increasingly organized as (transnational) corporate networks linked to each other through capital networks and interlocking directorates. Whether or not a firm remains within the network depends on its profitability. Less successful firms are sold on the market for corporate control. Firms can be bought and sold at any time on the market for corporate control, and each and every transaction constitutes a potential threat to the managers of these firms. The decisions on acquisitions and sales are taken by those managers who simultaneously represent the owners *vis-à-vis* the dependent firm. The market for corporate control has served substantially to increase the competition between managers. Managers must not only establish a place within the bureaucracy of large corporations; what is decisive for the stability of their career is to get access to the elite network which has internalized the control function of ownership as well as that of peer control. The more central their position in this network, the less they are threatened by the market for corporate control (see Fig. 5.1).

Pound (1992) characterizes recent changes in the control structure of large corporations as an evolution away from market control (e.g. hostile takeovers) to a 'political model of corporate governance'. Institutional investors have used their voting power to change the internal governance structure of large US corporations to make them more responsive to their shareholders. In this chapter, we have argued that market forces have been internalized in the network of large corporations and are thus controlled by the group of multiple-directors. The control structures of *individual* firms tend to become ineffective, if they are not paralyzed, by the interfirm network of multiple-directors who are electors and are elected, are supervisors and are supervised.

6

Education and Career of Multiple-Directors

Managers with the greatest number of high-ranking positions in the large firms form the 'core' of the economic elite. Such persons are not merely a member of a board of a leading corporation, but by virtue of their seat on a number of (supervisory) boards can also exert an influence on decisions in other large firms. We assume that this group of managers collectively performs the function of an *entrepreneur* within the German and British network of large corporations.

In this chapter, the educational background and the professional careers of the British and German multiple-directors are analyzed. We are particularly interested in the question whether these big linkers were 'entrepreneurs' at any time during their life course (Heinz 1991), or whether they started their careers right from the beginning as 'bureaucrats' in the large corporations. To expand the comparison we also consider data on the professional career of managers in France and the United States.[1]

Before the analysis of the professional careers of multiple-directors is presented, some theoretical concepts have to be discussed. First, the question of who is an 'entrepreneur' will be addressed. It will be shown that the definition given by Schumpeter cannot be applied to the manager–entrepeneur who holds a leading position in the large corporation. The organizational structure of firms has been transformed several times during the past century and with it the role of the entrepreneur in the economic system. It will be argued that it is not the individual manager, but the *group of interrelated directors* who fulfill the entrepreneurial function within the corporate economy.

Second, the professional careers of the British multiple-directors are compared to those of their German counterparts. It will be shown that the career paths of German managers are more standardized and professionalized than those of the British managers. In Section 6.2, the concepts of standardization and professionalization and the meaning of elite integration and homogenization will be briefly discussed, before we start in Section 6.4 to present the empirical data on the career paths of multiple-directors. The sample of directors has been drawn from the members of the elite network which has been analyzed in the previous chapter.

[1] I thank Hanne Konz, Jordi Klingel, and Christian Brandt for the data collection.

6.1. DEFINING THE ENTREPRENEUR

A classic definition of the entrepreneur is that of Schumpeter, writing in 1928: 'The essence of entrepreneurialship lies in the recognition and implementation of new opportunities in the economic sector'. In a path-breaking process of 'creative destruction', the entrepreneur replaces antiquated traditions with new technologies and organizational structures. In keeping with the popular terminology of his era, Schumpeter referred to the entrepreneur as a *'Führer'* (leader): 'The role of the entrepreneur is nothing but that of the "leader" in the economic sphere'. Hirschman observed that, in Schumpeter's view, charisma forms the basis of the entrepreneur's authority, and that 'his leadership, his willingness to assume risk, his breaking through old patterns of finance . . . almost made him look like a rebel against society'.[2]

Seen in a broader perspective, this concept of the entrepreneur imbues him with the aura of the driving force behind social change. In forcing through his innovations, the entrepreneur breaks through the sorts of traditional taboos and bureaucratic routines that impede progress, legitimizing his pioneering innovativeness in terms of economic rationality, the constraints of competition, or simply by his 'charisma'. In fact, the constant process of modernization over the past 150 years can be seen as growing out of a chain of technical and organizational innovations that have first been implemented in the economic system, but later transformed the entire society. The initiators of this modernization process have been 'entrepreneurs'.

In his book on the modern industrial society, however, Galbraith (1967) discounts the allegedly heroic role of the entrepreneur. He argues that the entrepreneurial 'leader' has been replaced by technocratic teams of scientists and managers working together to plan and routinize technological, organizational, and commercial innovations.[3] This bureaucratized form of innovation places a high value on control and predictability. It strives to rescue its products from the risk of market failure by technical planning and supervising of the entire process from innovation to production and to marketing.

Galbraith who emphasized the pivotal role of scientists and managers in the process of innovation seized, however, only one aspect of the historical change. It has to be taken into account that the technical, organizational, and financial context within which the 'entrepreneur' operates has changed over time and that the role of the entrepreneur has been transformed accordingly.

The family business—in which the founder serves as both owner and manager, bears the risk of his decisions, and mobilizes all resources—was dominant until the end of the nineteenth century (Pohl 1981). This form of business structure was replaced by the large-scale corporate enterprise typical of the era of manager capitalism. Here it is the responsibility of the top management to 'recognize and implement

---

[2] *Sources*: Schumpeter (1928: 482–3); Schumpeter (1950: 83); Hirschman (1958: 16). See also Redlich (1964: 46–8); Livesay (1995).

[3] 'There is no name for all who participate in group decision-making or the organization which they form. I propose to call this organization the Technostructure' (Galbraith 1967: 74).

new opportunities' (i.e. to take strategic decisions), while the risk entailed by these deci-sions falls to the stockholders,[4] and the mobilization of production factors is delegated to specialized departments (e.g. financing, personnel).

The grounds upon which entrepreneurs legitimate their decisions have also changed over time. The type of (charismatic) business leader described by Schumpeter as being *the* characteristic capitalist entrepreneur is now seen historically as merely a marginal figure and one relegated to the 'heroic' phase of capitalism. Such a figure finds no place in the type of organization described by Galbraith, one built upon bureaucratic rationality and the routinization of innovative processes.[5]

Not only have the organizational form and legitimating basis of entrepreneurial decisions changed, but also the *content* of whatever may be termed 'innovation' and 'new opportunities'. Fligstein (1990) investigated the professional specialization of top-level managers in US companies, that is, those persons who most clearly repres-ent the entrepreneurial function. He found that most of them had been production engineers or technicians until the interwar period, after which they were largely replaced by marketing specialists, who themselves began to be overtaken by finance specialists in the 1960s. These alternating phases demonstrate the changing nature of what 'innovation' has meant over time. Today 'innovation' is no longer understood as the routinized product development of a specialized company department,[6] but rather as 'genius' finance techniques of hostile takeovers, mergers, and restructuring (Kaufman and Englander 1993).

Technical innovations have not lost their value, but they are often developed by small companies which, upon achieving market success through their innovations, are then bought up by large enterprises on the market for corporate control. The innovat-ive capacity of many large enterprises in fact consists principally of their buying and selling the 'right' companies at the 'right' time.

If we now ask who performs this entrepreneurial function in the large corpora-tions, the obvious answer is that the top-level managers are the 'entrepreneurs'. They define the goals of the organization and determine the course of its future develop-ment. The thesis taken here, however, is different: it is not the *individual* manager who performs this socioeconomic function, but rather it is performed within the *network* of enterprises that are linked to one another by interlocks.

---

[4] The function of 'risk bearing' is emphasized by Knight (1934). See also Redlich (1964: 110–19). Schumpeter (1954: 555–6, 645) differentiates between 'capitalists' and 'entrepreneurs', with the capitalist delivering the resource of capital and thus bearing the risk, while the entrepreneur bears no risk at all but rather is responsible for the creative combination and recombination of production factors (land, capital, labor, technology).

[5] The phase of 'charismatic' leadership generally ends when the founder of the company leaves it (see Strouse (1999) in the case of J. P. Morgan and Feldman (1998) in the case of Hugo Stinnes).

[6] The Minnesota Mining and Manufacturing Company (3M) long served as a respected example of what it meant for a business to be innovative, constantly attracting attention by its new products and regu-larly appearing on the list of 'most admired companies'. This is a company in which technical innovation has become routinized, with 611 newly registered patents (innovations) in 1998. Since the mid-1990s, however, 3M has been considered on Wall Street as 'boring' and 'unimaginative'. Currently, the financial analysts of investment and pension funds obviously expect a different kind of 'innovation'. *Source: New York Times*, 6 July 1999, p. C7.

The decisions taken by large enterprises are so interdependent that no one manager is able to take action effectively by herself. She may be able to 'perceive' economic opportunities within her own horizon, but 'implementing' them almost always requires the cooperation of other, similar managers, upon whose resources she depends, and who are affected by any decisions that she takes. These relationships have been described as networks of (mutual) resource dependence (Pfeffer and Salancik 1978) or as (asymmetrical) interdependencies (Keohane 1984). It is thus the overall group, the network of managers who are bound to one another through interlocks that ultimately controls the cognitive, technical, and economic resources required for the perceiving and implementing of new opportunities.

This interdependence can be illustrated by an example taken from the history of the industrialization process in Germany: the power station which was later to become the largest in Europe, the *Rheinisch-Westfälische Elektrizitätswerke (RWE)*, was founded in 1898. One of the persons named to the supervisory board of the new company was the 28-year-old Hugo Stinnes.[7] Stinnes had very early 'perceived' that electricity represents in effect 'refined' coal, that it is easier to transport energy in this 'refined' state, that the electrical motor would ultimately replace the steam engine, and, most importantly, that economies of scale could be achieved only if electricity production were taken over by a regional monopoly that could provide inexpensive energy to the entire area rather than by each municipality attempting to produce its own electricity. The members of the supervisory board represented the various interests that would be affected by such plans: the mayor of the community who awarded the licence for the production of electricity; a banker who provided financial resources; the top-manager of the firm which delivered the steam turbines; the owner of a large steel combine; and finally Hugo Stinnes himself on whose pit the power station was to be constructed. While Stinnes had correctly 'perceived' the potential of electricity, he could not implement his vision alone. The entrepreneurial function belonged to the overall network of those representing the various interests and cooperating across sectoral boundaries. The innovative idea stemmed from Stinnes, but its realization required action by a network.[8]

Baumol examined the innovation policies of enterprises in the United States in the 1990s and found that the foremost weapon in the competitive struggle is not price but innovation.[9] Technological innovation, as Baumol argued, has become as much a routine aspect of the company as production and marketing. Furthermore, companies enter into technology-sharing compacts with one another, in particular with

---

[7] Hugo Stinnes (1870–1924) inherited coal pits from his father; by the turn of the century he was one of the most influential entrepreneurs in Germany. Together with August Thyssen (1842–1926) he restructured and founded numerous mining and steel companies.

[8] See Feldman (1998: 41–5); Klass (1958: 102–30). The automobile and the airplane (which both diminished the role of the railroads) are further examples of entrepreneurial innovations that could only have been implemented within the context of a network of interrelated companies (providing the infrastructure for automobiles and airplanes.)

[9] *Source:* 'Rewriting the book on capitalism's engine', *New York Times*, 5 June 1999, p A17. Quotations in this paragraph are from this source.

competitors. In this system of collaboration among rivals, each company guarantees the others licensing rights to its own innovations.[10] The network, therefore, generates a pool of innovations that are available to all members of the network. The possible problem of 'free riders' is eliminated by accepting for membership only those firms that can regularly add their own innovations to the common pool. Such collaborative agreements create networks that not only share innovations but also are bound to one another by a common pool of scientists. 'The scientists, especially the engineers, often required [technology-sharing compacts] as a condition of their employment: they simply refused to work for a company that would not allow them to communicate with their peers'.

This example of the innovation pool illustrates how the innovative function can be 'socialized' within a collective network of enterprises that are bound both by contracts and by a shared scientific community (Barnett *et al.* 2000).

This section concludes with the argument that in the context of the corporate economy, the entrepreneurial function is no longer fulfilled by a single individual, but by a network of interrelated managers. The speed with which technical innovations can diffuse within the network and the degree of *collective* control that can be exercised over entrepreneurial decisions depend upon the comprehensiveness of the network (i.e. the degree of inclusion of all stakeholders) and its density (i.e. the intensity of communication between members).

6.2. TYPOLOGY OF CAREER PATTERNS

Before the analysis of the professional careers of multiple-directors is presented, some of the concepts of elite research are briefly summarized (e.g. differentiation, standardization, individualization). These concepts are used here as instruments to describe the patterns of professional careers and the differences in the career paths of British and German multiple-directors.

6.2.1. *Differentiation*

Modern societies encompass a number of subsystems, including the economic, political, and cultural. The elites of the respective subsystems remain isolated from one another if they are recruited from within the respective subsystem, and if their professional paths seldom cross those of elites from the other subsystems. Differences in social background, education, and career stages are, thus, an indicator of the extent of differentiation between societal elites. Germany offers an example of relatively high differentiation, as economic elites generally serve an apprenticeship, supplemented

---

[10] The compacts may even be transnational. E.g. the US firm Perkin-Elmer (precision optics) has a technology-sharing compact with Hitachi 'for the right to license innovations that either company might adopt. Under the compact, each company provides a menu of innovations under development, any of which it promises to make available for a fee that often ranges from 6 to 7.5% of the price of the product that incorporates the innovation. Perkin-Elmer has entered about 100 other compacts since World War II'.

by a university degree in business administration, and career posts exclusively in large enterprises. Only seldom does an individual cross over either from or to, for example, the political system. In France, on the other hand, there is less differentiation: elites from the two systems frequently attend a common elite *lycée*, receive degrees from the Polytechnique or École Nationale d'Administration, and work together in the civil service (Grands Corps d'Etat).

In the following analysis, we use the number of job spells that a multiple-director has spent in other social systems (e.g. in the state bureaucracy or in government) as an indicator to measure the degree of differentiation of the economic elite.

6.2.2. *Integration*

In characterizing an elite it is important to ascertain whether it is integrated horizontally or vertically (Birnbaum 1978b; Useem 1980). In the case of *horizontal* integration, members of the elite can shift fairly easily from one organization to another. Such fluctuations can also be described as horizontal elite circulation. Here, a manager who is on the board of one enterprise often changes the employer and joins the board of another enterprise. Top managers are almost exclusively recruited from a 'pool' of upper class individuals ('establishment'). The elite forms a relatively closed social class, and the boundary between the highest level and other, lower levels of management is largely impermeable.

With *vertical* integration, on the other hand, individuals remain within a single enterprise and compete for the few positions on the top. Potential applicants are selected within and recruited from an internal labor market; this vertical mobility can lead to the highest management levels. Here the elite is socially less closed, and the boundary between upper and lower levels of management is permeable.

We use the number of years which the multiple-director spent in the company before reaching the highest level of management as a measure and operationalization for the level of vertical integration.

6.2.3. *Institutionalization*

The term institutionalization here refers to statutory or corporativist regulations of occupational training and professional practices. An example of an occupation that is highly institutionalized in modern society is that of the physician; that of the artist, on the other hand, illustrates the other end of the institutionalization continuum. A somewhat weaker concept is that of *standardization*, which denotes merely the similarity of career patterns[11] among those with the same occupation, without these necessarily being the result of formal regulations. French managers show a high degree of standardization, the British a low degree, with Germans taking an intermediate position.

---

[11] A career pattern is a specific *sequence of job spells* that a manager has passed through during her professional life.

We use different measures to operationalize the degree of standardization of the professional career: the degree of variation of the variables 'educational level' and 'subject studied'; and the heterogeneity of the sequences of job spells.

6.2.4. *Individualization*

The concept of individualization is the opposite of institutionalization and refers to the dissimilarity of career patterns (Mayer 1996). It has been claimed that careers are particularly individualized and that life styles have become more and more heterogenous in today's postmodern society (Beck 1983). Heterogeneity, destandardization, and deinstitutionalization are seen as the result of the increasing range of options from which one can chose, regarding education (which school, how long, what subject?), working time (full or part time?), and occupational interruption (e.g. sabbatical).

In the present context, we are less concerned with the level of individualization within the total population than whether there is a difference between social strata, that is, whether the political or *economic elite show more standardized career paths* than the middle class. Sociological research has shown, for example, that the marriage restraints in almost all societies are more rigid and mandatory for the upper than for the lower strata. The view taken here is that career patterns leading to economic elite positions are more standardized than those leading to lower level positions.

It has to be noted, that this hypothesis of greater standardization of elite career patterns cannot be tested with the present dataset as this includes information only on top-level managers; however, it can be supported by plausible arguments, for example, the factual uniformity of careers.

6.2.5. *Selectivity*

Every society has only a very limited number of elite positions. Even the concept of elite implies a high degree of selectivity in recruitment. Societies differ as regards the age at which selection occurs, the selecting institutions, and the selection criteria (e.g. on-the-job performance versus formal educational degrees). In France, for instance, the selection for elite positions takes place in the elite *lycées* and the *Grandes Ecoles*, that is, very early in the life course, while in Germany the selection of the economic elite is postponed until fairly late and occurs in the internal labor market of large enterprises.

6.2.6. *Professionalization*

The tailoring of educational training directly to the subsequent occupational function indicates a high degree of professionalization of this occupation. The physician again serves as an example here, whose position is highly professionalized. The top managers of British enterprises show less professionalization than their counterparts in Germany. This can be seen in the following comparison of two 'standardized' career patterns.

British manager   Elite secondary ('public') school → degree in English literature from Cambridge University → a position in the house of the royal family → member of the board of directors of a large British enterprise. Such a career path is highly selective (i.e. exclusive), but hardly professionalized.

German manager   High school diploma (*Abitur*) → apprenticeship in a bank → university study of business administration → employment in a bank → upward mobility in the internal labor market → member of the bank's management board. This career path is professionalized, and the selection takes place within the company itself.

The degree of *homogeneity of an elite* will be measured by the following criteria: the elite in a social subsystem is highly differentiated; the sequence of job spells is relatively standardized; the selection for elite positions occurs early in the life course; the career paths are highly professionalized. The members of a 'homogeneous' elite often stem from the same social stratum and/or attended the same elite university. They share similar professional experiences and—in the case of the economic elite—have hardly ever worked in the state bureaucracy or in government.

6.3. THE EMPIRICAL STUDY

The point of departure for this empirical investigation was a list of 308 German managers holding four or more positions in the corporate network of the 694 largest firms in (West) Germany. In Britain, all managers holding three or more positions and half of those occupying two positions in the corporate network of the 520 largest firms were listed (302 multiple-directors). The following analysis is based on a subset of these managers. We were able to collect fairly complete information on the professional careers of 200 German and 180 British 'big linkers'. We tried to follow the professional career of each manager up to the end of 1995.

In the first step, descriptions of professional careers were taken from handbooks and the financial press.[12] In the second step, a total of 280 questionnaires were sent to German managers to close information gaps in their professional career; we received responses from 143 managers.[13] Financial constraints made it impossible to send questionnaires to British managers, and the proportion of missing values is consequently greater in the British dataset. The data that were collected refer to the following variables: social background (parents' occupations), education (level, subject), sequence of career phases (from first professional position to current top-level position), name of the company (parent, subsidiary), hierarchical position and duration of individual career phases (job spells). Because the data on social background were very sparse in both the German and the British datasets, this variable had to be omitted from the analysis.

---

[12] For German managers, the following handbooks were used: 'Leitende Männer und Frauen der Wirtschaft', Hoppenstedt (Darmstadt), various annual volumes; 'Archiv für publizistische Arbeit—Munzinger Archiv: Internationales biographisches Archiv' (Ravensburg), various annual volumes. Schmidt and Römhild: Wer ist wer?—The German Who's Who? (Lübeck). For British managers: A & C Black: Who's Who? (London), various annual volumes.

[13] Cf. Jordi Klingel: Top manager in der deutschen Wirtschaft. Trier 1995: Universität Trier (Diplomarbeit).

TABLE 6.1   *Average founding year of largest corporations*

Position	G	F	UK	US
1–50	1901 (5)	1910 (11)	1915 (10)	1898 (2)
51–100	1900 (4)	1938 (18)	1906 (6)	1899 (6)
101–150	1910 (10)	1942 (18)	1924 (15)	1906 (4)
151–200	1910 (10)	1938 (19)	1940 (19)	1898 (2)
201–250	1922 (8)	1949 (26)	1923 (11)	1906 (7)
Total	1909 (37)	1935 (92)	1922 (61)	1901 (21)

Note: G: Germany, F: France, UK: United Kingdom, US: United States. Position: position in the ranking list.
Figures in columns give average founding year for each class in the ranking list. Figures in parentheses give number of firms in each class which were founded after 1960.

Previous studies have usually examined the social backgrounds and professional careers of top managers in the 200 or 500 largest corporations in the different countries.[14] The present study, however, concentrated on those with multiple-directorships and who, therefore, play a role in the network of connected enterprises. The economic elite considered here is thus a subset of the elite described by the other studies. Most of those managers investigated here are executive directors of one firm and nonexecutive directors of two or more other firms.

6.4. FOUNDERS VERSUS HEIRS

The analysis of the career paths of multiple-directors starts with the question of whether some of the managers in our sample had been founders of their firm. For Schumpeter, the entrepreneur was essentially a company founder, one who sought to realize his innovative ideas in his own enterprise. However, our sample includes no such company founders. As Table 6.1 shows, the 250 largest firms in Germany were founded on average in 1909. This rather advanced age of large enterprises is typical not only of firms in Germany but also those in France, Britain, and the United States. While French firms are somewhat younger on average (due to the delayed industrialization), even there the large enterprises of the country look back proudly on a long tradition. Surprisingly, of all the four countries it is not Britain that has the oldest firms, but the United States. It is also in the United States that one finds the lowest proportion of firms founded after 1960: only 21 from a total of 250 (see Table 6.1 last column, last line).

The managers in our sample are in effect 'heirs' of their companies inasmuch as the firms had generally existed long before they joined them. Their job was thus to secure the continued existence of the firm and guarantee its relative position in the

---

[14] The principal studies of managers in Germany and other European countries are summarized in Hartmann (1997). Comprehensive studies of western German entrepreneurs and managers are presented by Kruk (1972) and Stahl (1973). For the United Kingdom, see Giddens (1974), Fidler (1981), Barry (1998), Whitley (1973), Hill (1995). For the United States, see Useem (1980, 1984), Useem and Karabel (1986). For France, see Bauer and Bertin-Mourot (1995, 1999), Birnbaum (1978a,b).

ranking lists of the nation's enterprises. This strategic goal—ensuring that the company remains among the largest enterprises in the future—is common to all the managers in our sample.

Within the network of affiliated corporations there is both competition and cooperation. On the one hand, firms compete with one another for the highest possible position on the ranking list, and this regardless of their economic sector (DiMaggio and Powell 1983). On the other hand, however, the top managers are able to coordinate their strategies and to regulate competition. By hindering new companies, for example, to join the exclusive club of the largest firms, the established enterprises are collectively able to obviate a possible cause of their eventual decline. It is this type of strategy which imparts a cartel nature to the corporate network.

The advanced age of the enterprises that today belong to the 250 largest in the country indicates that most grew out of the second industrialization phase (automotive, chemical, machine engineering, insurance, banks), while those of the third industrialization (microelectronics, telecommunication, professional services) have hardly found access to the exclusive circle of large enterprises.[15]

Large enterprises protect their position by a series of strategies that are only indirectly related to anything that Schumpeter would have understood as 'creative destruction'. These include mergers, acquisitions, and complete transformations of the company's product structure.[16] The majority of company *founders* have an 'idea', but frequently no resources for realizing their idea. For the top managers in our sample, the case is just the reverse: they have at their disposal substantial resources, but are in search of an 'idea'. They usually find their ideas on the market for corporate control, where young and dynamic firms are up for sale. Deciding which firms to buy and which parts to sell belongs to the most important entrepreneurial decisions that top-level managers are required to make.

6.5. THE FIRST JOB IN THE COMPANY

Even if the multiple-directors in our sample did not found the firms that they lead, one could suspect that many of them had originally founded their own company at the beginning of their career, and that they only later assumed a top position in one of the largest enterprises. Although our dataset has many gaps, we can say that of the 200 German managers of whom we have information, only nine have ever been self-employed, thus fewer than 5 percent. Even these nine were not founders of their companies but had inherited them from their parents.

---

[15] The following example illustrates that this is changing, even though slowly: in November 1999, the following firms left the Dow Jones Industrial Index: Sears Roebuck (1886), Union Carbide (1886), Chevron (1879), Goodyear Tire & Rubber (1898). They were replaced by the following four firms: Home Depot (1978), SBC Communications (1877), Intel (1968), Microsoft (1975). The average founding year of firms in the Dow Jones Industrial Index before 1999 was 1888. After the younger firms had been included, the average founding year was 1894.

[16] Examples include the German combines Mannesmann (from pipe manufacturer to telecommunications) and Hoechst (from industrial chemicals to 'life science').

TABLE 6.2   *Average number and duration of job spells*

	Germany	United Kingdom
Number	6.3 (0.31)	6.0 (0.36)
Duration	5.6 (0.85)	5.8 (0.81)
% large corp.	69.7	56.4
Total (*N*)	1262	1072

Note: Number: average number of job spells (until end of 1995); duration: average duration of job spell in years; large corp.: proportion of job spells spent in the largest corporations. Figures in parentheses: coefficients of variation.

For each of the German and British managers in our sample, we divided the career path into discrete 'job spells', each clearly distinguished in terms of job description, duration, and position in the firm.[17] We thus defined a total of 1262 such job spells for the 200 German managers and 1072 for the British managers (Table 6.2, last row).

Table 6.2 shows that the German managers had an average of 6.3 job spells (British managers, 6.0), with an average duration of 5.6 years (British, 5.8). Of all the job spells among the German managers, 69.7 percent were in one of the 694 largest firms in the country (British, 56.4 percent in one of the 520 largest). These figures show that managers spend a considerable amount of their career within the enterprises that they later lead.

This is also clear in Table 6.3, which is divided into three parts. The upper panel shows the percentage of managers who in their first, second, and third job spells were already employed by one of the nation's large enterprises. About one-half (49.7 percent) of German managers began their career (first job spell) with one of these firms, but only one-third (33.8 percent) of British managers. By the third job spell, 67 percent of German managers and 56.2 percent of their British counterparts were employed by a large firm. This shows that especially German managers had, very early in their career, joined the enterprise of which they were later to assume the top leadership position.

The middle and lower panels of Table 6.3 show the sectors in which the managers were employed during their first and second job spells. Of the German top managers, 49.7 percent entered their professional career with a large enterprise, 26.5 percent in a smaller company (i.e. not one of the 694 largest in the country), 16.6 percent in the scientific system (e.g. at a university), and 6.1 percent in the civil service or politics. A striking proportion (14 percent) of British top managers began their careers with a position in the country's military. While there was no mention of such a position among the Germans surveyed here, it is probable that a considerable number of them did in fact serve as (professional) soldiers, even if they do not mention this in their

[17] An example of the information that we tried to collect for each job spell is the following: section head (*position*), Daimler-Benz (*enterprise*), 1960–5 (*duration of job spell*), Stuttgart, Germany (*location of enterprise*).

TABLE 6.3 *Distribution of job spells*

	Germany (%)	United Kingdom (%)
% largest companies		
1st job spell	49.7	33.8
2nd job spell	57.1	47.4
3rd job spell	67.0	56.2
Distribution		
First job spell		
Largest corporation	49.7	33.8
Other firms	26.5[a]	37.6
Military service	—	14.0
Scientific system	16.6	2.2
Political system	6.1	3.4
Second job spell		
Largest corporation	57.1	47.4
Other firms	30.2[b]	39.2
Military service	—	1.8
Scientific system	3.7	2.9
Political system	7.4	7.0

Note: *% largest companies*: proportion of managers (in percent) who are employed in one of the largest companies during their first/second/third job spell. *Distribution first/second job spell*: proportion of managers who are employed in one of the different sectors during the first/second job spell (e.g. private firm, military, politics).
Percentages given in the two lower panels of Table 6.3 do not add up to 100%, because sectors in which managers were employed are not completely listed.
[a] Among them 9 German self-employed managers; [b] among them 7 German self-employed managers.
Number of job spells in the analysis (Germany): 1st job spell: $N = 181$; 2nd job spell: $N = 189$; 3rd job spell: $N = 194$. United Kingdom: 1st job spell: $N = 178$; 2nd job spell: $N = 171$; 3rd job spell: $N = 169$.

public autobiographical data. This indicates the way in which cultural values influence the 'construction' of autobiographies.[18]

The proportion of those who were later to have multiple-directorships of large enterprises in Germany and who by their second job spell were not yet employed in the economic system is relatively low: 11.1 percent (3.75 percent at universities, 7.4 percent in the civil service). The corresponding figure among the British managers was 11.7 percent. Thus, the proportion of managers who by their second career position were employed in the economic system was just under 90 percent in both

[18] Autobiographies are 'constructions' inasmuch as they comprise selected (and deselected) events from the entirety of life events. The German managers prefer to portray their career as an unbroken chain of advancements and successes. At least until the early 1990s, service as a professional soldier was not considered among these managers to be a career post that should be mentioned with those that came afterward. One must also note the historical era in question here: since the average birth year was 1934, a sizable proportion will have entered professional life in the years following the war.

TABLE 6.4   *Highest degree earned*

	Germany (%)	United Kingdom (%)		United States[a] (%)	
No college	9.1	No college	30.9	No college	6.6
College (FHS)	3.5		—	Bachelor	40.5
University	24.2	University	61.9	Master	46.3
Doctoral degree	63.2	Doctoral d.	7.2	Ph.D.	6.6
Σ	100.0	Σ	100.0	Σ	100.0
Apprenticeship	25.9	Oxbridge	22.3	Ivy League	24.2
	—	Fellow	40.0		—
N	198		152		800

Note: [a] CEOs of the 800 largest US firms. Ph.D.: Doctor of Philosophy; Ivy League: 11 US universities/colleges, among them Harvard, Yale, Princeton, Dartmouth.
FHS: 'Fachhochschule' (technical/commercial colleges); Fellow: Fellow of Learned Societies/ Professional Associations. Oxbridge: Universities of Oxford and Cambridge.
The proportion of managers who attended elite universities (Britain, US) or obtained an apprenticeship certificate (lower panel) are included in the percentages of the upper panel.

countries, the major difference being that a greater proportion of Germans than British had already joined a large company even before this second position.

Only a relatively small proportion of any positions from the overall total were in politics or public administration: 4.1 percent in Germany (of 1262 positions) and 6.7 percent in the United Kingdom (of 1072).[19] This indicates that only little interpenetration takes place between the economic and the political/administrative elites.

6.6. PROFESSIONAL EDUCATION

Table 6.4 presents comparative figures for the educational certificates of German and British multiple-directors. This table also shows the highest degrees earned of the chief executive officers (CEOs) of the 800 largest firms in the United States.[20] It must be noted here, however, that because of the differences in educational systems, direct comparisons can be misleading in some instances. In the upper panel of Table 6.4, the 'standard' degrees for each country are presented; the lower panel specifies some

[19] Although the percentage of British managers who held at least one position in the public sphere is not substantially higher than the corresponding percentage of German managers, there is a difference among those who did hold such a position. Among the 21 Germans who held at least one public position, there were a total of 52 public job spells, or 2.5 per person. Among the British, on the other hand, there were 18 managers who had held a public position, and a total of 72 such positions had been held, or an average of 4.0 for each. This means that those in Britain who spend some time in the political/administrative system remained for a longer period in their career in that system than did their counterparts in Germany.

[20] This dataset was provided by *Forbes* for the year 1997 (on CD-ROM). Further information on the sample is given in *Forbes*, 19 May 1997, pp. 172–236. It has to be noted that the British and the German sample on the one hand, the US sample on the other, have been selected on the basis of different criteria. The European managers are multiple-directors in the largest firms, the US-managers are COEs in the 800 largest firms, regardless of their interlocks with any further enterprises.

educational certificates which are of particular importance in the respective national labor markets, for instance, the apprenticeship in Germany or degrees from elite universities in Britain (Oxford and Cambridge) and from the 'Ivy League' institutions in the United States.

In Germany, the two most frequently obtained certificates are the apprenticeship certificate (25.9 percent) and a doctoral degree (63.2 percent). While an apprenticeship signals practical experience and familiarity with the German enterprise culture, the doctoral degree symbolizes the 'high culture' of science. In fact, judging from the percentage of those who have a doctorate, it appears that *not* having one is certainly an obstacle to achieving the highest managerial positions in large German enterprises.[21]

There are also a number of characteristic features among the British top managers. For example, 33 percent graduated from an elite ('public') secondary school (attended primarily by upper class children)[22] and 32 percent from an elite university (Oxford, Cambridge, University of London, London School of Economics). Although a remarkable 30.9 percent of British managers did not graduate from *any* university,[23] 42.6 percent of these had attended a 'public' school (including eight from Eton). There appear to be two large and fairly distinct educational subsets in the British sample, each with about one-third of the total: those graduating from an elite university and those graduating from no university.[24] Despite this evident heterogeneity in the overall group of British managers, however, one can say that about two-third of British managers possess a high level of 'educational capital', acquired either at elite secondary schools or at elite universities.

In the case of managers in the United States, it is notable that only very few (6.6 percent) are not university graduates. One-quarter in fact attended elite ('Ivy League') universities. Tuition at these exclusive universities is very high, and receiving a degree from one of them is seen as guaranteeing career promotion (Useem and Karabel 1986; Mills 1956).

Table 6.5 compares the four university subjects that were most frequently studied by the managers. Again, there are substantial differences between the three countries. In Germany, for example, there are four times as many with a law degree as in the United States; in the latter, on the other hand, 36.1 percent studied engineering or

---

[21] The gender variable is not discussed here. Among the 180 British managers, there are three women: Louise Botting, Lady Elspeth Rosamund Morton; Yvette Monica Newbold. Among the 200 German managers, there is one woman: Ellen Roth Schneider-Linnée.

[22] We included in the category of 'elite' secondary schools 20 institutions, among them Eton, Harrow, Charterhouse, and Rugby. 22 managers of our sample attended Eton, 4 managers attended Winchester, etc. See Bauer and Bertin-Mourot (1999), who report 36% of CEOs in the 200 largest British firms having attended 'public' schools.

[23] The comparatively high proportion of British managers without university degree is not an artifact of our sample. Barry (1998: 6) examined 1000 members of the boards of directors of the 100 firms listed on the London stock exchange (index: FTSE 100). He found that 30.5% of these 1000 managers had no degree.

[24] Approximately 40% of British managers are 'Fellows' of a 'Learned Society', e.g. the Royal Society of Literature, or a professional association, e.g. Chartered Engineers. University graduates tend to have such memberships more frequently than nongraduates.

TABLE 6.5   *The four most important university subjects*

	Germany (%)	United Kingdom (%)	United States (%)
Law degree	35.0	12.4	9.1
Economics/business	36.7	20.6	38.0
Engineering	18.9	$\sum$ 14.4[a]	$\sum$ 36.1[a]
Natural sciences	8.3		
Humanities	—	18.6	17.0
$\sum$	98.9	66.0	83.1
N	180	97	743

Note: *N*= Number of managers with college/university degree who indicated their university subject in the biographical information. (Many British managers do not give information on the university subject in their biographies.)

[a] For British and US managers, degrees earned in engineering and natural sciences cannot be separated. Percentages give the sum of both degrees. Humanities: this category includes a broad collection of subjects (philosophy, sociology, history, theater science, etc.)

natural science. About one in six managers in both the United States and the United Kingdom took courses in the humanities at university, while in Germany there were none with this background.

In Germany, there appears to be a very short list of subjects which can lead to top management positions, as 98.9 percent of those in our sample holding these positions studied one of four subjects. The variance in subjects is substantially greater in the British sample, where the four most frequently reported subjects account for only 66 percent of the total.[25] In reference to the concepts discussed in Section 6.3, we could conclude that the career paths of German managers are more standardized and professionalized than those of their British counterparts. On this variable, managers in the United States take an intermediate position, with 83.1 percent having studied one of the four most frequently named subjects.

It is also worth noting that 8.9 percent of the US managers founded the company of which they are CEO. None of the European multiple-directors is the company founder.

6.7. INTERNAL VERSUS EXTERNAL RECRUITMENT

To describe the recruitment strategy of the various enterprises, we examined the variable of duration of employment with the company preceding attainment of the top management position (Table 6.6). Enterprises with *external* recruitment of top management hire persons specifically for the highest leadership positions who have no prior experience with the company at lower management levels. Bauer and Bertin-Mourot (1995) refer to these persons as 'parachutists', appearing from out of the blue, as it were, to take command of the enterprise. We expect enterprises that tend toward this recruitment strategy to show a specific set of characteristics.

---

[25] In fact, the variance is even greater when one considers the very broad definition of 'humanities'.

TABLE 6.6   *Years employed by the company before promotion to the top position*

Years	Germany	United Kingdom	United States
0	25.3	37.9	25.8
1–5	16.6	19.0	15.2
6–10	17.8	9.4	9.4
11–15	16.6	16.4	8.6
15+	23.7	17.2	41.0
N=100%	169	116	766

Note: Percent in columns add up to 100%.
0: less than 1 year in the company (= 'parachutists').

First, the positions which 'parachutists' assume are likely to be defined in 'political' terms. They can be thought of as political in the sense in which politicians are abruptly placed atop an administrative apparatus, serving first as defense minister, for example, and then as finance minister. The role that is expected of them has little to do with the content of the ministry (or company), and no special substantive training or experience in the area or the organization is necessary. Furthermore, enterprises that prefer this type of recruitment strategy tend to have an only weakly defined internal identity, for otherwise they could not be represented to the outside world by a 'leader' who is in effect foreign to them.[26]

Enterprises that fill top management positions from the external labor market rather than from within also tend to be characterized by a relatively wide social divide between its elite and the rest of the company. By recruiting its leaders not from those who have proven themselves within the organization, the company turns to a market of candidates who by virtue of their social background (e.g. upper class), education (e.g. 'public' schools, Grandes Écoles), or membership in special circles (exclusive clubs) make up what can be called the 'establishment'. These elites share certain features of social distinction (Bourdieu 1984), and it is these features that close this external market off to members of the middle and lower classes (horizontal integration of the economic elite).

Other companies, however, hire their top managers from within the organization, promoting persons who have proven themselves over many years in the company. Enterprises characterized by such *internal* recruitment strategies usually have well developed internal labor markets. At least theoretically it may be possible for someone to rise from the watchman's gate to the CEO's office. Here, the leadership position is less defined in 'political' terms, but rather demands substantive competence in the given sector or organization. These companies generally also have a clearly defined 'profile', and any newly named top manager who had not already proven

---

[26] Managers who have been promoted within the company to the top are usually bound by 'tacit contracts' with the workforce. 'Parachutists' who enter the company without a history in it, may find it easier to restructure the firm and to lay off parts of the workforce.

himself within the organization would hardly stand a chance of winning acceptance by the workforce.

As Table 6.6 shows, 37.9 percent of our British sample of top-level managers are 'parachutists', as opposed to 25.3 percent in Germany and 25.8 percent in the United States. Most striking in the data on American managers is the very high proportion (41 percent) who spend 15 years or longer in the enterprise of which they had become CEO. In these cases, the highest company manager had risen almost exclusively through the internal labor market of a single enterprise.

Countries differ greatly in typical management recruitment patterns: in the United States and Germany, recruitment tends to be internal, while in Britain and France 'parachutists' appear to dominate. The survey data of Bauer and Bertin-Mourot (1995: 64) show that 60 percent of the Présidents-Directeur-Général (=French CEOs) of the 200 largest enterprises in France are 'parachutists', among whom graduates of the *Polytechnique* and the *École Nationale d'Administration* are particularly well represented.[27] We relate the different recruitment strategies to two different types of elite integration: horizontal integration in the case of Britain and France (horizontal circulation of the 'establishment'), and vertical integration in the case of Germany and the United States (social mobility within the internal labor market).

6.8. SPEED OF PROMOTION

This section discusses three questions. First, how quickly have the managers risen to their present positions? Second, is the speed of promotion similar across the different countries, or are there systematic differences? Third, if differences do exist, what variables explain them? On average, the multiple-directors attained the top position in their enterprises between the age of 45 and 50 years; however, as the following figures show, their promotion can extend over a long period of time.[28]

Figure 6.1 presents the density function of the German and British managers in the sample. On the horizontal axis is the number of years since the beginning of the professional career, and on the vertical is the (empirical)[29] probability of being appointed in a particular year to the board position. Two features are particularly noteworthy here. First, in looking at the overall sample, this promotion can occur at any time in the career, from immediately upon entering the firm to 42 years thereafter. The rise to the highest management position is thus *not* standardized in the sense that most

[27] Typically, these persons begin their careers in the civil service (Grands Corps) and later shift to the private sector, where they assume a management position of a large enterprise. This practice, known as *pantouflage* resembles that of *amakudari* in Japan (Usui and Colignon 1995).

[28] Kruk (1972: table 28) shows that in the early 1970s, most German top managers were appointed to the management/supervisory board while they were aged between 40 and 49 years.

[29] We make no assumptions as to the theoretical distribution of the density or survival functions. It appears that the empirical distribution for British managers could be approximated by a standard extreme value distribution, and that for German managers by a log-logistic distribution. Since we have no plausible explanation for these differences, no theoretical distribution was assumed. For the regression analyses, the nonparametric Cox estimation was used (cf. Table 6.7 below). On the procedure see Blossfeld *et al.* (1986: 36–43), Lawless (1982).

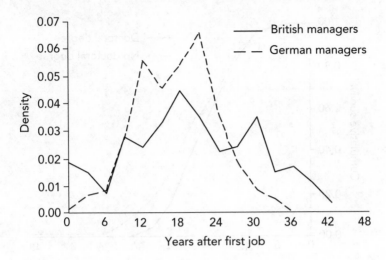

FIG. 6.1   *Promotion of German and British managers (density function)*

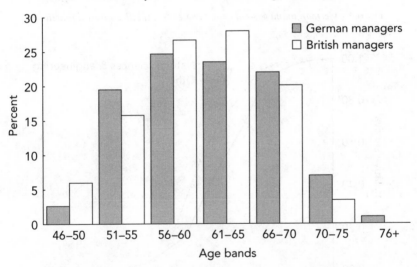

FIG. 6.2   *Age distribution—German and British managers*

managers reach the top position within a certain age spell. Nevertheless, the figure also shows that there is a 'typical' age for the promotion, namely about 15 years after the beginning of the professional career. It is at this point that the curve reaches its peak for the German managers. (The age distribution of managers is shown in Fig. 6.2.) The second striking feature refers to the difference between German and British managers. The promotion pattern in Britain is even less standardized than it is in Germany, that is, the curve is less steep.

Figures 6.3–6.6 show the cumulative survival rates for the British and German managers in relation to a number of variables which may be presumed to have an

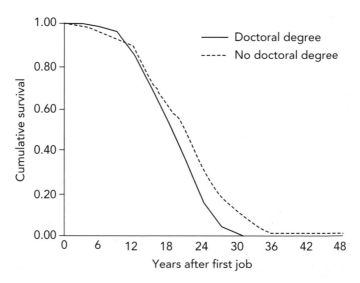

FIG. 6.3   *German managers—doctoral degree (cumulative survival function)*

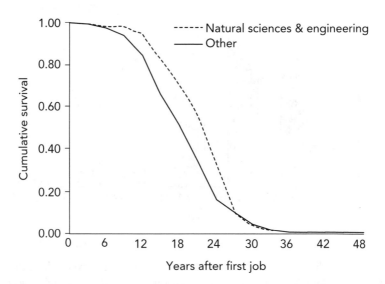

FIG. 6.4   *German managers—engineering (cumulative survival function)*

effect on the speed of promotion. On the horizontal axis is the number of years since the beginning of the professional career, and on the vertical axis is the survival rate, which indicates the proportion of those who had at that point *not yet* been appointed to a directorship. The curve runs horizontal at the time of beginning of the professional career (vertical axis = 1), indicating that none of the future managers had yet

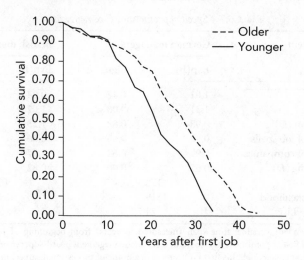

FIG. 6.5 *British managers—older/younger cohort (cumulative survival function)*

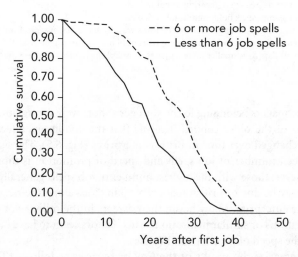

FIG. 6.6 *British managers—number of job spells (cumulative survival function)*

arrived at the top of the enterprise. After 40–50 years, all managers in the sample had attained a directorship, and the curve levels off (value 0). The steeper the curve, the higher is the promotional speed of the managers.

Figure 6.3 demonstrates that German managers with a doctoral degree rise more rapidly than those without. In addition, there is a relationship with the university subject that was studied: those taking courses in natural science or engineering rose less rapidly than those who did not. The fastest risers were managers with a law degree (Fig. 6.4).

TABLE 6.7   *Speed of promotion (Cox-regressions)*

Independent variables	German managers		British managers	
	Exp(*B*)	Sign.	Exp(*B*)	Sign.
Age	1.01	0.47	0.94	0.00
Education	1.31	0.00	1.07	0.30
1st position (*D*)	0.98	0.88	1.25	0.24
Number of job spells	0.97	0.63	0.86	0.01
Number of companies	0.97	0.62	1.07	0.28
Engineering (*D*)	0.57	0.00	0.82	0.51
N	178		167	
−2 Log Likelihood	1519		1398	
Change (−LL)	24.7		34.9	

Note: Dependent variable: time span (measured in years) from beginning of professional career until first appointment to a board of directors/management board/supervisory board.
1st position: manager held his first position (= beginning of professional career) in one of the largest German/British companies. *D*=dummy variable. Number of companies: number of different (independent) companies the manager joined during his professional career.
Engineering: first degree in engineering or natural sciences.
Sign.=level of significance; bold: significant variables.
If the coefficient Exp(*B*) is larger than 1, then this variable has a *positive* effect on the *speed of promotion* (a *negative* effect on the *number of years* until first appointment to a board position).
If the coefficient Exp(*B*) is smaller than 1, then this variable has a negative effect on the speed of promotion.

In Britain, managers belonging to the younger cohort were more rapidly promoted than managers of the older cohort. It seems that the conditions affecting mobility patterns have changed over time in British enterprises (Fig. 6.5). The significant relationship between number of job spells and speed of promotion is more difficult to interpret, however: those with the highest number of job spells generally rise the least rapidly. This may be due to British managers taking jobs along their career path that are outside the enterprise. Many began their careers in the military or as officials in interest associations or similar institutions. Such factors seem to have had a dampening effect on the speed of promotion (Fig. 6.6).

We can summarize the results of the Cox regressions as follows (Table 6.7): the most rapid risers among German managers were those with doctoral degrees who did *not* study natural sciences or engineering, but law or economics. The effects of these two variables are statistically significant. In Britain, on the other hand, the only variables with significant effects are age and number of job spells: those younger and with fewer job spells having risen more rapidly.

Despite obvious differences in the results for German and British managers, one can make the following observation for both samples: frequent change of job and/or company did *not* have a positive effect on the speed of promotion. Deliberate concentration on the internal labor market of a given enterprise appears to offer the same opportunity as frequent change of position.

6.9. CENTRALITY

The multiple-directors in Germany and Britain are linked to one another in a network of interlocking directorates. Each has, in addition to his top management position, parallel directorships on the boards of other companies. The number of persons who a manager meets in her various positions as director is referred to in network analysis as 'degree'. The higher one's 'degree', the more managers she meets, and thus the more 'central' her position in the network.[30]

Network membership entails influence and power. Particularly, the 'central' managers have contacts to numerous other enterprises, and these provide additional channels of information to which they would not be privy if confined to merely their own company. As members of other boards of directors, they are in a position to influence decisions of those enterprises as well as those of their own. Finally, they are presumably in a position to mobilize resources to ensure the success of their own strategic plans.

A regression analysis was computed to identify those variables which explain the degree (centrality) of a director. We take the degree as an indicator for the relative *opportunity* for exerting influence within the network. The independent (explanatory) variables refer both to the individual (e.g. age) and to the organization (e.g. status of the organization). The variables are selected according to specific hypotheses.

Age The manager's age is positively related to his centrality (variable 1). The older he is, the more opportunities he had to gather 'social capital' (Bourdieu 1980).

Educational level The higher the manager's educational status (e.g. doctorate, elite university degree), the greater is her prestige and the more central is her position in the network; similar considerations apply for an aristocratic title (variables 2 and 3).[31]

Honorary doctorate The direction of causality with this variable cannot be determined unequivocally. Either the manager receiving this title enhances his prestige and thus his role in the network, or, conversely, his centrality in the network (and social visibility) leads to his being awarded the title. Similarly, it is not clear what the causal relationship is with 'decoration by the Crown',[32] which is the variable used for the analysis of British managers (variables 4 and 9).

---

[30] The 'degree' is the column (or row) sum in a (symmetrical) matrix. In the present case, the two matrices consist of the 200 German/178 British managers in our sample who occupy three or more directorships.

[31] In the British sample, 12.4% of managers had aristocratic titles such as Baron, Earl, and Viscount, and 32.2% bore the title of 'Sir'. In the German sample, 4.4% had the aristocratic 'von' in their name. Kruk (1972: table 51, appendix) studied 300 managers who were members of the supervisory board of German large firms in the early 1970s and found 7.7% to have aristocratic names, while among 1230 members of the management board, 3.5% had aristocratic names. Comparing these figures with our data, we conclude that the proportion of 'aristocrats' among members of German top management has decreased since the early 1970s.

[32] 'Decorations by the Crown' comprise a list of state honors with ranking defined by tradition. The highest is the Victorian Cross, e.g. and the Knight/Dame Grand Cross of the Royal Victorian Order is at rank 10. The most frequent 'decoration' awarded to managers in our sample is the Knight of the Thistle (rank 4), which 54 had received. For a description of the various honors and their ranking, see Debrett's Peerage Limited: Debrett's Distinguished People of Today. London, 1990, p. 41.

Number of job spells   We hypothesize that managers who have had numerous positions during their career have thereby acquired a relatively wide circle of connections which increases their chances of being named to multiple directorships.

Chairmanship   Managers who are chairmen of the board have a greater visibility and prestige, which enhances their chances of acquiring additional directorships. The same sort of consideration applies in the case of managers with a position on the board of a prestigious firm, that is, one of the 100 largest in the country (variables 6 and 7).

Interest association positions   Managers of large enterprises often have leading positions in one or more interest associations, both in Germany and in the United Kingdom.[33] We presume that this greater social visibility increases the probability of being invited to join the board of directors of another company (variable 8).

Club membership   Biographical data for British managers often include information on membership in various clubs. This specifically British variable (no. 10) is included in the regression analysis along with the equally British variable of 'decorations by the Crown' (variable 9).[34]

The results of the regression analysis confirm some of the above hypotheses. The highest significance levels were shown by the variables 'prestigious firm' and 'interest association' (variables 7 and 8). Managers who hold a position on the board of one of the 100 largest German/British firms, *and* several positions in interest associations tend to be very 'central' in the network, i.e. they come into contact with a great number of managers who themselves meet a great number.

The variables 'age' and 'number of job spells' are significant only in the German sample: the older the managers and the more job spells they had during their professional career, the more 'central' they are. Among the British directors, the variables 'decorations by the Crown' and 'club membership' are positively related to centrality, but the relationship is not significant. We assume therefore, that the social networks that arise through club memberships do overlap with the British network of interlocking directorates, but not substantially.

The regression analysis shows, that the variables with the greatest explanatory power in both the German and the British sample are not those describing characteristics of the individuals themselves, but rather of the enterprises with which they are associated. German managers who tend to have a high centrality index are those with a seat on the board of one of the country's 100 largest enterprises and/or leading positions in either the Confederation of German Industry (BDI) or the Confederation of German Employers' Associations (BDA). The conclusion that we can draw is, therefore, that it is not the personal 'charisma' of the manager himself but rather the prestige of his position which opens the doors to directorships on the boards of other enterprises.

The results presented in Table 6.8 also show, that the explanatory power of the model is not very high: for the German sample, about 24 percent of the variance is explained ($R^2 = 0.24$), for the British sample only 12 percent ($R^2 = 0.12$). We assume that the

[33]   Among Germans with multiple directorships there were 46.4% who had such positions, and among the British 74.4% (see also Useem 1984).

[34]   Club membership on the part of the directors of the 27 largest British financial institutes is analyzed by Whitley (1973: 621); for the United States see Kono *et al.* (1998: 867).

TABLE 6.8   *Centrality (degree)*

Independent variables	Germany		United Kingdom	
	β	Sign.	β	Sign.
1 Age	0.12	0.09	−0.07	0.38
2 Education	−0.09	0.20	0.03	0.66
3 Aristocratic title	−0.09	0.19	0.01	0.91
4 Honorary doctorate	0.07	0.34	0.12	0.17
5 Number of job spells	0.15	0.03	−0.03	0.72
6 Chairman of the board	0.11	0.10	−0.05	0.51
7 Prestigious firm (rank)	0.40	0.00	0.26	0.00
8 Interest association	0.16	0.02	0.16	0.07
9 Decorations by the Crown	—	—	0.13	0.14
10 Clubs	—	—	0.11	0.14
N	177		172	
R^2	0.24		0.12	

Note: Dependent variable: centrality (degree); β: standardized regression coefficients; Sign.: level of significance (α); bold: significant coefficients.
Prestigious firm: 100 largest firms in Germany/Britain.
We computed a stepwise regression for Britain. The regression coefficients for the variables 1–8 hardly change when the additional variables (9,10) are entered; R^2 increases from 0.11 to 0.12. The regression for Britain is, therefore, shown only once.

lower explanatory power of the model for the British managers is due to the greater heterogeneity of this group of managers with respect to their education and career paths.

6.10. CONCLUSIONS

This section summarizes the results of the empirical analysis in regard to typical patterns of professional careers and nationally specific features. In particular, we ask: how standardized the careers of multiple-directors are, whether there are significant differences between the two countries and, finally: are these multiple-directors 'entrepreneurs'?

First, the degree of institutionalization in managers' careers does not appear to be as high as it is in the 'professions' (e.g. law, medicine). However, among German 'big linkers', we do find substantial standardization, for example, in the level of educational degree achieved (63.5 percent have a doctorate), the university subject studied (71.7 percent took either law or economics/ business administration), and the early entry into a large enterprise (49.7 percent as the very first occupational position). Less standardization is seen among top managers in Britain—in educational background, subjects studied, and in the breadth of noneconomic positions held during the career. Many among the British sample spent rather considerable periods during their careers in the military, employed by the royal family, posted to foreign missions, leading interest groups or economic associations before they assumed the leadership of a large business enterprise.

The economic elite, insofar as they are represented in this sample of managers with multiple directorships, comprises a highly differentiated and homogeneous social group that lacks strong ties to the political system. Only few of the 'big linkers' spent any time during their career working for a political party or the government, and by their second occupational position 85–90 percent had already joined a private enterprise (Table 6.3). *Interpenetration* between economic and political elites is thus low. At least regarding the level of leadership personnel, one can conclude from the present data that the state and the economy are separate entities, and this applies both for Germany and Britain.

This conclusion contrasts to the case of France, where almost one-half (44.5 percent) of the country's top-level managers spent a decade or longer working in the civil service before switching to a leadership position with a private enterprise (Bauer and Bertin-Mourot 1996: 55). As regards France, at least until the early 1990s, one can speak of a strong *infiltration* of large enterprises by the government bureaucracy.

In Britain there exists what one can conceive as an 'elite circulation' at the leadership level. Managers can switch ('horizontally') with relative ease from the board room of one company to that of another, without previously having had to 'learn the ropes' of the new company and achieving promotion through its internal labor market. British companies tend to recruit top managers rather from the external, and not from the internal labor market. The qualities that count on this market are not the 'tacit knowledge' of the firm or product-specific experiences, but are rather more symbolic in nature—'public' school background, 'Oxbridge' degree, aristocratic title.[35] This social exclusivity of the highest leadership positions in the British economy (the 'establishment') insulates it and protects it from meritocratic mobility by those from lower social strata.

The typical career pattern in Germany, however, as in the United States, is based upon 'vertical' recruitment, and the highest level of management shows more social integration with the rest of the enterprise rather than with an external 'peer' group. In companies that recruit their top managers internally, it is crucial for new leaders' success that they have spent time in the organization and developed substantive competence and social acceptance within it. The contrast is particularly striking between the United States and France: 41 percent of CEOs in the largest American enterprises had spent 15 years or longer in their firm before being appointed to its top management position, while 60 percent of PDGs in the largest French companies had spent less than one year in the company. In principle, the difference between Germany and Britain is similar, if somewhat less pronounced (Table 6.6).

Examining the careers of German top managers gives the impression that the occupational path which the person took was designed specifically with the aim in mind of entering the boardroom of a large company. All the steps along the way seem to lead the eventual corporate leader up the management ladder of one of the nation's outstanding enterprises. In Britain, however, looking at the early stages in the

---

[35] As we have seen above, these are not necessarily overlapping qualities. It is important that candidates possess symbolic status on the basis of at least one of these features.

career path of an eventual corporate leader seldom betrays the ultimate success that she is destined to achieve. British managers boast not the qualities of business management expertise, knowledge of the economic sector, or experience in the enterprise that he leads but rather qualities of royal honors, aristocratic titles, elite educational certificates, and a proud chain of up to thirty positions on various boards of directors and in interest organizations.

In terms of symbolic goods, even the most esteemed top-level corporate leader in Germany would seem embarrassingly impoverished beside, say, David George Coke Patrick Ogilvy, 13th Earl of Airlie, Knight of the Thistle, Knight Grand Cross of the Royal Victorian Order, British Officer in Malaysia in 1948–9, since 1984 Lord Chamberlain of Her Majesty's Household, and the distinguished occupant of eight seats on corporate boards of directors.

What is important here is not necessarily whether such accounts of (selected and *de*selected) qualities reflect the true capabilities of candidates for or holders of management positions. All presentations of this sort are ultimately 'constructions', and the important thing here is the type of qualities that persons *choose* to vaunt of themselves. And in this their choice shows as little 'individualization' in Britain as it does in Germany. The British establishment sets strict constraints on the type of 'qualities' expected of leaders, regardless of how idiosyncratic these may appear in terms of economic rationality.

The two countries differ, however, not only as regards the *criteria* for the selection of economic elites but also the *timing* of selection. An indicator of the age at which the two economic systems institutionalize the selection process is provided by the academic degrees which top managers possess. If the proportion of top managers who attended an elite institution is relatively high, then, the selection process took place relatively early in the life course and the members of the lower social classes are more or less excluded from the market for elite positions.[36] In Britain, about one-third of managers attended an elite secondary school and about a quarter graduated from one of the elite universities. In France, which as we have seen, is even more extreme in this regard, 50 percent of the PDGs of the country's 200 largest firms attended either the Polytechnique or the École Nationale d'Administration.

The doctorate that is commonly held by German managers offers no comparable equivalent to British titles and honors. It is a form of symbolic goods that has effective market value only in combination with other qualities (e.g. apprenticeship, practical occupational experience). This indicates that selection of German managers takes place comparatively late. After joining an enterprise, the new employee undergoes constant scrutiny to evaluate his potential for promotion.

Regardless of the criteria and timing of selection, however, the processes of selection are highly institutionalized in the various countries—even though in different ways. The market for top managers is not open to dilettantes or self-made men who have no form of professionalized training to show. In this sense, then, the managers are indeed professionalized, as relatively high educational standards are set for them.

---

[36] See Bauer and Bertin-Mourot (1996: 48); Windolf (1997: 120).

In Germany, France, and the United States, this means a degree from the 'right' university or in the 'right' subject, while in Britain it may also mean a certificate from the 'right' secondary school (Table 6.4).

If we now ask, returning to 'entrepreneurship', whether the managers in this sample can be called 'true entrepreneurs' or are merely bureaucrats, the answer must in fact be that the question is misleading, because it assumes a premise which is incorrect. Many authors who criticize the top managers of large corporations as unimaginative bureaucrats (Scheuch and Scheuch 1995) refer to the romantic image of 'creative destroyers' painted by Schumpeter, or of middle-class company founders, or of anecdotal 'genius' garage entrepreneurs. Large corporations which were founded around the turn of the nineteenth century and which have grown into giant empires over the last century cannot be led by garage entrepreneurs—regardless of how gifted they are. These corporations need an efficient and reliable administrative apparatus (the 'visible hand' of management) without which they would disintegrate. Today's managers of these enterprises are quasi-fiduciaries who have to ensure the continued existence of the inheritance, and in this sense they could be called 'conservative'.

Their goal, however, extends beyond maintaining the mere existence of the company, for they must also protect its ranking among the other large enterprises in the country. Daimler-Chrysler, for instance, intends to remain the largest and foremost industrial concern in Germany. Potential and actual leaders of the enterprise are judged against this organizational goal. If the company also manages to be 'innovative', this would surely be welcomed, but only on the condition that its innovativeness does not threaten its place in the overall corporate landscape of the country.

Large enterprises are united by interlocking directorates and form a defensive cartel, which protects them not only against their 'peers' among the corporate giants but also against smart upstarts. In the exclusive circle of large business enterprises, one finds only very few *parvenus*, and this is the case not only in Germany but also in the other countries examined here (Table 6.1). Through their economic cartel and their social closure, these giants are able either to thwart the growth of new potential rivals or to devour them on the market for corporate control.

PART III

POST-SOCIALIST NETWORKS

7

Corporate Networks in Eastern Germany

7.1. GROWTH PARADIGMS

While developing countries are burdened with the struggle to overcome their relative backwardness and reduce the gap between themselves and industrial nations, the latter encounter problems of institutional sclerosis and the resulting danger of backsliding. These problems have been termed by Abramowitz (1986), respectively, as 'catching up' and 'falling behind'. The considerable differences in these two situations attest to the wide discrepancy in development levels throughout the world, with some countries being effectively postmodern while others remain premodern.

Newly unified Germany presents a microcosm of this discrepancy as the result of two regions being joined that show very different development levels, with the east struggling to 'catch-up' while the west tries not to 'fall behind'. For the German government, the discrepancy means a constant policy dilemma, as the demands of telescoped modernization differ greatly from those required to check institutional sclerosis. Many of the conflicts over economic transformation which the country has faced since unification in 1989 can be traced to this dilemma (Czada 1998).

A number of countries have proven particularly successful at 'catching up' over the past 50 years, and in most cases their success has taken place in the context of a specific growth paradigm—one based not upon unbridled market competition but rather upon controlled competition. Examples include Japan, Taiwan, postwar West Germany, Brazil, and a number of other Latin American countries.[1] Countries, on the other hand, that have faced the problem of institutional sclerosis and proven especially able to combat it (e.g. United States, United Kingdom) have generally done so with the help of deregulation, privatization, and increased market competition. One can generalize from these examples that successful catch-up strategies involve *less* competition while successful anti-stagnation strategies rely on *more* competition. Within any one country only one or the other strategy can be taken with any promise of success—not both simultaneously, and this is the dilemma facing post-unification Germany.

It has not been long since Korea, Taiwan, and Mexico were accustomed to being classified within the world-system theory along with countries clearly belonging to

A previous German version of this chapter was published in *Kölner Zeitschrift für Soziologie und Sozialpsychologie* 51 (1999), pp. 260–82 (co-author: Sebastian Schief).

[1] See Leff (1978), Goto (1982), Orrù (1997), Hamilton (1996).

the periphery or semi-periphery (Smith and White 1992; Van Rossem 1996). In recent years, however, their rapid economic growth and aggressive export policies have significantly narrowed the gap between them and countries at the center (core), and they now offer industrialized nations serious competition. Analyzing the growth paradigm pursued by these countries is particularly interesting in forecasting the likely economic future of the former East Germany, which by 1989 had attained a level of economic development roughly comparable with a number of countries in the semi-periphery (Müller-Krumholz 1993).

By 'growth paradigm' we understand a system of institutions that direct macroeconomic processes, in particular the regulation and supervision of market competition (North 1990). Important elements of the paradigm include corporate networks, the 'invention of tradition' (Hobsbawm 1983), business ethics, and the level of qualifications, and technical expertise. Below, we examine two of these elements which are of particular importance for the transformation process in East Germany: corporate networks and the reconstitution of traditions.

7.1.1. *Corporate Networks*

Corporate networks, which coordinate the economic activities of their various constituent firms, are among those features that always draw substantial emphasis in comparative economic analyses (Granovetter 1995). The structure, density, and stability of these networks vary from country to country, as does its institutional basis. At the core of such a network one often finds, for example, single families (Taiwan), groups of families (Korea), large companies and banks (Japan), or a combination of families and financial institutions (France). These often come to symbolize the country's economic success—the *keiretsu* in Japan, the *chaebol* in Korea, the *guanxiqiye* in Taiwan (Numazaki 1996), the *grupos económicos* in Chile,[2] and the *Konzern* in West Germany.

These networks may provide protection without necessarily sacrificing the autonomy of their member firms. Competing firms are integrated within more or less densely connected networks, but they are not subjugated to the discipline of a rigid bureaucracy. Evans (1992: 171, 23) used the term '*embedded autonomy*' to point to these conflicting objectives which actors try to accomplish in their networks.

The existence of networks offers a substitute to open market competition, transforming the economic conditions into a system of 'controlled competition'. Experience shows that successful countries have not built their institutions along a neoliberal model of competition but have reconstituted their own respective traditions and integrated new business enterprises into a complex system of networks which provide effective protection to specialized companies. As is shown below, this sort of mutually protective networks is lacking in East Germany; in its place we find a unilateral dependence upon West German combines.

---

[2] For instance, Grupo Fernandez Leon, Grupo Angelini, etc.; see also Zeitlin and Ratcliff (1988).

7.1.2. *Traditions*

While in western countries the process of modernization entailed the dissolution of most premodern institutions, many Newly Industrializing Countries (NICs) preserved certain traditional forms of their economic organization. For example, familial or social ties often became a basis for the building of large business concerns. In some cases one finds a conscious reconstruction of the past, such as in Japanese companies with their quasi-feudal employment relations (e.g. lifetime jobs, seniority principle). 'Japan of the 1920s, and again in the post-war period, was much more of a cut-throat jungle than it is today. Not the ethics of relational contracting... nor the lifetime employment system, seem to have been at all characteristic of earlier periods of Japanese industrialization' (Dore 1987: 188; Gordon 1991).

The textile and clothing industry of northern Italy relies upon the traditional extended family for a kind of 'flexible specialization'.[3] In the case of Hungary, Szelényi (1988) has described the reestablishment of prewar business traditions in the course of economic reforms over recent years. These examples demonstrate that modernization is not necessarily a linear process, but one that can reach back into the past and reintegrate protective, premodern traditions.

In many countries, remnants of a religious past continue to underpin the social integration of economic networks, and this is true not only for the Protestant ethic in the West (Weber 1969: 282), but also for the Confucian ethic in some of today's NIC (Whyte 1996). Deutschmann (1989) has described the Japanese 'worker-bee syndrome', and East Asian politicians often praise what they see as typically Asian 'virtues', which they set in opposition to Western 'decadence' (Zakaria 1994).

Traditional forms of economic organization provide a comparative advantage because financial capital, technical expertise, loyalty, and protection may be mobilized which are not available in the market. For many countries, the 'reconstruction of history' has proven beneficial in today's context of global competition. We argue below that East Germany over the past 40 years has undergone two revolutions which have destroyed not only the political, but also the economic institutions of the country. The resulting institutional vacuum has enabled external actors to gain effective dominance there with relative ease.

Family associations form an institutional basis for the growth paradigm in some, but not in all countries (e.g. Taiwan, Korea). The economic success and modernization which France has enjoyed since the Second World War has relied upon a network-like relationship between state, traditional families, and the financial sector. In Germany, on the other hand, such familial relationships are *not* the characteristic form—rather the combine structure (*Konzern*), which includes capital networks between the financial sector and large industries, and corporatist control by virtue of

---

[3] See Piore and Sabel (1984: 213–16). In Italy, 99% of companies are owned by families. There, as in France, it has often been possible within only a few decades for such a family-owned company to achieve a leading position among the country's large-scale enterprises; examples include the Benetton, Berlusconi, and Merloni families. See *Le Monde*, 15 May 1998: 16–17.

interlocking directorates (including employees' representatives in those firms which are covered by the law on codetermination).

In none of these cases are the structures entirely new creations, but rather they grow to some extent out of traditions that have either continued unbroken from the past (e.g. the family associations in Taiwan) or have been newly reconstituted along historical lines (e.g. combine structure and codetermination in Germany).

We argue here that successful catching up strategies in the context of today's market globalization depend to a large extent upon specifically tailored growth paradigms. In practical terms, a growth paradigm consists of an institutional framework which provides protection from competition, but which, on the other hand, does not entirely eliminate competition. The analysis of East German corporate networks in the following sections focuses on two questions: what are the structural characteristics of the network there, and is this form of network a suitable institutional setting for 'catch-up' modernization in East Germany?

7.2. POLITICAL EXCHANGE IN NETWORKS

Seen as exchange systems, market, bureaucracy (hierarchy), and networks produce different transaction costs, lead to the trading of different types of goods, and are integrated by different social mechanisms. Here, the analysis focuses on transactions within networks which may be more efficient than market transactions, but also more discriminatory against outsiders.

The *market* creates a system of mutual functional dependence: each market participant depends upon every other participant (Swedberg 1994). There exists neither a formal authority structure nor a formal membership. The system is, at least in theory, open to everyone; no prospective participant is excluded on the basis of particularistic criteria. Legitimation of the system is guaranteed by the exchange of equivalents: participants trade goods of the 'same' value, as expressed in prices. However, there are many types of goods upon which no price is set, and which are, therefore, not sold in the market but rather are exchanged through social networks, for example, loyalty, protection from hostile takeovers, and (insider) information.

A *network*, on the other hand, can take any of several different forms and can rest upon various types of social integration. Networks between companies can consist, for example, of interlocking directorates or of capital participations (property rights). Social relationships defined outside the economic system are often exploited for the sake of economic exchange. Examples include intermarriage circles among upper class families, alumni associations of elite universities, old-boys' networks among age cohorts, and the former nomenclature in excommunist countries. Some of these relationships descend into mafia-like networks of corrupt 'crony capitalism'.

The economic efficiency of networks stems in part from their high degree of flexibility. Transactions within a given network may in fact take place at market prices and differ little from those in a competitive market setting. On the other hand, transactions within a network may be organized in a very different way, and are then referred to as 'political exchange' (Marin 1990). In these transactions, it is often impossible to set a 'value' on the service rendered (e.g. loyalty). The rule of equivalency of exchange does not hold in this case, as 'more' can be traded for 'less' without calling into question the legitimacy of the exchange. Moreover, payment can be deferred to a later date; here we can speak of 'barter credit'.[4] It is sometimes the case that multiple trading partners enter a 'circular' exchange network, with one receiving services for which another delivers the payment—in the expectation that at some point in the future the ledger will be balanced.[5]

Access to networks is generally based on particularistic selection criteria, such as kinship, possession of a degree from an elite university, membership in a particular political party, or even a certain age.[6] The group of persons thus defined are permitted to participate in the network and to compete within it, thus, not eliminating competition but rather controlling and regulating it. Even within the network, continued membership requires that payment eventually be made for services rendered, although the definition of services and payments may be somewhat flexible. A crucial characteristic of this system of controlled competition is its exclusion of outsiders—hence the protection to those trading within the system from extreme forms of competition. Thus, while full competition in open markets (universalism) is one means of achieving economic efficiency, the particularistic discrimination of controlled competition and trading within networks is another (Whitley 1990).

Transactions which in the broadest sense can be seen as economic can be organized in a given country either through the market, through the bureaucracy (hierarchy), or through networks. In every country there is a characteristic distribution structure which determines the proportion of transactions that take place in each of these three types of exchange systems. The distribution structure varies with the institutional and cultural context. In any given country, the largest proportion of transactions is assigned to the exchange system which promises comparative advantages in the global competition. When social and institutional resources are available to facilitate the social integration and control within groups (e.g. 'trust'), more transactions tend to be organized by networks than by the market or the bureaucracy (Fukuyama 1995). This

---

[4] The following illustrates the exchange relations between Chinese families in Singapore: 'When my father started out in the building construction business, Mr. Chai, the owner of one of the leading construction companies helped my father a lot. He channelled quite a lot of business to my father and helped our company to take off the ground. This was very important because my father was new to the industry' (Kiong 1996: 140). In this case the favor remained as an indebtedness until 'payment' was made years later. The timing and form of payment may be unspecified. Protective networks are also created by '*clientelismo*', which in its various forms is characterized by patronization (Graziano 1984).

[5] Dore (1987: 184) terms such transactions 'relational contracting' and illustrates them in the following example from the Japanese steel industry, which competed with cheaper imports from Korea: 'None of the major trading companies would touch Brazilian or Korean steel, especially now that things are going so badly for their customers, the Japanese steel companies. Small importers are willing to handle modest lots. But they will insist on their being landed at backwater warehouses away from where any domestic steel is going out, so that the incoming steel is not seen by a steel-company employee. If that happens, the lorries taking the steel out might be followed to their destination. And the purchaser, if he turned out to be a disloyal customer, would be marked down for less than friendly treatment next time a boom brings a seller's market'.

[6] Jacobs (1976: 80) characterizes these relationships as 'personalistic, particularistic, non-ideological ties between persons—based on a commonality of shared identification'.

is not only because networks reduce transaction costs, but also because they free productive resources (e.g. cooperation without bureaucracy).

In countries which since the Second World War have shown the greatest success in economic 'catching up', a larger proportion of transactions tend to take place in networks than is the case in countries that were already modernized, and that are at the center of the world system. Essential features of the growth paradigm of many countries include the relative limitation of a nation's trading to particularistic networks and the temporary protection thus provided from the competition in the global market.

Access to networks can be defined by various sets of criteria. In networks principally made up of individuals, membership is defined by particularistic attributes.[7] Age, sex, kinship, or ethnic attributes may be used as selection criteria to control access. Networks can also be based primarily on organizations, such as in the Japanese *keiretsu* groups and the German *Konzern*. In this case, membership depends upon the characteristics of the organization, for example, its age, size, and success (growth rate). However, networks based upon organizations are not necessarily more 'open' or 'universalistic' than those based upon individuals. In Chapter 3, it was shown that, for instance, the West German corporate network constitutes a very 'closed' society.

Upon its unification with the Federal Republic of Germany, East Germany took over unchanged the political, economic, and cultural institutions of West Germany. Furthermore, the business community of the east is dominated by western influence, as most companies there are owned either by firms or by investors from the west. One might presume from this that the structure of the corporate network in the east mirrors that in the west. As will be shown in the following sections, however, this is not the case.

7.3. EMPIRICAL STUDY

The population for the analysis in this chapter consists of all East German firms that in April 1996 had a minimum of 500 employees. Above this threshold level, the company works council can demand the establishment of a supervisory board.[8] This institution provides seats for owners and/or managers of other firms, and is the locus for interlocking directorates. Data were drawn from all handbooks published on German companies. In addition, we asked Hoppenstedt publishing company to put together additional data on companies with more than 500 employees that had not published data on themselves. Data were thus collected on a total of 315 companies, 39 of which were excluded, however, for belonging to the public or quasi-public sector.[9] The

---

[7] This is the case, e.g. with membership in the various family networks in Taiwan, which are defined either by kinship (*tongzong*), by regional origin (*tongxiang*), or by age cohorts (tongnian). Each of these three characteristics (kinship, region of origin, age) may be accepted as a signal of 'similarity', on the basis of which a new member may be accepted into the network (Numazaki 1996: 71–6, 300).

[8] See sect. 77 of the German *Betriebsverfassungsgesetz* (1952). In companies with more than 2000 employees, codetermination is regulated by the *Mitbestimmungsgesetz* (1976).

[9] Examples of those excluded are (government-run) transportation facilities, hospitals, theaters, schools, etc.

remaining 276 companies form the basis of our sample. Among these 276 are the 16 largest banks and savings societies in East Germany. Financial institutions were included in order to ascertain interlocking directorates between the financial sector and other firms.

Three-fourths of the enterprises in our sample have the legal form of a limited liability company. The law pertaining to this form of enterprise mandates the publication of only a few data, and firm reports consequently often fail to list the names of the members of the supervisory board. In 1996, we conducted a written and a subsequent telephone survey of the companies for which the names of supervisory board members or owners were missing from published accounts. These inquiries were addressed in each case to the works council of the respective company.[10] With the help of the published data and our written and telephone surveys, we were able to determine the names of supervisory board members, management board members, and managing directors of 224 enterprises. Data on the remaining firms were incomplete and are excluded from some analyses for the sake of comparison to the West German sample.

In the 276 companies considered, we obtained the names of 1714 persons in the above leadership positions; our analysis of interlocking directorates is based on this sample. Furthermore, we determined which of these 1714 individuals also have positions on the supervisory board or management board of any of the 600 largest West German companies or of a West German company which itself is the proprietor of one of the 276 companies in our East German sample.[11]

The results of this analysis are presented in Table 7.1. Column 2 shows the distribution of the 1714 persons in leadership positions in the 276 East German firms. Of these, 93.9 percent have only a single position, and 0.4 percent have four or more positions. When we look not exclusively at positions in East German firms but include also positions that these 1714 persons hold in West German companies (column 3), there is a different distribution: 82.5 percent have a single position, and 3.7 percent have four positions or more. Column 4 presents the positions which 8952 West German managers hold in the 694 largest West German companies. That the percentages in columns 3 and 4 are virtually identical shows that the distributions in east and west are the same if one includes the West German positions of eastern managers. One can conclude from these figures that almost all eastern managers who are involved in interlocking directorates in the *eastern* part of the country are big linkers in the network of the *West* German combines. In the following sections, we shall demonstrate that this is in fact the case.

---

[10] We addressed ourselves to the works councils because we assumed that firms which had not published the names of its supervisory board members would also not report them in such a survey. Questionnaires also included items referring to company codetermination. Both the text of the questionnaire and the raw data are available on request.

[11] Some of the parent companies of the East German firms are not among the 600 largest in West Germany. These additional companies were also examined to determine whether one of the 1714 persons in the East German sample had a leadership position in them.

TABLE 7.1 *East German managers and their positions*
(comparison with West Germany)

Number of positions	EG %	EG+WG[a] %	WG[b] %
1	93.9	82.5	83.1
2	5.1	10.8	10.4
3	0.6	3.0	3.1
4+	0.4	3.7	3.4
$\sum$ persons	1714	1714	8952
Positions	1850	2308	11,866

Note: EG: East Germany; WG: West Germany.
[a] Column 2 shows the *sum* of positions, which 1714 *East German* managers hold in East German *and* West German companies (survey: 1996).
[b] Column 3 shows number of positions, which 8952 West German managers hold in the 694 largest West German corporations (see Table 5.1).

7.4. CAPITAL NETWORKS IN EAST GERMANY

Capital networks arise when enterprises themselves are the proprietors of other companies; the linkage between firms in this case is thus based on property rights. This type of network exists in many but not all countries.[12] The structure of the network is often hierarchical, such as in the West German *Konzern*, in the French *groupe financière* (Morin 1994), and in the Korean *chaebol*, where, in the latter case, capital networking strengthens patriarchal control of a family-based group (Ungson *et al.* 1997). The structure of a capital network may, however, also be horizontal, in which case it resembles a clique, such as in the Japanese *keiretsu* groups and in the reciprocal linkages of the West German financial core and among the largest Czech banks. [13]

The structure of capital networks in East Germany can be described relatively easily: among the 276 East German companies in our sample, there exist a total of only 11 capital relationships, which means a network density of only 0.02. The matrix of the East German capital network is almost empty and it is, therefore, impossible to identify a specific network configuration.

The reason why there are no capital networks among East German firms becomes clear when we examine who the proprietors of these firms are. Table 7.2 lists the various types of owners and the concentration of shareholdings in East German firms. For the 276 companies, we identified a total of 478 shareholdings (1.6 per company). Of these, 59 percent are western interests—either West German companies or private investors in West Germany or elsewhere in the west (see column 'all shareholdings'). In only 10 percent of cases are the owners East German. However, here one must note

---

[12] In Chapter 4, it was shown that in the United States there are virtually no shareholdings among the largest 500 corporations. Therefore, the matrix of capital networks for these corporations is almost empty.
[13] The reciprocal structure of the financial core in the Czech Republic resulted from the method of privatization (voucher privatization). For details, see Figs 8.1 and 8.2.

TABLE 7.2 *Distribution of ownership in 276 East German companies*

Type of owner	Proportion of stock owned (%) (ownership concentration)						All shareholdings	
	–4.9	5–9.9	10–24.9	25–49.9	50–74.9	751	(N)	(%)
West (German) owner								
Nonfinancial firms	50.0	29.4	27.6	23.8	45.7	42.7	172	36.0
Financial firms	4.5	—	12.1	2.9	8.7	3.1	21	4.4
Families/individuals	—	11.8	8.6	15.2	13.0	4.6	42	8.8
Foreign interests (west)	18.2	7.8	5.2	5.7	6.5	13.8	47	9.8
East German owner								
Nonfinancial firm	—	2.0	1.7	3.8	2.2	5.6	18	3.8
Financial firm	—	—	1.7	—	2.2	0.5	3	0.6
Families/individuals	13.6	23.5	3.4	—	6.5	3.6	27	5.6
Public bodies								
THA	—	2.0	1.7	9.5	—	8.2	28	5.9
Communities	—	—	10.4	5.7	8.7	8.7	33	6.9
State	—	2.0	1.7	4.8	—	4.1	15	3.1
Owner unknown (missings)	13.7	21.5	25.9	28.6	6.5	5.1	72	15.1
All shareholdings								
N	22	51	58	105	46	196	478	—
%	4.6	10.7	12.1	22.0	9.6	41.0	—	100

Note: Each column adds to 100%. For example, 22 shareholdings (= 4.6%) make up less than 5% of company stock. These 22 holdings are distributed as follows: 50.0% to nonfinancial firms in the west, 4.5% to financial firms in the west, etc. The bottom row adds to 100% and presents the percentage of holdings falling within the respective share-size category. The last column gives the proportion of shares owned by the respective type of owner. There is a relatively high proportion of missing values. In many of these cases, we were able to identify the name of the owner, but we do not know whether the owner is a West(German) or an East German owner. These cases were classified as 'owner unknown'.

that nine of the twenty-one East German enterprises that own other East German firms are themselves owned by western interests; ultimate control rests in the west in these nine cases. Thus, genuine capital networks among East German firms is virtually unknown, since capital relationships typically run from west to east (in a total of 193 cases).[14]

Table 7.2 also shows that 242 of the proprietors that we identified own at least 50 percent of the nominal capital of the East German firm.[15] Since for each company there can be only one majority shareholder, the number of these shareholdings is equal to the number of firms. There are 242 majority shareholdings; therefore, the

[14] See Table 7.2, column 'all shareholdings': 172 shareholdings by nonfinancial companies and 21 by financial institutes, thus a total of 193 west–east capital relationships (West German firms/banks as owners).
[15] The figure of 242 majority shareholdings is the sum of the 46 that own 50–74.9% and the 196 that own 75% or more (second to the last row in Table 7.2).

proportion of large firms which are controlled in East Germany by a majority share-holder is 87.7 percent. This means that in East Germany, the concentration of owner-ship is higher than in West Germany.[16] In only 4.6 percent of cases is the holding smaller than 5 percent. This high degree of ownership concentration precludes the existence in East Germany of 'manager capitalism'. Most executive managers in these firms were born in East Germany, but they are under close control of a majority owner who is in most cases a West German combine.[17]

The structure of the East German network is the direct result of the method used to privatize the state-owned enterprises (SOEs) (Windolf 1998). Upon unification, the *Treuhandanstalt* (THA) became the legal successor to the former East German state as proprietor of these enterprises. A first step in the privatization process was to reduce the SOEs in size by mass dismissals to relatively small firms, most of which were then sold by the THA to investors in the west. The population of the former East Germany was not involved in the privatization (e.g. as was the case in the Czech Republic, through a system of share vouchers). Although in many cases the previous company management from the communist era attempted to purchase the company for themselves ('nomenclature privatization'), these attempts were generally rejected by the THA. The networks into which the privatized firms consequently became integrated were thus those in the west, with the firms themselves serving merely as *isolated* eastern outposts of western interests, rather than forming independent, specifically eastern networks of their own.

As noted above, our sample of 276 firms includes 210 limited liability companies and 48 joint stock companies, most of which are owned by western enterprises or investors. The advantage of this legal form is that the owners can reduce the risks inherent in investment, for they are liable in these cases only to the extent of their investment (i.e. the nominal capital). We have also noted above that 88 percent of East German firms have a majority owner. The practical significance of these figures can be explained in the following way: almost all large firms in East Germany have a majority owner who has *unlimited control* over the firm, but only *limited liability* for debt. The owners are in most cases West (German) corporations or investors whose genuine interests are not located in East Germany. The following example illustrates one of the consequences of this constellation of interests.

In August 1992, the THA trust sold two East German shipyards to a West German engineering firm, the *Bremer Vulkan Verbund* (BVV). The sale contract stipulated that the THA would not receive money for the East German shipyards, but was obliged to pay 351 million Euro as a subsidy to the West German owner (BVV). This kind of 'deal' was not uncommon in East Germany; in many privatization cases the 'sale price' was not paid by the purchaser to the THA, but by the THA to the pur-chaser. The only condition in this case was that 172 million Euro of the overall 'price'

---

[16] Fifty-one percent of the large West German firms are controlled by a majority shareholder (50%+); see Table 3.1.

[17] While most executive managers are born in East Germany, the seats of the supervisory boards (nonexecutive positions) are almost exclusively filled with top managers from West Germany (Windolf 1998).

was stipulated as an investment allowance, which meant that the purchaser should use these funds only for investment purposes. The German Finance Ministry attempted to impose further conditions on the use of this allowance, but these were rejected by the BVV. A subsequent 'cash-concentration' contract between the BVV and its subsidiaries gave the parent company the right of direct access to the assets of its subsidiaries, including the two East German shipyards, with their considerable public subsidy. This move, however, was not enough to save the BVV from going into receivership in May 1996. The bankruptcy of the parent company implied the bankruptcy of the two East German shipyards and the loss of 351 million Euro. The THA then brought suit against the BVV for improper use of the investment allowance, but lost the case in the German Supreme Court.[18]

This case illustrates the power that the parent has over its subsidiaries, including the right to force it to take actions that are detrimental, even suicidal, to it—for the sake of the parent. The case is not an isolated one; the German courts have pondered the legality of many such practices on the part of western investors toward their newly purchased eastern firms.

Also, the 'plundering'[19] of subsidiaries by the parent company is not limited to East German firms; in fact, the West German courts have deliberated for years over such shady practices by parent companies.[20] Nevertheless, the method by which eastern firms were privatized offered western investors a unique opportunity to exploit the possibilities allowed them by German law. The firms in East Germany which they bought at a low (or 'counter') price were often not in themselves in any way attractive to potential buyers except for their land and physical plant and, therefore, were ripe objects for such 'plundering'.

This is not to imply that the majority of western investors acted out of fraudulent motives in acquiring subsidiaries in the east. The point here is rather to demonstrate the difference in the nature of corporate networks in the east and west. Virtually all large companies in the former East Germany that survived national unification and economic privatization did so at the price of being sold to West German enterprises (see Table 7.2), which are permitted to do with their subsidiaries as they please. The East German corporate network thus consists principally of firms that are legally and economically dependent upon western interests. Whereas the corporate network in the west *protects* companies against external influence (cooperative capitalism), the corporate network in the east *exposes* them to external influence.

7.5. INTERLOCKING DIRECTORATES

There are a number of functions which interlocking directorates can fulfill, for example, sharing of information, reducing resource dependence, and strengthening the social integration of economic elites (Koenig *et al.* 1979). Almost none of these apply,

---

[18] Source: *ZIP/Zeitschrift für Wirtschaftsrecht*, vol. 19, 1998, pp. 561–8.
[19] This term has been used by the German Supreme Court for such cases (see *NJW* 1997, p. 69).
[20] See Lutter (1984), Michalski and Zeidler (1996).

TABLE 7.3 *Interlocking directorates in East Germany*

	East German firms		West German firms	
East German firms N = 276	*Matrix A* Directed ILD Undirected ILD	24 170 Σ194	*Matrix B* Directed ILD Undirected ILD	6 453 Σ459
West German firms N = 623	*Matrix C* Directed ILD Undirected ILD	221 453 Σ674	*Matrix D* West German corporate network (cf. chapter 3)	

Note: ILD: interlocking directorates.

however, in the case of East German firms. Most of the managers who play a prominent role in the East German network come from the west and occupy a comparable position in the network there as well. As has been shown in the previous section most large firms in the east are owned by West (German) corporations and, as a result, no autonomous corporate network could develop since 1989. The principal function of interlocking directorates is to reinforce the *control* of West German owners over East German firms. This corporate network does not strengthen the autonomy of its member firms (embedded autonomy), but rather increases their dependence.

Table 7.3 shows four different combinations of how East/West German firms may be linked to each other: interlocks among East German firms (matrix A); interlocks between East and West German firms (matrix B); interlock between West and East German firms (matrix C), and interlocks among West German firms (matrix D).

We begin with an analysis of interlocking directorates among the 276 East German companies themselves (matrix A). Here we find 24 directed and 170 undirected relationships.[21] The total number of 194 relationships yields a density of 0.18. When we consider, however, the number of relationships that are directed from west to east, we find that these are much more frequent (matrix C), with 221 directed and 453 undirected relationships among the total of 674. This means that East German companies are not predominantly linked to each other, but are connected to West German corporations many of which are owners of East German firms.

We also examined the possibility of relationships being directed from east to west (matrix B). These directed interlocks are of particular interest because an East German executive manager who sits on the supervisory board of a West German corporation has considerable influence on the decision-making process there. We were able to identify only six instances of this, and in each case the person in question had

[21] In a *directed* relationship there is a 'sender' and a 'receiver'; e.g. the member of the management board of firm A is sent to sit on the supervisory board of firm B (asymmetric relationship). When the same person sits on the supervisory board of a western and that of an eastern company, one can speak of an undirected relationship. Since undirected relationships are symmetric, the numbers in matrices B and C are the same (N = 453).

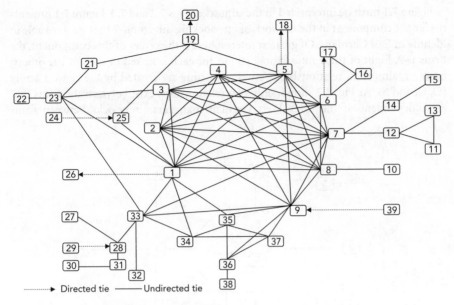

FIG. 7.1   *Largest East German component (1996)*

come from the west and had begun his career there.[22] We found no instance of an East German manager who had been co-opted onto the supervisory board of a West German company. As with capital-based networks above, it is also the case with interlocking directorates that the direction of influence is from west to east.

Burt (1992) uses the term 'structural holes' to refer to gaps in a corporate network which can be strategically exploited by dominant actors. Figure 7.2 presents a group of actors (O, G, and S)[23] who play a central role in a network which consists of nine East German firms, that is, these managers sit on the supervisory boards of the firms 1–9 in Fig. 7.2. The three managers (O, G, S) are members of the management board of a large West German combine. The East German firms themselves have a few local ties but are not linked directly with one another. Thus, there are 'structural holes' between these firms, and these are bridged over by the central actors (O, G, and S), who are able to monopolize the relationships between these firms. The exchange of information and resources between the firms is indirect, passing over the actors in the center.

---

[22] E.g. Lothar Späth, former governor of the West German state of Baden-Württemberg, is managing director of a company in Jena (in the east) and also has a seat on the supervisory board of a company in Munich (in the west). Claus Grobecker, former Minister of Finance in the western city-state of Bremen, was managing director of a company in Rostock (in the east) and also had a seat on the supervisory board of a company in Bremen (in the west).

[23] The persons concerned here are members of the management board of the combine Preussag: Gaul (G), Offermann (O), and Schoeneberg (S). Preussag is a West German combine that owns many power stations in Germany.

Figure 7.1 must be interpreted in the context of Figs 7.2 and 7.3. Figure 7.1 presents the largest component in the network of interlocking directorates that we were able to identify in East Germany. Of greatest interest here is the center of this component, the firms 1–9. Eight of these nine form a clique, for each is linked to each of the others; however, almost all relationships between the nine are created by the central actors (O, G, and S). As Fig. 7.2 shows, only two relationships exist between the firms that are independent of the three West German managers (interlocks between firms

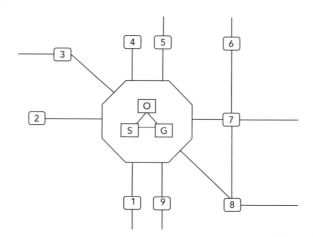

FIG. 7.2   *Structural holes*

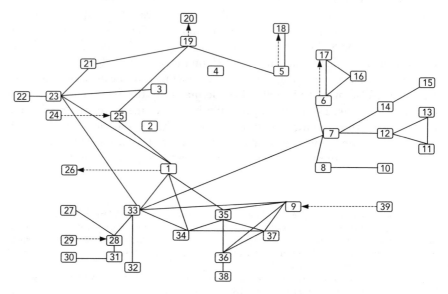

FIG. 7.3   *Largest East German component (ties of managers O., S., and G. omitted)*

6–7–8). The constellation in Fig. 7.3 is the result of subtracting the relationships which are created by the central actors. The center of Fig. 7.3 shows a 'hole' that remains when the ties created by the central actors are eliminated. The large component shown in Fig. 7.1 disintegrates into two components in Fig. 7.3.

This example illustrates to what extent the East German network (if there is such a network) is dominated by West German top managers. The notion of a 'structural hole' describes the strategic position that these managers hold in the East German network. They provide a 'bridge' among East German firms many of which would be isolated without these central actors.

Finally, we considered how many of the managers who are important in the network of interlocking directorates come from the west. Of the 1714 managers in Table 7.1, 105 (6.1 percent) have two or more positions. We asked how many of these managers had begun their careers in the west or at the time of the survey had their center of activity in the west (e.g. as a member of a supervisory board on a western company). Even if we assume that all of the persons who cannot be clearly assigned to the west are in fact from the east, we still find that about 80 percent of these persons who are important in the East German network are West German managers.

7.6. CONCLUSIONS

We presented the thesis above that the process of catching up is favored not by the elimination but by the regulated limitation of market competition. It was further argued that countries which are particularly successful in catching up, structure their domestic market in terms of networks that provide protection without necessarily sacrificing the autonomy of their member firms (embedded autonomy). The analysis of the East German network has shown that the ownership structures which have been created by the privatization process after 1989 discourage the formation of such networks. There are only very few independent relationships among East German firms; the capital network and the network of interlocking directorates is dominated by western owners (structural holes).

This structure did not arise by historical chance but is the direct result of political decisions: it was created by the method used between 1990 and 1995 to privatize the SOEs of communist East Germany which were previously state owned. The unequal distribution of property rights in the large East German companies was strongly influenced by the privatization process.

A second argument emphasized the role of traditions and the deliberate 'reconstruction of history' in the process of creating efficient economic organizations and institutions. Most of these institutions are not entirely new creations, but they have grown to some extent out of traditions.

Twice in the past half-century East Germany has experienced a revolution that destroyed the foundations of its political and economic institutions. The enterprises that had been founded in the nineteenth century, and that established a cartel network were expropriated following the Second World War by the new communist government. Persons belonging to the former 'bourgeois' elite were either dismissed from all leadership positions or simply liquidated. The large socialist combines subsequently erected in East Germany were dismantled just as radically by the THA after national unification in 1989. At that time it was no longer possible to build on prewar economic networks as these had long since ceased to exist, nor was it possible to reconstitute some of the socialist networks as these shared the discreditation of the communist regime. Stable networks rest on the reconstitution of traditions, and the accumulation of 'social capital' takes time. It was in the resulting vacuum that external actors were able to gain dominance in the east after 1989.

In no other postcommunist country have western interests been able, as effectively as in East Germany, to dominate the new economic structures. In the context of considering their competitive advantages on the global market, western enterprises regard the specific conditions of their East German subsidiaries as being of only marginal significance. In the best-case scenario, the eastern company was modernized by its western parent and accorded a meaningful position in the overall business plans of the company. In a less advantageous case, the eastern company was degraded to nothing more than a peripheral assembly plant. In the worst-case scenario, it was plundered dry by the parent company.

The microeconomic conditions thus existing in virtually all of the East German companies are reflected today in the general macroeconomic situation of East Germany: the post-unification domination by westerners has prevented the development of an autonomous economic network which can protect it from external influences.

8

Privatization and Corporate Networks in Eastern Europe

8.1. WHAT TYPE OF CAPITALISM?

The revolution of 1989 brought an end to almost all the world's socialist regimes, opened the way to a Western style market economy, and made it possible for the populations of East European countries to choose their economic and political institutions. Yet, 'capitalism' is not a homogeneous system, but exists in many variants and institutional combinations: US-style market capitalism is different from the corporatist systems in Sweden and Austria, and Japan and East Asian countries have not replicated Western models, but have developed different economic and political orders. What type of capitalism is evolving in Eastern Europe? Which model oriented political choices and what are the real outcomes? The present analysis concentrates on the constraints on and unintended consequences of such choices.[1]

Vladimir Dlouhy, Czech Minister for Industry and Trade, commented on the voucher privatization: 'Despite heroic attempts of the architects of Czech voucher privatization to create a US-style capital market, we have finished with something much closer to the German system of "corporate banking ownership" (Dlouhy and Mládek 1994: 169). Similar observations were made for the Russian privatization program: '...as the programme passed from conception to implementation it turned out to be much more favourable to worker ownership than its authors had intended' (Rutland 1994: 1112). Two years after reunification, East German industrial output was down by 73 percent on its previous level (Dornbusch and Wolf 1994). Would the architects of the East German privatization program have advocated a policy of rapid and complete privatization if they had known that the immediate economic results would be so disastrous?

A distinction can be made between the institutional *model* which oriented political choices in Eastern Europe, the theory that linked the model to the intended outcome (the socioeconomic *technology*), and the *real outcome*—to the extent that we can already observe it. These distinctions imply three different questions: which type of

This is a revised version of a paper first published in *European Journal of Sociology*, XXXIX (1998), pp. 335–76. Reproduced with permission.

[1] *Abbreviations* used in this chapter: CEE: Central and Eastern Europe; CSFR: Czech and Slovak Federal Republics; ESOP: Employee stock ownership plan; IMF: International Monetary Fund; MBO: Management buy-out; SOE: State-owned enterprise; THA: Treuhandanstalt (State Privatization Agency in Germany).

capitalism was chosen in Eastern Europe? Which technologies were used to achieve this aim, and here 'gradualist' and 'shock' technologies can be distinguished.[2] And finally, how large is the gap between the model and the real outcome?

East European citizens almost unanimously rejected the former socialist regime, but they were much more divided in their preferences as to the shape of the new society. Politicians faced a variety of choices, among them a liberal market economy, a 'third way' to welfare capitalism, or the reconstruction of historical models of society which existed during the interwar period in Eastern Europe.[3] These choices were constrained by lack of internal support and by growing external pressure. Public opinion surveys in Eastern Europe show that the enthusiasm for a 'pure' market order withered away the longer the shock therapy lasted and the more apparent its consequences became (Czapinski 1995). External pressure, exercised by the World Bank and the IMF, also constrained political choices. In all CEE countries, World Bank and IMF advisers were engaged to monitor the reform programs, and financial assistance from Western governments depended on the IMF's stamp of approval.[4]

In the following sections different aspects of the transformation process and the 'new' type of capitalism will be addressed:

1. First, the economic elites adopted a new *ideology* to legitimize the emerging unequal distribution of ownership and control in post-socialist societies. It will be argued here that the work of Hayek and Polanyi has structured a controversy between the proselytes of a liberal market order and those who have criticized the excesses of 'wild east' capitalism (Section 8.2).
2. Second, the *privatization process* created a new social structure which is characterized by an unequal distribution of ownership and control of the former state-owned enterprises (SOEs). In Section 8.4, the different privatization methods will be analyzed to show how these methods influenced the distribution of economic power and the process of class formation.
3. Third, most East European countries have enacted a new corporate law that defines the *governance structure* of the privatized firms. The analysis in Section 8.5 shows to what extent these laws restrict property rights and whether employee ownership may be a substitute for codetermination.

---

[2] Differences between gradualism and shock therapy are defined here in terms of the *speed* of the transformation and *not* in terms of policy objectives (model of capitalism). These two dimensions are sometimes mingled, and shock therapy (high speed of adjustment) is then identified with a liberal market order while gradualism (low speed of adjustment) is associated with a mixed economy (welfare capitalism). At least theoretically, these two dimensions may be cross-classified to provide a differentiated categorization for the transformation process. For a discussion of the two strategies see Murrell (1993); Brabant (1993); Hoen (1996); Pickel and Wiesenthal (1997).

[3] See Szelényi's (1988) hypothesis of an 'interrupted embourgeoisement' in Hungary; for Poland see Walicki (1990).

[4] See Blejer and Coricelli (1995: 73–4); Balcerowicz (1995: 353). The ideological orientation of some advisers can be judged by the following quote: 'We believe that the free-market reformers are politicians whose political constituency is the productive part of the economy, and whose political enemies represent the unproductive part' (Boycko *et al.* 1995: 48).

4. Fourth, members of the nomenclature were able to 'reproduce' their power position either by acquiring property rights, that is, they became owners of the former SOEs, or by gaining control over the governance structure of the privatized firms. The process of the *reproduction of elites* (circulation) is analyzed in Section 8.6.

Thus, four characteristics of the emerging model of capitalism in Eastern Europe are addressed: the ideology, the privatization methods, the governance structure of large firms, and finally the reproduction of the economic elite. The analysis will be limited to four post-socialist countries: East Germany, Hungary, Poland, and the Czech Republic.

8.2. THE IDEOLOGY: HAYEK VERSUS POLANYI

Balcerowicz (1995), Polish finance minister from 1989 to 1991 and architect of 'shock therapy' in Poland, described his policy objective as 'to put into place the least imperfect of the real world economic systems, namely, the competitive capitalist market economy' (p. 345). He entered the government in 1989 'with a strong "anti-gradualist" attitude toward economic reform' (p. 342) and asserted that 'the worst possible scenario for me was to preside over an economic programme that was politically acceptable but failed, because it was not sufficiently radical and consistent' (p. 344). In the event, Poland's transformation policy during the period 1989–91 turned out to be second only to East Germany in its radical approach.

Leszek Balcerowicz in Poland, Václav Klaus in the Czech Republic,[5] Yegor Gaidar and Anatol Chubais in Russia, and a few other reformers who had belonged to a counter-elite in Eastern Europe developed their ideas of a new economic order before 1989. In doing so, they were strongly influenced by neoliberal ideas of a free market society (Blejer and Coricelli 1995). The model they wanted to implement was neither the West German 'Soziale Marktwirtschaft' nor the Swedish model of welfare capitalism, but a radical alternative to the socialist economy which they had opposed for many years. Their ideological orientation can be broadly characterized by Hayek's (1963) notion of a 'spontaneous order'.

8.2.1. *The Spontaneous Order*

A spontaneous order is self-generating and regulated by endogenous forces, that is, the spontaneous order is created by the unplanned interaction of individuals and not by an external agency, such as governments or centralized bureaucracies. Furthermore, a spontaneous order is not governed by a hierarchy of preferences or a unitary system of ends (e.g. an egalitarian society). It is 'open' to any purposes that may be followed by the actors. A spontaneous order has no unifying policy objective (Hayek 1976: 108).

Hayek argues that modern societies have become so complex and are dependent on the knowledge and expertise of so many people that they can only be regulated by

---

[5] Václav Klaus (1997: 18), Czech Prime Minister, argued that 'the markets both at home and abroad were not...waiting for (gradualistic) experiments and that something like a sophisticated gradualism could not have been realized in a complex, pluralistic, democratic, open society'.

a spontaneous order. No central government or bureaucracy can ever acquire the information that is necessary to regulate complex modern societies. Any government interference with the spontaneous order produces suboptimal results and distorts an efficient allocation of resources.

Is the spontaneous order the product of an unpredictable social evolution or may it be implemented by political fiat? Hayek (1963) argues that 'if we understand the forces which determine such an order we can use them by creating the conditions under which such an order will form *itself*' (p. 5, emphasis added). To clarify his argument, Hayek points to an example in the natural sciences: 'There are in the physical world many instances of complex orders which we could bring about only by availing ourselves of the known forces which tend to lead to their formation... We can never produce a crystal or a complex organic compound.... But we can create the conditions in which they will arrange *themselves* in such a manner' (Hayek 1973: 39–40, emphasis added).

Social engineering can set up the external conditions under which a spontaneous order may appear, but it can never determine the network of exchanges and the structure of interactions in such an order. Policy makers in Eastern Europe set the general rules of the game (macroeconomic policy), hoping that the 'crystal' would spontaneously emerge.[6]

The 'spontaneous order' became the dominant ideology of a small elite group who had experienced the inefficiency of a centralized planned economy and the political repression of socialist regimes and who had no sympathies after 1989 for 'third-way' experiments. The opposition to gradualist approaches and mixed systems has perhaps been most clearly expressed by the prominent Russian reformer and architect of the Russian privatization program, Yegor Gaidar: 'I would say that the gradualist approach to transforming a communist economy is the strategy of a communist or totalitarian regime trying to adapt to new realities... Gorbachev tried the step-by-step approach and it led nowhere' (Gaidar 1995: 4,30).

8.2.2. *The Self-adjusting Market as Utopia*

Notwithstanding the discussion above, the more the consequences of 'pure' market competition became apparent, the more the enthusiasm for a spontaneous order withered away (Tittenbrun 1995: 30). Rising unemployment, falling incomes, and the dismantling of the socialist welfare state discredited the radical reform programs. Former communist parties exploited the general dissatisfaction with privatization and deregulation policies, and in some countries were able to regain power in parliamentary elections (Szelényi *et al.* 1996).

The work of Hayek on the one hand and Polanyi on the other has structured a controversy between the proselytes of a liberal market order and those who have criticized

---

[6] Pickel (1997) interprets the transformation in East Germany as an example of 'holistic social engineering'. However, it is questionable whether the spontaneous order implies holistic social engineering in the sense in which Popper (1970) understood this term. A more adequate interpretation shows that a spontaneous order requires *abstention* from politics or, to phrase it in more modern terms: the spontaneous order assumes the 'end of politics'. See also Pickel and Wiesenthal (1997).

the excesses of 'wild east' capitalism. Before we proceed, it will, therefore, be useful to summarize briefly Polanyi's critique of a self-regulating market, which is another notion for Hayek's spontaneous order.[7]

Polanyi (1957: 3, 81) argues that 'the idea of a self-adjusting market implied a stark utopia' and that by setting up a self-regulating market for labor and land 'mankind was forced into the paths of a utopian experiment'. Polanyi goes on to argue that 'a self-adjusting market could not exist for any length of time without annihilating the human and natural substance of society'. Thus, it can be said that the spontaneous order is utopian and self-destroying at the same time. If such a 'radical' order were implemented in pure form, it would destroy the fabric of society.

The claim that a self-regulating market 'annihilates' society is far from being self-evident and will be discussed next; then the question of why it is 'utopian' will be addressed.

The idea that a pure market order destroys society has a long tradition, so much so that Hirschman (1982: 1466) felt justified in calling it the 'self-destruction thesis' of social science. He shows that it can be traced back to conservative and romantic critics of the industrial revolution as well as to the writings of Marx and Schumpeter. Schumpeter's notion of 'creative destruction' is particularly illuminating here (1950: 83): a self-adjusting market 'incessantly revolutionizes the economic structure from within, incessantly destroying the old one, incessantly creating a new one. This process of Creative Destruction is the essential fact about capitalism'. A pure market order is creative, but also destructive, and Polanyi's argument is that society cannot survive permanent destruction in the long run. Competition in self-regulating markets continuously creates social conflict, and the more perfect competition is, the more intense social conflicts become (Simmel 1955: 82).

The idea of a spontaneous order is also *utopian*. The aftermath of the 1989 revolution has seen a curious resurrection of utopian ideas. While at the end of the nineteenth century the communist utopia of a classless society was compared to the evils of 'real' capitalism, this time the utopian idea of a self-regulating, competitive market society has been contrasted with the economic disaster and bureaucratic repression of 'real' socialism (Murrell 1995). The velvet revolution marks a switch of utopian ideas, from the utopia of a communist society to that of a self-regulating market. Stiglitz (1995: 3) argues that some American economists became the 'symbol of an ideology' and that many people in Eastern Europe were seeking an 'alternative belief system'.

8.2.3. *Institutional Environment*

In a third step and as a conclusion, it is argued here that a spontaneous order cannot survive without an institutional environment. The institutional environment reduces

[7] See Mendell and Salée (1991). The relative attractiveness of Hayek and Polanyi in this debate can be broadly assessed by the frequency with which these authors are quoted in scholarly articles: during the period 1992–97, Hayek was quoted on average 180 times per year in social science articles (many of which are written by East European social scientists); Polanyi's average is 93 per year. Source: Social Science Citation Index 1992–97.

the transaction costs of markets, regulates competition and social conflict, and makes the outcome of 'pure' market processes more predictable. The institutional environment is defined here as 'the set of fundamental political, social, and legal ground rules that establishes the basis for production, exchange, and distribution. Rules governing elections, property rights, and the right of contract are examples of the type of ground rules that make up the economic environment' (Davis and North 1971: 6).

Polanyi (1957: 149) describes the process by which the spontaneous order is embedded into a set of protective institutions as the 'countermove against economic liberalism'. The implementation of a spontaneous order constitutes one part of the movement; the counter-movement refers to the process of institution building that frames the spontaneous order within a set of economic institutions.[8] The sequence of reform and 'revisionist' counter-reform during the transition period and the political recycling of former communist party members in Russia, Poland, and Hungary can be interpreted as such a 'double movement' (Polanyi 1957: 150).

There was hardly any controversy among the new political elite in Eastern Europe about the implementation of a spontaneous order: the Western-style market economy was and still is an accepted model in terms of welfare, modernization, and democracy. A great deal of controversy arose, on the other hand, about the question as to the institutional environment in which the spontaneous order should be embedded.

All capitalist systems have implemented a 'spontaneous order', in one way or another. Where they differ is in their institutional environment, which they have inherited from their pre-capitalist past[9] or which they have deliberately adopted by political design (e.g. codetermination).

During the last two decades an intense ideological battle has been fought between owners and managers (principals and agents) about who controls the large corporation and who is entitled to appropriate corporate profits (Jensen 1989). The controversy has focused on the questions of which social classes control the means of production (managers versus shareholders), and which type of regulation should prevail (state regulation versus liberal markets). This ideological contest has also structured and oriented the debate in Eastern Europe. After forty years of experience with socialism, the bureaucratic mode of regulation has lost its legitimacy, and it is, therefore, not surprising to see reformers in Eastern Europe join the ranks of those who most vehemently defend property rights and the discretionary power of ownership.

---

[8] In his later writings Hayek replaces the notion of market equilibrium with that of an 'order', and he comes closer to acknowledging the importance of institutions for a market society. 'The concept of an "order" which ... I prefer to that of equilibrium, has the advantage that we can meaningfully speak about an order being approached to varying degrees, and that order can be preserved throughout a process of change' (Hayek 1978: 184). Hayek (1976: 12) also admits that this order is not only coordinated by prices and competition, but also by (abstract) rules.

[9] 'Trust', which is created and maintained in social networks and kinship relations, is an example of an inherited institutional condition (Fukuyama 1995).

The unconstrained freedom of a spontaneous order rather than the bureaucratic regime of a welfare state became the new 'utopia'.[10]

The transformation of the bureaucratic mode of control into private ownership has been accompanied by a transformation of ideologies. Under socialism, the members of the nomenclature defined their status as 'professionals' who controlled the SOEs and a system of 'rational redistribution';[11] under the new regime they regain this control by appropriating property rights in privatized firms. Members of the nomenclature who had de facto control over the means of production under socialism were the first to acquire property rights in SOEs by spinning off subsidiaries or by asset stripping (nomenclature privatization). The question to what extent the former economic elite was able to reproduce its social position is closely linked to the methods and control mechanisms of privatization. In many countries, privatization laws were modified to allow managers and employees to control the privatization process and to acquire shareholdings of 'their' firm at preferential rates. Control over the privatization process was an important (although not the only) instrument for the former nomenclature to reproduce its social status.

8.3. THREE SCENARIOS

The argument, that after 1989, societies in Eastern Europe had a 'choice' (Stiglitz 1995: 3) as to which type of economic and political order they wanted neglects the constraints of institution building. Research into modernization processes has provided abundant evidence that the implementation of Western institutions in countries with different traditions and value systems frequently fail. The outcome is often 'partial modernization' (Eisenstadt 1973)—a concept which points to the frictions and backlashes of modernization, elements that have also been encountered in the transformation process in Eastern Europe.

Three scenarios are discussed here which tentatively describe possible outcomes of the transformation and privatization process: (1) a 'pure' market order, (2) regulated state capitalism, and (3) a dependent semi-periphery economy. These scenarios are based on the assumption that all Eastern European societies have successfully implemented a 'spontaneous order' and, therefore, are 'market' societies, but that they differ in their institutional environment and with respect to the internal and external constraints they have to face.

(1) *'Pure' market order*   The revolution of 1989 revealed that socialism had lost legitimacy and that citizens in Eastern Europe accepted even radical reforms to change their political and economic order. The ultimate outcome of the transformation

[10] Among others see Klaus (1997), Balcerowicz (1994; 1995), Gaidar 1995. Blejer and Coricelli (1995) have interviewed the leading East European reformers asking them to describe their educational and professional careers and their political programs. See also Frydman and Rapaczynski (1994).

[11] The term 'rational redistribution' is based on Polanyi's (1957: 47) distinction between reciprocity and redistribution, and is used by Konrad and Szelényi (1979) to explain the specific ideology of the socialist nomenclature.

process in this scenario is likely to be a 'lean' state,[12] the implementation of 'perfect' competition, and the dismantling of institutions seen as obstacles to achieving such an outcome (e.g. workers' councils or the socialist welfare system). Countries switch from one utopian model of organizing a society (communist society) to another utopia (self-adjusting market). Their societies are, of course, also embedded in a specific institutional environment, because *laissez-faire* itself has to be enforced by the state (e.g. antitrust law).

Furthermore, these countries are likely to implement a liberal property rights regime and to follow the precepts of neoclassical advisers with respect to privatization: ownership in the means of production must be highly *concentrated* to create a class of owners who are able and willing to monitor the managers of firms. Ownership must be also distributed to *outside* owners because insiders (e.g. employees) do not have incentives and resources to enforce the restructuring of the firm and to provide the capital (Carlin and Aghion 1996: 380–4; Frydman and Rapaczynski 1994: 143–50). This institutional order is supposed to be a new *universalistic* model of capitalism and the one most appropriate to competition in a global market place.

(2) *State capitalism* This scenario emphasizes the historical heritage and the importance of path dependency. Each economy is embedded in a set of institutions many of which survive even revolutionary upheavals (e.g. the workers' councils in Poland; more generally social networks). It is assumed that the depth and speed of change is inversely related to the transaction costs of change (Liebowitz and Margolis 1995). Institutions whose remodeling causes high transaction costs (e.g. constitutions) are less likely to be changed than those whose change can be obtained at lower costs (e.g. traffic regulations). Property rights in the means of production and the distribution of ownership among different social classes are among the most fundamental social institutions and their change may cause high costs. It is assumed here that in a considerable number of cases the de facto control of former managers (nomenclature) and employees over the productive assets of society will be transformed into private property rights. In other words, those social actors who had control over firms before 1989 will now own them.

The post-socialist countries will be transformed into a mixed economy characterized by strong central governments, a high degree of economic regulation, various forms of institutionalized worker participation (e.g. codetermination), and— depending on their economic performance—a more or less generous welfare system to compensate the losers of the reform (Kornai 1996). In this scenario, the outcome of the East European transformation is something in between 'pure' capitalism and the previous socialist system. This hypothesis may also cover attempts to consciously 'reconstruct' history by reviving the models of the interwar period or even of the late nineteenth century (Walicki 1990).

---

[12] Frydman and Rapaczynski (1994: 142) report that dissidents who had joined the Czechoslovakian government after 1989 'considered the speediest possible elimination of the power of the state to be the main initial objective of their privatization program…' Having experienced the oppressive nature of the socialist state, they wanted it to 'wither away' as quickly as possible.

(3) *Dependent economy*   While the second scenario reflects the constraints of history, the third scenario emphasizes the constraints imposed by the global market, in choosing an economic and political order. In a competitive global market the internal institutional environment of a country depends on its position in the 'role structure' of global trade. A country that is located in the semi-periphery or even the periphery of the global trade system—as defined by the type of goods it imports and exports— cannot support the institutional environment that we typically find in countries which are situated in the 'center' of global trade (welfare state, corporatist labor relations, higher education). And vice versa, the institutional environment of a peripheral country would be inconceivable for a country in the center (Van Rossem 1996).

East European countries lost their position in the socialist world system[13] following its dissolution, and they are now struggling for a new position in the emerging global capitalist system. The institutional environment and thus the type of capitalism which evolves in these countries is heavily dependent on the outcome of this competition and hence on the position in the role structure of global trade that these countries are able to conquer.

In a recent analysis of the Hungarian economy, Kornai (1996: 964) argues that 'Hungary became a premature welfare state', which its economy cannot afford, and he blames the Hungarian government for having preserved the relatively high level of social welfare typical of the socialist countries before 1989 (rational redistribution). The former socialist countries have to reconstruct their institutional environment, including a new welfare system.[14] The new economic relationships between Eastern and Western Europe *could* resemble a hierarchical network structure which is characterized by hegemony on the one side and dependence on the other.

It is still too early to decide which of these scenarios is a correct description of the transformation process in Eastern Europe. However, the analysis of the privatization methods and of institution building which is presented in the following sections will show in what direction these countries are moving.

8.4. PRIVATIZATION METHODS

Ownership patterns vary considerably between different capitalist countries. For instance, in Germany there is a relatively high concentration of ownership in the large firms, while ownership in US and British corporations is fragmented. Most large industrial firms in Germany are owned by other industrial and/or financial firms, while investment funds are the dominant owners in Britain and the US (type of owner). The degree of ownership concentration and the type of owners to whom the former SOEs have been sold are important variables that allow us to assess the

---

[13] The Council for Mutual Economic Assistance (CMEA) was a 'closed' socialist world system in which some countries (e.g. the former SU, East Germany, CSFR) had relatively comfortable positions.

[14] By the end of 1995, the Hungarian government embarked on emergency surgery: it imposed an austerity package that reduced social benefits, laid off 13 percent of civil servants while freezing the wages of those who remained, devalued the currency by 8%, and imposed an 8% surcharge on imports. *Wall Street Journal*, 16 July, 1997, p. 17.

redistributive effects of privatization and the degree to which economic power is concentrated in Eastern Europe.

At the extremes we find, on the one hand, East Germany with a very high ownership concentration and with most large firms owned by West German/foreign combines, on the other, we have Poland, where more than 1500 firms are in employee ownership. While employee ownership has received widespread acceptance and legitimation in Poland, the ownership patterns which have been created in East Germany became more and more controversial. The patterns of social inequality are strongly influenced by the prevailing distribution of property rights in and/or by the de facto control over the productive assets of a country.

The network configuration is also an important variable with which to characterize patterns of control and influence in the emerging market economies. For instance, the '*keiretsu*' (clique structure) is a central network configuration in Japan, while the concern, which links many subsidiary firms to a parent company, is the dominant configuration in Germany.[15] Table 8.1 summarizes some of the structural variables characterizing the privatization process in Eastern Europe; they will be explained in more detail in the following sections.

A number of different methods and instruments have been used to privatize the former SOEs, among them voucher privatization, auctions on the market for corporate control, MBOs, ESOP, bankruptcy, joint ventures with foreign firms, etc. Even though almost all methods were tried at some point during the transformation period, in most countries only one or at most two of them were used as the *dominant* policy instrument for privatization (see Table 8.1, column 1).

The privatization methods can be distinguished according to whether they were administered by the central government and submitted to hierarchical control (top-down privatization), or whether actors in the firms themselves had a substantial influence on the choice of owners and on the conditions of privatization (bottom-up privatization). Centralized policy instruments were used predominantly in those countries which had weak reform movements (or none at all) and had been governed by an entrenched socialist bureaucracy before 1989 (East Germany, CSFR). Decentralized policy instruments ('spontaneous' privatization) were dominant in countries which had already granted considerable autonomy to the firms and their managers during the eighties.

In Poland, for instance, workers' councils were introduced in 1981; they negotiated production plans and influenced the selection of directors. Similar structures, although less decentralized, were introduced in Hungary in the late 1960s.[16] These structures survived for some time after 1989 and provided institutional support for an organized resistance against centralized privatization plans. Voucher privatization in the CSFR and the privatization by the Treuhandanstalt (THA) in East Germany

---

[15] See Fig. 3.1 in Chapter 3. An example of a network in the financial sector (Czech Republic) is given in Table 8.2 below; Stark (1996) presents several Hungarian capital networks.

[16] 'By the abolition in 1968 of compulsory plan directives, part of one of the fundamental property rights, that of control, passed to the management of the state-owned enterprise' (Kornai 1996: 983).

TABLE 8.1 *Privatization in four countries*

	Dominant method of privatization	Most frequent type of owner	Concentration	Cross-share-holdings	Open to new owner[a]	% State ownership	Codetermination	Employee-ownership
Czech Republic	Voucher (top-down)	Investment funds/financial	Medium	Financial/banks	Yes	40[b]	>33	4.4[c]
Hungary	Spin-offs/market for corporate control	Holdings/foreign (integrated ownership)	Medium/high	Inter-enterprise	Limited	42–50[b]	>33	(36,000[c] employees)
Poland[d]	a. Spontaneous (bottom-up)	Individuals families	—	No	Yes	—	—	20[c] (450,000 employees)
	b. Commercialization	state	High	No	Limited	54[b]	>33	
East Germany	Market for corporate control (top-down)	West-German combines	Very high	No	No/limited	>5	33–50	Minimal

Note: [a] Open to new owners/second or third wave of privatization.
[b] End of 1995; *Source:* World Bank (1996: 53, table 3.2); Hungary: Mihályi (1996).
[c] Estimates, see Earle and Estrin (1996: 29, table 1.1).
[d] Poland upper line (a) privatization of small/medium-sized firms; lower line (b) state sector (largest industrial combines).

(privatization on the market for corporate control) are examples of a privatization process that was centrally predesigned and subject to a bureaucratic control from above.

Privatization plans have also been influenced by macroeconomic variables and changes in the political environment. For instance, a comeback of the former communist parties in general elections[17] usually delayed privatization plans and strengthened the bargaining power of managers and employees in the SOE. The inflation rate also influenced the outcome of the privatization process. A high inflation rate (e.g. in Poland and Russia) reduced the scope for 'outsiders' to use financial means to outbid insiders in auctions for SOE. In many cases, privatization became a non-financial transaction between the state and the new owners (spontaneous/nomenclature privatization).

Summarizing these arguments, the following hypothesis can be put forward: if the former socialist economy was relatively decentralized before 1989, if there was a strong comeback of former communist parties in general elections, and if there was a high inflation rate after 1989,[18] then we expect to observe a privatization from 'below' and a strong influence on the privatization process exerted by the actors in the SOE. In the following sections, the privatization process in four countries is analyzed in more detail.

8.4.1. *Voucher Privatization in the CSFR/Czech Republic*

In the Czech Republic shareholdings in the former SOE were offered to all citizens more or less gratis. Each adult citizen could acquire a voucher booklet at a price of 1035 CSK (=35 US$; *c.* 25 percent of the average monthly income of a worker). These vouchers could be used to acquire shares in state enterprises, which were offered, for sale, in a centrally organized and computerized auction. The privatization process took place in two waves. In the first wave, 1491 companies were offered for privatization, in the second wave, 861 (of which 185 had already been offered in the first wave; Coffee 1996: 136).

Before the auctions started, the managers of the SOE had to submit a privatization plan to the Ministry of Privatization.[19] Even though some managers preferred an

---

[17] In 1993, the former Polish communist party (Democratic Left Alliance) and its ally (Polish Peasants' Party) won nearly two-thirds of the seats in the Sejm (Tworzecki 1994). In 1994, the former Hungarian communist party (Hungarian Socialist Party) won an absolute majority in parliament (Szelényi *et al.* 1996).

[18] In Russia 73% of firms have chosen a privatization method which allowed managers and workers together to buy 51% of the voting equity of their firm at a nominal price of 1.7 times the July 1992 book value of its assets (Boycko *et al.* 1995: 78). The inflation rate was 144% in 1991 and around 2300% in 1992. It is obvious that this regulation provided firm managers with a wide margin for manipulating the book value and hence the purchasing power of managers and workers.

[19] By way of example, the following division of ownership was proposed in a privatization plan submitted by the management of PSP (an engineering firm): 65% voucher privatization; 10% direct sale to a Brazilian customer; 15% transfer to commercial banks (debt–equity swap); 5% transfer to local administration; 5% to National Restitution Fund. This plan was approved by the Ministry of Privatization. *Source*: Estrin *et al.* (1995: 24).

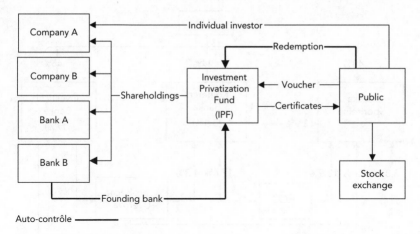

Fig. 8.1   *Voucher privatization in the Czech Republic (1997)*

MBO, this was usually not accepted by the Ministry. MBOs would have directly transformed bureaucratic control into private ownership. The fact that the Ministry was able (as was the German THA) to reject most MBO plans illustrates the relative strength of central government *vis-à-vis* local management.

Citizens had the choice of either spending their vouchers directly, by acquiring the shares of firms offered for privatization on the auctions, or of transferring their vouchers to investment funds which had been founded before the auction started. The transfer of vouchers gained momentum after Harvard Capital and Consulting (HCC)—an investment fund founded by Viktor Kozeny, a Czech graduate of Harvard University—promised to pay back ten times the value of the voucher booklet one year after the auction. This move turned out to be decisive for the outcome of voucher privatization: in the first wave 72 percent of all voucher holders transferred their vouchers to investment funds, in the second wave 65 percent. Thus the majority of the direct owners of privatized firms are not Czech citizens, but the investment funds (*Type of owner*, Table 8.1, column 2).

The degree of ownership *concentration* in 1490 firms which were privatized after the second wave is illustrated by the distribution of shareholdings among different types of owners: 40 percent are owned by investment funds (38 percent by the top ten); 37 percent are owned by individual investors, and 8 percent are still owned by the state. The shareholdings of investment funds and the state are concentrated in large firms,[20] while individual investors focused their shareholdings on smaller firms. A single investment fund is not allowed to acquire more than 20 percent of a firm's stock.

Figure 8.1 summarizes the process of voucher privatization; it also illustrates the way in which cross-shareholdings in the financial sector were produced (Fig. 8.2).

---

[20] The proportion of shares held by investment funds and the state in large companies is, therefore, larger than indicated by these average percentages. *Source*: Coffee (1996: 140, table 4.3).

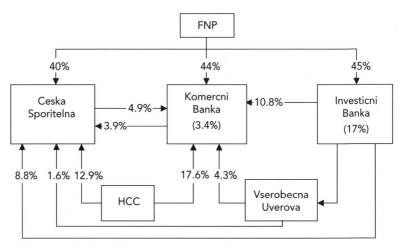

FNP: Fund of National Property (state ownership);
HCC: Harvard Capital and Consulting;
(17%) Auto-contrôle.

FIG. 8.2   *Shareholdings in the financial sector—Czech Republic (1997)*

A commercial bank (founding bank) creates an investment company and this investment company sets up several investment privatization funds (IPF). The citizens
exchange the vouchers they acquired from the Ministry of Privatization for shares/
certificates in the fund.[21] The IPF uses the vouchers for bids on auctions and acquires
the shares of company A, company B, bank A, and bank B. Because many investment
funds have acquired shares of Czech/Slovak banks, and given that most investment
funds were founded by banks, the financial institutions are linked to each other by
cross-shareholdings (i.e. the investment funds are intermediate owners). The IPF in
Fig. 8.1 acquires shares of its founding bank B and these shares provide what is called
here 'auto-control'. The HCC (and many other IPF) promised to pay back ten times
the value of the voucher booklet one year after the auction. This redemption of certificates is a second source of auto-contrôle. An example of the cross-shareholdings
that have been created in the financial sector is shown in Fig. 8.2.[22]

The voucher privatization process did *not* provide investment capital to the firms
to be privatized. The vouchers were purchased by citizens from the Ministry of
Privatization, which used the proceeds to finance the transaction costs of privatization (and budget deficits). On the auctions the voucher-money was recycled to the
Ministry. Legal ownership was transferred from the state to the IPFs (*c.* 40 percent)
and to the citizens (*c.* 38 percent). The Fund of National Property (state ownership)
still holds considerable shareholdings in the financial sector (see Fig. 8.2) and in

---

[21] The shares/certificates of the IPF are traded on the Prague Stock Exchange.
[22] *Sources*: Coffee (1996: 146–7), Brom and Orenstein (1994), Kenway and Klvacová (1996),
Palda (1997).

other firms considered of 'strategic' importance. Investment funds are professionalized owners who may exercise control by nominating representatives to the Board of Directors/Supervisory Boards of firms in their portfolios, but they do not provide *capital*.

Voucher privatization has created ownership structures which resemble to some extent those in Germany. German banks exercise their influence over large firms through three channels: direct ownership, proxy votes, and credit. The Czech banks cannot vote shares held by their customers (proxy votes), but they own many investment funds, which are the most important shareholders of privatized firms, and they also hold *direct* shareholdings in many Czech firms.[23] This structure and distribution of ownership in large Czech firms is 'open' to outside owners because the shares which are now owned by the investment funds are traded on the stock exchange and can be purchased by outside investors.

8.4.2. *Integrated Ownership Patterns in Hungary*

Paradoxically, a first step in the privatization process in Hungary was a form of 're-nationalization'. The SOE were transformed into joint stock or limited liability companies (commercialization) in order to restore the centralized control that had been lost to local managers during the eighties in the wake of the partial reform and decentralization of the socialist economy. Representatives of the state agencies[24] were nominated to sit on the Boards of Directors of the commercialized firms in order to monitor the process of restructuring and privatization.

In a second step, the large state combines were split into a number of independent firms (spin-offs) in which the parent/holding company holds (majority) ownership. This legal and organizational restructuring created networks of firms which are linked to each other by capital participation, and in which the Hungarian banks are also integrated by shareholdings.

The Hungarian government decided against distributing property rights in the SOE for free. Instead, equity stakes in firms were offered in auctions (market for corporate control) to Hungarian and foreign investors. Spin-offs and the deconcentration of the large industrial combines opened the way for a type of ownership which Stark (1996) has termed 'recombinant property'. Ownership of the subsidiaries and satellite firms was distributed among several types of owners: joint ventures with foreign investors were set up; private Hungarian firms acquired some of the shares; others were sold to managers and employees (MBO and ESOP).[25] The capital

---

[23] For instance, Investicni Banka holds more than 50 percent of shares in a pulp mill (Bicel), a dairy (Jihoceske Mlekarny), an electronic cables firm (Kablo Energo) and in the largest brewery (Plzenske Pivovary). *Source: Wall Street Journal,* 5 July 1996, p. 4.

[24] The state agencies entrusted with privatization were the State Property Agency (AVU) and the State Holding Company (AV); they were merged in 1995 and the new institution is now the State Privatization and Property Management Agency (APV). See Mihályi (1996).

[25] For instance, DKG (manufacturer of equipment for oil and gas production) negotiated a joint venture with Gasprom, a Russian conglomerate and important customer of DKG. DKG-East Ltd was

networks which were created by these financial operations also provided a considerable potential for (indirect) auto-contrôle (see King 1997).

The ownership structure that has been created in Hungary frequently integrates different types of owners within *one* firm. Foreign investors, Hungarian investors, families, managers, employees, the state, and the banks jointly hold shares in the privatized companies. Stark (1996: 1019) argues that these 'recombinant' ownership patterns are 'classic risk-spreading and risk-sharing devices that mitigate differences across firms'. While this argument is certainly correct, the integrated ownership pattern needs additional explanation.

From 1990 to 1995, the Czech Republic had an accumulated inflation rate of 120 percent, Hungary 155 percent and Poland 795 percent. This inflation, combined with a considerable loss of real income during the first years of transition, decimated private financial resources. Pooling financial resources from different social actors into an integrated ownership network was one of the measures adopted to make up for the shortage of finance capital. The participation of the state, which still holds a (minority) stake in many privatized firms, is welcomed by the new owner(s) because this participation provides physical assets to the network of other owners at zero interest.

It may be asked whether integrated ownership patterns remain stable in the medium term. It is at least questionable whether the state, banks, other Hungarian and foreign firms, and individual investors who have pooled their resources will be able to integrate their divergent interests within a joint corporate governance. More likely is a second round of privatization in the near future.

Before concluding this analysis, let us consider some statistical data that provide an overview of the privatization process in Hungary. In 1990, the assets of some 2000 SOEs were transferred to the State Property Agency. In 1994 (the year in which the former communist party obtained a majority in the Hungarian Parliament), the privatization process slowed down and public opinion became more hostile to privatization. By the end of 1995, about 25 percent of state assets had been privatized by sales in open or closed auctions; 25 percent 'disappeared through bankruptcy and liquidation'[26] and 50 percent are still owned by the state. Since then many banks, electric and gas utilities, and even parts of the telecommunication networks have been privatized, many of them being bought by foreign investors.[27]

---

founded in which DKG holds 51%, Gasprom 47 percent, and 2% is held by Hungarian trading firms. The privatization of Kanizsa Brewery is an example of a combined MBO and ESOP: 80% of its shares were acquired by a financial holding which was founded by 419 of the managers and employees of the brewery (45% of the workforce); 20% are still in state ownership. *Source*: Estrin *et al.* (1995: 155–63, 231–40).

[26] Quote from Peter Mihályi (1996: 207) who is Chief Economist of the Hungarian State Privatization and Property Management Agency (APV).

[27] It is difficult to give a precise percentage of how many firms are still in state ownership. For 1991, Hooley *et al.* (1996: 690) give the following estimate: 27.6% state owned; 12.6% state/private ownership; 34.1% private ownership; 7.1% state/foreign ownership; 9.6% private/foreign ownership; 9.1% co-op; sample size: 791 firms. It is estimated that by the end of 1996 about 30% of firms would still be owned by the state.

8.4.3. *Dual Ownership Structure in Poland*

In Poland denationalization started back in 1981, when 10 million members of 'Solidarity' forced the communist government to pass legislation which made state enterprises 'independent, self-managing, and self-financing' (Szomburg 1995: 85). A workers' council was elected by the workforce of the firm which had considerable influence on the nomination of directors, on the distribution of profits, and on the strategic decisions of the enterprise. These power structures survived after 1989. The various restructuring and privatization programs had to be negotiated between the Ministry of Privatization, the management, and the workers' council, which had a veto right. As in Hungary, commercialization was a first attempt by the government to 're-nationalize' the SOE and gain control over their assets before privatization programs could be implemented. In an SOE which has been transformed into a joint stock company the workers' council is dissolved and a Board of Directors/ Supervisory Board is nominated. These new structures are unlikely to eliminate the power of the workforce, but they certainly weaken it.

The institutional environment in which privatization took place in Poland after 1989 has to be taken into account in order to understand its outcome. First, there was an established opposition (Solidarity) which was at the same time a trade union, a political party, and a social movement and which—while opposing the socialist regime—did not for that reason support the shock therapy advanced by some neoliberal ministers in the government. Second, there was institutionalized worker codetermination on the shop floor with strong organizational links to the central government which was able to monitor the privatization proposals for each SOE. The power of the workers' councils is based on a high union density rate in the large SOE (70 percent). Third, there was growing disenchantment among the rank and file with economic conditions, which manifested itself in strikes in many cases lacking official union backing. In 1990, only 250 strikes were registered; in 1992/93, this figure rose to 6000 per year.[28] Fourth, Polish central governments were relatively weak: between 1990 and 1994, five different Polish prime ministers were in office (Hungary: one prime minister); after the 1991 elections, twenty-nine political parties were represented in the Polish Parliament; the party with the greatest electoral support received only 12 percent of the votes (Webb 1992: 166; Korbonski 1996). The relative balance of power was in favor of the actors in the SOE and any attempt on the part of central government to break up the coalition between management and workers on the shop floor faced tough opposition.

Three different procedures were enacted for privatizing a Polish SOE (Winiecki 1995; Kowalik 1994):

(1) *Public offerings*   Polish or foreign investors are called upon to submit their bids for the 500 largest SOE scheduled for this privatization program. Before being offered in the market for corporate control, each SOE was transformed into a joint

---

[28] *Source:* Blazyca and Dabrowski (1995: 68). In Hungary, 10 strikes were registered in 1992 and 17 in 1993 (Makó and Simonyi 1997: 224, table 1).

stock company (commercialization) and evaluated individually by a specialized consulting firm. Employees of the firm may acquire up to 20 percent of the shares at 50 percent of the selling price. However, in less than 5 percent of the cases was the Ministry of Privatization successful in finding a Polish or foreign investor. Spin-offs, which would have made a production site or a department of a large SOE more attractive to outside investors, were frequently blocked by managers and/or workers' councils.

(2) *Mass privatization*   This method is a complex voucher program which was intended to speed up the privatization process and to distribute ownership of about 510 medium-sized Polish firms[29] to Polish citizens at nominal registration fees (20 zlotys, about 6.20 US$). Fifteen National Investment Funds (NIFs) were established which received 60 percent[30] of the shares of the 510 SOE; 25 percent of the shares remain with the State Treasury; 15 percent are distributed free of charge to the employees of each company. In February 1996 the mass privatization program, which was highly controversial among the political parties, was approved in a referendum by the Polish people.[31] About 25 million Poles acquired a voucher which can be swapped for shares in the fifteen NIF, that is, each voucher entitles its holder to one share in each of the fifteen funds. In June 1997, the fifteen NIF were listed on the Warsaw Stock Exchange and each citizen can now swap his/her voucher for shares in the NIF. The privatization program is open to outside/foreign investors who started from the outset to acquire vouchers 'over the counter' from Polish citizens. The fifteen NIF are managed by consortia of Polish and international consultants and financiers who receive up to 3 million US$ in fees to restructure and modernize the 510 firms in their portfolio.

(3) *Privatization through liquidation*   This procedure was set up for the privatization of small and medium-sized SOEs. The assets of firms included in this program may be sold in toto or separately to one or several buyers. The law also allows leasing of the assets to a potential buyer; assets may also be transferred after the firm has been declared bankrupt. These forms of 'spontaneous' privatization cover a whole variety of transferring property rights to managers, employees, or outsiders, and they were only loosely controlled by the central government (nomenclature privatization, MBO, ESOP, spin-offs, asset stripping, etc.).

The most successful of all programs discussed here was privatization through liquidation. Several thousands of small and medium-sized firms have been privatized more or less 'spontaneously' and the assets have been transferred in most cases to those individuals who managed the firms before. The 'unintended' outcome of the privatization program so far has been a *dual structure of the Polish economy* (see Table 8.1).

[29] These are second-tier firms, not the giants of Polish industry; they account for about 6% of GDP. *Source: Wall Street Journal*, 13 June 1997, p. 14; 22 Nov. 1996, p. 8B.

[30] In fact, the procedure is more complicated: The 60% of the shares are not distributed equally among the 15 NIFs. Each NIF receives 33% in 34 firms while the remaining shares are distributed equally among the other 14 NIFs (27% : 14 = 1.93%). The government was seeking to create a controlling block in each firm to be owned by one of the NIFs.

[31] However, only 32% of eligible voters cast ballots, far less than the 50% minimum needed to make the referendum legally binding. *Wall Street Journal*, 21 Feb. 1996, p. 10.

First, there is a very dynamic sector of private *small* to medium-sized firms, many of which were able to start up because their owners appropriated, one way or another, the assets of former SOE. Winiecki (1996: 314) calls this the 'generic private sector' which has been created by privatization from below. Second, there is a sector of *large* industrial and service companies which are still owned by the state and are likely to remain in state ownership for the medium term.

In a survey of seventy-five Polish companies (case studies), Pinto *et al.* (1993: 255) find that the firms still owned by the state have undertaken far-reaching restructuring activities and that the stereotype of an inflexible dinosaur is unwarranted. The authors conclude that 'Poland's experience shows that rapid changes in ownership may be unnecessary, and that restructuring before privatization may be desirable'.

In the early eighties, Kornai (1980) argued that the chronic shortages and bottlenecks in socialist economies were due to centralized state ownership and the lack of competition. Economic reforms implemented in Poland and Hungary after 1989 provide empirical evidence that a macroeconomic policy of price and import liberalization, and the imposition of budget constraints on SOE can successfully eliminate shortages, and that ownership is important, but not *the* crucial variable.[32] Rather, rapid privatization was seen as the main cause for rising unemployment, and governments found it more and more difficult to gain public support for their privatization programs. By mid-1996, only a small proportion of large Polish SOEs have effectively been privatized. Szomburg (1995: 82) argues that a new kind of 'state capitalism' has been created and that the intentions of political actors are no longer to privatize the state-owned sector as quickly as possible, but to restructure it, to streamline its management, and to create a competitive environment for it.

8.4.3. *East Germany: Concentrated External Ownership*

The German approach to privatization was the most 'radical' of those compared here. During the 5 years of its existence (from March 1990 to December 1994) the THA privatized 90 percent of the former SOE in East Germany. Its privatization method can be broken down historically into three phases.

First, the large combines were fragmented into numerous individual firms, each of which was made a legally independent company. The first phase of privatization thus involved *atomization* of the industrial network of the former command economy (Albach 1993). Second, the individual firms were reduced in size by shedding labor. Through a gradual process of massive lay-offs, most of these companies lost over 80 percent of their pre-1989 workforce and were pared down to small or medium-sized businesses that were thought to stand better chances of survival. Third, these down-sized firms were offered for sale on the market for corporate control, where

---

[32] In a study of 706 Czech firms privatized by vouchers, Claessens *et al.* (1997: 12) found a significant positive relationship between concentration of ownership (investment funds) and profitability: the higher the shareholdings of the top 5 owners the more profitable the firm. If the National Property Fund (state ownership) still owns a substantial proportion of shares, this has *no negative* impact on the profitability of the firm. This result illustrates that state ownership *per se* does not preclude profitability.

buyers are almost exclusively other companies. The THA put more than 10,000 firms up for sale on this market.

The decision to sell East German firms as *corporate units* on the market for corporate control had two crucial consequences. First, it determined the size distribution of East German firms: the former large combines were unmarketable, and therefore their production networks had to be dissolved. Second, it determined the subsequent level of ownership concentration: by selling the firms to either single buyers or to small groups of investors it ruled out any possibility of a wide distribution of shares throughout the population. In this way a small group of large West German enterprises was able to take over most of the down-sized, competitive segments of the former East German combines. On average, 72.2 percent of all firms with more than 100 employees in East Germany belong to West German or foreign owners; this figure increases to 90 percent if only firms with more than 400 employees are considered (Windolf 1998: 339).

In divesting itself of the nationalized combines it was not the primary goal of the THA to obtain adequate compensation for the SOE, nor was it concerned to ensure that ownership in the former SOE was widely distributed among the citizens of East Germany (voucher privatization). On average, each firm which the THA was able to privatize involved a *loss* of 8.7 million Euro. The directors of the THA themselves reported in this regard that, 'We did not sell firms but bought investors' (Brücker 1995: 448). The privatization process in East Germany followed the neoliberal model: the concentration of ownership is very high and the owners (West German concerns) exercise 'external' control. The power of managers in the former SOE has been reduced as most East German firms are integrated into the control structure of a West German concern.

The rationale behind this privatization strategy is simple. The purchasing firms were able to offer three important resources which the East German firms needed in order to survive, and which could not be obtained in the short term by any other means: professional entrepreneurship, new technology, and financial capital. These were the three criteria which the THA applied in selecting among potential buyers. They had to put forth a cogent restructuring plan (entrepreneurial competence), be willing to make substantial investment (technological renewal), and demonstrate possession of the necessary capital reserves.

There was a widespread belief among the West German political elite that the 'window of opportunity' for reunification would be open for only a short period of time and that the cost of political and economic integration would be modest—compared to the economic power of West Germany. Both assumptions turned out to be wrong and have since been criticized as two among several 'unification myths' (Pickel and Wiesenthal 1997: 198–211). The price to be paid for this political miscalculation was high:

1. With the monetary union between and the political unification of the two Germanies, East German firms were exposed to full competition under European Union rules immediately after 1990. Whereas Poland and Hungary devalued their currency to attenuate the consequences of trade liberalization (Adam 1994), the

exchange rate between the East and West German mark (1 : 1) destroyed many opportunities for East German firms on Western export markets. In real terms, the East German currency was revalued by 300 percent.

2. In the late eighties, West German companies had underutilized production capacity which they were able to activate instantaneously. They are located at a short distance to the East German market and their brand names were well known to East German consumers because they had had access to West German television. The East German market which could not be sheltered for a transitional period by protective tariffs was swamped with goods produced by West German firms. This sudden demand growth fueled the short-lived reunification boom of West German industry after 1989; in East Germany, it was one of the factors that accelerated deindustrialization (Flassbeck 1995).

3. The macroeconomic shock therapy was an almost inevitable consequence of political reunification, by virtue of which East Germany had no longer control over its borders. Two years after reunification the East German economy had lost 73 percent of its industrial output (Poland: 39 percent), and unemployment was at 16.5 percent in 1992 (Dornbusch and Wolf 1994). Rapid deindustrialization was the price East Germany paid for political reunification.[33]

We have seen that in Hungary, and particularly in Poland, intermediate institutions existed which survived the revolution of 1989 and were activated to mobilize resistance against shock strategies (e.g. workers' councils in Poland). These institutions were lacking in East Germany: it did not have an influential and organized political opposition before 1989 and its economy was highly centralized, leaving to local management little autonomy. More important, any serious organized resistance against the shock therapy imposed by the THA would have questioned German reunification. A 'gradual' approach to privatization—supported by a devaluation of the currency, protective customs tariffs, and low wages—can only be implemented in a country that has at least some control over its borders.

The political calculation that the social costs of shock therapy could be softened and offset by generous transfer payments by the West German welfare state was only partly correct. It was correct in so far as East Germans accepted the 'bargain' and did not vote in the former communist party—as happened in Poland and Hungary. A communist comeback would have not only threatened political unification, but also the huge transfer payments from West to East Germany. Neither prospect was attractive to a majority of the East German electorate. But the calculation was wrong with respect to the economic consequences of the radical approach. Within two years, East Germany lost most of its industrial base and it is unlikely that it can be recovered in the near future under conditions of global competition (Boltho *et al.* 1997).

Compared to the economic restructuring of Poland or the Czech Republic, which did not receive huge transfer payments, privatization in East Germany is far from

[33] In 2001, the unemployment rate in East Germany (17.4%) is still more than twice as high as that of West Germany (7.2%).

being a success story. At least in relative terms[34] the East German economy has *not* out-performed the Polish or Czech economy, and the longer the new 'Wirtschaftswunder' fails to materialize, the more the outcome of privatization, that is, the unequal distribution of property rights and the dominance of West German concerns, suffers a loss of legitimacy and is criticized for its redistributive effects.

8.5. CORPORATE GOVERNANCE AND CODETERMINATION

Property rights are embedded in a particular institutional environment. Legal regulations frame the scale and scope of property rights and define their limits. The 'value' of property rights depends on legal constraints and on the specific network configuration within which these rights are exercised (see Fig. 8.2). The following analysis concentrates on three examples to illustrate in which way legal and non-legal institutions structure the scale and scope of property rights in privatized firms in Eastern Europe: (1) corporate law and laws on codetermination (corporate governance structure); (2) ESOP which has been widely used as a privatization method in Eastern Europe; and (3) fragmentation of ownership: if a large number of individuals own a firm *collectively* (e.g. a joint stock company), their property rights are diluted and sometimes reduced to a mere legal title (separation of ownership and control).

8.5.1. *Corporate Governance Structure*

The analysis starts with a brief description of the law of corporations in the different countries. The intention is not to go into the details of corporate law, but to show the ways in which the power of the different stakeholders (owners, managers, and employees) is structured *by law*. Firms which are incorporated as joint stock or limited liability companies have to comply with legal regulations, which define the governance structure of a firm. For instance, the German corporation law[35] stipulates that the owners of a joint stock company (general assembly) are not allowed to interfere with the operating business of the company. Members of the supervisory board cannot be members of the management board (and vice versa), and in firms with more than 2000 employees 50 percent of the members of the supervisory board must be representatives of the workforce; the general meeting elects the remaining members of the supervisory board. The supervisory board nominates the members of the management board (and not the owners).

Each of these regulations restricts the property rights of the firm's owners.[36] Owners cannot instruct managers directly, rather they have to comply with a bureaucratic

---

[34] Poland reached its pre-1989 level of Gross Domestic Product (GDP) in 1995, the Czech Republic in 1997. Compared with these countries, East Germany suffered the most dramatic loss of GDP after 1989 and had not reached its pre-1989 level of GDP in 1999.

[35] After 1990, this law also applied in East Germany.

[36] In 1976, the German Employers' Association took legal action in the German Constitutional Court arguing that the law on codetermination expropriates the owners (shareholders) of the large corporation (see: Entscheidung des Bundesverfassungsgerichtes zur Mitbestimmung, Bd. 50 (1979), pp. 290–318).

procedure. As employee representatives command a decisive voting block on the supervisory board, this power structure frequently fosters a coalition between the executive management and the representatives of employees.

The governance structure of incorporated firms in Poland, Hungary, and the Czech Republic combines elements of German and Anglo-Saxon corporation law. The *Czech* commercial code of 1992 can be taken as an example to illustrate the way in which property rights in large firms are constrained by law.

Companies have a management board and a supervisory board. The supervisory board is elected by the general meeting, the management board may be nominated either directly by the owners (general meeting) or by the supervisory board. In larger firms management boards frequently have five members: two members are senior managers of the company (one of them is chairman of the board), three are representatives of the owners. In companies with more than fifty employees, one-third of the members of the supervisory board must be employees elected by the workforce of the company (codetermination). Owners may be represented on the management board as well as on the supervisory board; the role of the supervisory board (which usually has 4–6 members) is restricted to legal supervision of management (auditing, control of the balance sheet).[37]

Stavomont Prahe, a construction firm in Prague, illustrates this governance structure: 92 percent of its shares were distributed through voucher privatization. Individual investors hold 25 percent of the shares; 55 percent are owned by thirteen investment companies (the three largest hold 46 percent); 10 percent are still owned by the state; employees of the firm hold 5 percent, and 3 percent were transferred to the restitution fund. Stavomont has a five-member management board, of which three members are representatives of the three largest owners (the three investment funds) and two members are senior managers of the firm. The supervisory board has four members: one employee, a construction engineer (professional), and two representatives of the two largest owners (investment funds; see Brom and Orenstein 1994: 911, 920–5).

With minor variations, this example is also applicable to the governance structure of large firms in Poland and Hungary. In all three countries there is no strict separation of supervisory and executive functions. Owners may exercise control rights on the management and the supervisory board simultaneously; a seat on the management board allows them to influence the strategic decisions of management directly. While German corporation law delineates the functions of the two boards very strictly, the corporate law in the other three countries opens the management of the incorporated firm to the owners.

It has been shown that in Poland and in Hungary state ownership in the large enterprises is still considerable (Table 8.1, column 6). Thus, the state may nominate a significant proportion of the members of one or both boards. The case of Poland

---

[37] In Germany, the supervisory board of large firms may have 20 or more members (depending on the total size of the workforce). The more (external) members a supervisory board has, the more opportunities there are for interlocking directorates between nominally independent companies. See regression analysis in Chapter 2, Table 2.7, variable 'Size of Board'.

illustrates the procedures used to fill these positions: in state-owned incorporated firms, the workers' councils have been dissolved and management and supervisory boards established. The Ministry of Privatization controls two-thirds of the seats on the supervisory board (one-third of the members are representatives of the workforce). Individuals eligible for the supervisory board must be over 25 years old and must have received higher education. The Ministry requires that applicants for membership pass an examination. In 1993, 3000 individuals passed the examination, and 2000 of them were appointed to board positions. The ministry also provides an intensive 100-hour training program for those who wish to take the examination (Leblanc-Wohrer 1996: 39). In the case of Hungary, Voszka (1994: 352) remarks that 'incorporation is estimated to create more than 20,000 well-paid posts', with remuneration in large firms equal to the salary of a tenured university professor (Török 1995: 19).

With the return to political power of the former communist parties in Poland (1993) and Hungary (1994), the structure of corporate governance has opened the door to political patronage and a comeback of the former socialist managers.[38] The still considerable importance of state ownership and the selection mechanisms for seats on the management and supervisory boards (which strengthen the role of owners) provide the institutionalized and *legitimized* channels through which the former economic elite (nomenclature) can secure its economic power position. Many surveys in Eastern Europe have provided empirical evidence for the high 'reproduction rate' of the economic elite after 1989. In the next section, the results of elite reproduction are analyzed in more detail. In this section, the economic resources, the legal regulations, and the institutionalized channels through which members of the economic elite have protected their (former) positions are described.

In all four countries discussed here, legal rights to *codetermination* constitute an important element of the structure of corporate governance (Table 8.1, column 7). In Hungary, Poland, and the Czech Republic, one-third of the members of the supervisory board have to be representatives of the workforce. In East Germany, the same regulation applies for firms with more than 500, but less than 2000 employees. As there are only few firms with more than 2000 employees, the 'one-third' codetermination is also the dominant type in East Germany.

A voting block of one-third can carry considerable influence if the other two-thirds of the shares are spread among thousands of individual owners (fragmented ownership). If this is the case, the employees on the supervisory board may represent the single most influential group and—entering a coalition with management—may effectively participate in the decision making within the firm. This constellation of interests is not typical for any of the CEE countries, however, particularly not for East Germany. The concentration of ownership in East Germany is higher than in West Germany: 90 percent of firms with more than 400 employees have a single or—at most—two or three (West German or foreign) owners. There is no managerial

---

[38] For election results in Poland, see Tworzecki (1994); for Hungary, see Szelényi *et al.* (1996); effects on economic policy are discussed in Winiecki (1996: 329).

capitalism in East Germany, but rather direct control by owners over the larger firms. Given this constellation of interests, employee representatives on the supervisory board may be able to obtain information, but they are hardly able to influence the strategic decisions of management.

The situation in Poland and Hungary is more complicated because here the state is still a majority owner in many large firms (Poland) or an influential minority owner (Hungary). But it has already been shown how the seats on the management and supervisory board are frequently filled with the members of the former nomenclature (political patronage). In the Czech Republic the investment funds hold voting blocks large enough to exercise control, but recent studies have shown that they do *not* use their voting power to control management, but leave control to the incumbent management.[39]

As a preliminary result of this analysis it can be said that, in Hungary, Poland, and the Czech Republic, managerial control over the firm is still strong *despite* a highly concentrated ownership. The bureaucratic power of managers *coexists* with ownership rights in the privatized firms. If the state bureaucracy or investment funds try to restructure the firm or to dismiss its management, the managers may find in employee representatives on the supervisory board a compliant ally. It seems that codetermination strengthens the role of managers *vis-à-vis* the owners, but does not provide genuine power to the workforce. In East Germany, corporate governance is clearly dominated by outside owners (West German concerns) and codetermination is a pure formality.

8.5.2. *Employee Stock Ownership*

Employee stock ownership has been furthered by various legal regulations and economic measures in the CEE countries, particularly in Poland, Hungary, and Russia (Table 8.1, column 8). It was the political price that had to be paid to reduce the resistance of managers and the workforce to central privatization plans (Nelson and Kuzes 1994; Gaidar 1995: 41). Three issues will be discussed here. Can employee stock ownership be used to strengthen the influence of the workforce? Is employee stock ownership stable in the medium term? To what extent is employee stock ownership used by managers to strengthen their control position?

Employee stock ownership plans (ESOP) may be implemented as a surrogate for higher wages or as an incentive for higher productivity; in this case, ESOP is an instrument of human resource management (and will not be discussed here). ESOP may also be introduced as a substitute for codetermination, however, and in this case it is almost a public good. Employee ownership can only be used as a control device if the employees as a group control *collectively* a substantial proportion of shares, and if this group has control over the sale of shares. Each individual worker will,

---

[39] Some fund managers explain that they do not have enough qualified personnel to supervise the companies in their portfolio, others believe that it is not their job to exercise direct control over the managers of companies they own. See Kenway and Chlumsky (1997) and Kenway and Klvacová (1996).

if there are no restrictions, sell his or her shares whenever it is in the interest of the individual household—regardless of the control interests of the employees as a group. Thus, employee ownership is vulnerable to 'defection' of which the Polish case provides some examples.

The workforce of Prochnik bought 20 percent of the firm's equity in 1991, this proportion was down to 8 percent by 1993, mainly due to the desperate economic situation of the workforce. Similarly, employees of Zywiec purchased (at preferential rates) 12 percent of their firm's shares that are traded on the Warsaw Stock Exchange; by 1993 the proportion of stock owned by employees was down to 6 percent. AT&T acquired 80 percent of Telfa and then purchased the remaining 20 percent held by the workforce; the employees of Phillips Lightning Poland who originally owned 20 percent, have since sold virtually all their shares (Tittenbrun 1995: 25–6).

In a survey of 200 Polish firms with employee stock ownership, 79 percent report restrictions on the free trade of shares: in 46 percent of the firms, management has to approve the sale of shares; in 33 percent employees of the firm have a right of first refusal of shares colleagues wish to sell (Jarosz 1996: 97). But it seems that these restrictions have not prevented employee ownership from being diluted. The same survey reports the following results: during the period 1993–5 the proportion of small shareholders (skilled/unskilled workers) in the 200 Polish firms decreased substantially while the proportion of managers with larger holdings increased. The outcome was a higher concentration of ownership in the hands of *management* (Jarosz 1996: 93).

In most Russian firms privatized by vouchers, managers, and the workforce collectively own 50 percent or more of their firm (insider control). The 'defection' of employees has so far been avoided because managers control the shares' register book, and they are able to prevent employees from selling their shares to outsiders by threatening them with dismissal (Rutland 1994: 1118).

Gurkov and Maital report for Russia that workers receive less information and have less influence on managerial decision making since they became shareholders of their firm (quoted in Bim 1996: 479). Similar observations were made in Polish ESOP firms: on privatization, the workers' councils were dissolved, and the small shareholdings that the firm's employees acquired did not compensate for the loss of institutionalized codetermination (Jarosz 1996: 85).

It seems that in many employee-'owned' firms, managers are able to combine property rights with the power of bureaucracy. As employee shareholdings are spread among hundreds of workers, individual property rights are dwarfed by the organized power of bureaucracy. The outcome of ESOP programs in Eastern Europe is paradoxical. Employee ownership is the privatization method that has received the strongest support and legitimation because it distributes ownership in the former SOE equally among the workforce. However, empirical evidence shows that if shares are distributed to individual workers, the control potential is likely to be lost by 'defection'. Only management seems able to prevent defection, but in this case, employee ownership strengthens managerial control.

8.5.3. *Fragmentation of Ownership*

Property rights are reduced to mere financial claims (dividends) if the shares of large corporations are distributed among thousands of owners. Rational choice theory has convincingly argued that a large number of small shareholders are unlikely to organize their interests. Lack of interest aggregation and information asymmetries between shareholders and managers have exacerbated the separation of ownership and control.

More recently neoliberal critics of managerial capitalism have reversed the argument: if ownership is highly concentrated in the hands of one or two outside owners, these investors should be able and willing[40] to control managers. Western advisers, many of whom are linked to the World Bank and/or the IMF, have consistently argued that the method of privatization in Eastern Europe should produce a highly *concentrated external ownership* (Carlin and Aghion 1996).

Ownership is highly concentrated in Poland, Hungary, and the Czech Republic, but it is doubtful whether it can be classified as 'external'. Foreign investors and multinational corporations which have bought many firms in these countries are certainly 'external' owners, but whether the investment funds in the Czech Republic are 'outsiders' is already questionable, and the Polish state is certainly not an external owner.

Many owners in Eastern Europe have de jure property rights, but lack resources which the German THA required, as selection criteria, of potential buyers in East Germany: financial capital, new technology, and entrepreneurial competence. None of the different types of predominant owners described in Section 8.4 are able to provide these resources. They are not 'external' investors, but may be classified as 'internal' owners. This is certainly true for the state-owned firms in Poland, it is correct to some extent for the investment funds in the Czech Republic, and still applies to many firms in Hungary.

On the basis of these ownership patterns, a specific type of Eastern European *managerial capitalism* has evolved. Even though ownership is highly concentrated, the new owners are unable to put pressure on managers because they do not provide essential resources to the firm, and therefore cannot threaten to withdraw them. Moreover, they are unable to discipline managers by threatening them with dismissal because of the acute shortage of managerial skills (see selection procedure for the Polish supervisory board, above). Within the institutional framework of the large firm, managers and owners are compelled to coexist. The 'new' owners are represented either by the state (Poland), by large financial institutions (Czech Republic), or by a network of other firms and the state (integrated ownership, Hungary). There is no separation of ownership and control, but rather a *balance of power* between managers and owners. Within these exchange networks, members of the former nomenclature were able largely to preserve their power position (see Section 8.6).

The case of East Germany is different: here, we have 'true' external ownership which is highly concentrated. As already mentioned, 72.2 percent of all firms with

---

[40] If there are only a few owners they have a greater incentive to bear the informational costs of control because they are also the beneficiaries of productivity gains resulting from efficient control.

more than 100 employees in East Germany belong to West German or foreign concerns. These owners differ from those in Poland and the Czech Republic in that they have a specific strategic interest in their property, they are able to enforce this interest because ownership and control are unified, and they have the resources to accomplish their aims.

In the former socialist countries, true 'external' ownership could only be obtained by selling the SOEs to foreign investors. This was the path chosen in the former GDR, but was not viable in the other East European countries for political reasons. Economic results obtained in East Germany have been poor, suggesting that concentrated *external* ownership is possibly not the most efficient institution for the transformation of a socialist economy.

8.6. REPRODUCTION OF THE ECONOMIC ELITE

The type of capitalism and its institutional order that is emerging in Eastern Europe has been shaped and structured to a considerable degree by the members of the political and economic elites. The way they have been socialized, their political affiliations and economic resources have had an important impact on the outcome of the transformation process and on the formation of capitalist institutions. Here, the question will be addressed as to what extent the former nomenclature was able to remain in elite positions after 1989 (elite reproduction). More precisely, it will be asked what proportion of the 'new' managers had already been directors of SOE before 1989.

The arguments will be presented in three steps. First, it will be asked under what conditions circulation (or reproduction respectively) of the former elites is likely to occur. Reproduction and circulation are two opposing concepts which describe the impact of revolutionary processes upon the ruling elites of a society and their ability to adapt their power resources to the new social structure. Second, empirical evidence is presented which shows to what extent the former economic elites have actually remained in power. Third, it will be asked which resources the nomenclature members used to protect their power position after 1989. Did they remain in elite positions because they acquired ownership of 'their' firms during the privatization process (resource: ownership/property rights), or did they remain in power because they were able to protect the firm's bureaucracy against the claims of the new owners (resource: bureaucratic power)?

8.6.1. *The Circulation of Elites*

After a revolutionary upheaval, the ruling elites of a society are likely to be replaced (high rate of circulation) if one or several of the following conditions are met:

1. The new elite enforces circulation by using *violence*. For Pareto the circulation of elites is a violent process epitomized by his famous dictum of history as being a 'cemetery of elites'.[41] An example of circulation imposed by force are the socialist

---

[41] 'Le aristocrazie non durano.... La storia è un cimitero di aristocrazie' (Pareto 1923: 262, § 2053).

revolutions which occurred in Eastern Europe after 1945, and during which the former 'bourgeois' elites were replaced (and often liquidated). In contrast, the 'velvet' revolution of 1989 was, by and large, a non-violent revolution in the wake of which liberal democracies were established in most CEE countries. Liberal democracies allow members of the former elites to use their social and political resources and to attempt to transform them into the new 'currency' (e.g. private ownership). Former communist parties were able to regain considerable political influence after general elections in Poland (1993), Hungary (1994), and Russia (1993). The non-violent character of the velvet revolution and the *open* political and economic structures established in Eastern Europe have created an institutional environment conducive to the reproduction of the former nomenclature (low circulation rates).

2. A second condition favorable to a high circulation rate is if, during a relatively long pre-revolutionary period, a *counter-elite* is able to develop skills and competencies and to accumulate resources required for high-level political or economic positions. This is likely to occur if the social structures and economic resources of the 'new' society—and its corresponding elites—mature gradually under the 'ancien régime'. The Solidarity movement in Poland fits this pattern to some extent, but its organization disintegrated after 1989 into several competing groups and lost its political momentum (Korbonski 1996). In other East European societies no organized counter-elite was able to develop before 1989.[42] So it was that most of the competent individuals capable of filling the many elite vacancies after 1989 were—one way or another—connected to the previous nomenclature. Therefore, the lack of a powerful counter-elite implies a low rate of circulation.

3. If access to new elite positions requires resources that are substantially *different* from those that guaranteed power positions under the previous regime, we expect to observe a high rate of circulation. Examples are Islamic revolutions imposing Islamic ideology and religious erudition as important selection criteria for elite positions in a theocracy. If such radical changes take place, many members of the former elite are likely to lose their positions because they are unable to meet the new selection criteria.

Both socialist and capitalist regimes in Europe are advanced industrialized societies which cannot survive without scientific, technical, and administrative competencies. Even if the level of sophistication is higher in the West, it has been shown that since the late sixties, party membership was not sufficient for recruitment into elite positions in the former socialist countries. These countries have high levels of tertiary education and they were transformed into 'meritocratic' societies long before 1989. Although some shifts occurred, technical and professional skills were not depreciated wholesale during the transformation process. Many scientists, engineers, and administrative experts remained in their positions and those waiting in the

---

[42] It is arguable whether the many small entrepreneurs which established themselves in market niches in Hungary and to some extent in Poland before 1989 (secondary economy) may be regarded as members of an economic 'counter'-elite.

'second line' were frequently promoted after 1989. The fact that scientific and technical competencies are important power resources in both capitalist and socialist societies leads us to predict low rates of circulation.

Summarizing the arguments it can be said that after 1989, three conditions coincided which helped to at least stabilize if not actually strengthen the position of the former nomenclature and may explain a high rate of reproduction of the economic elite: the non-violent character of the velvet revolution, the lack of a counter elite, and the similarity of resources that provide access to elite positions in socialist and capitalist societies. The latter condition points to the *structural similarities* of capitalist and socialist industrial societies (which had been emphasized by convergence theorists long before 1989).

8.6.2. *Empirical Evidence*

The economic elite, as defined here, consists of those individuals who have effective control over the *large* enterprises in each country.[43] Table 8.2 shows the origin of the new economic elite, that is, it indicates from which social strata its present members have been recruited (column 1). In Poland, 90 percent of directors and managers of the large firms had been in similar positions before 1989; in the Czech Republic, this proportion is 75 percent. As the data summarized in Table 8.2 are based on various sampling methods and different sample sizes, it is not meaningful to interpret variations between countries. It suffices to conclude that in each of the four countries at least three-quarters of the 'new' directors and managers of large firms were members of the socialist elite before 1989. Column 2 shows that almost 50 percent of these managers had been a member of the communist party and thus have in common similar educational and socialization experiences to which they were exposed within the party organization.

It has frequently been argued that members of the nomenclature 'converted' their political power into economic assets in order to preserve their previous positions. However, 'conversion of power' is a metaphor which does not explain the social transformation which allowed the former elite to maintain its position of power. The right-hand panel of Table 8.2 shows two different resources which may have been used by members of the economic elite who successfully reproduced their former social status: bureaucratic control and private ownership (property rights). Unfortunately, survey data which would allow us to assess the relative weight of these resources in the process of social reproduction are scarce.[44] Therefore, arguments often have to be based on case studies and qualitative data pertaining to the privatization process.

Many directors and managers have perpetuated their privileged positions because they were able to maintain *bureaucratic control* over the firm. In socialist countries, a similar separation of ownership and control existed as in Western managerial

[43] This definition is not exhaustive. The present analysis is limited to the transformation of large firms and, therefore, excludes officials of employers' associations and trade unions who are also members of the 'economic elite'.

[44] The comparative studies of CEE countries and Russia do not allow a cross-classification of the new economic elite with data on ownership. See special issue of 'Theory and Society' (1995), vol. 24, October.

TABLE 8.2 *Reproduction of the economic elite*

	% Reproduction		Resources		
	Former elite members	**Party member**	**Bureaucratic control**	**Ownership**	**N**
Poland	90	45	*Yes*	(yes)[a]	588
Hungary	90	49	Partly	Yes	489
Czech Republic	75	57	*Yes*	Partly	62
East Germany	85	47	No	No	426

[a] Small/medium-sized enterprise sector.

Sources: Poland: Wasilewski and Wnuk-Lipinski (1995: 682); Hungary: Szelényi *et al.* (1995: 708); Czech Republic: Clark and Soulsby (1996: 291); East Germany: Windolf (1998).

capitalism. The centralized state 'owned' the enterprises, but managers had a monopoly on information, they had acquired specific skills (human capital), and had privileged access to social networks which consolidated their local power. The former socialist managers were able to keep control of 'their' firms to the extent that this control *was not challenged by a new owner*. This is the case in Poland, where the state still owns most large enterprises and power relations have hardly changed, but also in the Czech Republic, where many investment funds are unable to exercise effective control. Some funds have several hundred firms in their portfolio and are represented on the management/supervisory board of only a few of these firms.[45]

Ownership is a second resource which enables individuals to take or retain control of a firm, but here it has to be explained how former nomenclature members succeeded in acquiring large shareholdings in former SOE. Several strategies were applied to 'convert' bureaucratic power into private property:

1. Privatization laws (many of which have been enacted under the pressure of former communist parties) allowed employees and managers to acquire shares of their firms at preferential rates. For Poland, Tittenbrun (1995: 25) reports, that 'in almost every company listed on the stock exchange the management group has substantial stakes'. These shareholdings range from 6 to 12 percent and have in some cases a value of several million US$. A study on Polish ESOP-firms shows that 72 percent of the current (1995) company presidents (who hold substantial shareholdings in the firms they manage) had been directors of the firm before privatization, that is, these members of the former nomenclature were able to transform their bureaucratic control directly into private ownership.[46]

[45] There is anecdotal evidence from case studies to suggest that former directors of large SOEs are co-owners of Czech investment funds. Later they were appointed as members of the management board of those firms which are in the portfolio of the investment fund (elite recycling; Clark and Soulsby 1996: 292).

[46] This is a representative sample of 218 Polish ESOP firms; 92% of the current managers have a higher education diploma. 50% of the current supervisory board members had been in managerial positions in the same firm before privatization (Jarosz 1996: 25, 101).

2. The high inflation rates during the transformation period destroyed the financial resources of potential competitors as owners and favored those who had direct access to the non-financial assets of the firm. They were integrated into local networks and had special information not available to external bidders. Many acquisitions of firms took the form of barter within exclusive nomenclature networks. In more general terms, it can be argued that the more decentralized the privatization process was and the more the members of the nomenclature were able to influence the rules of privatization, the greater their scope for acquiring control through ownership.

The acquisition of property rights was particularly important for *political* bureaucrats in order to maintain their social position. Before 1989, they were not directly integrated into the local power structure of SOE. The acquisition of shareholdings allowed them to transfer their status position from the political to the economic system. Survey data show that a small proportion of the new economic elite had been members of the political apparatus before 1989.[47] We assume that in many cases these transitions were made possible by the acquisition of shareholdings during the privatization process.

Finally, quasi-ownership may become an important source of control within capital networks. In this case, managers do not own a firm, but they control the firm which is the shareholder of another firm. It has been shown that this type of ownership (integrated ownership) is predominant in Hungary. Here, managers combine two resources within corporate networks: they exercise bureaucratic control over firm A and are quasi-owners of firm B in which firm A holds a sizable proportion of shares. The directors and senior managers of those firms which are connected by shareholdings exert as a *group* managerial power over and hold property rights in the whole network.[48]

The 'reproduction' of elites, which has been analyzed so far, is only one part of the transformation process, and a second part has to be taken into account. After 1989, many nomenclature members resigned, lost their jobs, or were dismissed by the workforce, and they have never regained positions of influence since then. In East Germany, the percentage of former managers who lost their positions is approximately as high as the percentage of workers who were dismissed (about 70–80 percent in the privatized firms).

Who stayed and which selection criteria were applied? The empirical evidence shows that, first, *age* was a significant variable: the older cohorts (socialist gerontocracy) almost completely disappeared and were replaced by younger managers. Second, *professional competence* was important: those who had technical competencies replaced nomenclature members who had mainly political control functions. Third, it seems that the 'new' economic elite has a more 'bourgeois' social background: their

---

[47] In Hungary, 3.8% of the new (1993) economic elite had been (non-economic) party or state officials in 1988; N=489 (Szelény *et al.* 1995: 711).

[48] King (1997) provides extensive empirical evidence for this kind of control within capital networks for Hungary and the Czech Republic.

parents having higher education and middle to higher managerial positions (in contrast to the 'working class' background of the older cohorts).[49]

Thus, while it is basically correct to say that the 'new' economic elite is essentially the old one, a number of important differences has to be taken into account: the new economic elite is younger, has a stronger professional orientation, and is to some extent more 'bourgeois'. One can argue that the former economic elite has been reproduced, but that *within* the elite considerable circulation has taken place.

Summarizing the above results, the following conclusions can be drawn. First, the proportion of current managers who had managerial positions before 1989 is *not dependent on the method of privatization* and its outcome. Just as diverse privatization policies as those applied in Poland versus East Germany, in Hungary versus the Czech Republic also have produced similar results. At least three-quarters of the 'new' managers had been in managerial positions under the socialist regime and almost half of them had been party members. This result suggests that ownership was not the dominant resource in the process of elite reproduction. The (economic) nomenclature remained in power because their members were able to retain control over the firm's bureaucracy. Technical skills, economic competence,[50] local knowledge, and social networks were—on balance—more important than property rights. In most firms, the *continuity* of the bureaucratic mode of control was not eroded by the 1989 revolution or subsequently by privatization, whatever form it took.

Second, notwithstanding the previous point, there is a large group of former nomenclature members who have acquired ownership in firms and who now exercise control because they are owners. They were able to exploit the 'window of opportunity' and quickly turned into capitalist entrepreneurs. This group of entrepreneurs is probably largest in Russia; it is larger in Hungary and Poland (spontaneous privatization) than in the Czech Republic; it is relatively small in East Germany. Their most important resources are property rights, and they are interested in protecting these rights.

Third, those members of the economic elite who reproduced their social position by virtue of their control over the bureaucracy are unlikely to tolerate a type of capitalism that would grant owners unconstrained property rights. They are more likely to enter into a coalition with their workforce in support of a corporatist or welfare variant of capitalism. This group represents the 'constraints of history' in the post-socialist societies in Eastern Europe (path dependency). The 'new' owners form the spearhead of a group of capitalists who promote the idea of a 'spontaneous order' and a 'self-adjusting market'. They have transformed the ideology of an enlightened nomenclature into the new creed of market competition and property rights, and they are unlikely to support third-way experiments or any kind of 'state capitalism'.

[49] See Wasilewski and Wnuk-Lipinksi (1995: 680–1) for Poland; Szelényi *et al.* (1995: 707–11) for Hungary; Windolf (1998) for East Germany. The 'embourgeoisement' of the managers is to some extent a cohort effect: the younger cohorts are simply more likely to have parents with college education (expansion of the educational system).

[50] In Poland, 86.4% of the new economic elite have a college/university diploma; in Hungary 94.1%; in the Czech Republic 77%; in East Germany 56,3%. *Sources*: Wasilewski and Wnuk-Lipinksi (1995: 682); Szelényi *et al.* (1995: 709); Clark and Soulsby (1996: 289); Windolf (1998).

The overall portrait of emerging institutions and constellations of interests is still inconclusive: there are social groups who favor a corporatist type of capitalism with strong constraints on property rights, but there are also forces that wish to move toward a more liberal and deregulated market capitalism. Only in East Germany is the control structure less ambiguous: even though many members of the former nomenclature have managed to save their job, they do not exercise control in most East German firms. It has been shown that these firms are owned *and* effectively controlled by West German/foreign firms or investors. From this point of view, East Germany is more 'liberal' and comes closer to the model of investor capitalism. The Czech Republic may also evolve in this direction if the investment funds are restructured in a third wave of privatization (e.g. hostile takeovers) and their shareholdings are sold to outside (foreign) investors (Coffee 1996).

8.7. CONCLUSIONS

The breakdown of socialism in Eastern Europe and the loss of legitimacy of socialist institutions left a vacuum in which neoliberal ideas and a 'utopian' capitalism flourished for some time. Neoliberalism was and still is an appealing alternative to those subjected to an 'economy of shortage' and to 40 years of political repression. The institutional and ideological vacuum provided a 'window of opportunity' for a small economic elite to disseminate their ideas of a new economic order and to preach radical changes and reform.

However, in practice, the outcome of shock therapy has been paradoxical: it did not destroy the power basis of the nomenclature, but rather stabilized it and provided the resources for the reproduction of the economic elite. Between 75 and 90 percent of the 'new' managers and directors had been in similar positions before 1989 and almost half of them had been members of the communist party. As Murrell (1993: 112) put it: 'Society vanquished the shock therapists'.

The type of capitalism that is evolving in some countries in Eastern Europe in some ways resembles Western managerial capitalism, but with certain significant differences. Privatization created a relatively high concentration of ownership. There is no clear-cut separation of ownership and control, but rather a *balance of power* between managers and owners. Some managers were able to seal off their positions from the direct influence of the new owners (Czech Republic) or they even strengthened their bureaucratic power by appropriating substantial shareholdings in 'their' firm (Poland, Russia); in the latter case, firm managers combine bureaucratic power with the power of ownership. Managers are not completely immune to control by owners, but they keep them at arm's length. In many cases, the new owners were unable to provide financial capital or technological know-how, and they cannot threaten to withdraw what they never delivered.

For the privatization agencies, the crucial question was not who has enough money to pay for the firms (because almost nobody in Eastern Europe had), but which selection criterion should be applied *instead* to distribute the assets of the SOEs. Perhaps unsurprisingly, those who were able to influence the rules of privatization and who were integrated into the former economic and political *networks* became the new owners. In Russia, but also to some extent in Hungary and Poland, former (economic) nomenclature members 'legitimately' appropriated former SOE in exchange for political support of the privatization process.

In East Germany, privatization was controlled by an external bureaucracy (THA) and the outcome was highly concentrated external ownership. The SOEs were sold to West German or foreign investors, less for money than for a promise to invest in new technology and to restructure the firms. But even here, 85 percent of the 'new' managers had been in similar positions before 1989. However, their position is weak compared to that of their equals in Eastern Europe. Highly concentrated external ownership reduces the power of managers to that of an 'agent'. The economic results of this privatization method, the one that comes closest to what neoliberal economists had recommended, are poor to say the least: East Germany has not outperformed its East European neighbors, and the controversy caused by the outcome of the privatization may cause political instability in the future.[51] Fundamental opposition is, for the time being, muted because of the high transfer payments from West Germany. But the *legitimacy* of economic institutions (e.g. the distribution of property rights) may be seriously challenged once this palliative is no longer available.

A final remark concerns the way in which the different privatization methods have transformed the class structure in Eastern Europe. It has been shown that the former enterprise directors and managers have taken over control or ownership (or both) in the privatized firms in Eastern Europe. However, this 'reproduction' of elites is only one part of the transformation process, and a second part has to be taken into account. After 1989, many nomenclature members resigned, lost their jobs, or were dismissed by the workforce, and they have never regained positions of influence since then. One can argue that the former economic elite has been reproduced, but that *within* the elite considerable circulation has taken place.

Concomitant to these changes in social structure, a shift in power resources and in ideological orientation has occurred. The political-bureaucratic power of the nomenclature has been replaced by managerial control and property rights in the economic system. The shift in ideology is more ambivalent. There is a group of young managers and entrepreneurs with strong neoliberal orientations. If the outcome of parliamentary elections in Poland is used as a guideline, this group accounts for perhaps 15 percent of the adult population.[52] But there is also a strong 'conservative' element which is being strengthened by the high proportion of votes for the former communist parties. The type of capitalism that is evolving in Eastern Europe will depend not in the least on the outcome of the power struggle between the two groups located at opposite ends of the political divide.

---

[51] The privatization method of the THA is not the only reason to explain the poor economic performance in East Germany. The reevaluation of the East German mark (300% in 1990) and the rapid increase of wages are, of course, also important in explaining the economic depression.

[52] In the 1997 parliamentary election, the 'Freedom Union' headed by Leszek Balcerowicz received 15.9% of the vote (*The New York Times*, 22 Sept. 1997, p. A7).

PART IV

OUTLOOK

9

From Corporatism to Shareholder Value

The market structures prevailing in Germany, France, or Japan since the Second World War have developed in one way or another along corporatist or statist lines. For more than a decade, however, there has been debate among social scientists as to whether these economic structures are viable in the context of today's global market. Does the German or French capitalism still have a future?[1]

Albert (2000) has argued that the structure of the worldwide financial market mandates a change in the capitalist regime, a change from the manager capitalism of the past to a capitalism based on shareholder value. In his view, a process of convergence is now underway which is leading the hitherto nationally specific capitalist patterns to a universal model, one in which—directed via the financial markets—shareholders exert a strong influence upon the operations of enterprises.

A somewhat different view to that of Albert interprets the various economic systems in which such features as corporate networks, relational contracting, and regulated competition play a prominent role as representing a lower level of economic development. The prognosis of observers from this approach is that neoliberal models of capitalism are destined to overtake and transform these relatively underdeveloped variants. Implicit in this view is that the 'innate' superiority[2] of market structures that have developed in the United States and Britain will ultimately force those in such countries as Germany, France, and Japan to adapt and to deregulate their own economies.

There is no doubt that Germany and France over the past decade have seen numerous alterations in their financial laws and substantial restructuring of their economic institutions, and that these changes could be interpreted as confirmation of the convergence hypothesis. Corporatist regulations on the labor and financial markets are being dismantled and replaced by a regime of market regulation. A special commission was established in Germany, for example, to identify the market segments most amenable to deregulation (Deregulierungskommission 1991). Britain has been using the European Union as a vehicle for the propagation of its neoliberal economic policy throughout the Common Market. The question that one can ask here, however, is whether these changes constitute a regime change or, rather, an adaptation within a regime to altered environmental conditions.[3]

---

[1] Comprehensive literature is available on this subject; see Streeck (1997), Albert (1991), Baudru and Kechidi (2000), Berger and Dore (1996), Morin (1998), Hall and Soskice (2001).

[2] Bratton and McCahery (1999: 246) speak of an 'evolutionary superiority claim'. See also Rajan and Zingales (1998), La Porta *et al.* (1997).

[3] See Krasner (1983). Hall (1993: 279) speaks of a 'policy paradigm shift' (e.g. from Keynesian to neoliberal economic policies).

The social sciences have developed a string of theories to explain institutional changes that we observed in the economic system in recent decades. Among these are the transaction-cost theories (lock-in effects) and theories on cultural evolution.[4] These concepts will be briefly summarized in the following section. In Section 9.3, we consider a number of examples to demonstrate the changes which corporate networks, the ownership patterns of large enterprises, and financial markets have undergone in Germany and France over the past decade. In Section 9.4, we return to the question of the future survivability of the economic institutions that developed in Germany and in France and that have been labeled by various scholars as 'Germany, Inc.' or 'capitalisme à la française'.

9.1. TRANSACTION COSTS AND 'LOCK-IN' EFFECTS

If we ask what type of institutions a society chooses in order to render markets more effective, transaction-cost theory offers a simple answer: society chooses those institutions that reduce transaction costs. As Williamson writes (1985: 17): '... the economic institutions of capitalism have the main purpose and effect of economizing on transaction costs'. In other words, the problem of the 'optimal' market order is resolved with reference to a meta-market in which institutions compete with one another. Those institutions will survive that, in the longer run, reduce transaction costs in a given country and thus raise its competitiveness. Competition on the meta-market for institutions, therefore, describes the mechanism through which institutions that have become an obstacle to innovation are replaced by new ones. Over time, the institutional structures developed in every country will become if not identical, then very similar (convergence).

However, historical and empirical studies show that in many countries there are institutions that—seen from a purely economic perspective—are inefficient, if not completely obsolete. If the meta-market of institutional competition were working perfectly, then inefficient institutions would be expected to die out over time. North (1990) refers repeatedly to transaction costs as a way to explain why such inefficient institutions nevertheless survive: institutional (or social) change itself causes transaction costs, and these can be very high (e.g. social reforms). The higher the costs, the less likely is social change. This clarifies the phenomena that North describes as 'lock-in' and 'path dependency'. A society is locked in to its institutional framework, and these institutions influence development paths in the future (path dependency). Inefficient institutions survive because the costs of social change are too high or at least appear to be so to the members of society.

Roe (1997: 167) illustrates the problem with the following example: 'We are on a road and wonder why it winds and goes here instead of there, despite that a straight road would be a much easier drive. Today's road depends on what path was taken before. Decades ago, a fur trader cut a path through the woods... Industry came and located in the road's bends; housing developments went up that fit the road and

---

[4] See Fog (1999), Boyd and Richerson (1985).

industry'. Home owners then continue to invest in their homes, making the losses that they would incur by a straightening of the road much too high.

The order of the keys on a typewriter is another example of the 'lock-in' effect that is often cited in the literature. Although experts do not consider the QWERTY-order of the keys to be optimal, this order has persisted unchanged (David 1985; Arthur 1989). In the literature on this topic, there are a number of explanations for such effects that are summarized in the following (Liebowitz and Margolis 1995).

(1) 'Sunk costs', meaning the economic and social investments made in a technology (e.g. nuclear power) or an institutional infrastructure (e.g. codetermination) by a society in the past, are one reason why institutions are not adapted to technological advancements or economic structural change. The costs incurred by adaptation would be higher than the expected benefits.

(2) In the network economy, consumers benefit from 'increasing rates of return': the more people there are in the society who own a cell phone (and therefore are 'reachable'), or the more people there are who use a certain software standard, the greater is the benefit for all the network members. One of the oldest examples illustrating the network effect is language.

The effect of 'increasing rates of return' is especially great in institutions whose efficiency increases through learning. For example, the longer the institution 'codetermination' exists, the more experience the involved actors have with it, and the more successfully they learn to arbitrate social conflicts using it, then the more efficient the institution of codetermination becomes.[5]

(3) The decentralized, uncoordinated decisions made by actors are another cause of the 'lock-in' effect, as the abovementioned examples of the winding road or the typewriter keyboard show. People make their decisions in a decentralized fashion and not concurrently in time, but sequentially, regardless of whether they are renovating their homes or learning to type. As each of these decisions to invest in the home or in personal skills are made, they incur 'sunk costs' at several points down the line, costs that make it appear 'uneconomical' to vary plans considerably, that is, to straighten the winding road or to learn to type on a keyboard featuring a different arrangement of keys.

Can this explain why there is codetermination in Germany, why cartels dominated the economic landscape until 1945, to be followed by corporate group structures, and why German businesses were financed chiefly through bank credit and not over the stock exchange? Can 'lock-in' effects explain why employees work their entire life at one firm (lifelong employment) in Japan, why companies have formed '*keiretsu*' networks and why unfriendly takeovers are taboo?

Let us return to the story of the winding road: Japan and Germany exemplify two societies in which the houses along the road were destroyed during the Second World

---

[5] '...complex technologies often display increasing returns to adoption in that the more they are adopted, the more experience is gained with them, and the more they are improved...(learning by using)' (Arthur 1989: 116).

War; then after the war, the road was forcefully 'straightened' by the occupational powers. In Germany, cartels were forbidden and large companies were decartelized (e.g. Krupp, Deutsche Bank); in Japan, the American occupational power also forbid certain forms of business groups (*zaibatsu*) and ordered their decartelization. By the mid-1950s, this development had been reversed. In Japan, business groups restructured themselves and regrouped under a new name (*keiretsu*). In Germany, the cartels were replaced by corporate groups (corporate networks).

The revival of traditional forms of economic organization cannot be explained by 'sunk costs' (the houses had been destroyed) and by a decentralized decision-making process (the occupational power was a key 'deus ex machina'). In the following, an alternative explanation is presented, in which it is argued that the (economic) institutions in a country are subject to a twofold selection, namely economic selection (reduction of transaction costs) and cultural selection (compatibility with the dominant culture/religion).

9.2. CULTURAL SELECTION

The key concepts of theories of social evolution are variation, selection, and retention (Campbell 1965). There is considerable variation in the legal and economic institutions of the different countries, and these variations constitute a pool of different opportunities from which each country is able to select. Through planned innovation (research), through creative destruction, through imitation or simply by accident, new variations are continually being created in every society.

However, not all variations survive. New institutions have to endure a twofold selection process. They are subjected to economic selection on the meta-market of institutions, where the decisive selection criterion is economic efficiency (reduction of transaction costs). They are also subjected to cultural selection, where the compatibility of an innovation with the basic values of the culture is the decisive criterion in selection. Variations (innovations) that are not compatible with the cultural or religious code of a society have little chance of survival. Should they be implemented anyway, they often create such social conflict that their economic advantages are reduced to nothing.

In the 1970s, the British government established a 'Committee of Inquiry on Industrial Democracy', the purpose of which was to recommend steps and measures for the introduction of a model of codetermination. The recommendations resulting from the committee's work have been largely ignored. Clegg (1979: 438) notes: 'Until recently British trade unions had never favoured trade union representation on company boards'. A similar thing happened to the Commission in Brussels, which failed in its attempt to introduce a model of codetermination that would have been obligatory for all EU member states. The plan was resisted not only by employers, but also by British and French unions, which declared that such codetermination was not compatible with their union 'culture' (Windolf 1993). In the following, an example of 'cultural' differences between the German and the Anglo-Saxon financial market will be discussed in more detail.

9.2.1. *Distribution of Risk*

La Porta *et al.* (1997: 1131) ask the question: 'Why do the United States and the United Kingdom have enormous equity markets, while Germany and France have much smaller ones?' The authors believe that the reasons for this lie in the different legal traditions of the various countries. Countries with a strong tradition of 'common law' protect shareholding investors better than do countries rooted in the traditions of Roman or of German law. The empirical evidence on which the authors base their thesis is not convincing, however. Therefore, we will attempt to offer another, more plausible answer to the question.[6]

Currently, multinational insurance companies are learning that the British public accepts high-risk[7] life insurances, while in Germany such policies are difficult to sell. The opposite is also true: life insurances with low risk are preferred by the German public but practically not sellable in Great Britain (Meißner 1999). How can this difference be explained?

One needs first to assume that the expected rates of return[8] for both types of insurance policies is approximately the same. There is always a trade-off between risk and return. The greater the possible return, the greater the risk involved, and vice versa. A risk-neutral investor is influenced by the expected rate of return and not by unlikely game winnings. In this context, the life-insurance preference of the British public demonstrates a behavior that can be labeled as 'risk-seeking', whereas that of the German public demonstrates 'risk-averse' behavior.

It is well known that the British government financed its colonial expansion through stock corporations as early as the eighteenth century and encouraged the public to buy shares, whereas France and later Germany financed their colonial expansion through issuing government bonds.[9] Government bonds were (at least in peacetime) a nearly risk-free asset, which could not be said for the colonial corporations. Swaan (1990: 250) argues that the introduction of social insurance in Germany in the late-nineteenth century resulted in German workers learning 'risk-averse' behavior.

With these two examples in mind, two hypotheses are proposed. First, risk-aversion and the player mentality (risk-seeking) are cultural patterns of behavior that vary between countries and yet remain relatively stable over time. Second, in

---

[6] With a sample size of 38 countries, it is fairly difficult to find a suitable indicator to measure the degree of legal protection to investors available in a country (criticism: *validity* of the independent variable). Furthermore, the variance of the dependent variable (=stock market capitalization/GNP) *within* each group is very high. The values vary, e.g. within the group 'English origin countries' between 1.46 (Malaysia) and 0.34 (Israel) (criticism: *intragroup heterogeneity*). See La Porta *et al.* (1997: 1147, table VIII).

[7] 'Risk' is defined by the *volatility* of the returns of a portfolio of securities. Volatility is measured by the *standard deviation* of rates of return. See Sharpe *et al.* (1995: 178).

[8] The expected return is defined by the probability distribution of a portfolio's returns. (High rates of return have a relatively low probability.)

[9] Vital for these operations were the various branches of the Rothschild Bank in Frankfurt, London, and Paris (Bouvier 1967: 58–90). For more, see also Barth (1999: 96–7).

Great Britain and the United States, entrepreneurial risk has been shouldered to a great extent by the public (small investors), whereas in Germany, this risk was assumed by the universal banks, which became co-entrepreneurs themselves in the late-nineteenth century. The distribution of mentalities throughout a society, that is, the ratio of risk-averse individuals and 'players', influences how entrepreneurial risk is distributed overall in capitalist societies.

Summarizing these ideas, it can be said that the German universal banks, as professional investors, guarantee the public quasi-'risk-free assets' and transform this capital into risky credit to industrial corporations. They can do this because they can eliminate a portion of the credit risk through diversification. The advantage for the borrowing firm is that they only need to enter a contract with one partner (the bank), and are not confronted with thousands of shareholders (reduction of contract costs). The banks also reduce their information costs because not every investor whose savings are invested into a company needs to be informed about it. Finally, German universal banks had already established a 'corporate network' by the end of the nineteenth century. This network enabled the most important decision makers of big business to be monitored through collective supervision.

In the United States, the Berle-Means corporation, with its hundreds of thousands of 'risk-seeking' investors, did not survive. The small investors were replaced by a system of 'risk-neutral' investment funds, which have matured from professional financial intermediaries into globally operating investors. Currently, individual shareholders only play a minor role on the American stock markets.

We can use a thought experiment to clarify the idea of the distributional structure of risk. We imagine that in each country, the entrepreneurial risk of all operating firms is 'measured' and added up to a 'total' sum of risk. This (total) risk is then distributed (and redistributed) among the various actors: entrepreneurs, banks, small shareholders, the state. The Berle-Means corporation, the investment funds, and the universal banks are institutions through which the burden of risk is distributed in very different ways, that is, their financial operations produce a different distributional structure of risk in each case. The question as to which structure is the most efficient (i.e. incurs the least transaction costs) is empirically very hard to answer.

9.3. INSTITUTIONAL CHANGES IN GERMANY AND FRANCE

In this section, we consider six examples to demonstrate the changes which the corporate networks and the financial markets have undergone in Germany and France over the past decade.

9.3.1. *The Declining Density of Networks*

One of the central characteristics of German capitalism is a relatively dense and centralized network incorporating virtually all the large companies. These companies are not only linked to each other by interlocking directorates, but also by capital networks. In Chapter 2, it was also shown that there exists a relatively high degree of overlap between the interlocks and the capital network and that the German banks had a central position in this network.

Tables 9.1 and 9.2 contain a part of the matrices on interlocking directorates in Germany and France, namely that part with the highest network density for 1990 and for the year 2000, respectively. Clique analysis was used to identify a core component of fifteen firms with the highest density. The figures in the table are the sums of directed and undirected interlocking directorates. The largest and most prestigious German corporations, such as Allianz (insurance), Daimler-Chrysler, Volkswagen, Deutsche Bank are connected to each other by interlocking directorates. Similar observations can be made for France (Table 9.2).

However, such closely intertwined structures no longer characterize the network in the year 2000 to the same extent as previously. Within 7 years, the number of interlocks between the fifteen enterprises which had made up the core in 1992/93 has declined by about 27 percent. This decline is reflected in the network density being reduced from 0.79 in 1993 to 0.58 in 2000. A similar development can be observed in France: the number of ties among the fifteen firms that made up the core in 1996 has been considerably reduced; the density of the core network decreased from 0.87 to 0.42.

Many companies remain closely related to others, and the overall density is still higher than that in the United States and in Britain; however, the specific forms of cooperation and control within the corporate networks are clearly losing in importance.

The dissolution of some corporate networks is particularly obvious in the case of Daimler-Benz (1992/93)/Daimler-Chrysler (2000). In 1992/93, the German corporation Daimler-Benz had a total of seventeen links to the other corporations which belong to the core component of the network (firm no. 5 in Table 9.1, left-hand panel). In the year 2000, the German–US corporation Daimler-Chrysler had only five links to the other corporations in the core component (right-hand panel of Table 9.1). This decrease in corporate links can be explained by the changing membership of the supervisory board of Daimler-Chrysler: in 2000, half of the supervisory board members are US managers who are not integrated into the German corporate network.

9.3.2. *State Regulation*

At the same time, the direct state regulation of financial markets has been intensified in Germany. Numerous laws have been enacted over the past decade replacing corporatist by direct state supervision of the financial markets.[10] For instance, a recent change in the German corporate law enhances the potential role that can be played in

---

[10] Since the early 1990s, the following laws have been enacted: 'Erstes Finanzmarktförderungsgesetz' (1990); 'Zweites Finanzmarktförderungsgesetz' (1994); 'Drittes Finanzmarktförderungsgesetz' (1998); 'Gesetz zur Deregulierung des Aktienrechts' (1994); 'Gesetz zur Kontrolle und Transparenz im Unternehmensbereich' (KonTraG, 1998); 'Gesetz zur Zulassung der Stückaktien' (1998); 'Kapitalaufnahme-Erleichterungsgesetz' (1998); 'Namensaktien- und Stimmrechtsausübungsgesetz' (2001). The 'White Paper' (Referentenentwurf) for the 'Third Financial Market Act' (Drittes Finanzmarktförderungsgesetz) had almost 400 pages. This long list of laws testifies to the increasing state regulation of financial markets in Germany. See Hommelhoff and Mattheus (1998: 249).

TABLE 9.1 *Interlocking directorates (core) Germany 1993/2000*

Germany 1992/93

	1	2	3	4	5	6	7	8	9	10	11	12	13	14	15
1	—	1	2	3	2	1	2	1	2	1	2	1	4	1	1
2	1	—	2	2	1	1	1	1	2	2	2	2	1	1	2
3	1	2	—	1	2	2	4	1	2	2	1	1	2		
4	3	2	1	—	1	1	2	1	1	2	2		1	1	5
5	2	1	2		—	2	1		1	1	2				
6	1	1	2	2	2	—	2	2	1	3	1	2	2	1	2
7	1	1	4	2	1	2	—	3	1	3	1	2	2	3	
8	1	1	2	2	2		2	—	2	1	1	2	2	1	
9	2	3	2	1	1	2	2		—	2	1	3	2	1	
10	1	1	2	2	1	1	1	3	2	—	1	1			1
11	2	2	1	2	1	2	1	1		1	—	1	1		
12	2	2	2	1	2	1	2	1	2	1	1	—			
13	1	1	2		1	2	2	1					—	2	
14	1	1	2	2	1	1	2	1	1	1	1	2	2	—	
15	1	3	2	5	1	1	3		1	1					—

Germany 2000

	1	2	3	4	5	6	7	8	9	10	11	12	13	14	15
1	—	2	2	3	1		2	1	1			2	2		1
2		—	2	2		2	2		3	4	3	1	1	1	2
3	2	3	—	1		2	2	2	3	1		2	1		3
4	3	3	1	—	1		2		3	1				1	1
5	1	1		2	—	2	1								
6		2	2	1		—	2	1	1						1
7	2	3	2	2	1		—	2	2	1	1	1	1	1	1
8	1		2	1		1	1	—		1	1		1		1
9		2	2	1	1	1	2	1	—	1	2	1		2	1
10	1		1			1	2	1		—	1		1	2	
11		2	1	1		1	2		2	1	—	1	1		
12	2	1	1		1	2	1	2	2		1	—	3	1	
13	2	1		3		2	1	2		1		3	—	3	
14		1					1				2	1	2	—	2
15	1	3	1	3	1	2	2	2	1	1	2	3	1		—

Note: Germany 1992/93
1 RWE; 2 VEBA; 3 Karstadt; 4 Allianz Holding; 5 Daimler-Benz; 6 Linde; 7 Thyssen; 8 MAN; 9 Münchener Rück; 10 Volkswagen; 11 Degussa; 12 Dresdner Bank; 13 Hochtief; 14 Commerzbank; 15 Deutsche Bank.
Density: 0.79 (dichotomized).

Germany 2000
1 RWE; 2 E.on (Veba); 3 Karstadt; 4 Allianz Holding; 5 Daimler-Chrysler; 6 Linde; 7 Thyssen Krupp AG; 8 MAN; 9 Münchener Rück; 10 Volkswagen; 11 Degussa; 12 Dresdner Bank; 13 Hochtief; 14 Commerzbank; 15 Deutsche Bank.
Density: 0.58 (dichotomized).

TABLE 9.2 *Interlocking directorates (core) France 1996/2000*

France 1996

	1	2	3	4	5	6	7	8	9	10	11	12	13	14	15
1	—	1	1	2	1	2		1	2	2	1	1	2		1
2	1	—	3	1	1	2	3	1	1		1	1	4	3	2
3		3	—	1	6	1		1	2	1	2		2	2	1
4	2	1	1	—	2	1	1	1	1	1	1	1	1	3	1
5	1	2	6	2	—		2	1	1	1	1	1	1	2	1
6	1	2	1	1	1	—	1	2	1	1	1	2	1	1	2
7	1	1	1	1	1	1		3	1	1	3		1	2	2
8	1	3	2	1	2	2	1		2	1	1	2	1	1	2
9	2	1	1	1	1	1	2	2		2	3	2	1	1	1
10	2	1	1	1	1	1	1	3	2	—	1	1	1	1	2
11	1	1	2	1	1	1	1	1	1	1	—	1	1	1	
12	1	1		1	1	3	1	3	2	1	1			2	1
13	3	3	1	1	2	1	1	1	2	2	1	2	—	1	1
14	1	3	2	3	2		1		2			2	2	—	2
15	2	2	1	1	1	2	1				1		1	1	—

France 2000

	1	2	3	4	5	6	7	8	9	10	11	12	13	14	15
1		a	a	a	a	a		a	a	a	b	a	a	a	a
2	a		1	1	2	a			2		b		4	2	1
3	a	1		1	a	a				1	b				
4	a	2	1			a		a	1	1	b	1	2	1	1
5	a	3		a		a	1	a	1	1	b	a	a	a	a
6	a	a	a	a		—									
7	a	2		a	1	a			2	2	b	1	2	4	1
8	a				1	a	2		b	b	b	b	b	b	
9	b	b	1	b	b	b		b	2	b	b				
10	a	1	1	1	1	a	1	1	1	1	b		1		
11		4			2	a			2		b	—		2	1
12	a	2	1	1	1	a			4				2	—	2
13		1	1			a					b			b	—

Note: France 1996
1 Groupe Paribas; 2 Générale des Eaux; 3 UAP; 4 Rhône Poulenc; 5 Saint Gobain; 6 CEP Communication; 7 BNP; 8 Crédit Comercial de France; 9 Elf Aquitaine; 10 Renault; 11 Galeries Lafayette; 12 Lafarge Coppée; 13 Alcatel Alsthom; 14 Société Générale; 15 Pinault-Printemps.
Density: 0.87 (dichotomized) (N = 15).

France 2000
1 (Paribas)[a]; 2 Vivendi (Générale des Eaux); 3 AXA-UAP; 4 Aventis (Rhône Poulenc); 5 Saint Gobain; 6 (CEP)[a]; 7 BNP-Paribas; 8 Crédit Commercial France; 9 TotalfinaElf (Elf Aquit.); 10 Renault; 11 (Lafayette)[b]; 12 Lafarge Coppée; 13 Alcatel Alsthom; 14 Société Générale; 15 Pinault-Printem.
Density: 0.42 (dichotomized) (N = 12).
[a] Company disappeared (merger, 1999/2000).
[b] Data not available for 2000.

companies by their supervisory board (e.g. rights to information, frequency of meetings), while reducing the number of supervisory board positions in different companies which any single person can hold. A further change makes these persons legally more liable to shareholders for their actions; shareholders representing, together, 5 percent of corporate equity can sue supervisory board members in the case of demonstrable malfeasance in the performance of their supervisory role.

A further example of the expanding state supervision is the altered law on company takeovers and mergers, replacing the previous voluntary code of practices in Germany.[11] This law mandates the rights and responsibilities of both the bidding and the target companies. One stipulation of the new law, for instance, is that any company acquiring at least 30 percent of another must make a public offer to purchase the shares in the hands of the remaining shareholders. This stipulation had also formed part of the previous (voluntary) code, but it had been widely disregarded.[12]

These examples illustrate the trade-off between corporatist self-regulation and state regulation.[13] When corporatist institutions (e.g. corporate networks) dissolve and at least in part lose their former regulatory function, the gap must be filled by state regulation. Similarly, the cartel of large German banks, which in the 1980s still controlled the financial markets, have now become subject to a fairly tight system of state regulation.

9.3.3. *The Dissolution of Stable Combine Structures*

A third example of the changes which economic institutions are undergoing, one finds in the ownership pattern within large industrial combines. A combine is a hierarchically structured network of firms that are coordinated by a central company for the sake of stable, long-term cooperation. These combines now appear to be becoming increasingly flexible and increasingly replaced by less stable holding structures and financial shareholdings.

The market for corporate control, where companies are bought and sold in toto, has undergone an enormous expansion, also in Europe. Here, parent companies acquire and sell off subsidiaries to other companies. By active, targeted participation in the market for corporate control, a steel combine, for example, can carry through a strategy of 'metamorphosis' to transform itself into a telecommunications combine (e.g. Mannesmann). Between 1988 and 1998, the German enterprise BASF sold 121

---

[11] See Börsensachverständigenkommission beim Bundesministerium der Finanzen: Übernahmekodex. In the United Kingdom, a voluntary 'City Code on Takeovers and Mergers' was agreed in 1967 (Woolcock 1996: 193).

[12] The rule hinders the construction of combines (business groups). It is frequently possible to gain effective control over a company by acquiring only 30–40 percent of its stock, in which case it is not necessary to finance 100 percent of its equity. In France, the *groupe industriel* also makes frequent use of this possibility. In the near future, a uniform legal regulation of takeovers and mergers will be available in the European Union with the 13th Company Law Directive (Takeover Directive).

[13] This trade-off can also be seen in the example of labor law in the United States. Until the mid-1970s, there existed a system of industrial relations in the United States which Stone (1981: 1510) has termed 'self-government by management and labor' (voluntarism). With the dismantling of this system, one finds 'an increased government intervention in the employment relationship'.

TABLE 9.3   *Market for corporate control 1988–98 (BASF)*

	Foreign	Germany	Total
Acquisitions	135	48	183
Sales	92	29	121

of its subsidiaries and bought 183 other companies (135 of which were outside of Germany) and thus transformed itself from an industrial chemicals giant into a combine based on gene technology (see Table 9.3).[14]

These transactions enhance the flexibility[15] of ownership relations: low-profit companies are sold off while others that promise higher profits are bought. The market for corporate control thus accelerates and globalizes the tendency for profit margins to balance out across competing firms and various economic sectors. Highly profitable firms can demand an inflated purchase price (thus diminishing their individual profit rates), while the price of companies yielding only modest profits declines (thus raising their individual profit rates).

A reform in German tax law (capital gains tax) will facilitate the 'flexibilization' of combine structures. Beginning in 2002, enterprises will no longer pay tax on profits resulting from the sale of subsidiary companies, provided that the sale takes place after a speculation period of one year.[16] This means that the trading of entire companies is regarded in the same light legally as the trading of individual shares (Höpner 2000).

9.3.4. *US Investment Funds own German and French Corporations*

A fourth example of institutional restructuring is provided by the changing ownership patterns in France and Germany. In France, the privatization of large state enterprises simultaneously with the liberalization of financial markets has transformed the ownership structure of French firms substantially.

A large proportion of the nationalized enterprises in France were privatized during the periods 1986–8 and 1993–5, and private corporations were invited to participate in the sales as buyers. The intention behind this policy was to create corporate networks resembling the *keiretsu* groups in Japan and thus to protect French companies from acquisition by foreign corporations ('cross-shareholdings'; see Table 9.4).

The majority of shares were offered to the public on the Paris stock market. At the same time, regulations on the capital market were abolished, thus enabling foreign

---

[14]   *Source*: 'Die BASF ist ohne Quantensprünge auf dem Weg zur Globalisierung', *Frankfurter Allgemeine Zeitung*, 22 September 1998, p. 25.

[15]   This 'flexibility' of ownership patterns within a combine is different from market 'liquidity' of shares (free float).

[16]   Coffee (2000: 14–15) argues that the 'explanation for concentrated ownership may be that German tax laws either caused this system or, more likely, enforced its persistence well after competitive forces would otherwise have compelled its dismantling'. However, the example of BASF (see above) illustrates that corporate shareholdings are not dismantled, but 'flexibilized'.

TABLE 9.4   *Ownership structure of large French and German corporations (2000)*

French firms	Cross-share holdings[a] %	US/British funds[b] %	German firms	US/British funds[b] %
AGF	11.4	8	Allianz	5
Alcatel	16.9	40	Bayer	21
Alstom	23.8	47	BASF	21
Aventis	0.9	32	Daimler-Chrysler	17
AXA UAP	21.0	28	Deutsche Telecom	33
Renault	10.0	14	Deutsche Bank	19
St Gobain	15.6	22	E.ON	25
Total Fina Elf	12.8	20	Münchner Rück	19
Vivendi Universal	14.6	25	Siemens	24

Note:
[a] Proportion of equity held within the 'hard core' (noyau dur); see Morin (1996: 1253).
[b] Source for US/British funds: *Le Monde*, 15 juin 2001, p. 22 and www.lemonde.fr
Source for cross-shareholdings: D. Baudru and S. Lavigne: Investisseurs institutionnels et gouvernance sur le marché financier français, Conference paper, LEREPS Toulouse (29 juin 2001).

investors to take part in the privatization sales. As a result, the relative influence of foreign institutional investors did indeed climb, particularly that of United States investment and pension funds.

The proportion of stock in the hands of foreign investment funds can be expected to continue to rise. There are two reasons for this. First, French combines are closing many cross-shareholdings because of their low profit margins. Second, many of the small (private) investors who originally acquired stock in the companies have in the meantime sold their shares. The opportunities thus offered have been seized upon by the United States investment funds.

Foreign investment funds own a smaller proportion of the stock in German than in French enterprises. This is due largely to the difference in enterprise structure, for in Germany, the owners of companies are frequently other companies, and their stock is therefore bound within the combine instead of being offered for sale on the stock market where it could be purchased by such investment funds.

9.3.5. *Free Float*

The Frankfurt and London stock exchanges have decided to alter the way in which they calculate their market indices (e.g. DAX, FTSE). Until now, the formulas used to calculate the relative weights[17] of the various corporations making up a financial index have been based upon all of the company's stock, including that 'bound', and thus non-purchasable, in the hands of other firms. In the future, however, the stock

[17] The 'weight' of a single corporation is determined by its own market capitalization, calculated as a percentage of the total market capitalization of all firms included in the index.

exchanges in Frankfurt and London will calculate the respective weights only on the basis of freely purchasable stock ('free float').[18]

Freely floated stock makes up less than half of all the company's stock in the case of many German corporations. The result of the policy change will be a relative loss of importance on the part of those firms whose stock is not liquid but rather is owned largely by other firms.[19]

When the company's relative weight on an index falls, its stock is less frequently purchased by investment funds, which means that the stock price of this company tends to fall. In this way, the stock market exerts pressure upon the enterprises to diminish their corporate networking and to 'liquidate' their shareholdings in other firms. The policy of 'flexibilizing' or dismantling the combine structure, as described above, is thus enjoying support of the stock exchanges in Frankfurt and London.

It is particularly the investment funds that have put pressure upon the management of the stock exchanges to alter their weighing formulas. When an index fund is created, it must reflect the structure of a stock index. When a company's stock has a low liquidity, that is, when in proportional terms it is largely bound in the hands of other companies, the stock price of its shares is highly volatile. Investment funds, therefore, have an interest in the relative index weight of a company being calculated only on the basis of freely floating stock.

9.3.6. *Investment Funds act as Referee*

Financial markets influence not only the external organizational structure of enterprises (e.g. the dismantling of business groups), but also their product and sales strategies. An example of this is the failed merger of Banque Nationale de Paris (BNP) with the Société Générale (SG) and Paribas. Here the investment funds acted as referee between competing management strategies.

After lengthy negotiations, the French banks SG and Paribas agreed a merger that promised substantial synergy effects and competitive advantages. In the agreed takeover, SG made a public offer on 1 February 1999 to the shareholders of Paribas, consisting of five of its own shares for eight shares in Paribas. This action was followed a few days later by the announcement by BNP of a planned takeover of both SG and Paribas. The managers of SG and Paribas rejected the move and declared their intention to continue with their own merger, independent of BNP. In a hostile takeover bid on 9 March 1999, BNP made the following public offering to the shareholders in SG and Paribas: eleven of its own shares for eight in Paribas, and fifteen of its own shares for seven in SG.

The weeks thereafter saw campaigns waged by the managers of SG and BNP among shareholders of the banks that they sought to take over. The takeover strategy of the former was to merge two banks; that of the latter was to merge three banks, thereby creating the largest unified bank in Europe. Shareholders in Paribas could

---

[18] See 'Streubesitz entscheidet künftig über Indexgewicht', *Frankfurter Allgemeine Zeitung*, 10 Aug. 2000, p. 29.   [19] E.g. the share of Deutsche Bank in Daimler-Chrysler is 11.92% (Year: 2000).

thus choose among three different options: continued independence (rejection of both offers), accepting the SG offer (merger of two banks), and accepting the BNP offer (merger of three banks).

The ensuing takeover battle was not carried out discreetly among the managers of corporate networks but was decided finally in open competition in the market for corporate control. The rivalry allowed the investment funds to exert direct influence upon the takeover strategies.

The campaign was waged, similar to an election campaign by politicians, with the leaders of the rival banks offering the shareholders ('voters') their respective management conceptions. The bank managers held their 'election speeches' at important financial centers such as New York, London, and Paris, where they sought the support of fund managers and economic analysts for their own programs.

The result was that 65 percent of Paribas shareholders exchanged their stock for shares in BNP, thus awarding BNP control over Paribas. On the other hand, however, only 37 percent of SG shareholders accepted the BNP offer. According to the ruling of the French supervisory agency[20] on 28 August 1999, SG was to remain independent, and BNP had to sell its acquired shares in SG. While BNP had won a partial victory, both takeover strategies were defeated, that is, that of SG to take over Paribas and that of BNP to take over SG and Paribas.

The outcome of such an 'election' in the stock market can thus be as problematic as that of a political election. At least, there is no guarantee that the decisions of autonomous and uncoordinated shareholders, 'voting' in the stock market, will produce an economically more efficient outcome than relational contracting in corporate networks between various groups of managers.

An important difference should be noted, however, between these 'elections' in financial and political markets, in that the former are less regulated than the latter. In most countries, there exists a code of practices regarding takeovers and mergers; however, this is frequently nonstatutory and leaves the involved parties with considerable leeway in allocating resources and implementing strategies (Woolcock 1996: 193).

Similarly public was the takeover battle waged between Mannesmann and Vodafone, in which the managers of the two firms spent together about 400 million Euro for PR campaigns waged on television and in newspapers. Mannesmann paid about 100 million Euro for investment bank fees, Vodafone about 320 million Euro. These expenses can be seen as the transaction costs of hostile takeovers.[21]

9.3.7. *Securitization of Debt*

The final example that is analyzed here to illustrate institutional changes refers to the institution of the German 'house' bank. The relationship between German banks and

---

[20] This committee (Comité des établissements de crédit et des entreprises d'investissement, Cecei) is headed by the governor of the Banque de France, Jean-Claude Trichet. One can assume that the influence of the French government on this committee is relatively strong. See 'La BNP ne prendra pas le contrôle de la Société générale', *Le Monde*, 29–30 Aug. 1999.

[21] *Source*: *Die Zeit*, 27 January 2000, p. 5; *Financial Times*, 4 February 2000, p. 16; *Financial Times*, 7 February 2000, p. 20.

enterprises as it has existed until now can be described as follows: enterprises maintain relatively stable and long-term affiliations with only a small number of banks. They finance their needs for external capital funds principally through credit provided by these banks. The enterprises frequently continue to enjoy the support of the banks even in times of crisis, thus becoming something of partners in the enterprise.[22] Finally, the banks have representatives on the supervisory board of the enterprise, where they obtain confidential information about the company, supervise its business affairs, and in critical situations can effect a change in company policy.

These stable patterns of long-term relations between banks and enterprises are currently in decline, occasioned by a process referred to as the 'securitization of debt'.[23] Here the enterprise obtains needed funds not from banks but directly from the international financial markets (e.g. through bonds). This change is examined below in three steps: (1) the rating of the enterprise, (2) the direct corporate borrowing in the financial markets, (3) indirect corporate borrowing through collateralized bond obligations.

(1) Companies can gain direct access to the financial markets only if their credit worthiness has been assessed by a well-known rating agency. The rating agency considers the company's performance, its strategy, and the quality of its management.

Carrying out the rating of an enterprise with total annual sales of 50–100 million Euro costs between 15,000 and 25,000 Euro; when sales amount to 500 million Euro, the assessment process may cost as much as 50,000 Euro. This process results in the awarding of a rating that may range from Aaa (best) to C (worst).[24] The higher its rating, the lower is the company's perceived credit risk and, therefore, the lower its borrowing costs.

In reaction to the Asian banking crisis, the Basel Committee on Banking Supervision determined that banks must in future establish the credit worthiness of every customer (borrower) in this way. Loans to enterprises with a rating of Aaa must be collateralized to only 20 percent by bank equity; the corresponding figure in the case of a B rating, on the other hand, is 150 percent.[25]

---

[22] The most recent example being 'Herlitz', a Berlin-based company which operates on the brink of bankruptcy. A German bank consortium rescued the company by transforming debt into convertible bonds. After this financial operation, the German banks will be the majority shareholder of Herzlitz. (*Source: Tagesspiegel*, 22 March 2001.) Many shareholdings of German banks in industrial firms may be traced back, one way or another, to rescue operations (e.g. Daimler-Benz, Klöckner).

[23] 'Direct raising of funds in the securities markets has affected the traditional role of banks as financial intermediaries. Securitization, the transformation of various types of financial assets and debts into marketable instruments, has been the vehicle for this disintermediation and for the massive expansion in the overall volume of the financial market' (Sassen 1991: 70).

[24] *Source:* 'Banken und Unternehmen sind auf das Kreditwürdigkeits-Rating nicht vorbereitet', *Frankfurter Allgemeine Zeitung*, 2 May 2000. Bonds which are rated Aaa are judged to be of the best quality. They carry the smallest degree of investment risk and are generally referred to as 'gilt edged'. Bonds which are rated C are the lowest rated class of bonds, and issues so rated can be regarded as having extremely poor prospects of ever attaining any real investment standing (Moody's Bond Ratings).

[25] See Presseinformation http://www.voeb.de/News/presse41.htm.

It is likely that in the coming years every medium to large-sized enterprise will undergo such a standardized rating assessment. This rating provides all potential lenders and investors with information which was formerly available only to 'house' banks. This means that the lending activities of banks no longer guarantee them exclusive access to information about their preferred customers. Rather, the information will be collected and analyzed publicly and according to uniform criteria.

(2) A large enterprise that has undergone the rating process can approach the financial market directly to meet its borrowing requirements in the form of bonds or convertible loans. The higher its credit worthiness is rated, the lower will be the company's costs incurred by borrowing. This leaves banks with the function merely of financial intermediary, that is, selling corporate bonds in the financial market.

The total volume of corporate bonds in the Euro market has more than octupled in the relatively brief span of only $2\frac{1}{2}$ years—from just under 10 billion Euro in January 1998 to more than 80 billion Euro in July 2000. Although enterprises pay an average of 1.2 percent higher interest on bonds than do governments, their costs probably remain lower in this way than if they took out bank loans.[26]

(3) If all of a bank's customers undergo a common rating assessment, that is, if all borrowing firms receive a score on a universally acknowledged credit worthiness scale—the bank is then in a position to pool the loans of all of its borrowers and to offer them to financial markets as collateralized loan obligations.

For example, Deutsche Bank in Germany commissioned the rating of 2200 medium-sized companies to which it had extended loans. It then combined all of these loans in a single portfolio and sold them to investment funds as collateralized loan obligations with a repayment period of 7 years. The expected losses due to borrowers' defaulting were distributed as follows: the first 2.25 percent loss occurring during the 7-year maturity period (the 'first-loss tranche') is borne by Deutsche Bank. The next 2.25 percent is assigned to a tranche with a lower rating; purchasers of these loans incur a relatively high risk but receive higher interest. A total of fifteen tranches were formed in this way, with a progressively declining proportion of credit risk. Since the probability that tranches 10–15 would suffer losses is very low, the purchasers of these securities receive lower interest.[27]

This leaves Deutsche Bank in the position as direct lender to its customers while selling the loans in the financial market to investment funds or other investors and thus recovering the capital paid out in the loans. These changes in financial practices entail a number of consequences.

First, the financial institutions attempt to externalize the risks associated with their financing business by 'selling' them in the financial markets. This tends to shift the risks from the financial institutions to investors. While this change in financial practice (pooling numerous loans into a single portfolio) eliminates the company-specific risks, a market risk remains which cannot be diversified, but which is no

---

[26] Source: *Frankfurter Allgemeine Zeitung*, 11 Sept. 2000, p. 40.
[27] Source: *Frankfurter Allgemeine Zeitung*, 10 July 2000, p. 24.

longer borne by the bank but by investors.[28] The investors who buy loans in this way from banks are frequently investment/pension funds.[29]

Second, investment/pension funds become not only the owners of enterprises but also their lenders. More than 50 percent of capital stock in the United States and in Britain is now in the hands of investment/pension funds. These funds can be expected to enjoy an increasing importance in financial markets as the result of this securitization of debt, for they will not only be buying stock in large enterprises but will also be extending loans to them. The risks entailed by this financing, however, will not be borne by the funds but by the individual investors (customers).

Third, the rating process tends to make the information about an enterprise a public good. In the past, there was generally an asymmetry in information about the enterprise between, on the one hand, its closely affiliated 'house' bank and, on the other, all competing banks and investors. This difference is largely overcome once universal rating is introduced, and the 'relational contracting' of the past is transformed into 'arm's length' market relations. This shift in the type of information collected illustrates the trade-off between an enormous gain in transparency of the firm and the loss of tacit knowledge which is no longer available for this firm.

Fourth, the relationship between the borrower and the ultimate investor is brokered by three intermediary institutions: (1) the bank which originally contracts the loan but then sells it; (2) the rating agency which assesses the credit worthiness of the enterprise; and (3) the investment fund, which uses the contributions of its customers to buy the collateralized bond obligations. This system creates new principal/agent relationships that entail relatively high transaction costs.

Fifth, the rating agencies are liable neither to the investor (e.g. for awarding the company an inappropriately high rating, only for it to prove insolvent later) nor to the company being assessed (e.g. for it receiving an inappropriately low rating and, therefore, having to pay excessive interest on loans). This means that the risk of moral hazards and opportunism is not diminished, but indeed perhaps rather augmented.[30]

9.4. FROM NATIONAL TO TRANSNATIONAL NETWORKS

The examples described above should not be considered to be a representative sample of institutional changes that recently occurred in Germany and France. However, they permit to give at least a tentative answer to the question as to whether these changes amount to a regime change or merely an adaptation of the system to altered environmental conditions.

---

[28] Market risk (= systematic risk) is the portion of a security's total risk that is related to moves in the market portfolio and cannot be diversified away.

[29] A similar financial technique is called '*Asset Backed Securities*' (ABS). Any asset can be 'collateralized' and sold as an ABS on the financial market (e.g. future licence fees of a pop star). See *Frankfurter Allgemeine Zeitung*, 26 March 2001, p. 40.

[30] A rating agency can, e.g. down-rate a firm to facilitate an affiliated investment fund's acquisition of the firm's corporate bonds at a lower price. For similar 'practices', see Handelsblatt, 7 Oktober 1998, p. 12. The expected loss of reputational capital may confine this kind of opportunism.

We have shown that the density of corporate networks decreased over the past decade in Germany as well as in France. We conclude from this that the institution of relational contracting within corporate networks has been weakened and is, to some extent, replaced by arm's length market transactions on the one hand, and direct state regulation on the other. The combine structure which used to be a prominent feature of German 'cooperative capitalism' (Chandler 1990) is being 'flexibilized' and partly dissolved. Dependent firms with low profit rates are sold on the market for corporate control and replaced by firms which promise high profit margins in the future. The European Stock Exchanges put additional pressure on the managers of combines to 'liquidate' their large shareholdings in listed companies.

In France, the state bureaucracy which exercised a decisive influence on the French economy retreated from the large state enterprises (privatization). The investment funds, in particular the United States pension funds, are becoming the most important owners of French listed corporations. They are able to influence the strategy and structure of these firms.

Finally, the role of the German 'house' bank is transformed by a process of increasing securitization of debt. Large firms are able to get direct access to the financial markets; information on these firms which used to be monopolized by the 'house' bank tends to become a public good. Investment funds which are already the owners of large firms acquire corporate bonds and collateralized loan obligations and thus also become the firms' creditors.

These examples and others that have not been described here seem to justify a pessimistic outlook regarding the chances for survival of the German capitalism. With respect to the future of this model, Streeck (1997: 53) argues: 'Market-modifying and market-correcting political intervention in the economy, including publicly enabled associational self-regulation, can take place only within nation-states, because it is only here that the public power necessary for the purpose can be mobilized. Economic globalization therefore erodes the conditions for such intervention and, by default but also by design, leaves only de-politicized, privatized and market-driven forms of economic order'.

It is undoubtedly correct that state regulation of markets is possible only within the boundaries of nation-states. On the other hand, however, it cannot be regarded as certain that 'associational self-regulation can take place only within nation-states'. As noted in Chapter 2, almost all economic sectors in Germany were regulated by a cartel in the period preceding the First World War, and this form of 'self-regulation' proved successful in the absence of *direct* state support. The corporate networks whose structure and function are analyzed in this book serve as a further example of 'self-regulation' by the markets that does not require the support of direct state intervention.

Germany is not the only country in which competition has been regulated. Similar market systems—albeit based on different institutions—are found in Japan (*keiretsu*), Korea (*chaebol*), and France (planification). In these countries, it is the enterprise together with the state (*keiretsu*, MITI) or the clan (*chaebol*) which serves as the basis for implementing the model of regulated competition.[31]

---

[31] See Gerlach (1992), Fukuyama (1995), Hamilton (1996), Orrù *et al.* (1997).

It is also correct that countries with a long tradition of regulated competition have been suffering economic downturn since the beginning of the 1990s. In Japan, the *keiretsu* networks are being dismantled. In Korea, the debts incurred by the *chaebols* led to economic crisis. In France, the nationalized companies are being privatized and the system of planification buried (Morin 1998). These developments show that economic systems which depend upon direct state regulation within the national context are no longer viable in the context of globalized competition. Models of self-regulation and the forms of regulated competition associated with them enjoy a chance of survival only if they can be reorganized at a transnational level.

The Common Market existing within the European Union represents such a transnational environment in which—if only to modest extent—economic institutions can be reconstructed which have in part lost their efficacy at the national level. Examples of such reconstructed institutions include the European Works Council, transnational equivalents of national collective agreements brokered by the European Commission, and a directive on mergers and takeovers that is meant to regulate the market for corporate control.

New forms of transnational market regulation can be expected to develop in the European Union. This is already being seen in cross-border mergers and transnational shareholdings, and interlocking directorates. Within the next decade, the German or French model of capitalism could be transformed into a 'European' capitalism, if with other structures and with other forms of market regulation. Once the relevant market is no longer the national but the European, attempts to implement a new market system must inevitably also look to the European level.

Appendix: Data Sources

WEST GERMANY

The West German sample of the 623 largest firms was drawn from all firms subject to the codetermination law, plus a number of other family firms as well as companies not subject to the codetermination law (e.g. banks in public ownership; publishing houses). In addition to the ownership structure of the 623 firms, we identified the persons filling 10,683 positions on the supervisory and management boards of these firms.

Information sources:

- *Handbuch der deutschen Aktiengesellschaften* (Hoppenstedt)
- *Handbuch der Großternehmen* (Hoppenstedt)
- *Konzerne in Schaubildern* (Hoppenstedt)
- *Leitende Männer und Frauen der Wirtschaft* (Hoppenstedt)
- *Wem gehört die Republik?* (R. Lietke, Eichborn)
- *Major Companies of Europe* (Graham & Trotman)
- *Die großen 500* (E. Schmacke, ed., Luchterhand)
- *Who Owns Whom in Continental Europe?* (Dun & Bradstreet)
- *Wer gehört zu wem?* (Commerzbank).

EAST GERMANY

- *Firmen der neuen Bundesländer* (Hoppenstedt)
- *Handbuch der deutschen Aktiengesellschaften* (Hoppenstedt)
- *Konzerne in Schaubildern* (Hoppenstedt)
- *Die großen 500* (Schmacke/Luchterhand)
- *Deutschlands Große 500* (Die Welt; Internet).

UNITED KINGDOM

The 520 largest British firms were drawn from a rank ordering (*The Times 1000, 1992–3*) of the 1000 largest firms in terms of capital stock. Information on capital ownership and the total of 5111 board positions came from:

- *Major Companies of Europe*, vol. 2 (Graham & Trotman)
- *Stock Exchange Official Yearbook* (Macmillan)
- *Who owns Whom?—United Kingdom & Republic of Ireland* (Dun & Bradstreet).

FRANCE

The 500 largest French firms were drawn from a rank ordering in: *Enjeux/Les Echos*: Les 500 premiers groupes français. Supplément au no. 98, 1994.

- *Dictionnaire DAFSA DESFOSSES des Sociétés* (Groupe DAFSA, Paris)
- *Des liens financières*, Tome I and II (Groupe DAFSA Paris)
- *Major Companies of France* (Graham & Trotman)
- *French Company Handbook* (Herald Tribune, Paris).

UNITED STATES

- *Five Percent Stock Holdings*, vols I and II (CDA Investment Technologies, Rockville MD)
- *13(f) Institutional Stock Holdings*, vols I and II (CDA Investment Technologies, Rockville MD)
- *D&B Million Dollar Directory* (Dun & Bradstreet).

NETHERLANDS

- *Financieel Economisch Lexicon*, vol. 1–5 (DELWEL Uitgeverij, Dordrecht)
- *Wie is Wie in Nederland*? 1994–1996 (F. Egmond; Den Haag: Uitgeverij Pragma).

SWITZERLAND

- *Verzeichnis der Verwaltungsräte* (Orell Füssli Verlag, Zürich)
- *Schweizerisches Ragionenbuch* (Orell Füssli Verlag, Zürich)
- *Who Owns Whom: Der Schweizerische Beteiligungsatlas* (Orell Füssli Verlag, Zürich).

ELITE NETWORKS, BIOGRAPHIES

- *Leitende Männer und Frauen der Wirtschaft* (Hoppenstedt)
- *Archiv für publizistische Arbeit/Munzinger Archiv* (Internationales biographisches Archiv, Ravensburg)
- *Wer ist wer*? (Schmidt and Römhild)
- *The German Who's Who*? (Lübeck)
- *Who's Who*? (A. & C. Black, London)
- Harris Corporation: Founding Dates of the 1994 Fortune 500 US Companies, *Business History Review* 70 (1996), pp. 69–90
- *Directory of Directors* (Reed Information Services, Essex)
- *D & B Million Dollar Directory* (Dun & Bradstreet)
- *French Company Handbook* (Herald Tribune, Paris)
- *Major Companies of Europe* (Graham & Whiteside)
- *D & B Europe* (Dun & Bradstreet)
- *Directory of Multinationals* (John M. Stopford, ed., Macmillan)
- *Directory of European Business* (Bowker-Saur, ed., Cambridge Market Intelligence, London).

With each of these source books we consulted several volumes (1993–2000).

References

Abelshauser, Werner (1984), 'The First Post-liberal Nation: Stages in the Development of Modern Corporatism in Germany'. *European History Quarterly* 14: 285–318.

Abramovitz, Moses (1986), 'Catching Up, Forging Ahead, and Falling Behind'. *Journal of Economic History* 46: 385–406.

Adam, Jan (1994), 'The Transition to a Market Economy in Poland'. *Cambridge Journal of Economics* 18: 607–18.

Adams, Michael (1994), 'Die Usurpation von Aktionärsbefugnissen mittels Ringverflechtung in der Deutschland AG'. *Die Aktiengesellschaft* 39: 148–58.

Alba, Richard and Moore, Gwen (1978), 'Elite Social Circles'. *Sociological Methods & Research* 7: 167–87.

Albach, Horst (1993), *Zerrissene Netze: Eine Netzwerkanalyse des ostdeutschen Transformationsprozesses*. Berlin: Sigma.

Albert, Michel (1991), *Capitalism contre capitalism*. Paris: Le Seuil. [English: *Capitalism against Capitalism*. London 1993: Whurr Publishers.]

—— (2000), 'Der europäische Kapitalismus im Rahmen der Globalisierung: Konvergenzen und Differenzen'. *Supplement der Zeitschrift Sozialismus* 5: 5–19.

Arthur, Brian (1989), 'Competing Technologies, Increasing Returns, and Lock-in by Historical Events'. *The Economic Journal* 99: 116–31.

Bachrach, Peter and Baratz, Morton (1970), *Power and Poverty. Theory and Practice*. New York: Oxford University Press.

Baker, George (1992), 'Beatrice: A Study in the Creation and Destruction of Value'. *The Journal of Finance* 47: 1081–119.

Baker, Wayne (1984), 'The Social Structure of a National Securities Market'. *American Journal of Sociology* 89: 775–811.

Baker, Wayne and Faulkner, Robert (1993), 'The Social Organization of Conspiracy'. *American Sociological Review* 58: 837–60.

Balcerowicz, Leszek (1994), 'Transition to the Market Economy: Poland, 1989–93 in Comparative Perspective'. *Economic Policy* 19: 72–97.

—— (1995), *Socialism, Capitalism, Transformation*. Budapest: Central European University Press.

Barnett, William *et al.* (2000), 'The Evolution of Collective Strategies Among Organizations'. *Organization Studies* 21: 325–54.

Barry, Richard (1998), *The One Thousand: The Men and Women Who Command the Heights of the UK's Economy*. Warwick: Institute for Employment Research (University of Warwick).

Barth, Boris (1999), 'Weder Bürgertum noch Adel: Zur Gesellschaftsgeschichte der Deutschjüdischen Hochfinanz vor dem Ersten Weltkrieg'. *Geschichte und Gesellschaft* 25: 94–122.

Baudru, Daniel and Kechidi, Med (1998), 'Les investisseurs institutionnels étrangers: vers la fin du capitalisme à la française?' *Revue d'Economie Financière* 48.

Bauer, Michel and Bertin-Mourot, Bénédicte (1987), *Les 200: Comment devient-on un grand patron?* Paris: Seuil.

—— —— (1995), '*L'accès au sommet des grandes entreprises françaises 1985–1994*. Paris: CNRS/Boyden.

—— (1996), *Vers un modèle européen de dirigeants? Comparaison Allemagne/France/Grande-Bretagne*. Paris: CNRS/Boyden.

Bauer, Michel (1999), 'National Models for Making and Legitimating Elites: A Comparative Analysis of the 200 Top Executives in France, Germany, and Great Britain'. *European Societes* 1: 9–31.

Bearden, James and Mintz, Beth (1987), 'The Structure of Class Cohesion: The Corporate Network and its Dual', in Mark Mizruchi and Michael Schwarz (eds), *Intercorporate Relations*. Cambridge: Cambridge University Press, pp. 187–207.

Beck, Ulrich (1983), Jenseits von Stand und Klasse? in Reinhard Kreckel (ed.), Soziale Ungleichheiten, Göttingen: Schwarz, pp. 34–74.

Bell, Daniel (1960), *The End of Ideology*. New York: Collier.

Bendix, Reinhard (1956), *Work and Authority in Industry*. New York: Wiley.

Berger, Suzanne and Dore, Ronald (1996), *National Diversity and Global Capitalism*. Ithaca: Cornell University Press.

Berle, Adolf and Means, Gardiner (1997 [1932]), *The Modern Corporation and Private Property*. New York: Macmillan.

Bhide, Amar (1993), 'The Hidden Costs of Stock Market Liquidity'. *Journal of Financial Economics* 34: 31–51.

Biehler, Hermann and Ortmann, Rolf (1985), 'Personelle Verbindungen zwischen Unternehmen'. *Die Betriebswirtschaft* 45: 4–18.

Bim, Alexander (1996), 'Ownership and Control of Russian Enterprises and Strategies of Shareholders'. *Communist Economics and Economic Transformation* 8: 471–502.

Birnbaum, Pierre (1978a), 'La classe dirigeante française'. Paris: PUF.

—— (1978b), 'Institutionalisation of Power and Integration of Ruling Elites: A Comparative Analysis'. *European Journal of Political Research* 6: 105–15.

Blazyca, George and Dabrowski, Janusz (1995), *Monitoring Economic Transition*. Aldershot: Avebury.

Blejer, Mario and Coricelli, Fabrizio (1995), *The Making of Economic Reform in Eastern Europe: Conversations with Leading Reformers in Poland, Hungary, and the Czech Republic*. Aldershot: Elgar Publishing.

Blossfeld, Hans-Peter *et al.* (1986), *Ereignisanalyse*. Frankfurt: Campus.

Blum, John *et al.* (1968), *The National Experience: A History of the United States*. New York: Harcourt, Brace & World.

Blumberg, Philipp (1987), *The Law of Corporate Groups: Tort, Contract, and Other Common Law Problems in the Substantive Law of Parent and Subsidiary Corporations*. Boston: Little Brown.

Böhm, Franz (1948), 'Das Reichsgericht und die Kartelle'. *Ordo* 1: 197–213.

Bok, Derek (1960), 'Section 7 of the Clayton Act and the Merging of Law and Economics'. *Harvard Law Review* 74: 226–355.

Boltho, Andrea *et al.* (1997), 'Will East Germany Become a New Mezzogiorno?' *Journal of Comparative Economics* 24: 241–64.

Bourdieu, Pierre (1980), 'Le capital social'. *Actes de la recherche en sciences sociales* 31: 2–3.

—— (1984), *Distinction: A Social Critique of the Judgement of Taste*. London: Routledge & Kegan Paul.

—— (1989), *La noblesse d'état: Grandes Écoles et esprit de corps*. Paris: Minuit.

—— *et al.* (1993), *La misère du monde*. Paris: Seuil.

Bouvier, Jean (1967), *Les Rothschild*. Paris: Fayard.

Boycko, Maxim, Shleifer, Andrei, and Vishny, Robert (1995), *Privatizing Russia*. Cambridge, MA: MIT Press.

Boyd, Robert and Richerson, Peter (1985), *Culture and the Evolutionary Process*. Chicago: Unviersity of Chicago Press.

Brabant, Jozef Van (1993), 'Lessons from the Wholesale Transformations in the East'. *Comparative Economic Studies* 35: 73–102.

Brancato, Carolyn (1991), 'The Pivotal Role of Institutional Investors in Capital Markets', in Arnold W. Sametz and James L. Bicksler (eds), *Institutional Investing*. New York: New York University Salomon Center, pp. 328–64.

Brandeis, Louis D (1995 [1914]), *Other People's Money and How the Bankers Use It*. New York: St. Martin's Press.

Bratton, William and McCahery, Joseph (1999), 'Comparative Corporate Governance and the Theory of the Firm: The Case Against Global Cross Reference'. *Columbia Journal of Transnational Law* 38: 213–97.

Brom, Karla and Orenstein, Mitchell (1994), 'The Privatised Sector in the Czech Republic: Government and Bank Control in a Transitional Economy'. *Europe–Asia Studies* 46: 893–928.

Brücker, Herbert (1995), 'Die Privatisierungs- und Sanierungsstrategie der Treuhandanstalt'. *Vierteljahreshefte zur Wirtschaftsforschung* 64: 444–60.

Brudney, Victor (1981), 'The Independent Director: Heavenly City or Potemkin Village?' *Harvard Law Review* 95: 597–659.

Buchanan, James (1991), *Constitutional Economics*. Oxford: Basil Blackwell.

Burns, Tom and Stalker, G. M. (1961), *The Management of Innovation*. London: Tavistock Publications.

Burrough, Bryan and Hellyar, John (1989), *Barbarians at the Gate: The Fall of RJR Nabisco*. New York: Harper & Row.

Burt, Ronald (1982), *Toward a Structural Theory of Action: Network Models of Social Structure, Perception and Action*. New York: Academic Press.

—— (1987), 'Social Contagion and Innovation: Cohesion Versus Structural Equivalence'. *American Journal of Sociology* 92: 1287–335.

—— (1992), *Structural Holes: The Social Structure of Competition*. Cambridge: Harvard University Press.

Burt, Ronald *et al.* (1980), 'Testing a Structural Theory of Corporate Cooptation'. *American Sociological Review* 45: 821–41.

Campbell, D. T. (1965), 'Variation and Selective Retention in Socio-Cultural Evolution'. *General Systems Yearbook* 14: 69–85.

Carlin, Wendy and Aghion, Philippe (1996), 'Restructuring Outcomes and the Evolution of Ownership Patterns in Central and Eastern Europe'. *Economics of Transition* 4: 371–88.

Carosso, Vincent (1970), *Investment Banking in America: A History*. Cambridge: Harvard University Press.

Chandler, Alfred (1990), *Scale and Scope*. Cambridge: Harvard University Press.

Claessens, Stijn *et al.* (1997), *Ownership and Corporate Governance: Evidence From the Czech Republic*. Washington: World Bank, Policy Research (Working Paper 1737).

Clark, Ed and Soulsby, Anna (1996), 'The Re-formation of the Managerial Elite in the Czech Republic'. *Europe–Asia Studies* 48: 285–303.

Clark, Robert (1980), 'The Four Stages of Capitalism'. *Harvard Law Review* 94: 561–82.

Clegg, Hugh (1979), *The Changing System of Industrial Relations in Great Britain*. Oxford: Basil Blackwell.

Coffee, John (1991), 'Liquidity versus Control: The Institutional Investor as Corporate Monitor'. *Columbia Law Review* 91: 1277–368.

—— (1996), 'Institutional Investors in Transitional Economies: Lessons from the Czech Experience', in Roman Frydman *et al.* (eds), *Corporate Governance in Central Europe and*

Russia, vol. 1: Banks, Funds, and Foreign Investors. Budapest and London: Central European University Press, pp. 111–86.

Coffee, John (2000), *Convergence and Its Critics: What Are the Preconditions to the Separation of Ownership and Control?* New York: Columbia University/Law School (Working paper).

Coleman, James (1990), *Foundations of Social Theory.* Cambridge: Harvard University Press.

Crouch, Colin (1977), *Class Conflict and the Industrial Relations Crisis: Compromise and Corporatism in the Policies of the British State.* Atlantic Highlands: Humanities Press.

Crozier, Michel (1963), *Le phénomène bureaucratique.* Paris: Seuil.

Czada, Roland (1998), 'Vereinigungskrise und Standortdebatte'. *Leviathan* 26: 24–59.

Czapinski, Janusz (1995), 'Money Isn't Everything: On the Various Social Costs of Transformation'. *Polish Sociological Review* 112: 289–302.

Daems, Herman (1978), *'The Holding Company and Corporate Control.* Leiden/Boston: M. Nijhoff.

Dahrendorf, Ralf (1959), *Class and Class Conflict in Industrial Society.* Stanford: Stanford University Press.

—— (1967), 'Die Funktionen sozialer Konflikte', in R. Dahrendorf (ed.), *Pfade aus Utopia.* München: Piper, pp. 263–76.

David, Paul (1985), 'Clio and the Economics of QWERTY'. *American Economic Review* 75: 332–7 (Papers and Proceedings).

Davis, Gerald (1991), 'Agents without Principles?' *Administrative Science Quarterly* 36: 583–613.

Davis, Gerald *et al.* (1994), 'The Decline and Fall of the Conglomerate Firm in the 1980s: The Deinstitutionalization of an Organizational Form'. *American Sociological Review* 59: 547–70.

Davis, Gerald and Mizruchi, Mark (1999), 'The Money Center Cannot Hold: Commercial Banks in the U.S. System of Corporate Governance'. *Administrative Science Quarterly* 44: 215–39.

Davis, Lance and North, Douglass (1971), *Institutional Change and American Economic Growth.* Cambridge: Cambridge University Press.

Demsetz, Harold and Lehn, Kenneth (1985), 'The Structure of Corporate Ownership: Causes and Consequences'. *Journal of Political Economy* 93: 1155–77.

Deregulierungskommission (1991), *Marktöffnung und Wettbewerb.* Stuttgart: Poeschel.

Deutschmann, Christoph (1989), 'The Japanese Organisation'. *Internationales Asienformum* 20: 73–94.

DiMaggio, Paul and Powell, Walter (1983), 'The Iron Cage Revisited'. *American Sociological Review* 48: 147–60.

Dlouhy, Vladimir and Mládek, Jan (1994), 'Czech Privatization'. *Economic Policy* 19: 156–70.

Dobbin, Frank and Dowd, Timothy (2000), 'The Market that Antitrust Built: Public Policy, Private Coercion, and Railroad Acquisitions, 1825 to 1922'. *American Sociological Review* 65: 631–57.

Domhoff, William (1983), *Who Rules America Now?* Englewood Cliffs: Prentice Hall.

Dore, Ronald (1987), *Taking Japan Seriously: A Confucian Perspective on Leading Economic Issues.* Stanford: Stanford University Press.

Doreian, Patrick and Woodard, Katherine (1994), 'Defining and Locating Cores and Boundaries of Social Networks'. *Social Networks* 16: 267–93.

Dornbusch, Rudiger and Wolf, Holger (1994), 'East German Economic Reconstruction', in Olivier J. Blanchard *et al.* (eds), *The Transition in Eastern Europe,* vol. 1. Chicago: University of Chicago Press, pp. 155–90.

Earle, John and Estrin, Saul (1996), 'Employee Ownership in Transition', in Roman Frydman *et al.* (eds), *Corporate Governance in Central Europe and Russia,* vol. 2. Budapest and London: Central European University Press, pp. 1–61.

Edwards, Jeremy and Fischer, Klaus (1996), *Banks, Finance and Investment in Germany*. Cambridge: Cambridge University Press.

——— and Ogilvie, Sheilagh (1996), 'Universal Banks and German Industrialization: A Reappraisal'. *Economic History Review* 49: 427–46.

Edwards, Jeremy and Nibler, Marcus (2000), 'Corporate Governance in Germany: The Role of Banks and Ownership Concentration'. *Economic Policy* 31: 239–67.

Eisenstadt, Samuel (1973), *Tradition, Change, and Modernity*. New York: John Wiley.

Estrin, Saul *et al.* (1995), *Restructuring and Privatization in Central Eastern Europe: Case Studies of Firms in Transition*. New York: Sharpe.

Eulenburg, Franz (1906), 'Die Aufsichtsräte der deutschen Aktiengesellschaften'. *Jahrbücher für Nationalökonomie und Statistik* 32: III. Folge: 92–109.

Evans, Peter (1992), 'The State as Problem and Solution: Predation, Embedded Autonomy, and Structural Change', in Stephan Haggard and Robert Kaufman (eds), *The Politics of Economic Adjustment*. Princeton: Princeton University Press, pp. 139–81.

Feldenkirchen, Wilfried (1988), 'Concentration in German Industry 1870–1939', in Hans Pohl (ed.), The Concentration Process in the Entrepreneurial Economy Since the Late 19th Century. Stuttgart 1988: Steiner, pp. 113–46.

Feldman, Gerald (1998), *Hugo Stinnes: Biographie eines Industriellen 1870–1924*. München: Beck.

Fidler, John (1981), *The British Business Elite*. London: Routledge & Kegan.

Flassbeck, Heiner (1995), 'Die deutsche Vereinigung: Ein Transferproblem'. *DIW-Vierteljahreshefte zur Wirtschaftsforschung* 64: 404–12.

Fligstein, Neil (1990), *The Transformation of Corporate Control*. Cambridge: Harvard University Press.

——— (1996), 'Markets as Politics: A Political-Cultural Approach to Market Institutions'. *American Sociological Review* 61: 656–73.

Fog, Agner (1999), *Cultural Selection*. Dordrecht: Kluwer.

Fohlin, Caroline (1999), 'The Rise of Interlocking Directorates in Imperial Germany'. *Economic History Review* 52: 307–33.

Frank, Ove (1981), 'A Survey of Statistical Methods for Graph Analysis'. *Sociological Methodology* 11: 110–55.

Franks, Julian and Mayer, Colin (1995), 'Ownership and Control', in Horst Siebert (ed.), *Trends in Business Organization*. Tübingen: Mohr, pp. 171–95.

Friedkin, Noah E. (1984), 'Structural Cohesion and Equivalence: Explanations of Social Homogeneity'. *Sociological Methods & Research* 12: 235–61.

Friedman, Milton (1970), *Capitalism and Freedom*. Chicago: University of Chicago Press.

Frydman, Roman and Rapaczynski, Andrzej (1994), *Privatization in Eastern Europe: Is the State Withering Away?* Budapest and London: Central European University Press.

Fukuyama, Francis (1995), *Trust: The Social Virtues of the Creation of Prosperity*. New York: The Free Press.

Gaidar, Yegor (1995), 'Russian Reform', in Yegor Gaidar *et al.* (eds), *Russian Reform/ International Money: The Lionel Robbins Lectures*. Cambridge: MIT Press, pp. 3–54.

Galbraith, John K. (1967), *The New Industrial State*. Boston: Houghton Mifflin.

Gall, Lothar *et al.* (1995), *Die Deutsche Bank 1870–1995*. München: Beck.

Gerlach, Michael (1992), *Alliance Capitalism: The Social Organization of Japanese Business*. Berkeley: University of California Press.

Gerschenkron, Alexander (1962), *Economic Backwardness in Historical Perspective*. Cambridge: Harvard University Press.

——— (1968), *Continuity in History and Other Essays*. Cambridge: Belknap Press (Harvard University Press).

Giddens, Anthony (1974), 'Elites in the British Class Structure', in Philip Stanworth and Anthony Giddens (eds), *Elites and Power in British Society*. Cambridge: Cambridge University Press, pp. 1–21.

Gierke, Otto von (1954 [1913]), *Das Deutsche Genossenschaftsrecht*, Bd. 4. Darmstadt: Wissenschaftliche Buchgemeinschaft.

Gordon, Andrew (1991), *Labor and Imperial Democracy in Prewar Japan*. Berkeley: University of California Press.

Goto, Akira (1982), 'Business Groups in a Market Economy'. *European Economic Review* 19: 53–70.

Gourevitch, Peter (1996), 'The Macropolitics of Microinstitutional Differences in the Analysis of Comparative Capitalism', in Suzanne Berger and Ronald Dore (eds), *National Diversity and Global Capitalism*. Ithaca: Cornell University Press, pp. 239–59.

Granovetter, Mark (1973), 'The Strength of Weak Ties'. *American Journal of Sociology* 78: 1360–80.

—— (1985), 'Economic Action and Social Structure: The Problem of Embeddedness'. *American Journal of Sociology* 91: 481–510.

—— (1995), 'Coase Revisited: Business Groups in the Modern Economy'. *Industrial and Corporate Change* 4: 93–130.

Graziano, Luigi (1984), *Clientelismo e sistema politico: Il caso dell'Italia*. Milano: Angeli.

Hall, Peter (1993), 'Policy Paradigms, Social Learning, and the State: The Case of Economic Policymaking in Britain'. *Comparative Politics* 25: 275–96.

Hall, Peter and Soskice, David (2001), *Varieties of Capitalism*. Oxford: Oxford University Press.

Hamilton, Gary (1996), *Asian Business Networks*. Berlin: de Gruyter.

Hannah, Leslie (1983), *The Rise of the Corporate Economy*. London: Methuen.

Hannan, Michael and Freeman, John (1989), *Organizational Ecology*. Cambridge: Harvard University Press.

Hardach, Gerd (1995), 'Zwischen Markt und Macht: Die deutschen Banken 1908–1934', in Wilfried Feldenkirchen *et al.* (eds), *Wirtschaft, Gesellschaft, Unternehmen*, Band II. Stuttgart: Steiner, pp. 914–38.

Hartmann, Michael (1997), Die Rekrutierung von Topmanagern in Europa. *Archives Européennes de Sociologie* 38: 3–37.

Hayek, Friedrich A. (1963), 'Kinds of Order in Society'. *New Individualist Review* 3: 3–12.

—— (1973), *Law, Legislation and Liberty, vol I: Rules and Order*. Chicago: University of Chicago Press.

—— (1976), *Law, Legislation, and Liberty, vol. II: The Mirage of Social Justice*. Chicago: University of Chicago Press.

—— (1978), *New Studies in Philosophy, Politics, Economics and the History of Ideas*. Chicago: University of Chicago Press.

Heinz, Walter R. (1991), *The Life Course and Social Change*. Weinheim: Deutscher Studienverlag.

Herman, Edward (1981), *Corporate Control, Corporate Power*. Cambridge: Cambridge University Press.

Hicks, John (1935), 'Annual Survey of Economic Theory: The Theory of Monopoly'. *Econometrica* 3: 1–20.

Hilferding, Rudolf (1915), 'Arbeitsgemeinschaft der Klassen'? *Der Kampf* 8: 321–9.

—— (1968 [1910]), *Das Finanzkapital*. Frankfurt: EVA.

Hill, Stephen (1995), 'The Social Organization of Boards of Directors'. *British Journal of Sociology* 46: 245–78.

Hirschman, Albert (1958), *The Strategy of Economic Development*. New Haven: Yale University Press.

—— (1970), *Exit, Voice, and Loyalty*. Cambridge: Harvard University Press.

—— (1982), 'Rival Interpretations of Market Society: Civilizing, Destructive, or Feeble?' *Journal of Economic Literature* 20: 1463–84.

—— (1992), 'Abwanderung, Widerspruch und das Schicksal der Deutschen Demokratischen Republik'. *Leviathan* 20: 330–58.

Hobsbawm, Eric (1983), *The Invention of Tradition*. Cambridge: Cambridge University Press.

Hoen, Herman (1996), 'Shock versus Gradualism in Central Europe Reconsidered'. *Comparative Economic Studies* 38: 1–20.

Hofstadter, Richard (1955), *The Age of Reform*. New York: Random House.

Hollingsworth, Roger and Boyer, Robert (1997), *Contemporary Capitalism: The Embeddedness of Institutions*. Cambridge: Cambridge University Press.

Hommelhoff, Peter (1982), *Die Konzernleitungspflicht: Zentrale Aspekte eines Konzernverfassungsrechts*. Heymanns.

—— (1985), 'Eigenkontrolle statt Staatskontrolle', in Werner Schubert and Peter Hommelhoff (eds), *Hundert Jahre modernes Aktienrecht*. Berlin: de Gruyter, pp. 53–105.

Hommelhoff, Peter and Mattheus, Daniela (1998), 'Corporate Governance nach dem KonTraG'. *Die Aktiengesellschaft* 43: 249–59.

Hooley, Graham *et al.* (1996), 'Foreign Direct Investment in Hungary'. *Journal of International Business Studies* 27: 693–710.

Höpner, Martin (2000), 'Unternehmensverflechtung im Zwielicht'. *WSI-Mitteilungen* 53: 655–63.

Iribarne, Philippe de (1991), 'Culture et "effect sociétal"'. *Revue française de sociologie* 32: 599–614.

Jacobs, Bruce (1976), 'The Cultural Bases of Factional Alignment and Divisions in a Rural Taiwanese Township'. *Journal of Asian Studies* 36: 79–97.

Jarosz, Maria (1996), *Polish Employee-Owned Companies in 1995*. Warsaw: Polish Academy of Science.

Jeidels, Otto (1905), *Das Verhältnis der Deutschen Großbanken zur Industrie mit besonderer Berücksichtigung der Eisenindustrie*. Leipzig: Duncker & Humblot.

Jensen, Michael (1989), 'Eclipse of the Public Corporation'. *Harvard Business Review* 89 (Sept./Oct.): 61–74.

Josephson, Matthew (1962 [1934]), *The Robber Barons: The Great American Capitalists 1861–1901*. New York: Harcourt, Brace & Co.

Kadushin, Charles (1995), Friendship Among the French Financial Elite. *American Sociological Review* 60: 202–21.

Kaufman, Allen and Englander, Ernest (1993), 'Kohlberg Kravis Roberts & Co. and the Restructuring of American Capitalism'. *Business History Review* 67: 52–97.

Kenway, Peter and Chlumsky, Jiri (1997), 'The Influence of Owners on Voucher Privatized Firms in the Czech Republic'. *Economics of Transition* 5: 185–93.

Kenway, Peter and Klvacová, Eva (1996), 'The Web of Cross-Ownership Among Czech Financial Intermediaries'. *Europe–Asia Studies* 48: 797–809.

Keohane, Robert (1984), *After Hegemony*. Princeton: Princeton University Press.

—— (1986), 'Reciprocity in International Relations'. *International Organization* 40: 1–27.

King, Lawrence (1997), *Strategies of Transition in Eastern European Capitalism: The Transformation of Property in Hungary and the Czech Republic*. Toronto: American Sociological Association (Conference Paper).

Kiong, Tong Chee (1996), 'Centripetal Authority, Differentiated Networks: The Social Organization of Chinese Firms in Singapore', in Gary Hamilton (ed.), *Asian Business Networks*. Berlin: de Gruyter, pp. 133–56.

Klass, Gert von (1958), *Hugo Stinnes*. Tübingen: Wunderlich Verlag.

Klaus, Václav (1997), 'Transformation of a Former Communist Country: Seven Years After'. *Deutsche Bundesbank (Auszüge aus Presseartikeln)* 35: 17–18.

Knight, Frank (1934), 'Risk'. *Encyclopaedia of the Social Sciences,* vol. *13*: 392–4.

Kocka, Jürgen (1969), *Unternehmensverwaltung und Angestelltenschaft am Beispiel Siemens 1847–1914.* Stuttgart: Klett.

Koenig, Thomas *et al.* (1979), 'Models of the Significance of Interlocking Corporate Directorates'. *American Journal of Economics and Sociology* 38: 174–86.

Kono, Clifford *et al.* (1998), 'Lost in Space: The Geography of Corporate Interlocking Directorates'. *American Journal of Sociology* 103: 863–911.

Konrad, Gyorgy and Szelényi, Ivan (1979), *The Intellectuals on the Road to Class Power.* New York: Harcourt Brace Jovanovich.

Korbonski, Andrzej (1996), 'How Much is Enough? Excessive Pluralism as the Cause of Poland's Socio-economic Crisis'. *International Political Science Review* 17: 307–17.

Kornai, János (1980), *Economics of Shortage.* Amsterdam: Elsevier.

—— (1996), 'Paying the Bill for Goulash Communism: Hungarian Development and Macro Stabilization in a Political-Economy Perspective'. *Social Research* 63: 943–1040.

Kotz, David (1979), 'The Significance of Bank Control Over Large Corporations'. *Journal of Economic Issues* 12: 407–26.

Kowalik, Tadeusz (1994), 'Privatization in Poland: Social Process or Another Shock?' in *United Nations Conference on Trade and Development (UNCTAD), Privatization in the Transition Process.* New York: UN Publications, pp. 141–61.

Krasner, Stephen (1983), *International Regimes.* Ithaca: Cornell University Press.

Kruk, Max (1972), *Die großen Unternehmer.* Frankfurt: Societäts–Verlag.

La Porta, Rafael *et al.* (1997), 'Legal Determinants of External Finance'. *The Journal of Finance* 52: 1131–50.

Lawless, J. F. (1982), *Statistical Models and Methods for Lifetime Data.* New York: John Wiley.

Lawrence, Paul R. and Lorsch, Jay W. (1967), *Organization and Environment.* Cambridge: Harvard University Press.

Leblanc-Wohrer, Marion (1996), 'Poland', in Dominique Pannier (ed.), *Corporate Governance of Public Enterprises in Transitional Economies.* Washington: The World Bank (Technical Paper No. 323), pp. 37–44.

Leff, Nathaniel (1978), 'Industrial Organization and Entrepreneurship in Developing Countries: The Economic Groups'. *Economic Development and Cultural Change* 26: 661–75.

Lehmbruch, Gerhard (1983), 'Neokorporatismus in Westeuropa: Hauptprobleme im internationalen Vergleich'. *Journal für Sozialforschung* 23: 407–20.

Lévy-Leboyer, Maurice (1980), 'The Large Corporation in Modern France', in Alfred Chandler and Herman Daems (eds), *Managerial Hierarchies.* Cambridge: Harvard University Press, pp. 117–60.

Liebowitz, S. J. and Margolis, Stephen (1995), 'Path Dependence, Lock-In, and History'. *The Journal of Law, Economics & Organization* 11: 205–26.

Liefmann, Robert (1923), *Beteiligungs und Finanzierungsgesellschaften.* Jena: Fischer.

Lincoln, James and Kalleberg, Arne (1990), *Culture, Control, and Commitment.* Cambridge: Cambridge University Press.

Livesay, Harold (1995), *Entrepreneurship and the Growth of Firms, vol. I and II.* Brookfield: Aldershot.

Lorsch, Jay and MacIver, Elizabeth (1989), *Pawns or Potentates: The Reality of America's Corporate Boards.* Boston: Harvard Business School Press.

Lutter, Marcus (1984), 'Die Sterbehaus-Konstruktion', in Walther Hadding *et al.* (eds), *Festschrift für Winfried Werner.* Berlin: de Gruyter, pp. 477–93.

Lütz, Susanne (1997), 'Die Rückkehr des Nationalstaates? Kapitalmarktregulierung im Zeichen der Internationalisierung von Finanzmärkten'. *Politische Vierteljahresschrift* 38: 475–97.

Makó, Csaba and Simonyi, Ágnes (1997), 'Inheritance, Imitation and Genuine Solutions: Institution Building in Hungarian Labour Relations'. *Europe–Asia Studies* 49: 221–43.

Marin, Bernd (1990), *Governance and Generalized Exchange: Self-Organizing Policy Networks in Action*. Frankfurt: Campus/Westview.

Mathis, Franz (1988), 'Kartelle, Fusionen und multinationale Unternehmen in Großbritannien, Frankreich, Deutschland, den USA bis 1914'. *Zeitschrift für Unternehmensgeschichte*, Beiheft 46: 79–96.

Maurice, Marc et al. (1982), *Politique d'éducation et organisation industrielle en France et en Allemagne*. Paris: PUF. (Engl: The Social Foundations of Industrial Power: A Comparison of France and Germany. Cambridge 1986: MIT Press.)

Maurice, M. et al. (1992), 'Analyse sociétale et cultures nationales'. Réponse à Philippe d'Iribarne. *Revue française de sociologie* 33: 75–86.

Mayer, Karl Ulrich (1996), 'Lebensverläufe und gesellschaftlicher Wandel', in Johann Behrens and Wolfgang Voges (eds), *Kritische Übergänge: Statuspassagen und sozialpolitische Institutionalisierung*. Frankfurt: Campus, pp. 43–72.

McCraw, Thomas (1984), *Prophets of Regulation*. Cambridge: Belknap Press.

Meißner, Bernd (1999), 'Zwei Welten des Anlagestils in Europa'. *Börsen-Zeitung*, 6. Februar 1999, p. B2.

Mendell, Marguerite and Salée, Daniel (1991), *The Legacy of Karl Polanyi*. New York: St. Martins Press.

Mestmäcker, Ernst-J (1984), *Der verwaltete Wettbewerb*. Tübingen: Mohr.

Meyer, John and Rowan, Brian (1977), 'Institutionalized Organizations: Formal Structure as Myth and Ceremony'. *American Journal of Sociology* 83: 340–63.

Michalski, Lutz and Zeidler, Finn (1996), 'Die Ausgleichshaftung im qualififiziert faktischen Konzern'. *Neue Juristische Wochenschrift (NJW)* 49: 224–9.

Mihályi, Peter (1996), 'Privatisation in Hungary: Now Comes the "Hard Core"'. *Communist Economics and Economic Transformation* 8: 205–16.

Mills, C. Wright (1956), *The Power Elite*. New York: Oxford University Press.

Mintz, Beth and Schwartz, Michael (1985), *The Power Structure of American Business*. Chicago: The University of Chicago Press.

Mishel, Lawrence et al. (2001), *The State of Working America 2000–2001*. Ithaca: Cornell University Press.

Mizruchi, Mark (1982), *The American Corporate Network 1904–1974*. Beverly Hills: Sage.

—— (1992), *The Structure of Corporate Political Action*. Cambridge: Harvard University Press.

—— (1996), 'What Do Interlocks Do? An Analysis, Critique, and Assessment of Research on Interlocking Directorates'. *Annual Review of Sociology* 22: 271–98.

Morikawa, Hidemasa (1992), *Zaibatsu: The Rise and Fall of Family Enterprise Groups in Japan*. Tokyo: University of Tokyo Press.

Morin, François (1974), *La structure financière du capitalisme français*. Paris: Calmann-Lévy.

—— (1994), 'Liaisons financières et coopération des acteurs-systèmes'. *Revue économique* 45: 1459–70.

—— (1996), 'Privatisation et dévolution des pouvoirs: Le modèle français du gouvernement d'entreprise'. *Revue économique* 47: 1253–68.

—— (1998), 'La rupture du modèle français de détention et de gestion des capitaux'. *Revue d'économie financière* 50: 111–32.

Müller-Krumholz (1993), 'Erfahrungen beim Versuch der Rückrechnung einer Volkswirtschaftlichen Gesamtrechnung für die ehemalige DDR', in Statistisches Bundesamt (ed.),

Rückrechnungen gesamtwirtschaftlicher Daten für die ehemalige DDR. Stuttgart: Metzler-Poeschel (Forum), pp. 94–101.

Murrell, Peter (1993), 'What is Shock Therapy? What Did it Do in Poland and Russia?' *Post-Soviet Affairs* 9: 11–140.

—— (1995), 'The Transition According to Cambridge', Mass. *Journal of Economic Literature* 33: 164–78.

Nelson, Lynn and Kuzes, Irina (1994), 'Evaluating the Russian Voucher Privatization Program'. *Comparative Economic Studies* 36: 56–67.

Newman, Philip (1964), *Cartel and Combine.* Ridgewood: Foreign Studies Institute.

Nörr, Knut (1995), 'Law and Market Organization: The Historical Experience in Germany from 1900 to the Law Against Restraints of Competition'. *Journal of Institutional and Theoretical Economics* 151: 5–20.

North, Douglas (1990), *Institutions, Institutional Change and Economic Performance.* Cambridge: Cambridge University Press.

Numazaki, Ichiro (1996), 'The Role of Personal Networks in the Making of Taiwan's Guanxiqiye (Related Enterprises)', in Gary Hamilton (ed.), *Asian Business Networks.* Berlin and New York: de Gruyter, pp. 71–115.

Offe, Claus and Wiesenthal, Helmut (1980), 'Two Logics of Collective Action'. *Political Power and Social Theory* 1: 67–115.

Olson, Mancur (1982), *The Rise and Decline of Nations: Economic Growth, Stagflation and Social Rigidities.* New Haven: Yale University Press.

Orrù, Marco *et al.* (1997), *The Economic Organization of East Asian Capitalism.* London: Sage.

Ouchi, William (1981), *Theory Z.* New York: Avon.

Pahl, R. E. and Winkler, J. T (1974), 'The Economic Elite: Theory and Practice', in Philip Stanworth and Anthony Giddens (eds), *Elites and Power in British Society.* Cambridge: Cambridge University Press, pp. 102–22.

Palda, Kristian (1997), 'Czech Privatization and Corporate Governance'. *Communist and Post-Communist Studies* 30: 83–93.

Palmer, Donald (1983), 'Broken Ties: Interlocking Directorates and Intercorporate Coordination'. *Administrative Science Quarterly* 28: 40–55.

Pappi, Franz *et al.* (1987), 'Die Struktur der Unternehmensverflechtungen in der Bundesrepublik'. *Kölner Zeitschrift für Soziologie und Sozialpsychologie* 39: 669–92.

Pareto, Vilfredo (1923), *Trattato di Sociologia Generale, vol. III.* Firenze: Barbèra.

—— (1968), *The Rise and Fall of the Elites.* Totowa, NJ: Bedminster Press.

Passow, Richard (1930), *Kartelle.* Jena: Fischer.

Pastré, Olivier (1992), *Les nouveaux piliers de la finance.* Paris: La Découverte.

Pejovitch, Svetozar (1990), *The Economics of Property Rights.* Dordrecht: Kluwer.

Pennings, Johannes (1980), *Interlocking Directorates.* San Francisco: Jossey-Bass.

Pfeffer, Jeffrey (1992), 'A Resource Dependence Perspective on Intercorporate Relations', in Mark Mizruchi and Michael Schwarz (eds), *Intercorporate Relations.* Cambridge: Cambridge University Press, pp. 25–55.

Pfeffer, Jeffrey and Salancik, Gerald (1978), *The External Control of Organizations: A Resource Dependence Perspective.* New York. Harper and Row.

Pickel, Andreas (1997), 'The Jump-Started Economy and the Ready-made State: A Theoretical Reconsideration of the East German Case'. *Comparative Political Studies* 30: 211–41.

Pickel, Andreas and Wiesenthal, Helmut (1997), *The Grand Experiment. Debating Shock Therapy, Transition Theory, and the East German Experience.* Boulder: Westview.

Pinto, Brian *et al.* (1993), 'Transforming State Enterprises in Poland'. *Brookings Papers on Economic Activity* no. 1: 213–70.

Piore, Michael and Sabel, Charles (1984), *The Second Industrial Divide.* New York: Basic Books.

Pohl, Hans (1981), 'Zur Geschichte von Organisation und Leitung deutscher Großunternehmen seit dem 19. Jahrhundert'. *Zeitschrift für Unternehmensgeschichte* 26: 143–78.

Polanyi, Karl (1957 [1944]), *The Great Transformation.* Boston: Beacon Press.

Popper, Karl (1970), *The Poverty of Historicism.* London: Routledge & Kegan Paul.

Pound, John (1992), *The Rise of the Political Model of Corporate Governance and Corporate Control.* Cambridge: Harvard University (Working Paper).

Powell, Walter W. (1990), 'Neither Market Nor Hierarchy: Network Forms of Organization'. *Research in Organizational Behavior* 12: 295–336.

Prais, S. J. (1981), *The Evolution of Giant Firms in Britain.* Cambridge: Cambridge University Press.

Presthus, Robert (1979), *The Organizational Society.* London: Macmillan.

Prowse, Stephen (1992), 'The Structure of Corporate Ownership in Japan'. *The Journal of Finance* 47: 1121–40.

Rajan, Raghuram and Zingales, Luigi (1998), 'Which Capitalism? Lessons from the East Asian Crisis'. *Journal of Applied Corporate Finance* 11: 40–8.

Rappaport, Alfred (1990), 'The Staying Power of the Public Corporation'. *Harvard Business Review* 90 (Jan./Febr.): 96–104.

Rawls, John (1971), *A Theory of Justice.* Cambridge: Harvard University Press/ Belknap.

Redlich, Fritz (1964), *Der Unternehmer.* Göttingen: Vandenhoeck & Ruprecht.

Riesser, Jacob (1971 [1905]), *Die deutschen Großbanken und ihre Konzentration im Zusammenhang mit der Entwicklung der Gesamtwirtschaft in Deutschland.* Glashütten: Detlev Auvermann.

Roe, Mark (1991), 'A Political Theory of American Corporate Finance'. *Columbia Law Journal* 91: 10–67.

—— (1994), 'Strong Managers, Weak Owners'. Princeton: Princeton University Press.

—— (1997), 'Path Dependence, Political Options and Governance Systems', in Klaus Hopt and Eddy Wymeersch (eds), *Comparative Corporate Governance.* Berlin: de Gruyter, pp. 165–84.

Royal Commission on Trade Unions and Employers' Associations (1980), *Donovan Report 1965–1968* (Chairman: Lord Donovan). London: Her Majesty's Stationery Office.

Rutland, Peter (1994), Privatisation in Russia. *Europe–Asia Studies* 46: 1109–31.

Sassen, Saskia (1991), *The Global City: New York, London, Tokyo.* Princeton: Princeton University Press.

Scharpf, Fritz W. (1985), 'Die Politikverflechtungs-Falle: Europäische Integration und deutscher Föderalismus im Vergleich'. *Politische Vierteljahresschrift* 26: 323–56.

Scheuch, Erwin and Scheuch, Ute (1995), *Bürokraten in den Chefetagen.* Hamburg: Rowohlt.

Schmidt, Ingo and Binder, Steffen (1996), *Wettbewerbspolitik im Internationalen Vergleich.* Heidelberg: Verlag Recht und Wirtschaft.

Schmitter, Philippe (1974), 'Still the Century of Corporatism?' *The Review of Politics* 36: 85–131.

Schmoller, Gustav (1906), 'Das Verhältnis der Kartelle zum Staate'. *Verhandlungen des Vereins für Socialpolitik* 116: 237–71.

Schönwitz, Dietrich and Hans Weber, Hans (1982), *Unternehmenskonzentration, personelle Verflechtungen und Wettbewerb.* Baden-Baden: Nomos.

Schreyögg, Georg and Steinmann, Horst (1981), 'Zur Trennung von Eigentum und Verfügungsgewalt: Eine empirische Analyse der Beteiligungsverhältnisse in Deutschen Großunternehmen'. *Zeitschrift für Betriebswirtschaft* 51: 533–58.

Schröter, Harm G (1994), 'Kartellierung und Dekartellierung 1890–1990'. *Vierteljahresschrift für Sozial- und Wirtschaftsgeschichte* 81: 457–93.

Schumpeter, Joseph (1928), 'Unternehmer'. *Handwörterbuch der Staatswissenschaften*, 8. Band. Jena: Gustav Fischer, pp. 476–87.

—— (1950), *Capitalism, Socialism, and Democracy*. New York: Harper.

—— (1954), *History of Economic Analysis*. New York: Oxford University Press.

Scott, John (1986), *Capitalist Property and Financial Power: A Comparative Study of Britain, the United States and Japan*. Brighton: Wheatsheaf.

—— (1990), 'Corporate Control and Corporate Rule'. *The British Journal of Sociology* 41: 351–73.

—— (1991), *Social Network Analysis*. London: Sage.

—— (1997), *Corporate Business and Capitalist Classes*. Oxford: Oxford University Press.

Sharpe, William *et al.* (1995), *Investments*. Englewood Cliffs, NJ: Prentice Hall.

Shleifer, Andrei and Vishny, Robert (1986), 'Large Shareholders and Corporate Control'. *Journal of Political Economy* 94: 461–88.

Simmel, Georg (1908), 'Die Kreuzung sozialer Kreise',. in Georg Simmel (ed.) P, *Soziologie*. Berlin: Duncker & Humblot, pp. 305–44.

—— (1955), *Conflict*. New York: The Free Press.

Smith, Adam (1979 [1776]), *The Wealth of Nations*. Baltimore: Penguin.

Smith, David and White, Douglas (1992), 'Structure and Dynamics of the Global Economy: Network Analysis of International Trade 1965–1980'. *Social Forces* 70: 857–93.

Stahl, Wilhelm (1973), *Der Elitenkreislauf in der Unternehmerschaft*. Frankfurt: Harri Deutsch.

Stark, David (1996), 'Recombinant Property in East European Capitalism'. *American Journal of Sociology* 101: 993–1027.

Stiglitz, Joseph (1995), *Whither Socialism?* Cambridge: MIT Press.

Stinchcombe, Arthur (1990), 'Weak Structural Data'. *Contemporary Sociology* 19: 380–2.

Stokman, Frans N. *et al.* (1985), *Networks of Corporate Power*. Cambridge: Polity Press.

Stone, Katherine van Wezel (1981), 'The Post-War Paradigm in American Labor Law'. *The Yale Law Journal* 90: 1509–80.

Streeck, Wolfgang (1997), 'German Capitalism: Does it Exist? Can it Survive?' in Colin Crouch and Wolfgang Streeck (eds), *Political Economy of Modern Capitalism*. London: Sage, pp. 33–54.

Strouse, Jean (1999), *Morgan: American Financier*. New York: Random House.

Suleiman, Ezra (1978), *Elites in French Society*. Princeton: Princeton University Press.

Swaan, Abram de (1990), *In Care of the State*. Cambridge: Polity Press.

Swartz, David (1985), 'French Interlocking Directorships: Financial and Industrial Groups', in Frans N. Stokman *et al.* (eds), *Networks of Corporate Power*. Cambridge: Polity Press, pp. 184–98.

Swedberg, Richard (1994), 'Markets as Social Structures', in Neil Smelser and Richard Swedberg (eds), *The Handbook of Economic Sociology*. Princeton: Princeton University Press, pp. 255–82.

Szelényi, Ivan (1988), *Socialist Entrepreneurs: Embourgeoisement in Rural Hungary*. Cambridge: Policy Press.

Szelényi, Iván and Szelényi, Szonja (1995), 'Circulation or Reproduction of Elites During the Postcommunist Transformation of Eastern Europe?' *Theory and Society* 24: 615–38.

Szelényi, Szonja *et al.* (1995), 'The Making of the Hungarian Postcommunist Elite'. *Theory and Society* 24: 697–722.

—— (1996), 'Interests and Symbols in Post-Communist Political Culture: The Case of Hungary'. *American Sociological Review* 61: 466–77.

Szomburg, Jan (1995), 'The Political Constraints on Polish Privatization', in George Blazyca and Janusz Dabrowski (eds), *Monitoring Economic Transition*. Aldershot: Avebury, pp. 75–85.

Tittenbrun, Jacek (1995), 'The Managerial Revolution Revisited: The Case of Privatisation in Poland'. *Capital and Class* 55: 21–32.

Tilly, Richard (1982), 'Mergers, External Growth, and Finance in the Development of Large-Scale Enterprise in Germany, 1880–1913'. *Journal of Economic History* 42: 629–58.

Török, Ádám (1995), *Corporate Governance in the Transition: The Case of Hungary*. Budapest: Hungarian Academy of Sciences/Institute of Economics, (Discussion Paper No. 35).

Tworzecki, Hubert (1994), 'The Polish Parliamentary Elections of 1993'. *Electoral Studies* 13: 180–5.

Ungson, Gerardo *et al.* (1997), *Korean Enterprise*. Boston: Harvard Business School Press.

Useem, Michael (1980), 'Corporations and the Corporate Elite'. *Annual Review of Sociology* 6: 41–77.

—— (1984), *The Inner Circle: Large Corporations and the Rise of Business Political Activity in the U.S. and U.K.* New York: Oxford University Press.

—— (1996), *Investor Capitalism: How Money Managers Are Changing the Face of Corporate America*. New York: Basic Books.

Useem, Michael and Karabel, Jerome (1986), 'Pathways to Top Corporate Management'. *American Sociological Review* 51: 184–200.

US Interstate Commerce Commission (1908), *Intercorporate Relationships of Railways in the United States as of June 30, 1906*. Washington 1908: Government Printing Office.

Usui, Chikako and Colignon, Richard (1995), *Government Elites and 'Amakudari' in Japan, 1963–1992*. Washington: American Sociological Association (Conference Paper).

Uzzi, Brian (1996), 'The Sources and Consequences of Embeddedness for the Economic Performance of Organizations: The Network Effect'. *American Sociological Review* 61: 674–98.

Van Rossem, Ronan (1996), 'The World System Paradigm as General Theory of Development: A Cross-National Test'. *American Sociological Review* 61: 508–27.

Voszka, Éva (1994), 'From Renationalization to Redistribution? in *United Nations Conference on Trade and Development (UNCTAD), Privatization in the Transition Process*'. New York: UN Publications, pp. 349–62.

Walicki, Andrzej (1990), 'The Three Traditions in Polish Patriotism', in Stanislaw Gomulka and Antony Polonsky (eds), *Polish Paradoxes*. London: Routledge, pp. 21–39.

Wasilewski, Jacek and Wnuk-Lipinksi, Edmund (1995), 'Poland: Winding Road from the Communist to the Post-Solidarity Elite'. *Theory and Society* 24: 669–96.

Wasserman, Stanley and Faust, Katherine (1994), *Social Network Analysis*. Cambridge: Cambridge University Press.

Webb, W. L. (1992), 'The Polish General Election of 1991'. *Electoral Studies* 11: 166–70.

Weber, Max (1956), *Wirtschaft und Gesellschaft, 1. Halbband*. Tübingen: J. C. B. Mohr.

—— (1969 [1920]), *Die protestantische Ethik, Band I*. München: Siebenstern.

Wegener, Bernd (1987), 'Vom Nutzen entfernter Bekannter'. *Kölner Zeitschrift für Soziologie und Sozialpsychologie* 39: 278–301.

Wehler, Hans-Ulrich (1974), 'Der Aufstieg des Organisierten Kapitalismus und Interventionsstaates in Deutschland', in Heinrich August Winkler (ed.), *Organisierter Kapitalismus*. Göttingen: Vandenhoeck & Ruprecht, pp. 36–57.

Whitley, Richard (1973), 'Commonalities and Connections Among Directors of Large Financial Institutions'. *Sociological Review* 21: 613–32.

—— (1990), 'Eastern Asian Enterprise Structures and the Comparative Analysis of Forms of Business Organization'. *Organization Studies* 11: 47–74.

Whyte, Martin K. (1996), 'The Chinese Family and Economic Development: Obstacle or Engine?' *Economic Development and Cultural Change* 45: 1–30.

Wieser, Carl Wolfgang Freiherr von (1919), *Der finanzielle Aufbau der englischen Industrie.* Jena: Gustav Fischer.

Williamson, Oliver E. (1985), *The Economic Institutions of Capitalism.* New York: Free Press.

—— (1991), 'Comparative Economic Organization: The Analysis of Discrete Structural Alternatives'. *Administrative Science Quarterly* 36: 269–96.

Windolf, Paul (1993), 'Codetermination and the Market for Corporate Control in the European Community'. *Economy and Society* 22: 137–58.

—— (1997), *Expansion and Structural Change: German, Japanese and American Universities 1870–1990.* Boulder: Westview.

—— (1998), 'The Transformation of the East German Economy'. *Polish Sociological Review* 124: 333–55.

Windolf, Paul and Wood, Stephen (1988), *Recruitment and Selection in the Labour Market.* Aldershot: Avebury.

Winiecki, Jan (1995), 'Polish Mass Privatisation Programme: The Unloved Child in a Suspect Family', in OECD/Centre for Co-operation with the Economics in Transition (ed.), *Mass Privatisation: An Initial Assessment.* Paris: OECD, pp. 47–57.

—— (1996), 'The Superiority of Eliminating Barriers to Entrepreneurship over Privatization Activism of the State'. *Banca Nazionale del Lavoro Quarterly Review* 198: 313–31.

Womack, James *et al.* (1990), *The Machine that Changed the World.* New York: Maxwell Macmillan.

Wood, Christopher (1994), *The End of Japan Inc.* New York: Simon & Schuster.

Woolcock, Stephen (1996), 'Competition among Forms of Corporate Governance in the European Community: The Case of Britain', in Suzanne Berger and Ronald Dore (eds), *National Diversity and Global Capitalism.* Ithaca: Cornell University Press, pp.179–96.

World Bank (1996), *World Development Report 1996: From Plan to Market.* New York: Oxford University Press.

Yamauchi, Koresuke (1994), 'Internationales Konzernrecht in Japan', in Marcus Lutter (ed.), *Konzernrecht im Ausland.* Berlin: Walter de Gruyter, pp. 154–70.

Zakaria, Fareed (1994), 'Culture Is Destiny: A Conversation with Lee Kuan Yew'. *Foreign Affairs* 73: 109–26.

Zeitlin, Maurice (1974), 'Corporate Ownership and Control: The Large Corporation and the Capitalist Class'. *American Journal of Sociology* 79: 1073–119.

Zeitlin, Maurice and Ratcliff, Richard (1988), *Landlord and Capitalists: The Dominant Class of Chile.* Princeton: Princeton University Press.

Ziegler, Rolf (1984), Das Netz der Personen- und Kapitalverflechtungen deutscher und österreichischer Wirtschaftsunternehmen. *Kölner Zeitschrift für Soziologie und Sozialpsychologie* 36: 557–84.

Ziegler, Rolf *et al.* (1985), 'Industry and Banking in the German Corporate Network', in Frans N. Stokman *et al.* (eds), *Networks of Corporate Power.* Cambridge: Polity Press, pp. 91–111.

Index